Comedy and Culture

Comedy and Culture
England 1820-1900

ROGER B. HENKLE

PRINCETON UNIVERSITY PRESS

Princeton, New Jersey

Copyright © 1980 by Princeton University Press
Published by Princeton University Press, Princeton, New Jersey
In the United Kingdom: Princeton University Press, Guildford, Surrey

All Rights Reserved
Library of Congress Cataloging in Publication Data will be
found on the last printed page of this book

Publication of this book has been aided by a grant from
The Andrew W. Mellon Foundation

This book has been composed in VIP Baskerville

Clothbound editions of Princeton University Press books
are printed on acid-free paper, and binding materials are
chosen for strength and durability

Printed in the United States of America by Princeton
University Press, Princeton, New Jersey

To My Mother
and in Memory of My Father
for Their Love
and Support

Contents

Preface

I am indebted to Brown University for several summer stipends that made possible work on this book, and thus indebted to Richard Salomon, whose generosity provided for the stipends. I wish also to acknowledge the assistance of the staffs of the John D. Rockefeller and John Hay Libraries of Brown, the Reading Room of the British Museum, and the Widener Library at Harvard. The following journals have kindly granted me permission to reprint, as part of chapter five of this book, portions of my articles: The Virginia Quarterly Review *(Winter 1973) for "The Mad Hatter's World,"* Critical Quarterly *(Summer 1974) for "From Pooter to Pinter," and* MOSAIC *(Summer 1976) for "Spitting Blood and Writing Comic."*

There are several people whom I particularly want to thank for their support during the writing and consideration of this book. Jerry Sherwood of Princeton University Press has been a deeply appreciated source of guidance and confidence from the first moment of its submission. My colleagues William Vanech and Robert Scholes have kept the faith. Dana R. Buchman not only gave me help with the book but also enthusiasm and continuing commitment to it which I have greatly appreciated. Tam Curry of Princeton University Press has done a splendid job of editing. And of course, my children Tim and Jennifer must be thanked for putting up with everything.

I told the students in my classes on British comic writers at Brown University that I would follow standard professorial procedure: I would appropriate all their ideas and then thank them for being "a valuable sounding board" for my thinking. They were a valuable sounding board, though it is possible that you may not think there is enough in here to have been worth stealing in the first place.

Three people are owed especially profound thanks. First, Donald Gray of Indiana University, whose readings of my book manuscript were a model of critical professionalism. Rarely does one have a reader who devotes as much attention to every aspect of argument, evidence, and expression, whose suggestions are so "right," and whose appreciation for what I am trying to do is so gratifyingly clear. He has guided me in making a number of important changes in the presentation of this book.

Ian Watt of Stanford has exercised the most significant intellectual and critical influence on my work. Not only is his The Rise of the Novel *the inspiration for all studies in literary developments in a social context, but his wisdom about approaches, premises, and interpretations has been invaluable to me. I suspect I am no longer even conscious of the extent to which I have drawn upon his rich appreciation of English literature, especially the comic novel, or upon his wit and perception, but I am distinctly aware of how much I owe him for his support, generosity, and shrewd insight.*

Finally, I want to thank my wife, Carol, who has encouraged and sustained me in the long years of work on this book. I have appreciated her faith in me more than I can say, and she has been a marvelous source of perspective and common sense. Of course, there have been some incidental benefits to her. Occasionally, when I paced around expounding to her my latest Great Thoughts about comedy, she found these insights so stimulating that she fell asleep.

Comedy and Culture

Introduction

> The great superiority of France over England is
> that in France every bourgeois wants to be an
> artist, whereas in England every artist wants to
> be a bourgeois.—*Oscar Wilde*

he genesis of this book lies in an observation
by the British critic L. C. Knights that "profitless
generalizations are more frequent in criticism of
comedy than in criticism of other forms of literature."[1]
Knights made that remark in 1933, before the rich and
valuable studies of comedy by Northrop Frye, Susanne
Langer, and Arthur Koestler were published, so the indictment is less valid than it once was. But the premise of
his complaint still holds: most of what has been written
about the nature of comic expression neglects the literary,
individual, and social contexts within which that expression
occurs. We still tend to speak about comedy as a general
concept, an idea, or a theory that somehow may be applied
to writers as diverse as Rabelais, Jane Austen, and Kafka.
We embrace such broad notions as the "comic rhythm," the
"mythos of comedy," or the "comic spirit" and then struggle to adapt them to individual works of various tones and
manners, of various times and cultures. The general concepts are undeniably provocative; and they enable us to
identify the larger structural patterns and attitudes of
characteristic comic works, such as *Tartuffe, Don Quixote*,
and *Huckleberry Finn*. But they do not account for the perceptible differences in the nature of the comedy in each

literary product. Nor do they allow us to discover why a writer chooses *comic* expression. Or why that expression should be so exuberant in some instances and so restrained in others.

The key questions that we need to ask about comedy cannot be adequately answered until we examine comic works within specific literary and cultural frameworks. We can account for the tone of a comic expression, for its manner of presenting its material, only if we can locate the writer's position in his society and discover what he is responding to, if we can understand his *use* of comedy. Abstract declarations about the function of the comic—as a means of undermining the social fabric, or conversely, as an accommodation to the prevailing social order—are relatively insubstantial unless we can watch the writer at work, maneuvering among the shibboleths and sacred assumptions of his day, coping with his own inhibitions, and breaking free into art and wit. Comedy is by nature highly self-reflexive; it operates through diversions and evasions that reflect the ambivalence or plain equivocation of the writers. Its very techniques, such as parody and paradox, betray these complex and often self-opposing impulses. It exaggerates, distorts, inverts, and plays with its material.

This book, then, is a study of comic writing along the lines that Knights suggested—within a specific social and literary context. It examines English comic writing, particularly in prose, that appeared during the years 1820-1900. I chose this time span for several reasons. The 1820s and 1830s, the pre-Victorian decades, were years of change into a new social order. They marked the acceleration of the Industrial Revolution, the period in which the image of the modern city was composed, the years in which vast numbers of people moved up and down the scale of the middle class evolving new life styles. The literary situation was unstable and reflected other spheres of instability. Against this stands a period of almost legendary solidity—the Victorian era. Though the Victorian period was a time of considerable intellectual ferment, its dominant sense of progress and affluence furnishes a special kind of backdrop to comic expression. Finally, in the later decades of the nineteenth century, dissatisfaction, disengagement, and forms of what we have come to call "alienation" surfaced with greater frequency and growing boldness, especially among intellectuals and artists. In the 1880s and 1890s, something of the pre-Victorian dandyism and extravagance reasserted itself, but the comedy at the end of the century was agonistic, antibourgeois, and experimental.

Nineteenth-century England was a logical choice for this sort of study for another reason as well: it was one of the most fertile periods of comic literature. It was the time of Dickens, Thackeray, Lewis Carroll, Meredith, and Wilde; it was the setting in which comic journalism enfranchised itself; it was the milieu in which the tone ranged from radical cynicism to indulgent humor. Although the atmosphere was apparently uncongenial to original comic theatre, it was one in which comic prose flourished as never before.

The receptivity of the Victorian age to comedy raises issues of comedy's social workings. Martin Turnell, in discussing French literature during the nineteenth century, argues that the English differed from the French by never using comedy to attack their social institutions. According to Turnell, the English comic emphasis on affectation, hypocrisy, and eccentricity implied that the underlying soundness of the English way of life would reassert itself if excesses in individual behavior were corrected.[2] Turnell writes from the vantage point of French letters where the estrangement of the artist from the middle class was established early in the nineteenth century and reigned as a governing principle for Baudelaire, Balzac, Flaubert, and their followers.[3] By comparison, Thackeray does indeed seem to be evasive, and Dickens too willing to gloss the evils of society in ideals of domestic virtue. Until the end of the century, though, English writers strove to speak to the middle class and probably adjusted their comedy accordingly. Wilde's epigram, quoted at the beginning of this Introduction, insinuates that the impulse to fall in line with the bourgeoisie gripped the mind of every English wit. All the more reason, I suggest, to explore the uses of comedy in expressing middle-class concerns and anxieties.

The writers I shall discuss were all "middle-class" in family background, in schooling, or in achieved social position. Their audience was also predominantly middle-class, although it tended to divide late in the century. And they wrote essentially about their sense of position within and with respect to the middle class. However imprecise the term "middle class"—the British historian G. Kitson Clark suggests that the best definition may simply be that "it was made up of those people who thought themselves to be middle class and were allowed by their neighbors to be so, or were accused of it"[4]—as we examine the comic expression of the Victorian period, the term will appear to comprise a certain set of concepts about one's positions and aspirations. Indeed, the differentiating factor between middle class and lower class may be that quality of *Angst* about one's possibilities, one's failures or dissatisfactions, or one's life style that makes up so much of comic expression.[5]

Let me also say that I am well aware of the dispute among sociologists of literature over the question of how representative artists are of their social positions or the attitudes of their social class.[6] I must stress, however, that it is not my objective to try to define the complex attitudes of the English middle class through the expressions of these writers, nor even to assert that they are adequately representative of all the aspects of that shifting, multifaceted body. My objective is to define the workings of comedy—its operations and its internal uses by a group of writers who, however influential they may have been (and surely Dickens, Thackeray, Carroll, and Butler were highly influential), were engaged in expressing what they perceived to be the social and cultural concerns of the time. Because it is comedy we are exploring here, the crucial factor is the *writer's* perception of what constitute middle-class cultural concerns or attitudes—how he defined those values and modes of living and how he responded to them.

Appropriately enough, it is also the writer's attitude that determines when a work is comic. Most of the theories of comedy—those of Freud, Langer, Henri Bergson, Koestler, Meredith—speak as if it were the attitude of the audience that is the ultimate determinative factor. Clearly comedy must have an attuned audience (and in many instances, as Meredith, Freud, and Bergson insist, a highly sophisticated audience), but the disparities among what men find amusing are so great—especially in the last two centuries when we are being asked to laugh at human wretchedness and grotesquerie—that audience response serves as a highly unreliable criterion. One man's rich human comedy can be another man's death of the soul. Consequently, all theorists must look as well for some constants in form (such as Frye's opposition between "free" and "blocking" characters) or in behavior (such as Bergson's "mechanical" encrusted on the "human"). *The* critical factor, though, is the attitude toward the subject matter that is transmitted to the audience by the artist. An assessment of the attitude, almost the intention, of the author, can thus be postulated from such admittedly elusive factors as tone, strategy, and intensity.

We can determine that an author's attitude is "comic," in my definition, if he has not approached or treated his material in a way designed to elicit from his audience the most potentially serious response to the subject matter. A comic attitude can be discerned when the text, enlightened with outside, contextual evidence, shows that the author is handling his subject in ways that (1) avoid emphasizing or intensifying its more psychically upsetting aspects or (2) reduce the intensity of the reader's confrontation with its social implications. After all, the selection of a comic approach is governed by a resolution to insinuate one's viewpoint without "preaching" or challenging the reader to make a committed response, and to enhance the pleasures that come from use of entertainment or play of wit. We will see how subtle this insinuation becomes as we look closely at mid-century domestic humor.

A comparison of Wilde's *The Picture of Dorian Gray* with his letter-memoir *De Profundis* provides a graphic example of the difference between a comic and a serious attitude in nineteenth-century English literature. Written within a few years of each other, both books take up Wilde's hedonistic relationships with young men; but one, *Dorian Gray*, stylizes the emotions in lavish strokes of paradox and arch wit, while the other presents a bleak and peevish journal of human agonizing. *Dorian Gray* is a novel of moral reform manqué; when the feelings of the hero in decline are presented, they are melodramatically overwrought, illustrating Wilde's dictum in his essay "The Decay of Lying" that when life, with its tedious morality, encroaches on a work of art, it creates bad art. *De Profundis*, though, a protest of Lord Alfred Douglas's betrayal of Wilde, is in deadly earnest—page after page in the horrible clarity and banality of total recall:

> At three in the morning, unable to sleep, and tortured with thirst, I made my way, in the dark and cold, down to the sitting-room in the hopes of finding some water there. I found *you*. You fell on me with every hideous word an intemperate mood, an undisciplined and untutored nature could suggest. By the terrible alchemy of egotism you converted your remorse into rage. You accused me of selfishness in expecting you to be with me when I was ill; of standing between you and your amusements; of trying to deprive you of your pleasures.[7]

We cannot mistake the author's attitude here; this material has been invested with its most personally profound psychic consequences.

It is important to keep in mind that comic treatment of

an issue does not mean that the artist considers it a matter lacking importance and serious implications. Rather, he makes a strategic choice to present serious concerns in a way that transmits the effect obliquely or ambivalently. Samuel Butler's late-century bombshell against the Victorian family, *The Way of All Flesh*, was written largely in intervals of recrimination and despair. Butler himself privately admitted that a "sense of grievance" informed the novel. No reader can fail to share in his condemnation of Father and Mother and Sunday Religion, but Butler consistently softens the impact of the reading experience through the wry comments of a narrator who urges us to be urbane and relativistic about all things.

The strategy of the author may shift within a single work, often reflecting a change in attitude during the course of the work. This appears to have happened in Lewis Carroll's *Alice in Wonderland*, when an attempt to vivify a life of adult self-indulgence—the selfish pleasures of whimsical behavior and games by one's own rules—turns into an outburst of authorial anxiety. The casual anarchy of Wonderland is suddenly seen to be vulnerable to the worst excesses of despotic will. What transforms a comically conceived existence into a nightmarish one is the insistence by the authority figures in the book (the Queen of Hearts, for example) that some vaguely criminal or immoral "meaning" must be attached to acts previously considered innocent and meaningless. This is a crucial change in attitude—from one that treats behavior as inconsequential and playful to one that emphasizes meaning and discomforting social or psychological consequences.

Clearly context is essential in enabling us to identify these shifts of authorial position. But there are some more objectively discernible factors that offer insights into the author's intent. Comedy transmits a characteristic vision of life—the *comic* view of human behavior. In order to explain this view, I shall draw upon some observations that Frank Kermode has made in his book *The Sense of an Ending*, a book not about comedy, but about the need in Western man to put arbitrary beginnings and endings upon the slices of time in his life.[8] Kermode adopts a term, "fictions," from Hans Vaihinger that I find valuable in discussing comedy. He defines the term not in the more limited sense of literary creations, but as notions that people invent to live by, or concepts that they consciously employ in order to explain or structure portions of their everyday lives and activities. These notions or concepts are "fictive" because they are temporary "working beliefs" that are understood (at some point at least) to be *created* for convenience in organizing or imaginatively grasping human activities. Some of these fictions only mark off small islets of individualistic behavioral indulgence, such as "hobbyhorse riding," while some can be the governing principles by which careers are justified and psychic defense structures are built. It is only when they are no longer provisional, no longer treated as fictive visions, that they become ossified into what Kermode calls "myths," that is, beliefs that people begin to accept as true or permanently desirable.

In a later chapter of his book, Kermode discusses the dilemma that Jean-Paul Sartre presented to himself in his novel *Nausea*. "The absurd dishonesty of all prefabricated patterns" (fictions) offended Sartre, yet the reality of a life without any patterns imposed upon it was ultimately "nauseous" to him, for it left man in the viscous, changing, amorphous flow of contingency, where human matter and human consciousness were subjected to disorienting chaos. Thus, although Sartre found it finally necessary to create fictions in order to live humanely, he found it equally necessary to realize that such patterns were fictive and only operational if one were to avoid sterility and self-delusion. Others writing about the nature of comedy have emphasized comedy's treatment of the changing, contingent elements in life. Bergson argues that we laugh when a man has fallen into patterns of action that are not flexible enough to withstand the upsets of human existence. Susanne Langer makes an eloquent case for a "comic rhythm" that depicts life as "physical or social events occurring by chance and building up the coincidences with which individuals cope according to their lights. . . . Destiny in the guise of Fortune is the fabric of comedy; it is developed by comic action, which is the upset and recovery of the protagonist's equilibrium, his contest with the world and his triumph by wit, luck, personal power, or even humorous, or ironical, or philosophical acceptance of mischance."[9] George Santayana stresses the same aspect of comedy: "This world is contingency and absurdity incarnate . . . Existence involves changes and happenings and is comic inherently."[10] Northrop Frye contends that comic plots move the action toward pragmatically free social situations.[11] Meredith's evocation of the comic spirit, "an oblique light, followed by volleys of silvery laughter," is his typically ornate way of describing life's flux operating on the rigidified fictions—the "myths"—of a culture, "whatever is overblown, affected, pretentious, pedantic, fantastically delicate."[12]

Yet comic works themselves are often highly complicated structures of ingenious or artificial behavior, and our enjoyment of them often lies in their very complications. When Face and Subtle in Jonson's *Alchemist* pile higher and higher their precarious house of cards, their deceit and disguise, our delight is not only in the inevitable debacle that will occur but in their contrivances. We appreciate the ingenuity and even the misled commitment of moral and immoral schemes. In nineteenth-century examples, consider our letdown when Pecksniff is humiliated, when the Anglo-Bengalee Disinterested Life Assurance Society's fraud is found out, when Quilp and Uriah Heep must skulk away from the scene. Elaborate plans and exotic constructs constitute a large proportion of the subject matter of comedy, and it is often the connivers, the perpetrators of farfetched hoaxes, the would-be empire builders who attract us through their vitality. There is something splendid in self-centered human intelligence.

Freud accounts for the effects of tendentious wit—that is, wit that carries in it an attack that is normally inhibited by the superego—by suggesting that the pleasure is attributable in large part to the complicated, oblique manner of presentation in which the tendentious thrust of comedy is clothed. The more devious the route to the laughter, the richer its cathexis. Hence we do not simply want to see life in all its randomness triumph; we do not simply await the flow of contingent reality breaking down human constructions. Our pleasure is found as often in the building up or digging in of men making their own "permanent" fabrications. Indeed, we cannot account for the success of Dickens' great comic inventions—Mrs. Gamp with her habitual bottle on the "chimley piece" and her imaginary admirer Mrs. Harris, or Pecksniff's reflexive piety as he places his fingertips together in the form of a church and gazes eloquently heavenward—by contingency and absurdity alone. We must include that other aspect of the comic vision, the emphasis on fictions, for many of our favorite comic characters are entrenched in their hypocrisy and self-protective patterns of behavior, which are hardly what Susanne Langer could call open, flexible, or life-celebrating.

If we realize, however, that the objective of almost all comic works in the last two centuries has been to make us understand that most of our habitual and self-defensive behavior is made up of fictions, in Kermode's sense, then we can see why comedy incorporates both the random chanciness of human existence and all manner of elaborate constructs and devices. Comedy's particular vision of life, and what it seeks to transmit to us, is that once a social code or a line of conduct ceases to be treated as a fiction and is instead sanctified and taken seriously by a society, or by influential individuals in it, then existence grows oppressive

and sterile. Comic works characteristically expose pompos-
ity and smug self-deception (what Frye calls the ritual
bondage in which so many authority figures find themselves) and undermine dull and inhuman mores. By top-
pling those authorities and delving cynically into the covert
sexuality that lies behind decency, or the timorous greed
that lies behind calls for "responsibility," comedy encourages us to understand what is masked by rigorous, somber
approaches to human behavior. Somehow the attitude that
we can define as "noncomic," the tendency to see things in
their most serious and consequential terms, contains the
potential of freezing and stultifying human response and
leads, comic writers tell us, to a vision that will prove painfully inflexible. Hence the pulse of chancy reality surges
through comic works, opening up the society to change
and adjusting its concepts so that all the psychologically
necessary patterning of human behavior can be conceived
as the building and adjusting of fictions. Comedy causes a
culture to look at itself in a new way.

There is, finally, another aspect of comedy that I intend
to trace through the nineteenth century. There appears to
be a process in the nature of comic invention that generates
some of comedy's characteristic forms. The process has
three discernible phases, and although the phases admittedly overlap and different phases predominate in different periods of literary history, they are present in most
comic works. The first phase is one of destruction or reductiveness; the second phase, one of elaboration and experimentation; and the third, one of closure of the comic
development.

We are most familiar with the first phase, for almost all
comedy seems to need to launch an attack on the fictions
that have become myths and on the rigid social situations
and literary conventions that are choking off the breath of
free imaginative development. Thackeray and Dickens
conspicuously began their careers with parodies of writing
styles that had become stultified or mannered. The burden

of distrust that comedy had to bear in a Puritan culture arose from the suspicion that comic treatment was randomly destructive. And indeed, the very origins of formal comic expression did lie in rites of fertility and spring in which old gods were symbolically dethroned, the relics of the dead seasons immolated, and the spontaneous anarchy of Saturnalia let loose. Hence, this first stage is one in which the techniques of blasphemy, ridicule, parody, mimicry, exaggeration, and grotesque reduction predominate.

The appeal of the destructive phase, the heady sound of crashing chandeliers and broken glass and of air being let out of stuffed shirts is almost too great to control at times, and there are many writers who let it spin out of control so that it dominates the entire work. Alvin Kernan observes that in conventional satires, an absolute frenzy of indignation and attack often envelops the narrating persona.[13] In fact, the distinction between comedy and satire inheres in the modifications that comedy makes in its destructive operations. As we shall witness in Jerrold and Dickens, two angry men who could hurt with their words and whose iconoclastic delights could often come close to getting out of hand, comic writers are restrained at some crucial point by their ambivalence toward their own positions and usually toward the objects of their attacks.

This necessary modification that comedy makes in its reductive operations is described by the psychoanalyst Ernst Kris:

> Things which simply arouse anxiety or unpleasure cannot be adapted to comic expression—to attempt to do so may produce an uncanny effect—until they have been reduced in intensity and undergone some degree of working over. A measure of elaboration is a prerequisite of comic expression, and at the same time comic expression accomplishes a measure of elaboration.[14]

Kris is talking here of the kind of lessening or deflecting of impact that I mentioned earlier as defining a comic attitude in an author, but he is also pointing out that the essence of comic expression is a "working over" of material, enabling the writer to handle it with control and poise. This serves the purpose of taking into account any ambivalence the comic artist may feel about the justice or propriety of his attack; an ambivalence that occurs frequently in middle-class writers criticizing their own affluent societies from the inside. It is the "wit work" of which Freud speaks that enhances the pleasure we get from tendentious wit. This is the point, in Arthur Koestler's formula, where the "higher forms" of comedy shade over from attack to artistic discovery.[15]

The very nature of comedy, then, forces it beyond the first stage of pure antagonism and reductiveness into artistic experimentation. I call this second phase the "elaborative" phase, drawing on Kris's terminology. The author's preoccupation with art grows in this phase, for it is here that he tends to flex his creative powers and experiment with new ways of playing with his subject matter. Listen to a description of this process from Wilde's *Dorian Gray*: Lord Henry "played with the idea, and grew willful; tossed it into the air and transformed it; let it escape and recaptured it; made it iridescent with fancy and winged it with paradox. The praise of folly, as he went on, soared into a philosophy. It was extraordinary improvisation. He was brilliant, fantastic, irresponsible." Having started with the conviction that sterile fictions need to be exposed as fictions and paralysis overcome, and having found that only through the transforming techniques of comedy is this achieved, the comic artist irresistibly seeks to continue the metamorphosis. By turning things on their heads, by dissolving and reconstituting, by riding the crest of change, they can ensure the vitality of humane values of freedom and creativity.

Consequently, the writer's impulse toward more and more elaboration strengthens as the creation goes on, just as the caricaturist finds himself dashing off one quick variation after the other. Gulley Jimson, the artist-comic hero of

Joyce Cary's comic novel *The Horse's Mouth*, says that "when you get inside, you get something that goes on going on—it's creation." In this phase, the writer dives into his own art, and self-parody and involution seize his writing. Dickens sensed these impulses strongly, and we can observe it in the delight he takes in elaborating his own inventions—the urge to keep Quilp on yet another dastardly mission and to give us another vignette of Mrs. Gamp—and in the analytically self-parodic aspect of it. "I think it is my infirmity," he said, "to fancy or perceive relations in things that are not apparent generally. Also, I have such an inexpressible enjoyment of what I see in a droll light, that I dare say I pet it as if it were a spoilt child."[16]

Yet Dickens went on to assert, "I . . . never give way to my invention recklessly, but constantly restrain it." The elaborative phase is likely to be the most exciting one for the artist, offering the potentiality of discovering new forms through experimentation, but it has alarming tendencies. The metamorphosis may get out of hand so that nothing holds together in any form that may be called artistic. Comedy is by its nature often anarchic, which can be disturbing to artists like Dickens and Carroll who value order. It is so close to "play" (as we shall see) that the artist may feel he is spinning a web out of his own insides and find the indulgences trivial or senseless. A writer who is highly conscious of a social responsibility may find himself playing too fast and loose with the ethical and social assumptions of his time. Dickens' restraint of comic elaboration is an example of the third phase in the comic process—that of closure.

Closure can be dictated by various considerations reflecting various emphases. It can be a reaffirmation of the normal or recognizable social order, freer than the one that the comic vision first attacked but in no sense radically reformed or changed. It can be a retreat back to the status quo, indicating that the comic venture was one of escape or whimsical imagination—a cry of anguish, perhaps, but nothing consequential. It can be an aesthetic closure, the adoption of an ending that brings the action or character development to a point of rest or that fulfills the governing image. It can be, as is the ending of *Dorian Gray*, a mock denouement, following the patterns of the hackneyed literature it has been parodying. Or it can be only the most perfunctory of closures, as those of Nabokov's novels are, in which the possibilities for elaboration remain indefinitely open; the book ends, but not the comic vision.

The attitude of the individual artist toward the form of his work is ultimately the determinative factor in deciding the nature of the closure, and whether to emphasize the reductive phase or the elaborative phase. Any generalizations, therefore, about historical changes in the emphasis of comic literature will be risky. We can suggest, though, that in a socially conscious period in which there is a certain suspicion toward artistic revel and improvisation, the elaborative phase will not predominate and therefore writers will be inclined to put a firm, socially responsible ending on their comic explorations. If, during such a period, there is uncertainty or cynicism about vestigial mores and social forms, comic works may be characterized by their reductiveness. During the unstable times of the pre-Victorian Regency, for example, the literature shows the strains of a reductive attack on old forms, coupled with the need to explore new modes of life, and yet a very pronounced social self-consciousness. Hence the works from this period, which we study in chapter one, are circumscribed, for all their elaboration. The artistic play is not allowed to follow its own tendencies. Though it is often self-parodic and involuted, it is not so in a creative way. It does not spring from the artist's instinct to follow his own inventions and whims in the search for new fictions and fresh artistic formulations. These writers compulsively return to conventional morality and relatively stereotyped literary visions. They probe the frontiers of their own art only haltingly, for they are writers of very limited creative expansiveness.

Thackeray and Dickens, on the other hand, are capable

of great expansiveness, and in the work of both men, we can see that their creations transcend the old formulas. As mordant social critics, they first of all excel in the reductive operation; but as acutely self-conscious fabricators, they move on to richer elaborations. Yet in Thackeray's great comic novel *Vanity Fair*, Becky Sharp's comic freedom and exploitation of sterile social fictions must apparently be curtailed because of her author's reluctance, finally, to renounce social order. The ambivalence that prompts the elaboration must, at last, idle down to vacillation and ironically uncommitted poise. Dickens, however, does not concede to his time: his comedy unfurls as he brilliantly metamorphoses his material, pressing further and further into analytical parody and transmogrification. But Dickens is bent on dominating his world with an embracing moral and social vision. He will not permit himself to give way entirely to the effusions of his natural creativity, even though he stretches his broad canvases more and more in *Bleak House* and *Little Dorrit* to accommodate it all—hence the arbitrarily imposed endings of his novels, all the teeming comic life swiftly bottled and corked. He is a child of an earlier, more puritanically self-controlled generation of comic writers.

Closure in Lewis Carroll's Alice books reflects an anxiety lest comic anarchy get out of hand. There is some of this to Dickens' thinking, but his writing shows none of Carroll's use of elaboration as a means of conceiving an alternative life style, free of the incursions of modern Victorian social responsibilities. Dickens' great advance in the uses of the elaborative phase of the comic process was to open up the possibilities for the transformative powers of art, while the characteristic expansion of the elaborative phase in the writers of the 1870s was to explore new life styles. The latter innovation is principally a form of social rather than artistic elaboration. As the major artists feel themselves more alienated, their agonistic reductiveness evolves more rapidly into experimental behavior patterns. This development in the internal forms of comedies continues through the end of the century to the point at which we find, paradoxically, that elaboration in life styles has begun to turn life into art.

Consequently, as major comic artists become less faithful to the commonly apprehended social realities and more inclined to think of human existence in terms of what I have called the comic vision—a contingent, ever-changing reality dissolving old fictions and prompting new ones—the reductive phases and elaborative phases intermingle and we get the impression of constant elaboration. Closure is dictated in these writers by aesthetic impulses rather than a need to return to social norms and responsibility. For example, Meredith and Butler are less inclined to resolve their stories with endings that affirm the hallowed English institutions and relationships. And as a result, their endings often strike us as weak, half-hearted. But Wilde solves the problem with patently artificial conclusions that are mock endings. And Beerbohm simply lets the pattern of elaboration continue forever; we are constantly turning over the dilemma of Enoch Soames' existence, and the "truth" of A. V. Laider's lies.

The formal properties, therefore, of comic works—the nature of the closure and the emphases on the elaborative rather than the reductive—reflect the changing uses of comedy during the nineteenth century. This provides an organizing principle for the study of this literature in this time span. As we turn now to the decades immediately preceding the Victorian period, we can observe the tensions within the comic phases begin to build.

1

1820-1845: The Anxieties of Sublimation, and Middle-Class Myths

The triflers of any epoch are an invaluable evidence of the bent of the public mind.
—*Thomas Love Peacock*

I

The dominating fictional phenomenon in England during the 1820s and 1830s was the novel of high fashion and coxcombry that came to be known as the Silver Fork novel. Its origins could perhaps be traced to the late eighteenth-century novels on manners, but nothing of a literary nature could quite account for its sudden popularity. The fashionable novel reflected the volatile social change of the times and the excited interest in aristocratic mores. The appetite of the growing middle-class reading public for glimpses behind the boudoir doors of the upper crust and into the gaming rooms of Crockford's, The Cocoa Tree, and other famous exclusive clubs was so keen that it loosed an onrush of novels under such titles as *The Diary of a Désennuée*, *Marriage of High Life*, and *Flirtation*.

In retrospect, these novels, whose mission was to unfold the shocking and absolutely fascinating intrigues of high society, seem to be rich grounds for the comic. The topics—the self-conscious pretensions of the nouveau riche and the jaded aristocratic establishment—were ripe for satire, playfulness, and exaggeration. The characteristic pro-

tagonist of a Silver Fork novel was an ambitious young man
with delicately exquisite features, carefully rehearsed wit, a
smattering of useful knowledge carelessly displayed, and
audacious pretensions. Disraeli epitomizes the qualities in
his young beau, Charles Annesley:

> But his manner was his magic. His natural and subdued
> nonchalance, so different from the assumed non-emo-
> tion of a mere dandy; his coldness of heart, which was
> hereditary, not acquired; his cautious courage, and his
> unadulterated self-love, had permitted him to mingle
> much with mankind without being too deeply involved
> in the play of their passions. . . . Perhaps the great secret
> of his manner was his exquisite superciliousness, a qual-
> ity which, of all, is the most difficult to manage.[1]

Usually the younger son of a propertied family and therefore of limited prospects, the Silver Fork hero apprentices
himself to a socially prominent dowager who schools him
in the arts necessary to attract both attention and the infatuation of the bored wife of a wealthy earl. His story is
only a thin pretext for the real attractions of such fiction,
however—the firsthand glimpses of the amorous ma-
neuverings that take place behind the façades of the great
houses of London and the cynical insights into the machi-
nations of politics at a time when social connections were
the entrees to power. Though everything is presumably
drawn from reality, nothing is genuine. *Ton* is all: the material is the quicksilver of light social comedy.

The most influential work of the genre, Edward Lytton
Bulwer's *Pelham, or the Adventures of a Gentleman* (1828), begins with the promise of such comedy. Pelham disposes of
his own youth in persiflage, convincing us that he is quite
capable of retailing any horrid anecdote about his family.
When he was a lad, for instance, his mother is said to have
looked over her lists of engagements at the end of an unusually dull social season and, having "ascertained that she
had none remaining worth staying for, agreed to elope

with her new lover."[2] In an excess of passion she got up at six o'clock in the morning to effect her escape. Discovering that she had left behind her favorite china monster and her French dog, however, she returned to fetch them. She appeared just as her husband had discovered her absence and was engaged in performing a ritual of his grief for the benefit of the servants ("he was always celebrated for his skill in private theatricals"). Although secretly anxious to be rid of her, Pelham's father was compelled for the sake of form to insist that his wife stay. Thus, Pelham mournfully reports, he was condemned to endure life with both a father and a mother.

A good beginning, certainly; it is precious, wicked, deceptively casual. But Bulwer suffers from the curious infirmity that beset almost all of the Silver Fork novelists: he does not have the nerve to treat his material comically. From the very beginning, the high-fashion writers apologized for the illusions and wit that made up the piquant sauce of their offerings. Robert Plumer Ward's *Tremaine* (1825), which along with Thomas Henry Lister's *Granby* (1826) established the vogue, opens on the defensive. Ward admits that his account of the boudoir crises and elaborate affectations of Regency high society may have played too loosely with morality. He hopes, though, that the reform of his rakish hero at the end of the novel serves as a "moral antidote" to all the colorful and social evils with which he has entertained us. He frets over his tone, wondering whether it "may appear extraordinary and little suited to the gravity of many of the subjects discussed." A mock "editor" asks rhetorically whether "the author was correct in his half-jesting, half-serious supposition that he was writing a treatise on moral philosophy, not a novel."[3] Ward resolutely keeps himself astraddle the issue of whether his account of the beau monde should be morally didactic or amorally comic, and then worries about its effect on his audience.

And sure enough, before long, Bulwer's Pelham begins

to fall into the tedious habit of mulling over the ethical questions we assumed he had long left behind him. He loses his engaging insolence, behaving less like the infamous puppy he was bred to be and more like a stiff hero from some eighteenth-century novel of moral uplift. To our dismay, we learn that we misconceived him all along: "Beneath all the carelessness of my exterior," he announces, "my mind was close, keen and inquiring; and under all the affectations of foppery, and the levity of manner, I veiled an ambition the most extensive in its objects, and a resolution" (179). Bulwer seems to have disguised the nature of his novel: what began as light, amoral, and comic, suddenly purports to be a study in character reform and the wages of frivolity. Yet in truth the novel becomes neither sort of book; rather, it oscillates between embellished vignettes of high society posturing and pedestrian solemnities about social responsibility. Like Ward, Bulwer refuses to settle on his own designs for his book and allows his tone to range all the way from satire to sentimentality.

According to Mrs. Catherine Gore, whose *Cecil: or, The Adventures of a Coxcomb* (1841) was probably the last great triumph of the vogue, the problem facing the Silver Fork novelist is to maintain one's nerve. "To make a good flippant writer," she announces ironically in her book's preface, "he must have acquired an easy versatility, a nice mixture of courage and caution, the one to startle his reader with some strange fantasy, the other to steer clear, while in his rapid course, of what may be dangerous."[4] Mrs. Gore's prescription would seem to produce a novel of mixed literary manners; and in fact, *Cecil*, like *Pelham*, is a work of strangely varied comic and "serious" effects. Mrs. Gore is just near enough to the Victorian period, however, to favor a weightier moral than her predecessors.[5] Cecil pays more dearly for his careless foppery, and we are rather moved by his genuine remorse when his impulsive determination to take his brother's only son on a furious ride through the forest results in the boy's accidental death. It is a moment fraught not only with significance but also with poignancy. It is a more telling indictment of superficiality and reck-lessness than we usually find in Silver Fork novels. But Mrs. Gore can no more keep the pitch than can Bulwer or Ward; no sooner does she become serious than she pulls herself up abruptly and launches into a set of fabulous adventures on the Continent, leaving behind all the pathos of Cecil's carelessness. Interestingly, Mrs. Gore brings Lord Byron into her novel as a character at this point. Byron was, after all, an appropriate presiding spirit for Silver Fork fiction because in both his life and his work he dramatized the agonies of ethical self-doubt and the joys of vaunting hedonism. Byron's self-mockery and his own conflation of posture and true nature emblemize the predicament of the English high-fashion novelists, who could be sure neither of their positions nor of their tone. "Tragedy,—comedy,—farce (what shall I call it?)" Mrs. Gore asks of the behavior of one of her characters. It is a good question.

Thus, it is almost logical that in *Pelham*, Bulwer grows so haplessly deaf to his own key that he must interrupt his narrative occasionally to remind the "sagacious reader" that some of his text is "writ in irony" and some in "ear-nest." Presumably his audience well understood that Pelham's extensive recitals of "maxims on dress" were not to be entirely accepted as the author's guidelines when they included such recommendations as "keep your mind free from all violent affectations at the hour of the toilet," and such observations as "there may be more pathos in the fall of a collar or curl of a lock, than the shallow think for." Yet Bulwer could never be sure and laced his subsequent editions with frequent disclaimers. And no wonder, for one of the lasting effects that *Pelham* had upon its time was to change the manner of dress. Bulwer's book is credited with influencing a major change in the color of men's evening clothes: from plum to black. Bulwer was obliged to state in the second edition of *Pelham* that "if mistaking the irony of Pelham, [young gentlemen and young clerks] went to the extreme of emulating the foibles which that hero attributed to himself—those were a thousand times more harmless . . . than . . . the mawkish sentimentalities of vice." But the clerks and young bucks found their new affectations rather pleasant. And the entanglement grew even more complex: Bulwer, a reserved and, to some, insolent young man, appeared to act the part of Pelham himself and was constrained for several years to deny publicly that he had made himself the heroes of his novels. When the youthful Benjamin Disraeli, who always carried off his self-expression with unchecked verve, appeared in canary waistcoats and velvet trousers, he half-facetiously claimed he did so in response to the spirit of *Pelham*. Bulwer thus found himself mocked by the fictions of his own tour de force.

The social novelists thus became ensnared in their social effects. Their own exploitation of the volatility of the times increased their attractiveness to certain rather impressionable or reckless souls. Henry Colburn, the most successful publisher of Silver Fork novels, indulged in shameless puffery, hinting in his blurbs that secrets of royal chambers were being disclosed and that his books were thinly fictionalized "portraits of living characters." As a matter of fact, this was often the case. Thomas Henry Lister's character Trebeck in *Granby* was so much like Beau Brummell that the latter swore "Lister must have known those who were intimate with me." Robert Plumer Ward was a lawyer and M.P. with numerous political and social connections that furnished real-life inspirations for his fictional scandals. Lady Charlotte Bury, author of *A Marriage in High Life* and *The Lady of Fashion*, was the daughter of the Duke of Argyll and lady-in-waiting to Caroline, the Princess of Wales; and one naturally assumes that the tidbits and general outlines of behavior in her novels were drawn from the most genuine of sources.

Novels like *Pelham* generated not only imitative behavior,

but a chain reaction of "literary" events that took on their own cultural significance. For example, Bulwer was plagued with an inauthentic "second series" of *Pelham* that appeared in the disreputable journal *The Age* and created almost as great a rage as the original. Also, scandal sheets modeled after Silver Fork novels flourished with manufactured details and speculations about the prominent and notorious. When Disraeli finally presented an "inside" glimpse into the operations of these very cheap sheets in *The Young Duke*, we turn almost a full circle—fiction exposing the true nature of newspapers that imitate the novels that purport to expose real life.

Thomas Carlyle found the entire situation so disgusting that he identified "Dandyism" as one of the besetting ills of the age. Grumbling over the "moon-calves and monstrosities" that it inspired, he expressed a fear that they would take on life. "What is it that the Dandy asks? . . . Solely, we may say, that you would recognize his existence: would admit him to be a living object."[6] Hollow, a set of walking fine clothes, the literary dandy was not yet a reality, but he symbolized the modern difficulty in differentiating the false from the substantial in human nature. Carlyle used *Pelham* as his special whipping boy, and Bulwer, exasperated that he was being persistently misread, was hurt and perplexed that the philosopher could have so misconceived the intentions of his book.

To a certain extent, it was not a purely literary problem after all. The Byronesque oscillations in mood—the posing and affectation, the mixed hedonism and moralism—had an actual foundation in the life that the fashionable novels studied. Something was happening in the 1820s and 1830s that Silver Fork dandyism and recklessness was accurately reflecting. Bulwer, for all his casualness as a novelist, could be a perceptive social critic. In the highly influential study of national character *England and the English* (1833), Bulwer reflected on his times:

The novels of fashionable life illustrate feelings very deeply rooted, and productive of no common revolution. In proportion as the aristocracy had become social, and fashion allowed the members of the more mediocre classes a hope to outstep the boundaries of fortune, and be quasi-aristocrats themselves, people eagerly sought for representations of the manners which they aspired to imitate, and the circles to which it was not impossible to belong . . . Hence the three years' run of fashionable novels was a shrewd sign of the times.[7]

The social historian-critic Maurice Quinlan agrees with Bulwer that a "revolution in manners occurred during the first quarter of the century." He finds it permeating every social stratum. The causes were "an expanding population, the advent of the industrial system, and the consequent increase in national wealth [that] afforded opportunities for many enterprising individuals to improve their economic condition."[8] "There is a continual ferment going on," Charles Greville noted in his memoirs, "and separate and unconnected causes of agitation and disquiet which create great alarm but which there seems to exist no power of checking or subduing."[9]

The nature of the changes in manners as people began shifting their social positions was unusually frenetic during these decades. The peace after the Napoleonic Wars left the English in a euphoria that found a ready outlet in self-induced excitements. Extensive social adjustment was made necessary as urbanization and a certain amount of rural economic dislocation put people into new situations for which the old styles of life seemed inadequate. The adjustments were particularly noticeable within the middle class, which was increasing in proportion and in its own sense of respective wealth. Ward, musing over his unstable times, says, "Not that I think the world worse now than it has been for perhaps the last hundred years. The upper and lower classes I should say are certainly not so; I am not so sure of the middle."[10] The contemporary critic R. H. Horne finds a great deal that is excessive in Mrs. Gore's *Cecil* but allows that "she excels in the portraiture of the upper section of the middle class, just at the point of contact with the nobility, where their own distinguishing traits are modified by the peculiarities of their social position. . . . All this external tumult, wrong-headed and hollow-hearted, proud, sensitive and irritable."[11] Many in the middle class had suddenly come into wealth and into the opportunities for leisure, and it is they who turned to the aristocracy—and to literature about the aristocracy—to discover manners and modes of life that would somehow befit and signify their new stations. The very rapidity of rise in class, and the corresponding danger of sudden plunge in fortunes, exacerbated the social turmoil. Bulwer notes:

> These mystic, shifting, and various shades of gradua-
> tion; these shot-silk colours of society produce this effect:
> That people have no exact and fixed position—that by
> acquaintance alone they may rise to look down on their
> superiors—that while rank gained by intellect, or by in-
> terest, is open but to few, the rank that may be obtained
> by fashion seems delusively open to all. Hence, in the
> first place, that eternal vying with each other; that spirit
> of show; that lust of imitation which characterize our
> countrymen and countrywomen. . . . As wealth procures
> the alliance and respect of novels, wealth is affected even
> where not possessed; and, as fashion, which is the crea-
> ture of an aristocracy, can only be obtained by resem-
> bling the fashionable; hence, each person imitates his fel-
> low.[12]

The Silver Fork novel, then, reflects the tenor of one segment of contemporary society, while purporting to mimic it for the purposes of ridicule and moral example. No wonder Bulwer kept confronting the irony of seeing his own fictional character Pelham set the style for young men on the make. No wonder the attempts to deny the reality of affectation and show were continually misfiring. And no wonder figures like Ward, Lister, and Lady Bury, whose literary backgrounds were slight and casual and whose chief claims to authorship were their firsthand knowledge of the court and beau monde, could not put the mores of such an excitable era under any kind of imaginative control. They were, for one thing, scarcely equipped to find the literary means to reconstitute their material in dramatically compelling and original ways. The more they ransacked earlier literature for formulas—the sentimental novel, the late eighteenth-century novel on manners, the Gothic novel, the turn-of-the-century tract literature of moral progress—the more inappropriate and artificial their expression seemed. For another thing, they found themselves in a position where the social imperatives that might regulate their fiction were in constant flux.

Freud's theory of the comic in his *Jokes and Their Relationship to the Unconscious* does not always prove to be useful in discussing the broader comic expression of literary forms (largely because Freud is concerned primarily with the psychic dynamics of laughter and wit). It does, however, help us understand the nature of the dilemma of this particular set of writers. Freud speaks of the tendentious thrust of much wit, its impulse to attack and criticize—and if anything, the Silver Fork writers fancied themselves as critics of haut monde behavior. Freud insists, though, that all such tendentiousness must be clothed in a clever, often artistically contrived, mode of expression; otherwise it will be unsettling rather than amusing. This he attributes to the demands of the superego, which urges us to conform to or mitigate any offense to the social (and thus ethical) "realities" of living in a civilized society. The expression of the joke, or the wit work, allows us to circumvent in part the superego's constraints. When, however, the realities of the time are so problematical and the governing social mores

so volatile as they were in the 1820s and 1830s, the imperatives of the superego are themselves in a state of flux. The
superego is, as it were, constantly defining and redefining
its terms. Judgment is likely to depend upon pure assertion
and to be arbitrary and self-conscious. Is it any surprise,
then, that Bulwer—who was often the walking superego of
his times and would oscillate between unconvincing
moralizing and barely modulated satire and extravagance—would find his comedy so uneasy?

The social content of Silver Fork fiction and the concerns
of Bulwer and others about the implications of their vision
suggest another unsettling dimension to the dilemma of
these writers. Bulwer was hypersensitive to his effect on
clerks and on the general public because he was aware that
a fundamental change in the depiction of human nature
was emerging in nineteenth-century literature. The emphasis on role playing reflected more than the period's opportunism and frantic image-seeking; Bulwer frets openly
in his novels over the dangerous conceptions that his
readers may be developing about human character. Thus,
for instance, we find him hastening to defend one of the
most melodramatic portraits in *Pelham*—that of the troubled soul Glanville who has nearly ruined himself in his
dogged stalking of the man who seduced his fiancée—by
insisting that he is no posturer. "Reader must bear in mind
that there was nothing artificial or affected in [Glanville's]
musings. . . . nothing of the dramatic brown studies and
quick starts, which young gentlemen, in love with Lara or
Lord Byron, are apt to practice" (192). The portrait of
Glanville is predicated, Bulwer is saying, on assumptions
about *human nature* that current experience seemed to be
casting into doubt. The notions about man's nature that
had prevailed in the eighteenth century held that the true
character of an individual was essentially a fixed quality,
and that the outer, social "personality" was often a façade.
To the humanistically oriented writer of the eighteenth
century, human nature was "fixed, stable and objectively

knowable." Whatever the "infinitely varied surfaces" of man, which Samuel Johnson labeled "disguises," the center was uniform.[13] Writers and critics through the time of Scott spoke of the truth of the human heart and the consistent qualities of goodness (or baseness) that external evidence often belied.[14] Such a concept is at the core of the eighteenth-century literature of the "man of feeling," whose basic inclinations are benevolent and good. It is a premise of the theory of comedy that Henry Fielding in *Joseph Andrews* and Oliver Goldsmith in his "Essay on the Theatre" express, for in arguing that comedy lies in the exposure of affectations and pretensions, they are assuming that a "true self" can be unearthed. The satiric operations of comedy in the eighteenth century are for the most part designed to expose the reality of the comic target's essentially base nature. Conversely, a man may exhibit outward faults and occasional rash behavior while, as in the case of Tom Jones, his inner being is sound. Such assumptions about character support the narrator's assertion in *Pelham*, vis-à-vis Glanville, that "a man may commit the greatest of crimes, and . . . it changes not the current of his being. . . . *One* crime, however heinous, does not necessarily cause a revolution in the system—it is only the perpetual course of sins, vices, follies, however insignificant they may seem, which alters the nature and hardens the heart" (300). By the same theory, Pelham, for all his youth and young manhood of cynical sycophancy, can still be a man of integrity at his core.

Against this, however, stands the phenomenon that the fashionable novels catch—the mania of the times for role playing and the uncanny interaction between fictions of self and human reality. The self-conscious projections of personality have become so complex that, as the fashionable tease Lady Harriet Vandelour observes in *Cecil*, "we are all pretending to be natural with all our might, till the affectation of nature has become as natural as any other affectation" (I, 74). Bulwer cynically observes in *England and the*

English that the inner/outer man disjunction can be twisted deceptively; many a public figure is excused for his ruthlessness or callousness by the virtuous example he sets in his private, domestic life. The truth is, Bulwer notes, that in many cases the outer man is the "real" man. "We ought to allow no such unreal distinctions," he insists in his essay "On English Notions of Morality"—"it is the whole man only we must acknowledge to be good or evil—not a part of him."[15]

The reason for this apparent "change in human nature," which occurred on or about 1825 (to paraphrase Virginia Woolf, speaking humorously of another such change a century later), was very likely the quality of modern urban life. The twentieth-century sociologist Cesar Graña looks back upon dandyism itself as a kind of desperate proclamation of individuality in the lonely city, an often pathetic but often spirited assertion of personality at a time of disorientation.[16] Bulwer, in fact, created perhaps the first vivid English portrait of the tortured city man in his next novel *Paul Clifford* (1830) but wrought it in his characteristically ambivalent, vexing manner. The subject of the portrait is a London lawyer, William Brandon, who has become literally encased in the role that he has adopted for getting along in the city. Brandon is being eaten away by a horrible personal secret but he has risen to great political eminence by acquiring an inscrutable mask of respectability and self-control. In one brief relaxation of that control, he tells his niece that the way of the world is false image: "Half of us are employed in saying white is black, and the other half is swearing that black is white. . . . The fool says what is false while the colours stare in his face and give him the lie; but the clever man takes as it were a brush and literally turns the black into white and the white into black before he makes the assertion, which is *then true*."[17] Brandon's own power of mind attains unbelievable proportions. He suffers, as a kind of poetic justice for his hardness, the agonizing pains of involuntary spasms of the face muscles—the dreaded tic douloureux—but betrays not a trace of it. More incredibly, he endures the symptoms of an onsetting paralytic stroke with equal composure. Even death cannot crack the façade: while "the right side of his face was partially distorted, as by convulsion or paralysis; . . . not sufficiently so to destroy the remarkable expression of loftiness and severity which had characterized the features in life" (454).

William Brandon is an early characterization of the hardened man of the city. He is that same mixture of suppressed emotion, imperious dignity, and Calvinistic rigor that we find in Dickens' great tycoons, Dombey and Merdle. His story is essentially the same as that of Dombey; the gradual tightening of the will under the pressures of finance until all other human qualities have been squeezed out—a man made over by the necessities of life. Dickens, however, renders Dombey as such a compelling portrait that he must inevitably color our lasting impression of the industrial tycoon. Dickens understands how the self-fiction reconstituted the man, how Dombey's role as a cold, calculating, willful entrepreneur had grown to be all of him and left him no flexibility to be other than his image. Dickens was the first great writer to show how a comic vision of life as a series of created fictions was the appropriate vision for the new urban consciousness. Indeed, though such a vision may be as old as man's literature, it never seems to have so aptly served as a governing image until the great nineteenth-century writers like Dickens applied it to their times. Bulwer was, as we shall later see, a substantial influence upon Dickens' perception of such people; Dickens may even have known the Brandon portrait. However, in Bulwer's hands, the impression of character could not acquire the power and conviction to emerge from the novel as a conceptual truth. Instead, it is defeated and rendered ludicrous by Bulwer's half-belief. It is almost as if Bulwer were caught between the convictions of his traditional concept of human nature and the imperatives of his comic vision; he adds just the comic touch—the power of a man to will his facial muscles into place during a paralytic stroke and to stare down the tic douloureux—that breaks the tone. Bulwer seems to have subconsciously realized that he was on a ground appropriate to the comic yet, as is characteristic of him, he proved unable to give himself entirely over to it.

Here, as in other instances, what Bulwer the cultural critic so cannily perceived about his time, Bulwer the popular novelist and beleaguered social arbiter steadfastly refused to acknowledge. He rejected the notion that one must view human behavior as a series of fictions because it contributed to the affected style of French culture. The conviction that there was one "essential" human nature in each person seemed particularly "English" (in the eighteenth century the notion had been associated with the solidness of English character), and the "new" way of looking at man was, appropriately enough, an insidious cultural influence from France. One of the characters in *Pelham* notes that the French excel in "memoirs, comedy, satirical observation on peculiar classes, and pointed aphorisms," because they are "fonder of considering man in his relation to society and the active commerce of the world." The English in contrast, favor the study of man "in the abstract," "man *in se*" (61). Indeed, novel after novel in the Silver Fork vein shows that affectation and Frenchified thinking go hand in hand. It is no accident that the haut monde incessantly drops French phrases and dotes upon the Parisian scene. Inevitably, such people fall into the grievous Gallic error of mistaking the surface for reality. A comic vision that suggested that life is little more than a series of willed fictions and that man exists in a state of contingency could only sap the integrity of the English self-image.

There is a deeper issue here, however—one that penetrates to the heart of the comic. The Silver Fork writers are unable to establish any clear demarcation between art and reality. Their fiction oscillates between invention and actuality. Even the purely fictional proves to be unstable, for it generates its own mocking "reality." If Freud is right in supposing that the impulse toward comedy originated in childhood play—in our fascination with and growing mastery of words, puns, and forms—then we may find that the source of the difficulties of the fashionable novelists lay in their inability to adhere to the first principle of "play": it must be divorced from actuality. Johan Huizinga, in *Homo Ludens*, his study of the play elements in Western culture, states that adult play requires that its product be separated from what we consider "ordinary" or "real" life.[18] Otherwise the element of mastery will be lost, and the player will fall into the anxieties and cross-purposes that characterize life. The essential premise of the comic enterprise may be the ability to conceive of one's activity primarily as play.

The issue is more complex, however, for comic writing almost always involves more than play, more than rehearsal of forms or controlled paradigms. It is a mode of engagement with life, of reworking, or reorienting, some of those very anxieties, desires, and contingencies of reality. Ernst Kris' formulations are helpful here, for while he acknowledges that play is the "starting point" of the comic, he also notes that it necessarily must progress into a second stage, which he calls "fun" and which incorporates other people and thus more of the nature of reality. Then one must move on to the art work, the "wit work" or elaboration, that is so essential to effective comic expression.[19] In these later stages something more complex is involved: "fun" and artistic elaboration both presume self-consciousness and a certain formal and rhetorical sophistication that accompanies art. Here, presumably, the separation of the artistic expression from actuality will be more difficult to retain. It is at this point that some sort of commitment to the primacy of art must be made.

When we compare Benjamin Disraeli's Silver Fork novels with those of Bulwer and Mrs. Gore, we see how critical the commitment to art can be. As a virtuoso's lark, Disraeli composed his own fashionable novels; and his second, *The Young Duke* (1831), contrasts tellingly with *Pelham* and *Cecil*. Disraeli's book contains none of the oscillation of tone and unintentional irony that mar the other two novels. It fulfills the comic promise of its subject. *The Young Duke* has all the verve that the posturing of the haut monde's dandyism calls for. Rather than backing away from the affectations of Silver Fork life and Silver Fork style, Disraeli boldly intensifies them. There is no stinting, no qualification, no looking over the shoulder. Disraeli's hero is wealthy beyond imagination. His twenty-first birthday, when he succeeds to his father's estates, is "an event which created almost as great a sensation among the aristocracy of England as the Norman Conquest." He inherits blocks of London, estates almost illimitable, an entire province in Ireland. To charm a mistress, he reconstructs the Alhambra in nine acres off St. James. He masters every frivolous pleasure: "His dancing was declared consummate. He galloped with grace and waltzed with vigour. It was difficult to decide which was more admirable, the elegance of his prance or the precision of his whirl."[20] He yields to none of Pelham's dreary *longueurs* of faltering self-esteem: the Duke, when alone, "fell into a reverie and mused on his magnificence. He could no longer resist the conviction that he was a superior essence, even to all around him. . . . His soul wandered in dreams of omnipotence" (36). *The Young Duke* sustains its nature as an exquisitely rendered comic bauble by appearing to deny any but the most stylized relationships to actuality.

Disraeli's novel succeeds because it asserts and revels in its own art whenever possible. It draws attention to its craft. Unlike Bulwer, Ward, or Mrs. Gore, Disraeli strives constantly for the epithet, the bon mot, the antithesis, the graceful phrase. He moves through his ornately dramatic incidents with patience so that the small talk is allowed to unfold naturally and the sounds and movements of the scene are not arbitrarily blocked off from the central ac-

tion. He seeks the fanciful analogy that mocks its own pretension: "Some sherry, with a pedigree like an Arabian,
heightened the flavour of the dish, not interfered with it;
as a toady keeps up the conversation which he does not
dare distract" (171). The comic and the artificial are made
to seem somehow the same, which is precisely what the
fashionable novel calls for. Bulwer and the others aimed
for this kind of unity with their haughty young heroes
dawdling over chocolate and fixing their ringlets, but they
achieved it only intermittently.

The spirit of *art* appears to be necessary for comedy. Disraeli committed himself to the fabrication necessary to
render the shameless, self-absorbed milieu of the haut
monde and capture the unstable, evanescent temper of the
1820s and 1830s. He believed, as Bulwer never quite could,
in the romantic possibilities of the human imagination to
conjure up new realities. Significantly, the change in the
concept of human nature that Bulwer, Carlyle, and Mrs.
Gore contemplated with such dismay lifted Disraeli's spirit.
He speaks unambiguously in *The Young Duke* of the role
playing of the times: "the great majority of human beings
in a country like England glide through existence in perfect ignorance of their natures, so complicated and so con-
trolling is the machinery of our social life!" (241). Disraeli
accepts the possibilities of the assumed persona because of
his own conviction that one can project one's personality,
one's own special vision, upon the actualities of the world.
The commitment to the workings of the imagination that
raises *The Young Duke* above its peers is the same power
Disraeli believes can be imposed on life. He was unique for
his time—for any time—in his confidence in his own abili-
ties to transform actuality according to his own vision. He
boldly reread history to draw sweeping analogies between
the Venetian constitution and Whig political theory. He
imagined a group of young illuminati, the Young Eng-
landers of his political novels, whose ambitious ideals
would change the political map. He dared to assert that vi-

tality could recharge that most languid of social classes, the English aristocracy. As John Holloway observes, Disraeli's work "cannot be accepted as describing the world as it is, one accepts it as having shifted for a moment to describing the world as it should be."[21]

Admittedly, Disraeli is something of an anomaly in these decades. Not until Oscar Wilde (who recognized his precursor in the connection that his *Dorian Gray* draws with Disraeli's first Silver Fork novel *Vivian Grey*) do we encounter another English writer with the panache to invent such apparent counter-realities as Disraeli does. To the writers of the early and mid-Victorian periods, Disraeli's nonpolitical fiction was scarcely worth taking seriously; to some, like Trollope, he was an insidious corrupter of taste. Trollope let loose waspishly in his *Autobiography*:

> Disraeli's glory has been the glory of pasteboard, and the wealth has been the wealth of tinsel. The wit has been the wit of hairdressers, and the enterprise has been the enterprise of mountebanks. An audacious conjurer has generally been his hero,—some youth who, by wonderful cleverness, can obtain success by every intrigue that comes to his hand. Through it all there is a feeling of stage properties, a smell of hair-oil, an aspect of buhl, a remembrance of tailors, and that pricking of the conscience which must be the general accompaniment of paste diamonds.[22]

No formula could better produce a Silver Fork novel. Still, Trollope has a point; Disraeli was off on a lark. His presentation was too abstracted to seem relevant to a generation so immersed in the ambiguities of social alignment. The direction taken by Victorian comic writing, as we shall see in Dickens, was toward an expression that would incorporate the middle-class writer's social ambivalence while still giving free reign to the imagination. The challenge posed by Disraeli's aesthetic success in the fashionable novel was quite real, though: British comic writers would be plagued by their inability to transform their socially charged material through the powers of art. For the generation immediately following, the comic was largely subordinated to what we must call "sociological" objectives.

" 'Ow I wish I was a heagle!"—*John Jorrocks*

I I

The fashionable novel was not the only brief fictional sensation of the pre-Victorian decades. In fact, the period was characterized by a surprising variety of comic expressions. Writings that would not normally be expected to incorporate comedy—such as the writings of Thomas De-Quincey on the horrors of crime—slipped frequently over the edge into mordant humor. Around the same time, a former sports reporter named Pierce Egan started a vogue for exuberant literary sketches of London low life. And Frederick Marryat, a retired sea captain, introduced the tales of naval and military adventure that were to become staples of boys' reading for the rest of the century and tapped a strong reservoir of wish fulfillment in a society feeling the first constraints of modern living. Robert Smith Surtees struck an oddly keen response for his episodes in the life of a cockney grocer whose insatiable fancy is to ride to the hounds. The variety seemed to reflect a spirit of experimentation; as if writers in a transitional period were seeking both a mode of literary expression and a language in which to articulate the fears and the excitement of the changing times.

The turmoil was stirred by a hectic publishing scene. Newspapers and magazines were being launched almost weekly in an effort to exploit the growing craving for information about politics, urban life, new fashions, and fresh entertainments. The new publications were inclined

toward "satirical" and "humorous" treatment of social and
political subjects, and as they jostled with each other for
position, they put a premium on spirit, even to the point of
recklessness. For instance, the manner of *Fraser's Magazine*
during William Maginn's editorship at this time has been
characterized by John Gross as "riotous Tory Bohe-
mianism."[23] That was a good image to have, for in order to
be popular, a journal needed to be a stimulant, bracing its
politics with wit and leavening it with episodes of adventure.

The emphasis on action was another striking aspect of
literary expressions of the 1820s and 1830s. In fact, if there
is anything that distinguishes the predominant mode of
comedy in the pre-Victorian decades from that of the later
periods, it is the impulse of the writers to externalize the
strains and concerns of the times, to find outlets in activity
and broad social interaction. Hugh Dalziel Duncan, a
sociologist who believes that literature functions mainly as
a symbolic presentation of feelings transformed into social
values, suggests that this may be characteristic of popular
literature: "such literature does not weigh ends and means
but charges objects and experiences with sentiments useful
in common action."[24] Certainly much of what appears to be
purely entertaining depiction of life is charged with sentiments and informed by a discernible social positioning.
The sentiments and points of view are those of the nascent
middle class, responding to the shocks of social, especially
urban, change.

Pierce Egan's book furnishes a colorful example of Duncan's claim. Egan's novel, formally titled, *Life in London; or,
the Day and Night Scenes of Jerry Hawthorne, Esq. and his Elegant Friend Corinthian Tom Accompanied by Bob Logic, the Oxo-
nian, in Their Rambles and Sprees through the Metropolis*
(1823), an account of the adventures of three upper-class
young bucks in the depths of the city, is not so much a
novel as a production. It styles itself a "CYCLOPEDIA," or
a collection of essentially unrelated encounters and comic

pieces. Its manner is that of a carnival come-on: the printing type is set in exotic combinations of full capital letters and italics and seems to dance before the eye. The text is interspersed with poems, songs, and routines; it is copiously illustrated; and the reader's attention is repeatedly drawn down to mock footnotes citing the likes of Messrs. Scissors and Paste or The Grub Street Gang. Egan further accents the work with a relentless patter of fast lines and quick jokes. In one footnote, for example, a person is described in this manner: "It had been said of SHUTER, that he was descended from respectable parents: this he denied by public advertisement; asserting that he owed his existence to an Irish Haymaker, from an amour with an oyster-wench."[25]

Dedicated to Laurence Sterne, appropriately enough, Egan's book flourishes its fictionality, its extravaganza/sideshow qualities: "The Metropolis is now before me: POUSSIN never had a more luxuriant, variegated, and interesting subject for a landscape; nor had SIR JOSHUA REYNOLDS finer characters for his canvass." "The *Camera Obscura* is now at work; the table is covered with objects for the amusement of my readers" (17, 19). Characterization is little more than a conjuring art, the author protesting that "the likeness of CORINTHIAN TOM is not taken with a *machine*," but requires "numerous lights and shades . . . the frequent rubbings out—the various tints—the fine workings-up—required to do justice to a head" (51). Egan's attitude seems to be that if it is specimens that his readers want, it is specimens they will get. He has a delightful time presenting his phantasmagoria and parades forth all manner of human items, dressed out and fully typed:

LIFE in London, all jostling against each other in the Park with the utmost *sang-froid* . . . —the IMPURE and the *Modest Girl* . . . the FLASH COVE and the *Man of Sentiment*—the FLAT and the *Sharp* . . . the HEAVY TODDLERS and the *Operators* . . . the DUKE and the

"Dealer in Queer" . . . the PINK OF THE TON and his *"Rainbow"* . . . the SURGEON and *Resurrection Man* (154).

Egan knows his public. He knows what he is selling to whom—easy generalizations about the lower orders for the "edification" of a middle-class audience. "LIFE IN LON-DON will be seen without any fear or apprehension of danger either from fire or water; avoiding also breaking a limb . . . or picking up a Cyprian and being exposed the next morning before a magistrate for being found disor-derly. . . . HAWTHORNE and laughing TOM are now about to relate their *adventures* for the benefit of *fire-side* heroes and sprightly maidens, who may wish to 'see life' without receiving a *scratch*" (19).

Although other writers may be less extravagantly arch than Egan, instance after instance of the displacement of middle-class uneasiness about urban life is brought into broad comic sociological portraiture. One cannot but re-mark on the number of comic writers of this generation who are keenly involved with the poor. Dickens founded part of his success on his ability to "capture" the lot of the victims of the city in comic portraits. Henry Mayhew, whose four-volume *London Labour and the London Poor* of the 1840s and 1850s is credited with being the first exhaus-tive sociological study of the lower classes—and a real eye-opener—apprenticed himself by writing farces and burles-ques. The readability of Mayhew's social treatise can be as-cribed to his ability to sketch the colorful gesture, the manic oddity. Douglas Jerrold of *Punch* and the poet Thomas Hood, two writers who felt most strongly about the poor, were primarily satirists and humorists. And the great illustrators of the London scene, such as George Cruikshank, alternated between Hogarthian tableaux of the Progress to Ruin and deftly coy domestic sketches.

George Orwell complained about this comic treatment of the poor a century later. When the proletariat "do find their way between the covers of a book," he said, "it is nearly always as objects of pity or as comic relief."[26] P. J. Keating's recent study of the working classes in Victorian fiction substantiates Orwell's claim.[27] Part of the reason writers portrayed the workers and the poor in this way is that vestigial notions of literary decorum remained from the eighteenth century in which fictional arbiters like Fielding proclaimed that the lower classes could be fitly dealt with only in comedy. Orwell is alleging class condescension, however, and there is little doubt that the middle class is trying, through its literature, first of all to *place* the urban lower classes. It is trying to categorize an alien subculture of people and trying to do it in a way that minimizes their *human* characteristics.

Beyond placement, however, is displacement; the writers addressing a middle-class sensibility are abstracting their public's apprehensiveness about the human condition of the time into sociological formulations. Comic novels of the city like Egan's did not just describe and classify, they acceded to the fond beliefs of the upper classes that the metropolitan poor were not terribly sensitive and complicated. Traditional attitudes held: lower life was generally depicted as colorfully grotesque—brazen, crazy, or thoughtlessly violent—or as the reverse—drab, servile, or depressing. Corinthian Tom spoke what his readers liked to think when he said that the "Lower Orders really Enjoy themselves." Egan himself was aware of the travesty of this position; his cynicism about what his audience of "fireside heroes" wanted was what led him into that highly self-mocking, burlesque manner. The writers of such literature during this period all seem to have relied on comedy to keep their balance between the more ambiguous actuality and the colored, stereotyped versions that pleased the public tastes.

Critics of the early Victorian period have noted this tendency toward social objectification. Robert Scholes and Robert Kellogg remark that the English novel tends to "maintain a persistent hospitality toward the typical and allegorical."[28] We are at the beginning, with *Life in London*, of the heyday of the Victorian novel—the novels of Thackeray, Dickens, Trollope, and George Eliot—in which social objectification of human problems is the salient characteristic. The critic C. H. Rickword suggests that British fiction essentially skips over the Richardsonian psychological novel in the early decades of the Victorian period and favors instead the Fieldingesque model of exteriorization of internal thoughts and emotions. "Outward actions have to be invented that will recreate, and not merely illlustrate, inward happenings."[29] Presumably this is prompted in part by the sense, amply supported by the social upheavals all around, that much of what *seems* different about life and one's attitudes is a broad social phenomenon and not something internal. Orwell continues to be naggingly right, nonetheless; when it comes to representing class anxieties, the middle class of this time generally prefers to displace them into modes of expression that seem only indirectly to convey the complexity of emotional situations and the specifics of class response.

Thus, even the real terrors of the potentiality for social chaos that lies in the disordered spread of the city are cast into abstractions of unmodulated action. A new subculture surely was arising in London, and it had frightening proportions in its size, speed of change, and potentiality to violence. The literature of the time reflects the nature of that subculture in the teeming, roiling, unsettling London scenes of Dickens and Thackeray among others.

The subculture is reflected in a different way in the curious abstraction of manic energy in a book such as Frederick Marryat's *Snarleyyow: or the Dog Fiend*. *Snarleyyow* is about the life-and-death struggle at sea, in port, and in various mysterious coastal havens, of a vicious, relentless bulldog named Snarleyyow and a skinny ship's boy named Smallbones. Snarleyyow—"ugly in shape," hairless from an "inveterate mange," walleyed, underjawed, a cur with a

"villainous and sour look"—is the prized pet of Captain
Vanslyperkin. The captain's own character "may be
summed up in the three vices of avarice, cowardice, and
cruelty." His favorite amusement, other than futile attempts on the hardened heart of the corpulent widow
Vandersloosh, is the torment and torture of Smallbones.
He sets the dog on him, keelhauls him, or simply orders
that the lad be whipped until sundown. Smallbones is vex-
atious because despite his "pale, cadaverous face, high
cheekbones and goggle eyes" of malnutrition and abuse, he
is indestructible and indomitable. He apparently lives only
to revenge himself upon the dog. Their encounters are
epic: "long was the struggle, and such was the savage energy of the lad, that he bit and held on with the tenacity of
a bull-dog, tearing the lips of the animal, his ears, and
burying his face in the dog's throat, as his teeth were firmly
fixed on his windpipe. The dog could not escape, for
Smallbones held him like a vise."[30] The ability of the an-
tagonists to survive the most dreadful mauling and sav-
aging—the dog loses an eye, is thrown overboard, kicked,
and poked; Smallbones is left to freeze to death, chewed
on, and beaten with a thick stick—is all that sustains the
tale, for *Snarleyyow* is a chronicle of almost pure, unmotivated meanness.

Nothing explains Marryat's intentions for this book
other than the desire to write an exciting, action-filled
story, and nothing ultimately explains the unnatural malice
of the characters except Marryat's overheated imagination.
He was not the kind of writer to ponder the philosophical
implications of his work, nor, for that matter, is there any
reason he should have been expected to. But books of this
sort, which are, if anything, comic in their exaggeration,
their manic incident, and their depiction of a contingent,
unstructured reality, raise intriguing questions about the
uses of the mode. Walter Allen calls *Snarleyyow* a macabre
farce and notes that it deals with what is almost uncanny in
human behavior.[31] In some cultures, writing of this sort is

to a great extent just sociologically descriptive; the inhumanity and the brutality reflect the desperate lot of a significant stratum of people—of the peasants and the
ignorant. We might think of some Slavic comedy, or Near
Eastern comedy. The characteristic detachment of the narrator and the nonjudgmental approach and unmodulated
prose of the author (Virginia Woolf calls it in Marryat's
case "a kind of bright hardness") indicate an acceptance of
the mayhem as a reality among certain classes of people,
who are presumably too dull, or too dehumanized by their
predicament, to register nuances of emotion. Such a comic
viewpoint is almost nonexistent in nineteenth-century English letters, however, where scarcely any depiction of lower
life can be delivered without a good ladling of sentimental
moral truisms. Ample evidence exists in Marryat's other
writing to indicate that making unemotional sport of the
brutish lot of the common folk is not in his nature. But
Snarleyyow seems to be taking us, half-seriously, into regions of human behavior that defy rational explanation, or
at least conventional explanation—into borderline areas
that are only dimly understood. Indeed, we might suspect
that a work like this is venturing into an area, of human
psychology or social or philosophical crisis, that is troubling
to the writer and his audience, but for which there are no
ready sciences of analysis.

As we advance into the consciousness that we call "modern," where the anxieties are more vague than they seemed
when society was more of a piece, we shall see that Freud's
notion of the dynamics of comedy appears to be inadequate. It is difficult, for one thing, to find a specific "target"
against which a tendentious attack makes its thrust; indeed,
the animosity (or defensiveness) that is implicit in Freud's
concept does not exist when the concern that comedy must
deal with is disquiet, alienation, or anxiety. We have already observed, in Bulwer's predicament of frantically trying to articulate and shore up the unstable ethical premises
of his time while also seeking to circumvent inhibitions

about them, that the superego is a highly problematical factor in attempting to diagnose the workings of the comic in a changing, relativistic situation.

Once again, Ernst Kris seems to offer the most helpful concepts for defining the operations of comedy under these conditons. When Kris redefines the psychology of comic artistry from the perspective of fifty years of twentieth-century literary expression, he speaks of a field of psychic concerns that is significantly different from Freud's. Comedy copes, Kris says, with "things which simply arouse anxiety or unpleasure"; more and more often in modern literature, it attempts to deal with vague apprehensions, with the "uncanny," with psychic fears too amorphous to fit into the socially conscious, socially corrective scheme of Freud. Kris comes to his comic insights from a study of caricature and its means of ritually subduing and transmitting the uncanny and from a study of the pathological. He is a Freudian, but his sense of comedy's scope exceeds Freud's in ways that are more useful to us in looking at nineteenth- and twentieth-century literature.

Thus, we see *Snarleyyow* as a venture, and surely a rather ingenuous one, into regions of psychic disorientation that elude precise definition and categorization. This accounts for its freedom from cloying social considerations, but also for the book's odd, floating disengagement, its refusal to pursue the implications of its bizarre material. Like many writers observing the changes of the century's early decades, especially the potentiality for violence in the lower spheres of London, Marryat only imperfectly understands the causes of his uneasiness. The significance of apparently spontaneous, anarchic expression of human energy cannot be assessed. Its outward manifestations are primarily social—increased crime, civil disorder, individual desperation. Surely what the English are confronting are the dislocations that accompany a shift from an agricultural/ commercial society to an urban/industrial one. But everywhere in the literature of the period are vague intimations that something more crucial is taking place, something that amounts almost to a philosophical disorientation. Something is at work in the nature of human behavior; something can be perceived about human psychology that confounds the old explanations. Marryat's creations behave demonically, as if charged by superhuman forces. As Eric Auerbach has demonstrated with Balzac, it is a feature of the Romantic imagination's apprehension of the new urban milieu to "sense hidden demonic forces everywhere and to exaggerate expression."[32] It is as if they are trying to encompass the latent power and uncanniness of the new situation.

The one writer of the time who seems to be able to take the powers of comedy directly to the source of this disquiet is one whom we do not think of as a comic writer at all, Thomas DeQuincey. In his essay "On Murder Considered as One of the Fine Arts," DeQuincey deftly exposes the period's abiding fascination with accounts of violence in the London netherworld by composing what he characterized as "a foam bubble of gaiety . . . this lecture on the aesthetics of murder."[33] He retells, with exquisite delectation, each sanguinary detail of the brief and brutal career of one John Williams, who decimated two households in London in 1812 with consummate and finicky savagery. In doing so, DeQuincey purports to cater to the "universal" tendency toward "critical or aesthetic valuation of fires and murders" by writing a "bagatelle to graze the brink of horror." One sly purpose is surely to satirize the era's ambivalent romanticization of the very capacities for terror that they feared. We are gratified to learn that Williams "wore a long blue frock of the very finest cloth and richly lined with silk." And we thrill to the description of his "tigerish" character:

> "You might imagine," said my informant, "that in his veins circulated not red lifeblood, such as could kindle into the blush of shame, or wrath, or pity—but a green sap that welled from no human heart." His eyes seemed

frozen and glazed, as if their light were all converged upon some victim lurking in the far background. So far his appearance might have repelled; but, on the other hand, the concurrent testimony of many witnesses, and also the silent testimony of facts, showed that the oiliness and snaky insinuation of his demeanor counteracted the repulsiveness of his ghastly face, and amongst inexperienced young women won for him a very favorable reception."[34]

DeQuincey's essay goes beyond parody or satirization, however. It is a brilliant exegesis of the elaborative powers of the comic imagination. DeQuincey's fugitive wanderings in London had been compelled by his own acute experiences of alienation and drift. His writings were extensive and deceptively circumlocutious attempts to fill the void of his life that was caused by personal loss and an acute sense of man's separation from God. For him, as for Carlyle and others of the period, the alien, bestializing disorder and emptiness of the modern urban experience was symbolic of other kinds of internal and philosophical disorientation: loss of order, loss of connection with God, division of self. DeQuincey penetrated deeply into the regions of anxiety and the uncanny that Marryat only dimly sensed. DeQuincey was conscious of the potential for duality, self-contradiction, and perversity in his own psyche. His literary work can be characterized as a marvelously complex process of elaboration of those intuitions and *aperçus*.

Kris contends that the comic venture is "double-edged," probing into those areas that are most psychically fearful and in constant danger of veering radically into manic disequilibrium unless the elaboration of the dangerous material is full and sufficient. Comedy's sources in the pleasure of mastery of the strange and disquieting appear to require the venture into these areas, nonetheless, for it provides a psychologically satisfying analysis and aesthetic control of those very things that would otherwise haunt the mind.

DeQuincey's "bagatelle" on murder as a fine art constitutes, then, an elaboration of the potential for human perversity that was seemingly unleashed by modern urban
conditions. He painstakingly describes the exfoliations of
evil in the individual mind, seeking, as he does in much
of his writing, to achieve mastery of its nature through
exhaustive and exquisitely incisive representation of it. He
makes Williams' career a demonstration of the manner in
which perversity becomes an artistic composition. The
brute rejoices in slitting the throats of each of his victims,
even of babies who can tell no tales. He seeks to dispatch
every soul on the premises lest an omission ruin the artistic
symmetry of his horrors: "the household ruin was thus full
and orbicular." He leaves his signature of blood each time
in the hope that his deeds will be "more lasting than brass"
in the public's awed memory, pieces of art that "*he* would
condescend to own for a work turned out from his own
studio." In DeQuincey's wily depiction of the fine art of
murder, we are transported by comic elaboration through
the uncanny potentialities of the human psyche, carried
with the artist and the murderer on that double-edged
excursion.

Implicit in DeQuincey's demonstration is the extent to
which the individual human desire can go to pursue its
own psychic courses. Implicit in the era's fascination with
the macabre dimensions of lower life and criminal life is an
apprehension of the urge for self-assertiveness and its capacity for threatening social order. Something about the
times seemed to be raising disquieting avenues of rebellion
and perverse self-expression. However, DeQuincey's will-
ingness to articulate the psychic warp latent in that urge
through amoral comic elaboration of it was not shared by
his fellow writers. Rather, the inclination was to skirt the
psychological for the broadly social and to continue to
project the complexities of emotional and cultural response into action.

Some writers followed a different inclination, turning in

another, more "Victorian" direction toward the romanticization of the potentialities for self-expression that seemed to be slipping from the middle class. Here too, action was the outlet: adventure, rough and ready humor, and vigorousness. In this writing, however, the concern was not so much the alien underworld of city slums or the uncanny tracks of the psyche reacting to its own apprehensiveness; it was the change felt in the quality of middle-class life itself. A literary mode had to emerge to accommodate a generation chafing under moral and physical constraints of the altered life styles that accompanied the divisions of labor and the spatial and functional limitations that were imposed on individuals in a commercially oriented and more thoroughly organized society. Glimmerings of the oncoming Victorian conventionality were visible here and there in this generation; hence, comedic romances of adventure appeared that dreamed aloud the inchoate emotions of rebellion against the ordered, banal life that was steadily encroaching. A form of middle-class myth took shape that sustained the possibilities of freedom of action. The "green world" of the English countryside swelled again in the nostalgic imagination.

A novel by Robert Smith Surtees called *Jorrocks' Jaunts and Jollities* (1831) modernized the myth by drawing the new lower class into it and by reconciling the two spheres of society that had seemed so alien to each other. Surtees' hero, a cockney grocer, ascending by his energy and shrewdness into the middle class, brings the rough-edged vitality of the turbulent city into an idealized reprise of the older freedom of the eighteenth century's Squire Westerns and Tom Joneses. No commercial London affairs are so pressing that, come a good crisp day, Jorrocks will not drop everything for a day's riding to the hounds, or for an excursion to see the Cheltenham dandy put on the boxing gloves: "What true-bred city sportsman has not . . . put off the most urgent business—perhaps his marriage, or even the interment of his rib—that he might 'brave the morn' with that renowned pack, the Surrey subscription foxhounds?"[35] The sedentary city life, "thou Vampire Indolence," is what stiffens the soul. Industrial London with its choking fog and cramped quarters and narrow streets is symbolic of the life to which it condemns its luckless residents:

> "The deuce be in the fog," said Jorrocks, "I declare I can't see across the Strand. It's as dark as a wolf's mouth." . . . Here and there appeared one of those beings, who like the owl hide themselves by day, and are visible only in the dusk. Many of them appeared to belong to the other world. Poor, puny, ragged, sickly-looking creatures, that seemed as though they had been suckled and reared with gin. "How different," thought the Yorkshireman to himself, "to the fine, stout, active labourer one meets at an early hour on a hunting morning in the country!" (18).

"Who can wonder," the narrator asks, "that smoke-dried cits, pent up all week, should gladly fly from their shops to enjoy a day's sport on a Saturday?" (3). "In London, there's hardly room to swing a cat."

"Jorrocks is a sort of Don Quixote of the last Phase of a brutal chivalry," V. S. Pritchett remarks; "*Après moi* (he might have said) *le garage*."[36] Animal spirits run high, including, of course, that sure English indicator of *joie de vivre*, a stupendous appetite. "Why, wittles to be sure," says Jorrocks looking into the luncheon hamper. "You seem to forget we are going a woyage, and 'ow keen the sea hair is. I've brought a knuckle of weal, half a ham, beef, sarsingers, chickens, sherry white, and all that sort of thing" (99). It is a rough-and-tumble world, with headlong spills into the cesspool and quick fists; one has no truck with citified pantywaists: "Quite the lady," snarls the Yorkshireman of a swell decked out in well-waxed ringlets and polished patent leather boots. And it is preeminently a man's world. There is a Mrs. Jorrocks, but we are spared her frequent presence; and a good thing it is, too, for she has gooseberry eyes and a complexion like "a lump of beef—all red." Away with that Victorian domestic sentimentality. Being of an "emigrating disposition," Jorrocks harrumphs that he does not see why he should have to spend *every* Christmas at home.

Jorrocks' Jaunts and Jollities and its numerous sequels did not have immediate success. Distaste for low-bred heroes assured that fate; and the literary critics of the day generally condemned Surtees for his protagonist's coarseness. It held on, however, and grew into a minor popular classic, particularly as the Victorian age's domesticity and tameness became pervasive. It is the symbolic alternative of the frustrated male imagination; it is a return to boyhood pleasures; it is the comic green world:

> On they go—now trotting gently over the flints—now softly ambling along the grassy ridge of some stupendous hill—now quietly following each other in longdrawn files, like geese, through some close and deep ravine, or intermediate wood, which re-echoes to their never-ceasing holloas—every man shouting in proportion to the amount of his subscription, until day is made horrible with their yelling. There is no pushing, jostling, rushing, cramming or riding over one another; no jealousy, discord (2).

And then:

> Down Windy Lane, a glimpse of a few red coats may be caught passing the gaps . . . of the fence, among whom we recognize Jorrocks, with his long coat-flaps floating in the breeze . . . "Vot a pace! and vot a country!" cries the grocer, standing high in his stirrups (10).

The progenitor of this experience may well be the festive Saturnalias of the archetypal "merrie England" of pre-Elizabethan times. Those holidays of spirit and celebration are described by C. L. Barber in his *Shakespeare's Festive*

Comedy.[37] Like Jorrocks' escapes from the workaday world, they are temporary occasions in which the restraints that normally prevailed in civilized society were discarded for revel and play. Days of drinking and strenuous activity, they produced what Barber calls a "clarification" of man's relationship to Nature just when such a relationship was beginning to be problematical, and of a man's relationship with his fellows just when these were normally constrained by conventional mores. For Jorrocks, then, the hunt was a kind of communion: "no pushing, jostling . . . no jealousy, discord." The Saturnalian interlude, as Barber makes clear, was never respectful of even the pastoral ideals it was supposed to consecrate. In fact, the social order, and in particular class hierarchy, was often overthrown by the temporary ascendency of a gross, boisterous "lord of misrule," made king for a day. Jorrocks is lord of his small domain, the organizer and chief promoter of all the outings. In sequel novels, *Handley Cross* and *Hillingden Hall*, Jorrocks becomes vested in this role as master of the hunt. But in this transition, the urban lower classes and the essentially nonurban, older middle class find harmony.

Misrule and overturned order imply normal rule and order, however, so the release of festive comedy in the green world is temporary. The later aficionado of riding to the hounds Anthony Trollope employs a Saturnalian outing in *Barchester Towers*—the "Ullathorne sports"—explicitly reviving Elizabethan holiday games, in an effort to break up the sterility of the mid-century power politics that grips his community of characters. It is a short but emotionally liberating interlude. Similarly, Jorrocks' country vitality is bounded by a return to the city (and in the later sequels by his own developing sense of responsibility), so the experience is a conceptually restrained and limited one. Northrop Frye traces various "phases" of what he defines as the comic mythos that embody this kind of temporary alternative world. In their form, Jorrocks' adventures would seem to characterize Frye's second, or quixotic phase—an adolescent set of experiences by a runaway protagonist, unsophisticated in the ways of the world. We shall have occasion later on to see precisely how adolescent and regressive this comic alternative world can become in nineteenth-century England; at this point, however, it is robust. Frye believes that the phases blend into each other on a spectrum leading toward the still, isolated "penseroso mood of romance."[38] Thus, as comedy takes the new aspects of urban life and charges them with the desires, the vicarious excitement of alternative life styles, they become projected into various degrees of a contained, imagistically intensified "vision." They are primarily emotional states, receding from actuality as they become more idealized; tableaux rather than dramatizations.

The enchantment of the comic green world, the action within a frozen frame, and the contained exuberance of the temporary burst of vitality present the reader with a kind of suspension of normally contradictory qualities—of rest and control on the one hand, and of contingent, free-spirited life on the other. The two aspects hold each other in tension. Our realization that they will break apart and the green world and its joys dissipate suggests that the vision of such a world functions as a cultural myth. It is a temporary constellation of ideas, or more properly, of desires. The one clear desire is that which we have identified—adventure and individual freedom of action. The other desire is for security and general bourgeois comfort. (The sport of fox hunting rather nicely combined these qualities for many Englishmen.) The comedy of picaresque adventure upon which a book like *Jorrocks* is modeled, incorporating an eighteenth-century character mold of the robust, fun-loving squire, propagated an ideal of those twin desires for several decades. It furnished the pre-Victorian decades with an appropriate comic form for the expression of this newly poignant middle-class myth. It is almost as if a nation of potential shopkeepers, on the threshold of Victorian moderation, was stretching its country legs for one last time, having its last imaginative fling.

The comfortable inn at the end of the day's sport, the hamper full of veal, sausages, and sherry white are, of course, clues that even this final fling is domesticated bourgeois. The picnic basket and the good night's rest are ways of carrying the comforts of middle-class life along on those richly exciting experiences. The classic example of a book that celebrates this happy joinder of two modes of existence is, significantly, the most popular novel of the century—Dickens' *Pickwick Papers*. Surtees' book, though, is a worthy contemporary.

William Hazlitt, in his sixth lecture on "The English Comic Writers," describes the greatness of the literature of the eighteenth century in a way that makes clear how the elements of the myth are joined: the "genius" of Fielding, Smollett, and Sterne lies in their attention to the middle class. French writing is thin because it speaks of nothing but "the vices, the miseries and the frivolities of the great." Significantly, in France "there are no middle classes." "But in the period of our history in question, a security of person and property, and a freedom of opinion had been established, which made every man feel of some consequence to himself . . . : there was a general spirit of sturdiness and independence."[39] In an historical and economic study published in 1835, *History of the Middle and Working Classes*, John Wade says that the "first benefit derived by all classes: from the rule of law in England is *personal security*. . . . The next most important benefit derived from the supremacy of the law consists in the liberty of *locomotion*. . . . This is certainly liberty; and if we add to it the other advantage of personal security in its exercise, we may truly call it enjoyment, and one of the most gratifying results of civilization."[40]

Hugh Dalziel Duncan says that literature often enables a culture to sustain the importance of certain ways of life or ways of thinking about them. He adds that the conversion of a culture's aspirations or concerns into representative action allowed them to be accommodated by the religious, economic, and social institutions of the time. The tendency of early Victorian literature to objectify human problems and put them in social terms was not only a means of displacement of internal concerns but also a way of fitting the changes in life that everyone was beginning to feel into more traditional relationships—those of country life, those of the home, and so on. Thus, whenever the urge to rebel or the impulse to go adventuring grew potentially antisocial, it was resolved in favor of middle-class stability. For instance, Jorrocks, in the sequel novels *Handley Cross* and *Hillingdon Hall*, progressed steadily into an Establishment figure—a squire and a justice of the peace—with his coarser edges much less visible. Charles Lever, a contemporary novelist whose *Harry Lorrequer* (1839) was a highly popular account of brawling and sporting in Ireland and England, followed the same progression. When, in later novels like *The Knight of Gwynne*, he became more "serious," his protagonists took to being "gentlemen." For a better understanding of what a mid-nineteenth-century gentleman signified, we must look at Thackeray. We now turn to him and to two other writers, Peacock and Jerrold, who set themselves up as critics of the unexamined idealizations of the pre-Victorian decades.

2

Peacock, Thackeray, and Jerrold:
The Comedy of "Radical" Disaffection

"The world being a great theatre of evil . . .
laughter and merriment make a human being
no better than a baboon."—*Mr. Toobad*

I

*I*n chapter one, we observed the inclination of
several pre-Victorian writers to displace whatever
anxieties they may have had about the age into pure
comic action. In doing so, they produced what is often a
characteristic comic "environment," or mode of presentation. Their works have a nerveless, anesthetic quality: passions and intensities are sacrificed to ludicrous effect, and
the most appalling mayhem takes place matter-of-factly.
We see this clearly in Marryat's *Snarleyyow*, where fiendish
violence erupts without any apparent motivation, where
death and dismemberment have no meaning, no direct
significance in terms of the work, and where serendipitous
good luck occurs with equally little cause. Comedy repli-
cates the manner in which things seem to happen in life—
unexpectedly, irrationally, and often dispassionately.

This has made comedy a particularly appropriate mode
for rendering modern life, which it is relatively common
to look upon as absurd or emotionally unsatisfying. Twentieth-century man has become, the argument goes, so
alienated from his natural expression that his acts frequently appear unmotivated. Indeed, in the diffuse,
mechanized, bureaucratic modern society, the possibilities

for translating one's intentions into socially significant action are often pathetically remote. Certainly, people do make existential choices that lead to action or inaction and people do make themselves and others miserable by sheer force of will, but in the larger complex of human affairs these are relatively fugitive and ineffectual expressions. Their very futility makes it natural for us to try to view them unemotionally, to treat them as distant comedy. Thus, while the seventeenth century could have a theory of comic behavior that depended, as Ben Jonson's "humours" concept did, upon something physiological and natural to man, and while even earlier comic misadventure could be attributed to some humanly incomprehensible but nevertheless operative *scheme* of Fortune, by the beginning of the twentieth century we have Bergson's mechanical man theory and the Kafkaesque.

Comic method—the treatment of characters and events in a comic work—can, then, have a philosophical significance as well as the sociological implications that we noted in the previous chapter. Uncomplicated, two-dimensional cutout characters, with "type" mannerisms and comic-book names, can stand for the dehumanization of modern conditions. Chance, ludicrous happenings can be considered symptoms of a world without teleological direction in which individual action can have no impact. Evil and violent twists of fate can mean that the human lot is an uncontrolled, alienated, frustrated existence in which perversity is at least some kind of gesture of humanness. If all this turns out to be genuinely funny, presumably that is because there is no other sensible way to respond to life.

In twentieth-century British literature, Evelyn Waugh's novels depicting the frenzy of life after the Great War provide hard, glossy, and often hilarious specimens of this kind of mordant, emotionless comedy. In *Decline and Fall*, the character "little Lord Tangent" is accidentally wounded in the foot by a starter's pistol at a boys' school game, develops gangrene, and loses the foot, all in a few witty textual asides. A more prominent character, Mr. Prendergast, has his head sawed off rather abruptly by a religious lunatic. Captain Grimes, on the other hand, puts out no effort, lays few plans, is invariably "in the soup," and yet inexplicably lands on his feet. He is naturally lucky. Throughout this random chronicle, Waugh's characters allude to religion as if it might once have been vaguely relevant to all this, but it is eminently clear that spirituality and moral convictions no longer have bearing on success or failure in this world. The luckless Prendergast, indeed, was the most earnest of divines.

I look ahead to Evelyn Waugh at this point because his comic fiction is part of a line that can be traced back to the early nineteenth-century satirist of the Regency and Romanticism, Thomas Love Peacock. The line includes Peacock's son-in-law George Meredith and the Aldous Huxley of *Point Counter Point*. They all wrote what are characterized as "comedies of ideas," in which the principal objective appears to have been the presentation and spoofing of various current philosophies and social and political positions. The works vary widely in the effort they make to suffice as novels—from Meredith's careful plotting to Peacock's spare scenarios for extended debate—but they all belong to a peculiar subgenre, related by their relish of the comicality of intellectual transfixion and pedantry. Peacock is by no means sui generis, as I shall note later, but the prefiguration in his writings of modern issues of alienation and impotence and of the particular comic milieu that we observe so often in modern literature makes him an intriguing object of study. Peacock is relating the source of the modern sense of life to the Romantic imagination. He identifies those disquieting intuitions about human nature that we have observed troubling other writers in the 1820s and 1830s and attributes them to the follies of Romantic introspection and idealism. It is almost as if he achieved a sudden intellectual *aperçu* of the modern condition and then, for reasons that are equally telling about his time, confounded his insight with retreat into bluff, self-protective English conservatism.

I should make it clear at the outset that the world view set forth in Peacock's comedies is not that of Waugh or Huxley; and it is not properly our twentieth-century dark comic vision of an absurd or inexplicably disjointed existence. Peacock does not proceed from the ethical relativism or philosophical doubt of later commentators. Nor is his world the violent one of Waugh and Huxley. It is true that the heroine of Peacock's novel *Melincourt* (1817) is nearly ravished and that a man is shot to death by the way in *Crotchet Castle* (1831), but those happenstances do not really signify. And when the protagonist of Peacock's *Nightmare Abbey* (1818) reaches the moment when only suicide makes sense, he quaffs another glass of Madeira instead. Peacock nonetheless does identify the characteristics that were to become so much a part of the modern picture of malaise and alienation—the inability of individual effort to reform the world, the curious disjunctures between motivation and action, between cause and effect, and the inexplicable obtuseness of man and his institutions. And he identifies these characteristics from a curious standpoint, for he does not appear to be reacting, as are so many of the writers we consider, to a social condition. His books provide almost no social context; they are extended comic symposia. Clusters of people assemble for a weekend, or are thrown together, and then they talk about human nature or "philosophical" issues deep into the night, utterly oblivious to any palpable, living world that may exist outside them. They thrive on etherealized "idea." It is almost as if Peacock himself does so, too, for his deliberate critical disengagement from his time stems not from anything that could be called personal alienation, but from a simple, dry, *intellectual* detachment.

Peacock's novels register the inundation of ideas and problems that England experienced as it adjusted itself to the French Revolution, Romanticism, and the Industrial Revolution. The accelerated discussion of man's nature, man's relation to God, political economy, and so forth, is Peacock's topic—the massive strain of trying to digest Hegel, Kant, Rousseau, Malthus, Coleridge, Bentham. His idea-oriented writings bear an affinity to the literary anatomy, which in the hands of its great practitioners—Rabelais, Burton, and later Joyce—is a means of absorbing a sudden effusion of ideas and putting them under some sort of whimsical control. Peacock differs from the anatomists, however, in his lack of interest in dominating or sorting out his material. Rather than putting all the ideas to use—even if a playful use—Peacock believes that the plethora of theories about the nature of man and the state of things produces nothing in the way of concrete effects. His fictional characters pop off at each other like champagne corks and contain mostly fizz. Lord Feathernest speaks for us all when he cries out in the midst of a pompous debate about whether the poem "Chevy Chase" or "Paradise Lost" gives a deeper insight into the truth of things: "I do not know what you mean by the truth of things."[1] The persistent woolgathering of Peacock's comic exponents of Kantian metaphysics, or of Benthamite political economy, prompts more than one participant to announce, "A dry discussion. Pass the bottle, and moisten it."

One Peacockian gentleman snaps, "It is *as notorious*, sir, *as the sun at noonday*, that theory and practice are never expected to coincide." This is Peacock's theme, and through it he cannily registers the early nineteenth-century manifestations of those unnerving disparities, disjunctures, and failures of aim that make up the ludicrous scenes of so much of the comedy of the last two centuries. There are intimations from the curmudgeony Peacock that things are coming slightly unglued. Mr. Toobad, the millenarian doomsayer of *Nightmare Abbey* who slouches about proclaiming that "the Devil is among us, having great wrath," clearly muddles the issue. But when Scythrop, the novel's protagonist, decries the sordid state of contemporary life, he waxes half-eloquent: "Evil, and mischief, and misery, and confusion, and vanity, and vexation of spirit, and death, and disease, and assassination, and war, and poverty, and pestilence, and famine, and avarice, and selfishness, and rancour, and jealousy, and spleen, and malevolence . . . all prove the accuracy of [Toobad's] views."[2] Most disquieting about Peacock's comedy is its highly successful exploitation of the ludicrousness of individual attempts to impose one's will upon actuality.

Peacock begins poking some easy fun at Romantic visionaries. Although a sometime intimate of Percy Shelley, and a man whose own creative orbit seems to have swung erratically around him, Peacock derived a great deal of amusement from what he considered to be Shelley's lack of common sense; so the reformist ideals of the Romantics constitute the initial field of comic play. *Nightmare Abbey*'s Scythrop is unabashedly Shelley, with his fancies of social mission: "He now became troubled with the *passion for reforming the world*. He built many castles in the air, and peopled them with secret tribunals, and bands of illuminati, who were always the imaginary instruments of his projected regeneration of the human species" (10). Sylvan Forester, the hero of *Melincourt* and also modeled after Shelley, is equally visionary. The sum of Forester's efforts is an abortive antisaccharine league, a futile consumer boycott of sugar designed to wipe out the West Indian slave trade; and of Scythrop's schemes, a thin volume called "Philosophical Gas; or, a Project for a General Illumination of the Human Mind," which sells seven copies.

Peacock goes beyond the spoofing of certain Romantic excesses, however; he builds comedy out of one's total inability to effect change in modern society. It is not enough that his books are populated by irrelevant people; we expect that of the comedies of ideas. But they return again and again to an abiding theme—the interrelationship of intention and idea with action in the world, or, as Scythrop puts it, the difficulties of a transcendental technology. In *Melincourt,* the principal subject of debate is the possibility of social reform. The characters argue it up and down the hills and dales of the English countryside and through the consumption of numerous bottles of claret. What plot there is to the novel concerns the love of Anthelia Melincourt, a handsome young woman who seeks the hand of one who matches her high philantropic ideals. Joined to such a man at last (who is, naturally, Sylvan Forester), she exclaims:

> "O Forester! you have realised all my wishes. I have found you the friend of the poor, the enthusiast of truth, the disinterested cultivator of the rural virtues, the active promoter of the cause of human liberty. It only remained that you should emancipate a captive damsel, who, however, will but change the mode of her durance, and become your captive for life."[3]

Social reform has clearly been too much on her mind.

Nightmare Abbey "refines" the issue to the problem of converting one's intentions into action. Scythrop and his father translate a dispute over whom Scythrop shall marry into one on "liberty of action," which the son defines as the "co-natal prerogative of every rational being." "Liberty of action, sir?" responds his father, "There is no such thing as liberty of action. We are all slaves and puppets of a blind and unsympathetic necessity." "Very true, sire; but liberty of action, between individuals, consists in their being differently influenced, or modified, by the same universal necessity; so that the results are unconsentaneous . . ." (19). Another character, Flosky, a parody of Coleridge, is also engrossed with the issue, but on a typically arcane level. Poised to write after having lain "*perdu* for several years" in the darkness of Kantian metaphysics, he composes his magnum opus on the "Categories of Relation, which comprehend Substance and Accident, Cause and Effect, Action and Reaction." The divans of the Abbey are adrape with precious types who have resigned active involvement in life in anticipation of its futility, effecting the malaise that will subsequently become symptomatic of dispiritedness. The Honourable Mr. Listless finds modernity "very consolatory and congenial to my feelings. There is, as it were, a delightful north-east wind, an intellectual blight breathing through modern works; a delicious misanthropy and discontent, that demonstrates the nullity of virtue and energy." He need, therefore, engage himself very little and has acquired a servant, Fatout, to relieve him of the wasted efforts of action and even of thought:

> *The Honourable Mr. Listless.* I have thought very seriously of Cheltenham, I assure you: very seriously and profoundly. I thought of it—let me see—when did I think of it? (*He rang again, and Fatout reappeared.*) Fatout! when did I think of going to Cheltenham and did not go?
>
> *Fatout.* De Juillet twenty-von, de last summer, Monsieur.
>
> *The Honourable Mr. Listless.* So it was. An invaluable fellow that, Mr. Larynx—invaluable, Miss O'Carroll.
>
> *Marionetta.* So I should judge, indeed. He seems to serve you as a walking memory, and to be a living chronicle, not of your actions only, but of your thoughts.
>
> *The Honourable Mr. Listless.* An excellent definition of the fellow, Miss O'Carroll, excellent, upon my honour. Ha! ha! he! Heigho! Laughter is pleasant, but the exertion is too much for me (25).

Indeed, we might suspect that Peacock, to the extent that he bothered to take seriously so insignificant a literary form as the novel, found it particularly congenial to parody because of its claim to being a means of explaining the motivations and circumstances that lead to concrete effects and because of its pretensions to impose a meaningful structure upon human life.

The delusion of the Romantics, as Peacock saw it, arose from a foolish belief in the power of the individual imagination to transform reality. The vision that convinced Disraeli he could transfigure actuality was of a piece with the puerile fantasizing of all the sensational literary vogues. It was a disease that addled the mind, producing households full of the functionally incompetent: "There never were so many idle persons as there are at present in England," Peacock remarks. It engendered a literature of bombast and self-indulgent posing. Mr. Listless unwraps the latest product of the fictional "avant-garde," a long Byronesque poem called "Paul Jones": "Hm. I see how it is. Paul Jones, an amiable enthusiast—disappointed in his affections— turns pirate from ennui and magnanimity—cuts various masculine throats, wins various feminine hearts—is hanged at the yardarms" (26). While Disraeli, then, would take the Romantic inspiration of his time and fly with it to comic caprices, and while Bulwer would waver indecisively between warring impulses, Peacock employs comedy as a cautionary art.

Peacock is admirably deft at his analysis of the effects of the Romantic consciousness. He is alert to the changes in self-conception that Romanticism has been causing. The Romantics saw man as a creature of rich self-created possibilities, as one whose nature is not in the fixed tension between permanent internal "character" and outer social façade, but in an evolving, responding, self-changing process. Introspection and awareness of one's divided dispositions were potentially generative. Peacock detects in these notions a source of the disquieting instability of the social persona that we have previously noted in the age—and, of course, a source of the self-analytical bent that leads one to explore the darker, perverse caprices of the psyche. Like many a critic of his time and afterwards, Peacock attributes it all to acute Romantic solipsism: "Our life is a false nature," moodily rants Cypress, the Byron parody in *Abbey*; "it is not in the harmony of things; it is an all-blasting upas, whose roof is earth, and whose leaves are the skies which rain their poison dews on mankind" (67).

Still, Peacock's canniness is remarkable. He detects the preposterous in all ideas, those that are venerable as well as those currently *de rigueur*. In *Melincourt*, Peacock introduces Sir Oran Haut-ton, an orangutan whom Sylvan Forester has cultivated and successfully put up for election as a member of Parliament, an ape so well-bred that his manners are impeccable (he is equally accomplished in flute and French horn and is the ideal dinner companion, although he regrettably does not converse). This characterization ostensibly spoofs Rousseauistic notions about primitive man but at the same time, it mocks the benevolist theories about the human heart on which eighteenth-century concepts of character were premised. Indeed, Sir Oran proves to be as stout and true as a simian Lord Chesterfield. Correspondingly, in the later novel *Crotchet Castle* (1831), the avant-garde political economist Mr. MacQuedy (pronounced "Mac Q.E.D.") argues that man is a product of his education. Individual qualities of character are acquired in response to social impressions so that any person can be "saint or sinner, aristocrat or democrat, judge, counsel, or prisoner at the bar." This is another explanation, presumably, for the phenomenon of personae conforming to roles in modern life; but it is poppycock, as becomes apparent when the discussion focuses on whether Achilles could have been molded into one of the contemptible editors of the shallow reviews that Peacock despised so heartily. Dr. Folliott, who represents Peacock's thinking as well as anyone in the novel, scoffs at the proposal (while asking for a second helping of main dishes): "And I say, sir—chicken and asparagus—Titan made him of better clay. I hold with Pindar: 'All that is most excellent is so by nature.' "[4] Thus, by invoking a little Greek wisdom, all the fashionable nonsense about human nature can be smashed flat.

Peacock's balanced perspective—or maybe it was his cantankerous skepticism—enabled him to observe the social pressures of the age and perceive the falseness of the middle-class social myths that were being devised to accommodate those pressures. He would have none of the romanticization of those writers who converted the period's sense of social and emotional displacement into illusions of adventure. Nor would he be content with the kind of hearty, unthinking assertion of bourgeois values that characterizes Surtees. As Peacock's spoofs make clear, the new state of the world was not one in which activity was essentially correlated with either feeling or value, even symbolically.

Peacock and the other two writers I discuss in this chapter, Thackeray and Jerrold, were acutely aware of the social disjunctures of the transition into Victorianism and into what we have come to call modernism. And all three were skeptical of the way that the popular culture would transfigure the disjunctures into middle-class myths. They vary in their comic approach to the situation: Peacock engages in an essentially satiric exposure of the "philosophies" and attitudes of the times; Thackeray first parodies and then elaborates on the fictions of the period; and Jerrold savagely attacks the Establishment mentality of early Victorianism. They were all able to identify the sources and the nature of the malaise that was part of the modern condition, in the inability to translate intention into action, in the divided post-Romantic sensibility, or in the emotional/intellectual position we have come to call alienation. But the other remarkable quality that these three rather acerbic commentators share is the tendency, in the last analysis, to retreat into their own varieties of conservatism. As we examine the writings of each, we observe a gradual evolution into some sort of social and emotional retrenchment or accommodation.

Mario Praz argues, in fact, that Peacock was one of the transitional figures who bridged Romanticism and the bourgeois Biedermeier mentality that he contends dominated British Victorian literature. I must say that I find Praz's argument somewhat vague and insufficiently substantiated.[5] But certainly there is an attraction in all Peacock's books toward the bourgeois comforts of a good tight country house, a splendid meal, and the proprietary claret. To hear Dr. Folliott of *Crotchet Castle* expatiate on a fine salmon or turbot or on a choice lobster for breakfast on a May morning is to discover the ultimate rhapsodies of Peacock's fictional world. G. K. Chesterton, in an essay on Dickens and Christmas, identified the atmosphere of Peacock's comic works as peculiarly English. The Italians, Chesterton says, find the blue sea and the open sky idyllic; but the English savor an enclosed place, like a cottage with a cozy seat by the fire and a wind howling outside. "The ideal of comfort belongs peculiarly to England. This comfort is an abstract thing."[6] Peacock himself gave up his early poetic aspirations for a desk at the East India Company and a semireclusive and apparently elegant existence.

Peacock was not a Victorian bourgeois, however. If anything, he was a kind of anachronistic eighteenth-century Augustan in disposition. He found a corrective to all the post-Romantic and urban dislocation in the classics—in his Plato and Thucydides, his Seneca, and his Marcus Aurelius. He felt that the crisis of the time was *cultural* and that by returning to the classic cultural virtues of balance and restraint one could surmount the modern self-absorption and restlessness of spirit. The position is an intriguing one, for, as we shall see in chapter six, Victorian comedy did take a turn toward a "high culture" line, led by Peacock's sometime disciple George Meredith.

It is equally true, however, that having asserted the values of high culture, Peacock found he could do very little with it in human terms. We do not have to share the Victorian ideals of Peacock's near contemporary James Spedding, who in a major essay in the *Edinburgh Review* faults Peacock for a lack "of that latent reverence and sympathy" that "awakens within that 'sweet recoil of love and pity'," in order to concur with Spedding's main point: Peacock's invocation of classical literature and thought produces little that is *humane* as an alternative to Romanticism. It is a retreat for the most part—to the study and to old verities of another time and place. As Spedding goes on to say, we see in Peacock's writings "only the working of a scepticism truly impartial and insatiable, which, after knocking down all the opinions which are current in the world, proceeds to set up an opinion made up of all that is *not* current in the world, that when that falls too, the desolation may be complete."[7]

We cannot discover any more by examining the life of the man. "Doubtless," as Spedding comments, "his spirit has a home of its own to go to, or it could not so take its ease in its inn." But Peacock guarded that spirit's home as jealously as any man of the century. We catch quick glimpses into an early disappointment in love, an excursion into Shelleyan Romanticism, and a poignantly troubled marriage, but they are closed over immediately. His granddaughter observed that the pattern of his later life was to preserve his geniality through elaborate efforts to avoid personal commitment; he "would not be worried, and just got away from anything that annoyed him." And nothing could be more impersonal than his books on comedy.

Thus, we have in Peacock a curious phenomenon of the early Victorian period—a man whose disengagement is almost a purely intellectual and cultural one. Eighteenth-century satire lives again in Peacock's writing, but not within any Augustan frame of reference. He intuits that a pervading cultural crisis is at hand, he perceives that its sources lie partly within the disposition toward human nature that arises out of the Romantic revolution, but he can take these intuitions no further. Peacock's critiques do not bite into the age. They exist as detached modalities, with disturbing implications, but without integrating force. It falls upon a later generation, whom we shall discuss in chapters six and seven, to synthesize Peacock's sense of cultural crisis, his essentially stoic disposition, and his intellectualized comedy into a critical position that engages with the nature of the Victorian period and provides both a critique of and an alternative to the prevalent bourgeois expression. What Peacock observes rather abstractly in the 1820s develops into a vision fifty to seventy years later. In the meantime we turn to others—Thackeray and Jerrold—whose responses are decidedly more visceral.

a certain . . . jocose sneering good-humoured
scandalous sentimental sort of way.
—*William Makepeace Thackeray*

I I

To move from Peacock to Thackeray is to move from a writer who is classically detached, who projects almost no distinctive literary personality, to a man who is intimately associated with his readers, who is gregarious and familiar, sometimes almost oppressively so. "At that famous period of history," begins Thackeray's first "novel," *Catherine*, "when the seventeenth century (after a deal of quarrelling, king-killing, reforming, republicanizing, restoring, re-restoring, play-writing, sermon-writing, Oliver-Cromwell-izing, Stuartizing, and Orangizing, to be sure) had sunk into its grave. . . ."[8] Immediately we find ourselves in the hearty embrace of an expansive narrative companion, a man who tells a story or recounts an anecdote easily because he knows that his audience is responding to him—laughing, sneering, and growling, as he does himself. Thackeray's great strength early in his career was his ability to establish that relationship. He learned the trick during extensive apprenticeship as a journalist and writer of comic sketches for *The Morning Chronicle, Punch, The Corsair, Fraser's*, and various other magazines, newspapers, and journals. Speaking through one of his many improbable narrative personae—Michael Angelo Titmarsh, Charles James Yellowplush, or George Savage FitzBoodle (the "third best whist player in Europe")—Thackeray set the personal manner and relationship to his material that was to determine his later comic and social vision as a novelist.

The personal-sketch journalism that Thackeray practiced created by its very nature an intimate interaction between author and reader. It had to attract the reader's attention immediately, so it was compelled to address concerns or interests that were on the reader's mind. Because the attention span that periodical essays can command is brief, the writing must be trenchant and economical. And the topicality of the material requires that the sketch writer have a reasonably sure sense of his reader's social attitudes. The manner of the occasional sketch had been passed down to the early nineteenth-century journals by their eighteenth-century forebears whose audience was a relatively restricted one of urbane, generally aristocratic readers. Thackeray retained that manner and successfully adapted it to an early Victorian reading public that was considerably more diverse and less worldly. It was, though, a public hungry for knowledge of the world, readers eager to share new experiences. And Thackeray exploited this hunger by flattering his audience with the inference that it was as "knowing" and shrewd in the ways of life as he was. In his expansive manner, Thackeray draws the reader along with him in shared attitudes. He proceeds with the confidence that we are as quick as he to spot a sham or humbug and that we are canny enough to detect the irony in any disingenuous account of suspect morality.

An early Thackeray narrative like *Catherine* is built upon this illusion of shared cosmopolitanism and of shared moral referents. We hardly need more to size up a situation or a character than this: "If Miss Cat, or Catherine Hall, was a slattern and a minx, Mrs. Score was a far superior shrew. . . . Yet . . . Mrs. Score put up with the wench's airs, idleness, and caprices, without ever wishing to dismiss her from the Bugle. The fact is, that Miss Catherine was a great beauty; and for about two years, since her fame had begun to spread, the custom of the inn had also increased vastly" (438). And woe to him who cannot read the world from its clear appearances: "The reader, if he does not now understand why it was that Mr. Hayes agreed to drink the corporal's proffered beer, had better just read the foregoing remarks over again, and if he does not understand *then*, why small praise to his brains" (447). When a writer, especially in his first works, makes asides of this kind, it is an indication of his besetting operating concerns. Of all the major writers of the nineteenth century, Thackeray is the most determined to establish and exploit formulas of characterization and judgment.

Thackeray's use of formulas is attributable to his early training as a caricaturist and sketch writer. It is not necessarily a sign of lack of craft, however—especially in Thackeray's hands. E. H. Gombrich, in his study of the artistic process, *Art and Illusion*, suggests that almost all of what we consider to be innovation in the plastic arts begins with the exploitation of what he calls schemata, or familiar, formulaic renditions of subject matter. He argues, for example, that the eighteenth-century landscape artist William Constable derived his "unique" way of observing and recreating massive cloud patterns from his variations on schematic cloud pictures in a drawing book by Alexander Cozens. " 'Perception,' it has recently been said, 'may be regarded as primarily the modification of an anticipation.' . . . We notice only when we look *for* something."[9] What we look for is what we are accustomed to seeing, which the creative artist-observer then begins to modify, partly by testing against experience, but more often through variations on the scheme. Thackeray's "apprenticeship" appears to be a good example of this kind of operation by a writer, for what he does is induce his reader to apply familiar schemata of observation and interpretation about human behavior and then work his own creative innovations upon us. We observe the same intimacy between artists and audience in Thackeray that Gombrich notices in painting; a remarkably strong collaboration is necessary in order for the beholder to follow the lines of development and insight of the artist.

Another thing that we immediately sense when reading Thackeray's first works is the imaginative exuberance. Once we grasp the individual or the situation according to its scheme, Thackeray shows us how we can "fill it in," how from outward indicia we can project the entire rich "story" and "message" behind the appearance. Thackeray was, appropriately, an interested observer of painters, and especially of caricaturists, whose fertile field is, after all, the physiognomy and the gesture. He writes admiringly of Daumier in his *Paris Sketch Book*; and in an isolated piece on the nineteenth-century English caricaturist and comic illustrator George Cruikshank, Thackeray shows his own *verbal* caricaturing ability brilliantly. He expatiates on a Cruikshank illustration of some pompous well-fed men and women in a pew:

> Miserable sinners indeed; O what floods of turtle-soup; what tons of turbot and lobster-sauce must have been sacrificed to make those sinners properly miserable. My lady there, with the ermine tippet and dragging feather, can we not see that she lives in Portland Place, and is the wife of an East India director? She has been to the Opera over-night (indeed her husband, on her right, with his fat hand dangling over the pew-door, is at this minute thinking of Mademoiselle Leocadie whom he saw behind the scenes)—she has been at the Opera over-night, which with a trifle of supper afterwards—a white-and-brown soup, a lobster salad, some woodcocks, and a little champagne—sent her to bed quite comfortable. At half-past eight her maid brings her chocolate in bed, at ten she has fresh eggs and muffins, with, perhaps, a half-hundred prawns for breakfast, and so can get over the day and the sermon till lunchtime pretty well. What an odor of musk and bergamot exhales from the pew— how it is wadded and stuffed, and spangled over with

brass nails—what hassocks are there for those who are not too fat to kneel—what a fluttering and flapping of gilt prayerbooks; and what a pious whirring of Bible-leaves one hears all over the church as the doctor blandly gives out the text. To be miserable at this rate you must, at the very least, have four thousand a year.[10]

The expansiveness of Thackeray's imagination is incredible. Beginning with Cruikshank's acute perception of detail—the "fat hand dangling over the pew-door," the "ermine tippet and dragging feather"—he creates a fully fleshed and moving world. He has the peculiar advantage of the man of experience, for he seems to know instinctively the secret lives behind the boudoir doors. And characteristic of Thackeray also is his rich evocation of detail—the turbot, the half-hundred prawns, the fluttering gilt prayerbook leaves, the odor of musk and bergamot. He is entranced by the phenomenal richness of the things of the world. Just as in caricature, there is a tension present in Thackeray's work. It is as if the grotesque propensities and inner perversities of the caricatured individual were trying to break free by distorting the mouth and face and eyes and dictating the telling cock of arm or leg. Within every subject that Thackeray sketches in words, there is the tension of its hidden activities and weaknesses—its story. The mind learns to grasp the pattern or scheme of the situation immediately and then to multiply the colorful existence behind it.

The implications of this are intriguing in terms of the nineteenth century's continuing concern about human nature and in terms of Thackeray's fictional characterizations. It suggests that if we can see the outer man in his pose, we can imaginatively project what he is really like, how his day passes, and what his impulses are. Thackeray, in a manner again dictated by his journalistic training moves from exterior observation to reconstruction of the inner man. We are able to perceive the true nature of the subject because experience furnishes us—artist and

reader—the likely schemata from which to surmise the motives. And if the power of observation and invention has
enough in details and scenes at its command, the specifics
of a man's hidden existence exfoliate lavishly. Such a view
of life encourages us to assume that most human beings are
inextricably caught up in their social roles. What experience and necessity has required of them has cast them into
the mold that we observe and can readily interpret.

Such a vision necessarily affects Thackeray's rendition of
human interaction in his novels and other fiction. Once the
quality of an individual character is identified and the pattern of his likely motivation apprehended, the character's
response to other people is so predictable and unchanging
that scenes in a novel are not likely to produce complex
psychological or moral movement. The characters will not
alter their opinions and nature in response to each other
but will persist in their roles and mannerisms. Percy Lub-
bock, for one, has made the observation that Thackeray
does not make the most out of the dramatic possibilities of
his fictional scenes: we do not see people in the agonies of
change of attitude or self-discovery. Edwin Muir, in his
book *The Structure of the Novel*, deals with this quality by
calling Thackeray's books prime examples of the "character novel," which he distinguishes from the "dramatic
novel." In the character novel, we do not witness human
development or the working of change over the course of
time; rather, we have a relatively unchanging, static world
in which people play their characters against each other.
The advantage of the "character novel," Muir suggests, is
the full picture of society that it affords us, of "how people
live in civilized society." Its emphasis is on vitality; "the
scene seems crammed to bursting-point" with diverse
humanity.[11]

Thackeray's first pronouncements on art, in *The Paris
Sketch Book* (1840), are founded on the premise that art
uniquely communicates the nature of *social* life. "I have
often thought that, in respect of sham and real histories, a

similar fact may be noticed; . . . all who . . . are inclined to follow the easy and comfortable study of novels, may console themselves with the notion that they are studying matters quite as important as history."[12] *Tom Jones*, he argues, "gives us a better idea of the state and ways of the people, than one could gather from any more pompous or authentic histories." Thackeray, a large, vital, and restless man, thrived on the worldly experience of London, Paris, and all cities. His appetite for curious material was prodigious. He wanted to experience many things and learn as much as possible about his world; his early writings, up to and including *Vanity Fair*, show a preeminent desire to capture the teeming, roiling, comical variousness of his time. What he admires in Daumier's works is their capacity to "form a very curious and instructive commentary on the present state of society in Paris, and a hundred years hence, when the whole of this struggling, noisy, busy, merry race shall have exchanged their pleasures or occupations for a quiet coffin (or a tawdry lying epitaph); . . . when the follies here recorded shall have been superseded by new ones, and the fools now so active shall have given up the inheritance of the world to their children; the latter will, at least, have the advantage of knowing, intimately and exactly, the manners of life and being of their grandsires."[13] The qualities that we noted in Thackeray's narrative method serve to transmit such a moving reality—the quick eye for sizing up people by thinly disguised pretensions; the rapid filling in of a crowded, typical scene of characters, each engaged in his own folly; the sense of a shifting, tumultuous life. All of this gives us, in the prose itself, a sense of constant movement. It is Thackeray's gift to instill in his readers a fuller imaginative vocabulary for their own observation, judgment, and enjoyment of life—to give them the formulas, the experiential richness, the eye for detail in a time when the novel as well as journalism saw its mission as providing vicarious experience.

"The Snobs of England, by One of Themselves," which

ran in *Punch* in 1846 and 1847, refines Thackeray's approach further. It provides extensive mock categorizations of social strata. The essays analyze the Snob Royal, Great City Snobs, Clerical Snobs, Political Snobs of various persuasions, Continental Snobs, Country Snobs—the gamut of snobbery. Thackeray was driven, as was the young Dickens, to try to subsume all of English life in his literature. Both men sought to include and analyze every manifestation of life. But where Dickens, as we shall see presently, began to reconceive life in accordance with his own desires and imaginative insights and could not rest with simply description, Thackeray contented himself with schematic, comic classification. In the Snob papers, however, the social criticism bites more sharply than in the previous sketches, for what unites snobs is not only their emphasis on appearance—they are all playing roles—but their devotion to social status. People indulge in snobbism as a means of asserting higher social class or of putting down those of lower class. Pump, of the moneyed City firm of Pump and Aldgate, marries the daughter of the aristocratic, blooded Stiffneck, because he needs social prestige and Stiffneck needs a hundred thousand pounds to pay off his mortgages. This arrangement grates Stiffneck, who sneers that Pump's grandfather was a bricklayer: "Your pedigree begins in a workhouse; mine can be dated from all the royal palaces of Europe. I came over with the Conqueror: I am own cousin to Charles Martel, Orlando Furioso, Philip Augustus, Peter the Cruel, and Frederick Barbarossa."[14] There *is* movement in social classes, as Thackeray sees it, but it is the spasmodic accretion of successive roles and produces little in the way of character development:

> So, when the City Snob's money has been washed during a generation or so, has been washed into estates, and woods, and castles, and town mansions, it is allowed to pass current as real aristocratic coin. Old Pump sweeps a shop, runs messages, becomes a confidential clerk and

partner. Pump the Second becomes chief of the house, spins more and more money, marries his son to an Earl's daughter. Pump Tertius goes on with the bank; but his chief business in life is to become the father of Pump Quartus, who comes out a full-blown aristocrat, and takes his seat as Baron Pumpington, and his race rules hereditarily over this nation of Snobs.[15]

A dismal social prospect, though entertainingly depicted. More venality is observed in the Snob catalogue than in anything Thackeray has done before. A self-satisfied, materialistic society emerges. Thackeray is no less exuberant in his imaginative creation but he is now quite cynical in his assessment. His characters are frozen in their pretensions. "You cannot alter the nature of men and Snobs by any force of satire." "And it seems to me that all English Society is cursed by this mammoniacal superstition; and that we are sneaking and bowing and cringing on the one hand, or bullying and scorning on the other, from the lowest to the highest."[16] In "The Snobs of England," Thackeray penetrates for the first time to that stultifying vice of the Victorian age—respectability. "It is among the Respectable class that the greatest number of snobs are found."

In the course of nearly ten years of journalistic sketch writing, Thackeray acquired an even deadlier eye for the myths of his countrymen. He was ready to take on Victorian respectability with a vengeance, because he had penetrated all the fond social illusions of the generation of the 1830s and 1840s. In 1847 he produced a series of short comic tales, called "Novels by Eminent Hands," that parodied the major fictional growths from the pre-Victorian period. He did a parody of the Newgate novel called "George de Barnwell," a take-off on Disraeli's *Coningsby* entitled "Codlingsby," a mock novel of adventure called "Phil Fogarty: A Tale of the Fighting Onety-onth" (attributed by him to a certain Harry Rollicker), and a Silver Fork parody with the title of "Lords and Liveries." In

every case, he not only put his superb powers of mimicry to
the task of exposing the excesses of the particular style but
he held up for ridicule the myths about society and human
nature that we have identified within each of these literary
expressions.

In "George de Barnwell," for instance, Bulwer's evoca-
tions (in his Newgate novels romanticizing criminality) of
eighteenth-century ideals about the goodness of human
nature and his prescription for social reform are shown to
be deceits covering larceny and licentiousness. De Barnwell
is working at a grocery store, moodily descanting on the in-
effable: "Figs pall; but oh! the Beautiful never does. Figs
rot; but oh! the Truthful is eternal. I was born, lady, to
grapple with the Lofty and the Ideal. My soul yearns for
the Visionary."[17] Moved by these considerations and by his
passionate nature, "His genius breaks out prodigiously. He
talks about the Good, the Beautiful, the Ideal, etc., in and
out of all season, and is virtuous almost beyond belief."
And he robs the till, which sets him off on a glorious life of
outlawry. In the last chapter, we behold him heroically facing the gallows and explaining why he committed murder:

> "And wherefore, sir, should I have sorrow," the Boy re-
> sumed, "for ridding the world of a sordid worm; of a
> man whose very soul was dross, and who never had a
> feeling for the Truthful and the Beautiful! When I stood
> before my uncle in the moonlight, in the gardens of the
> ancestral halls of the De Barnwells, I felt that it was the
> Nemesis come to overthrow him. 'Dog,' I said to the
> trembling slave, 'tell me where thy gold is. *Thou* hast no
> use for it. I can spend it in relieving the Poverty on which
> thou tramplest; in aiding Science, which thou knowest
> not; in uplifting Art, to which thou art blind. Give Gold,
> and thou art free.' But he spake not, and I slew him."[18]

There is no sympathy in Thackeray for the romantic exile,
that myth of rebellion as noble expression that Bulwer
thought spoke so eloquently of modern man's deepest psy-

chic needs. It is all humbug and cant. The very notion of surmounting one's social bounds in order to attain heroic self-realization is pure speciousness to Thackeray's mind, for the basis of his whole vision is the conviction that man is caught *within* his society. Thackeray's realism is a hard-headed assessment that we are all creatures of our social milieu, and what he has chronicled in his sketches is a very dense, demanding society that cannot be imaginatively re-molded. The fiction that tries to do it is false dreamwork. *Here* is the literary viewpoint that so markedly differentiates Thackeray from Dickens; for while the latter sought to dominate his material and put it into some kind of moral and emotional form, Thackeray could only see the possibility of describing and analyzing his fictional worlds. This accounts for much of the dissatisfaction that is felt by twentieth-century readers and critics with *Vanity Fair*, for it is our disposition now to expect a governing conceptual vision.

We must consider most of Thackeray's work to be reductive, in terms of my phases of comedy. He uses comedy to destroy the myths of the time. This is the initial function of parody—to break down styles or ways of thinking that have become stultifying. Just as caricature and the journalistic comic sketch explode the tension that exists within false form, so parody, by capturing the exact tone and manner, releases the material in the work from the bondage of affected rendition. A skilled parodist goes beyond pure imitation to wilder and more fanciful excess, sometimes rendering the style and characteristic attitude of his material better than those whose work he mocks. Thackeray, when taking on the Silver Fork novelists in his "Novels by Eminent Hands," can give himself up entirely to the comic potential of the genre, as Bulwer, Ward, and the others never could. The Earl of Bagnigge, protagonist of Thackeray's Silver Fork "Lords and Liveries," is far more stupendous in his gallantry and raffishness than Pelham or Cecil. "At three-and-twenty, he was a cynic and an epicure. He had

drained the cup of pleasure till it had palled in his un-
nerved hand. He had looked at the Pyramids without awe,
at the Alps without reverence. . . . Bitter, bitter tears did
[his mother] Emily de Pentonville weep, when, on [the
Earl's] return from the Continent, she beheld the awful
change that dissipation had wrought in her beautiful, her
blue-eyed, her perverted, her still beloved boy!"[19]

A writer as deft as Thackeray, with an imagination so
fertile, inevitably moves beyond the reductive phase in his
parody to the elaborative. We have seen it in his descriptions of the overstuffed worshippers; indeed, almost everything Thackeray writes unfurls. As I suggested earlier, the
metamorphosis, experimentation, and play that characterized the reductive, or breaking-down, process of comic
writing generates more and more improvisation. The artist
begins to carry on his own fabrications. We see this elaboration in Thackeray's novel parodies—as in the description
of de Bagnigge who, disguised as a butler named Jeames,
rescues his beloved Miss Amethyst when her carriage
horses go out of control (partly due to the incompetence
and cowardliness of de Bagnigge's archenemy, Borodino):

> But if those steeds ran at a whirlwind pace, Jeames was
> swifter. To jump from behind, to bound after the rock-
> ing, reeling curricle, to jump into it aided by the long
> stick which he carried and used as a leaping-pole, and
> to seize the reins out of the hands of the miserable
> Borodino, who shrieked piteously as the dauntless valet
> leapt on his toes and into his seat, was the work of an in-
> stant. In a few minutes the mad swaying rush of the
> horses was reduced to a swift but steady gallop.[20]

In this instance, as in many instances in the parodies, a full
scene has been invented; the mimicry of a dead work has
taken dramatic and fully imagined life of its own. Thackeray's parodies of the novels are short, however, and the
elaboration always sharply curtailed. While Joyce might
later expand the parodic and elaborative impulse into its

own work of art in *Ulysses*, Thackeray would have none of this. The reason, again, was his ultimate confidence in his mordant, hard-headed realism. He would not lose sight of social reality for the sake of art's elaboration.

The English reality in Thackeray's comic masterpiece, *Vanity Fair*, is a stunningly chaotic one. It is a society in which all agencies of order, honor, personal integrity, and social hierarchy are breaking down. The gentry and the aristocracy are in a shambles, replaced by a shifting, treacherous system built on money and fortune. The prospect of social mobility energizes the middle and lower middle classes into opportunism, yet they are haplessly enmeshed in the broken traces of the old order—fascination for the peerage and concern for marriage into title. The dead hand lies heavily on the English social scene, as it does in almost all Victorian fiction through George Eliot. Whatever is decaying, like Sir Pitt and Lord Steyne, has a febrile intensity still; whatever is new and aggressive, like the Osbornes, is sapped of vigor and joy by its slavish avarice for the deadening forms of old means of prominence. John Ruskin is quoted as saying of Thackeray, "he settled like a meat fly on whatever one had got for dinner and made one sick of it."

Ruskin is hardly the man to appreciate Thackeray (or Dickens either, for that matter), but Thackeray, in a letter to Robert Bell about *Vanity Fair*, acknowledges, "if I had put in more fresh air . . . my object would have been weakened. I want to leave everybody dissatisfied and unhappy at the end of the story—we ought all to be with our own and all other stories. You have all taken my misanthropy to task—I wish I could myself; but take the world by a certain standard and who dares talk of having any virtue at all?"[21] Such a disillusioned version of human existence seems to be remarkably familiar to modern readers. In some ways, *Vanity Fair* is the first powerful statement of the conditions of urban despiritualization. But where Peacock's critique of life can be said to prefigure the later vi-

sions in which individual will and purpose has no effect or
relevancy to the working of things, Thackeray sees life as a
battle of wills, a contest for individual power. *Vanity Fair* is
informed by the imagery of war—from the scenes at
Waterloo to Rawdon's praise of Becky Sharp for being a
good general in social struggles. People in the novel are in
dominant and submissive relationships; the impetus of the
acquisitive elements is for control. They are constantly maneuvering for position and exploiting weaknesses. Implicit
in this is the assumption that human determination can
work its way. The characteristic early Victorian literary impression of the shape of life is of a contest of wills (Anthony
Trollope's later fiction becomes its most thoroughgoing
statement).

The irony that Thackeray observes in all this, of course,
is that human beings in such a society become self-
imprisoned. In *Vanity Fair*, old Osborne embodies the new
financial success; his consolidation of wealth and position is
contrasted to old Sedley's improvidence and ruin. Sedley
did not keep his eye on the main chance, while Osborne
lived the money market so completely that when he came
home to dinner in a bad mood the household whispered, "I
suppose the funds are falling." But the cost to Osborne in
human values is staggering. In his pride and rigidity, he
has disowned his son George. One of the most poignant
scenes in the novel shows Osborne as an old man, secluded
in his study, brooding over his son's childhood letters and
toys and a locket containing his hair:

> Turning one over after another, and musing over these
> memorials, the unhappy man passed many hours. His
> dearest vanities, ambitions, hopes, had all been here.
> What pride he had in his boy! He was the handsomest
> child ever seen. . . . He had the child before his eyes. . . .
> And this, this was the end of all!—to marry a bankrupt
> and fly in the face of duty and fortune! What humiliation
> and fury: what pangs of sickening rage, balked ambition

and love; what wounds of outraged vanity, tenderness even, had this old worldling now to suffer under![22]

Then, bitterly, forcefully, he obliterates his son's name from the family Bible.

All power in this world is encased in its rigid forms and self-imposed and societally imposed expectations. Just as old Osborne the tycoon is victim of his self-made fictions, so Lord Steyne the aristocrat is victim of the dessicating traditions of his race. "It was the mysterious taint of the blood: the poor mother had brought it from her own ancient race. The dark mark of fate and doom was on the threshold,—the tall old threshold surmounted by coronets and carved heraldry. This dark presentiment also haunted Lord Steyne. He tried to lay the horrid bed-side ghost in Red Seas of wine and jollity, and lost sight of it sometimes in the crowd and rout of his pleasures. But it always came back to him when alone" (457). The corruption is symbolic. Thackeray finds it manifest or latent everywhere. Though he does not diagnose it specifically in terms of living by fictions that have become ossified or that are by their nature dehumanized, he presents a human scene in which, with only one or two exceptions, there is no humane flexibility, no possibility of renewal.

Jos Sedley—fat, pompous, gourmandizer, ablush with his neuroses, and inspired only by rack punch and a copious table—is the grand comic epitome of hapless self-entrapment. He is a bolster, stuffed with his vanities, playing the charade of a personality:

> On returning to India, and ever after, he used to talk of the pleasure of this period of his existence with great enthusiasm, and give you to understand that he and Brummel were the leading bucks of the day. But he was as lonely here as in his jungle at Boggley Wollah. He scarcely knew a single soul in the metropolis: and were it not for his doctor, and the society of his blue-pill, and his liver complaint, he must have died of loneliness. He was

> lazy, peevish, and a *bon-vivant*; the appearance of a lady
> frightened him beyond measure. . . . His bulk caused
> Joseph much anxious thought and alarm; now and then
> he would make a desperate attempt to get rid of his
> superabundant fat; but his indolence and love of good
> living speedily got the better of these endeavors at re-
> form (29).

Jos would be a pathetic piece of baggage, virtually inarticu-
late with all his *Pooh*s and *I say*s and *egad, sir—this claret's
very good*s, if Thackeray (who was himself sometimes "the
fat contributor" to *Punch*) did not enjoy his character so
richly. Here rests an apparent anomaly of the comic-
reductive writer, for his most devastating portrayals are
alive and relished creations of imagination. This is doubly
true of Thackeray, whose mission as a writer was to make
us appreciate life, and who had the ambivalence of a man
who knows the actuality of human behavior too well. So,
rather than a bleak wasteland of dispirited inaction, *Vanity
Fair* is one of the most vital, engaging, *living* books in the
English language.

Sir Pitt Crawley and his ménage, for example, reflect the
degeneration of a kind of ideal of animal spirits that the
Squire Westerns of English literature embody—the ras-
cally, wenching, brawling, country gentry. And he is splendid. "Sir Pitt Crawley will do anything," complains the
rector's wife. He installs Becky Sharp as his mistress under
the very nose of his wife, chafes his sons and relatives mer-
cilessly, drinks to all hours with Horrocks the butler, and
smells of the stables. When Becky leaves for better game,
Sir Pitt accelerates his pell-mell decline: "Since the departure of Becky Sharp, that old wretch had given himself up
entirely to his bad courses, to the great scandal of the
county and the mute horror of his sons. The polite families
fled the hall and its owner in terror. Sir Pitt went about tip-
pling at his tenants' houses; and drank rum-and-water with
the farmers at Mudbury and the neighbouring places on

market days" (319). Thackeray's narrator intones disdainful maledictions upon Sir Pitt's career: "Here was a man . . .
who had the habits and the cunning of a boor: whose aim
in life was pettifogging: who never had a taste, or emotion,
or enjoyment, but what was sordid and foul; and yet he
had rank, and honours, and power somehow: and was a
dignitary of the land, and a pillar of the state" (86). When
the old reprobate is committed to the grave, the narrator
lets us know that the maggots had begun their work on the
body long before. But Sir Pitt dominates every scene he
plays, and no reader can escape sensing the author's enjoyment of him.

Thackeray's ambivalence in attitude—sermonizing on
the one hand and serving up the gamiest of specimens on
the other—troubles readers of *Vanity Fair*. Thackeray can
present the most wicked vignettes of domestic insipidity—
the ultragood Lady Jane Sheepshanks (need the name say
more?) sitting in old Miss Crawley's drawing room singing
"little songs and hymns" while the old woman nods and
her spinster companion Miss Briggs sheds tears of happiness—yet he can write of his doll-like heroine Amelia
with what appears to be unfeigned, and *very* saccharine,
sentimentality. We shall look further into these disparities
of viewpoint in Thackeray presently, but from what we
know of the man, it does appear that he was genuinely cynical and sentimental by turns. His narrative persona, as
Kathleen Tillotson has pointed out, is not the vehicle of a
single, organizing vision, but a human being much like
Thackeray himself. If it defeats our expectations of literature as a way of organizing and commenting on experience
for us, it is probably *our* fault in asking that life be presented with no annoying inconsistencies.

Admittedly, there are times, especially near the close of
the novel, when the imagery that Thackeray employs is at
odds with the presumed attitude. For example, while extolling Amelia's final happiness with Dobbin, he likens her to
a parasite entwined around a stout oak. This hints at a rad-

ical instability in approach. Generally, though, Thackeray's purposes in *Vanity Fair* are clear. Everything in his journalistic apprenticeship and everything that is vital in the novel illustrates his great receptiveness to the contingent reality of life. His openness, his cosmopolitan acceptance, and his vivid narrative voice indicate that the comic vision, as I have defined it, is vigorously at work here. The chaos of the world of the novel is a characteristic of life's chanciness and flux breaking down the old and the false new schemes for order. The disrespect for institutions is a respect for change. None of the old fictions will hold.

And, of course, the means by which actuality is made to expose what has become rotten is Thackeray's protagonist Becky Sharp. She is a perfect comic agent. She is *energy* contrasted to Amelia's passiveness. She is infinitely adaptable. An accomplished mimic, Becky can assume whatever role suits her present purpose. In one of her grandest moments, the drawing room at Lord Steyne's is abuzz with speculation about her:

> She was an artist herself, as she said very truly: there was a frankness and humility in the manner in which she acknowledged her origin, which provoked, or disarmed, or amused lookers-on, as the case might be. "How cool that woman is," said one; "what airs of independence she assumes, where she ought to sit still and be thankful if anybody speaks to her." "What an honest and good-natured soul she is," said another. "What an artful little minx," said a third. They were all right very likely; but Becky went her own way, and so fascinated the professional personages (488).

She adroitly maneuvers the people around her, uncannily sensing their obsessive life fictions, the imagined roles they have for themselves—which are, of course, their weaknesses. Needing a coach in which to escape Brussels, she insinuates herself into Jos's good graces with flattery of the courage he does not possess and with archly simpering accusations that he is what he wishes he were—a reckless cad: "Are you preparing to join the army, Mr. Joseph? . . . Is there to be nobody left to protect us poor women?" "You men can bear anything. . . . Parting or danger are nothing to you" (295). Like Thackeray himself, she can read everyone's secret motives from shrewd observation of their behavior.

Becky can thrive as well among Bohemians in Germany as in Lord Steyne's drawing rooms; she can be Sir Pitt's coy wench and Miss Crawley's obedient young disciple. Although the sagas of feminine ingenuity date back to Moll Flanders and Pamela and beyond, Becky's shows the most versatility of them all, for though social prominence is naturally her goal, she does not lose heart no matter where she lands. This is the ability to ride with the waves of life at its finest. Becky represents something new in nineteenth-century English characterization. Observing what was happening around him—the old morality breaking down, the inherited social forms in disarray, and the world changing almost too rapidly to describe—Thackeray presents us, in Becky Sharp, with a specimen of the totally free soul. She is breaking loose to try an existence that is in tune with the caprices of fortune. No wonder she dominates the novel imaginatively and seems to "get away" from her creator. If a Becky Sharp cannot reappear again in Victorian literature, it is perhaps because no subsequent writer (not even Thackeray after *Vanity Fair*) could believe in the possibility of living without accommodating oneself through various fictions to at least some elements of the social order. Male and female Becky Sharps do appear in twentieth-century literature, as rebels and confidence men and latter-day picaros, but rarely do they present the bold, assertive contrast, the opening of potentialities, that we see briefly expressed in *Vanity Fair*.

Becky Sharp is a representative power to Thackeray. She is the power of the artist, caricaturist, and creature of worldliness. Her father was a painter of some little skill.

From him, and from the imperatives of her own precarious position as a déclassé, unfamilied, and unmarried young woman, she has developed into a great observer of people—so great, in fact, that she can project herself into the roles that others expect of her and mimic almost every female part in *Vanity Fair*. We learn of these powers through her skills as an actress: in Lord Steyne's fashionable evening of charades, Becky stuns the audience with her Clytemnestra: "A tremor ran through the room. 'Good God!' somebody said, 'it's Mrs. Rawdon Crawley' " (494). She is the consummate artist of the English culture that we have been describing, for she can assume all the *social* roles when writers like Thackeray are given to interpreting their times in social terms.

Becky's particular strengths are Thackeray's own strengths, of course. She functions as do his own imaginative and interpreting powers—seeing the formulaic characteristics of individuals from what they betray in outward talk and manner, quickly projecting and imaginatively vivifying such people, and making cynical dispositions of them. Yet, as the novel progresses, Becky herself is denigrated into a formula of the loose woman whose sins achieve their revenge. The confiding relationship that Thackeray always seeks to establish with his readers enables him to assure a change in their affective response to Becky when, three-fourths of the way through the novel, she betrays her trusting husband Rawdon and neglects her child. Up to that point everyone whom she had maneuvered deserved it, even Amelia, who is a sentimental simpleton for all her "good heart"; but Rawdon is one of the few in the novel to make some moral progress, and the cuffing of her own child seems too cruel. It is an adroit reading of audience attitudes on Thackeray's part, even if it runs against the grain of our response to Becky through the rest of the book. Thackeray intensified the attack on his protagonist from that scene on, degrading her further and

further. By chapter sixty-four, the invidious associations
have acquired particularly grotesque imagery:

> In describing this syren, singing and smiling, coaxing
> and cajoling, the author, with modest pride, asks his
> readers all round, has he once forgotten the laws of po-
> liteness, and showed the monster's hideous tail above wa-
> ter? No! Those who like may peep down under waves
> that are pretty transparent, and see it writhing and twirl-
> ing, diabolically hideous and slimy, flapping amongst
> bones, or curling round corpses. . . . When, however, the
> syren disappears and dives below, down among the dead
> men, the water of course grows turbid over her, and it is
> labour lost to look into it ever so curiously. . . . And so,
> when Becky is out of the way, be sure that she is not par-
> ticularly well employed and that the less that is said about
> her doings is in fact the better (617-18).

Such a passage shows Thackeray's narrative method at its
worst. It is evasive—an attempt to shed his authorial responsibility of "finishing off" his character in a dramatic
and adequately explained way. It is also an attempt to bury
the issues that are embodied in our previous responses to
Becky. And the imagery of the "hideous" serpent-syren is a
most heavy-handed invocation of affective response—as if
the comparison made the character so instinctively repug-
nant that we would be unable to prevent the revulsion
from welling up. It is, frankly, the reflexiveness of that
overwrought sensationalism of bad art that one sees in the
Silver Fork, Gothic, and Newgate writers.

Because Thackeray so devastatingly parodied such
writers, it is puzzling that he gives in at times to their propensities unless there is something about his own contact
with them that has tainted "art" itself. A potential liability
of reductive parody is the sort of critical penetration it requires into the parodied models themselves. When the literature parodied cannot stand so thorough an exploration
of its characteristic artifices, when its manner reveals it to

be a pretentious obscuration of its own false readings of human nature or of its own crassness or absence of thought, then an uneasiness about that literature arises in the parodist himself. Thackeray's refusal to allow himself to go very far beyond the reductive-imitative into extensive creative explorations of his own, his insistence on measuring all art against harsh actuality, instilled in him a distrust of the fiction-making process. His feelings toward art are surely more essential than, say, Bulwer's, for Bulwer never had the artistic capacity of Thackeray and never committed himself to the work of creating a comprehensive social vision as Thackeray does in *Vanity Fair*. Nonetheless, Thackeray's qualms about imagination's work (at least the work being produced by his contemporaries in the novel) surfaces constantly. He smirks at literary conventions throughout *Vanity Fair*: "We might have treated this subject in the genteel, or in the romantic, or in the facetious manner." Thackeray's misgivings about the fictive process were so obtrusive that they came to influence his great devotee Trollope and many others writing in the next decades. Trollope, in fact, went one step further and equated the falsities of the novel conventions—especially its need to manipulate characters—with falsity in human behavior, which he defined as the besetting ill of modern times. Bulwer's old dilemma, that novels treating of false behavior and role playing infected readers with the urge to indulge their own self-fictions, thus stays alive with slightly different emphases in Trollope and Thackeray. In consequence, role playing in actual life is further associated with the dangers of art.

Such an interrelationship of art and human behavior had been an English concern for almost two hundred years and it had a particularly unfavorable effect on the climate for comedy. The Puritan distrust of art, for its embellishment and its sensual appeal, inspired an even stronger suspicion of the comic. Puritan injunctions against levity were prompted by the suspicion that it denoted a frivolous disposition unfavorable to spirituality. Comedy spread disorder and disrespect. It was generally assumed that a man who could laugh about moral issues would soon find his own rigor slackening. The origins of comedy in "play" and "fun," its elaborative impulses, and its affinities to the experimental spirit of art inevitably brought it into conflict with a religious bent that was earnest, plain-speaking, and ever watchful. The proofs of spiritual adequacy and salvation in Calvinist beliefs were in good conduct and good works; frivolous diversions demonstrated an inclination to stray off a righteous course. John Bunyan, author of *Pilgrim's Progress*, one of the most influential and widely read works of English thought throughout the nineteenth century, equated the spirit of play—in language as well as in deed—with the Devil's temptation. Thus, in his spiritual autobiography, *Grace Abounding*, he defended his unadorned style, his lack of conscious art on these terms:

> I could also have stepped into a stile much higher then this in which I have here discoursed, and could have adorned all things more than here I have seemed to do: but I dare not: *God* did not play in convincing of me; the *Devil* did not play in tempting of me; neither did I play when I sunk as into a bottomless pit, when *the pangs of hell caught hold upon me*: wherefore I may not play in my relating of the tale, but be plain and simple.[23]

Such distrust of comedy, modified but not essentially alleviated, became a kind of moral-aesthetic assumption for the lower middle class whose roots of belief were in Puritan religions. It created the atmosphere that led to the closing of the theatres in the seventeenth century, and it formed the basis of value system of countless critics from the Restoration on. The uneasiness about comedy's operations—especially its tendency to ridicule, to play fast and loose—accounted for a spurious but tenacious critical distinction between wit and humor in the eighteenth and much of the nineteenth centuries. Later, we shall have occasion to speak more of this distinction and of the pervasive, and in some ways invidious, Puritanical suspicion of comedy. But it is worth noting here that "wit," roughly defined to be the intellectual capacity to make specious connections and disjunctions among ideas or images, became associated generally with pretension and role playing. In part, this was because of the reliance upon wit in Restoration comedy whose characters were shallow poseurs for the most part and whose immorality was often shocking to contemplate. The Restoration dramatist William Congreve acknowledged that excesses of comic irreverence sprung from the disposition to treat men in their social personae, when they were so often "under a Voluntary Disguise." Wit, usually the product of artistic sophisticates, inevitably came to be associated with a human behavior model. And in all, a complex of notions sets itself rather deeply in the middle class—a complex that associates immorality with levity, with play, with artistry, with intellectual wit, with affectation, and with false nature. It is a complex that was still highly influential in the thinking of Thackeray's time—so much so that Carlyle and Ruskin, powerful cultural spokesmen with a Puritan bent, characterized fiction on occasion as "lying" and factitious. Thackeray's attitude toward comedy curtailed his ventures of both imagination and wit; this is one reason that Becky Sharp is checked in her fanciful, amoral career as representative of comic art.

   The narrative viewpoint of *Vanity Fair* is thus fraught with Thackeray's conflicting impulses—those of the man of worldliness versus the exponent of domesticated values; and those of the lifelong lover of caricature and art's powers versus the cynical and faintly self-righteous censor of art's ethical "dangers." M. H. Abrams, in *Natural Supernaturalism*, offers an analysis that assists us in putting these conflicts of viewpoint in larger perspective. He suggests that the "stages of transition in England from the Romantic to the Victorian preoccupation with alienation and community" can be marked by Carlyle's writings, particularly

"Characteristics," the essay appearing in 1831. Carlyle was much admired by Thackeray and was indisputably one of the most influential diagnosticians of the ills of his time. The contention of Carlyle's works was that man's happiness and psychic health consist, as Abrams recounts it, in his instinctual sense of wholeness.[24] The evil of the current age was "Inquiry," the consciousness that divided "the knowing self" and "the thinking self." This division of the intuitive from the analytical produced an ensuing self-consciousness and sense of alienation and caused a souring vision of the possibilities for natural human community. It led to a fragmented, often contradictory response to life. The narrative persona in *Vanity Fair* reflects this division between the analytical and the instinctively apprehended elements of man's makeup. Thackeray is himself the voice of the interpreting mind, already highly self-conscious and alienated, at times uneasily jocular; and he is the voice of certain intuitive qualities as well. Characteristic of Victorian expression, these intuitive qualities are moral qualities. Thackeray's narration brings into play certain understood ethical values, and they struggle for assertion—and even in some cases for relevance—in a literary operation that is hard-headed, often cynical, always worldly. How Thackerayan is his own remark that he was trying to write in "a certain agreeable jocose sneering good-humoured scandalous sentimental sort of way," for his prose (at least through the next novel, *Pendennis*) reflects the internal conflict of the analytical and the intuitive. Indeed, somewhat ironically, Thackeray now represents the Victorian degeneration of the intuitive, richer, moral self so celebrated by the Romantics—into a largely self-conscious, sentimental being who blithely accepted middle-class values of reverence, loyalty, duty, and so forth.

These innate moral sensibilities took on a form in Thackeray that proceeded directly from his vision of human behavior. Carlyle had taken the social pretension that he saw all about him as his evidence of disastrous self-alienation in the pre-Victorian period. "Dandyism" was his symbol of the extreme manifestation of the self-consciousness of the age. Carlyle was aware, as was Thackeray, of the "unnaturalness" that social adaptation in industrial society required—the separation from what was instinctual. Both men had strong misgivings about the apparent change occurring in human nature in which the outward persona was becoming paramount. Not only did Thackeray's observations of life around him confirm this trend but his own artistic method as journalistic sketch writer predisposed him to this means of interpreting human behavior. What the analytical mind of *Vanity Fair* demonstrates, and what Becky Sharp as mimicking comic agent exposes, is that all of London is playing roles.

In an effort to reconcile what his analytical insights and his moral intuitions told him, Thackeray conceived of a synthesis in the ideal of the "gentleman." His biographer Gordon Ray notes that Thackeray "attained his high position among his contemporaries chiefly by redefining the gentlemanly ideal to fit a middle class rather than an aristocratic context."[25] That is, Thackeray took a notion that flourished in aristocratic eighteenth-century culture, and which was premised on that century's belief in the consistency of human nature, and adapted it to a much different world. In *Vanity Fair*, Dobbin embodies the gentlemanly virtues; a later novel, *Henry Esmond*, is an excursion into an eighteenth-century setting, made largely to exemplify the concept of gentlemanliness in the protagonist Esmond. As Thackeray advanced in life, no longer the journalistic sketch writer, he became fonder and fonder of his concept, for it seemed to unite in one exemplar the qualities Thackeray had so long tried to reconcile. The gentleman is an integrally moral individual of such breeding that he is capable of negotiating the most problematical of modern situations. Yet, in Thackeray's formulation, he is also a worldly man, a man of experience—qualities the author had always admired. In addition, the conception of the gentleman accords with the modern reality that Thackeray observed but could not conscientiously accept: a social persona is crucial to survival and success. The very idea of the gentleman puts emphasis on manners; it is a concept defined in terms of social role, deportment, personal style. A "classic" synthesis.

Carlyle would have none of this and dismissed it as one of Thackeray's easy accommodations: "Thackeray had no convictions, after all, except that a man ought to be a gentleman, and ought not to be a snob." The critic Chauncey Wells suggests that it is Thackeray's instance of what Chesterton defined as the "Victorian Compromise," whereby the middle class, instead of insisting upon a clean sweep, a radical reorientation of social values after the Industrial Revolution, simply allied itself with the aristocracy in intent.[26] There is surely much sneaking admiration of the aristocratic life style in Thackeray's synthesis. In fact, there are indications, especially in *Henry Esmond*, whose protagonist is the model of the young gentleman, that Thackeray was aware of the thinness and the social arbitrariness of his own concept. The very mood of that novel is a departure from the realism that one sees in Thackeray theretofore. It is a Dumas-like romanticization of an adventurous age when personal glory was possible, a transportation to a period that never was, in which cardboard recreations of people walk stiffly around through artificially animated sequences. It is infused with bourgeois ideals of home and devotion. Yet elements of the jaded, irreverent Thackeray still persist, as in the strange love affair of Henry Esmond for the older woman Rachel, who has always been his mother in fact as well as image. The unmistakable suggestion of an incestuous love caused George Eliot to remark that "*Esmond* is the most uncomfortable book you can imagine. The hero is in love with the daughter all through the book, and marries the mother at the end." After attending to the glorification of Henry Esmond's noble qualities throughout the book, Thackeray suddenly presents us with a scene—the kind of surprising and unnerving episode that we find so often in his work—in which Beatrix says what we have all been thinking—that Henry is a stick. "I loved you once," she tells him, "but the old chill came over me, Henry, and the old fear of you and your melancholy; and I was glad when you went away." It is a stunning remark because it devastates the novel's hero so aptly and because it reveals that the author himself has been aware all the time of what is unsatisfactory about his leading character. Indeed, Thackeray is reported to have said to Trollope, "After all, Esmond was a prig."

These kinds of flashing self-insights—or perhaps they are equivocations—are simply *Thackeray*, and we must take him with such complications. His irreverence, such a tonic during the 1840s, never entirely left him; it was integral to his thinking. But it seems to have discomforted him more and more in later years as he assumed the position of literary lion. He cloaked it with offhandedness and bluff heartiness. Finally, in the series of highly popular lectures. Thackeray delivered in 1851 on "The English Humourists of the Eighteenth Century," we seem to lose track of the old cynical, crafty Thackeray altogether. In his lecture on Jonathan Swift, with whose skepticism one might expect he would have some affinity, he presents an ungenerous character assassination. He quotes at length, and with contempt, from Swift's letter supplicating favor from his patron Sir William Temple and asks rhetorically, "Can prostration fall deeper? Could a slave bow lower?"[27] Swift's signs of social and intellectual radicalism and human resentment annoyed Thackeray. They are poor form on Swift's part: "As fierce a beak and talon as ever struck—as strong a wing as ever beat, belonged to Swift. I am glad, for one, that fate wrested the prey out of his claws, and cut his wings, and chained him" (378). And they are also a measure of how removed the later Thackeray had himself become from angry criticism of the prevalent English social order.

Thackeray tries to explain in the lectures what he likes and does not like about the eighteenth-century comic writers by analyzing their lives. It is characteristic of the "humor" tradition of eighteenth- and early nineteenth-century British comedy that it was the nature of the man that was crucial. The tenor of the comedy and the quality of human nature were inextricably bound together. Thus, what infected Swift's wit was the Dean's own "lifelong hypocrisy." In Thackeray's writings about Sterne, we also see how thoroughly his individual philosophy was steeped in convictions that favored solidness and transparency of nature. What he disliked about Sterne was that the true character of the man never came clear. "How much was deliberate calculation and imposture—how much was false sensibility—and how much true feeling? Where did the lie begin, and did he know where? and where did the truth end in the art and scheme of this man of genius, this actor, this quack?" (529). Thackeray perceived, as perhaps only a man who sometimes shares the very same disabilities can perceive, the equivocation and ambivalence that reside in Sterne but, like most of his contemporaries, he could not perceive (or could not tolerate) the highly involuted complexity of Sterne's imagination. And, in any event, he could not abide the man's life, which seemed so full of opportunistic and quixotic instability.

Thackeray was more generous with Congreve, oddly enough, probably because it was becoming a sign of immature squeamishness to be offended by Restoration drama. He passes over the "immorality" of Restoration theatre easily enough. But his assessment about its hollowness is instructive. He writes of Congreve's art:

> Without the music we can't understand that comic dance of the last century—its strange gravity and gayety, its decorum or its indecorum. It has a jargon of its own quite unlike life; a sort of moral of its own quite unlike life too. I'm afraid it's a Heathen mystery, symbolizing a Pagan

doctrine; protesting—as the Pompeians very likely were, assembled at their theatre and laughing at their games; as Sallust and his friends, and their mistresses protested, crowned with flowers, with cups in their hands—against the new, hard, ascetic, pleasure-hating doctrine (407).

The allusions indicate that Thackeray saw the Saturnalian, life-celebrating quality of the Restoration comedy. But by this time it was alien to him; it was a comedy of form, a comedy generating its pleasures out of its language and play with its own conventions. This sort of thing we do not find in Thackeray the novelist after *Vanity Fair*. We see almost nothing of the metamorphosis of his own creations, the evocation of his own delights, the experimentation. Dickens' later work displays that kind of elaboration, but Thackeray, as we noted in his earlier parodies, stops himself short. In those earlier works, happily, there had been a love affair with language and with what the experienced observer could fill in with his imagination. By the 1850s, however, his delight in those things palled, and there entered instead, with greater and deadlier force, the social and moral imperatives that appeared, with him, to have been temperamentally prompted—they were almost emotional needs.

That such "emotional needs" existed is speculative for the most part, of course, even though we could assemble ample evidence to support the surmise from the facts in Gordon Ray's biography. Certainly the 1850s demanded a more conservative morality from its writers, and certainly Thackeray was not alone in espousing it. What is ironic in Thackeray's case is that a man who began his career so brilliantly exposing the humbug of the middle-class myths in the lesser literature should have spent his maturity solidifying variations of those myths. It is ironic, also, that a writer whose earlier work is almost premised on the changes in human nature, the necessity of living by fictions, and the rich possibilities of freedom that seeing life in terms of fictions opens up, should have striven so mightily to synthesize this knowledge with an older, outmoded concept of human nature. The ironies illustrate the importance of the comic vision of the time in serving to define life style. They also illustrate how self-conscious a life style was required by the bourgeois literary temperaments of the age.

Choose your friend as you would choose an orange; for his golden outside and the promise of yielding much, when well squeezed.
—*Mr. Punch*

III

Peacock and Thackeray were men with strong affinities to the eighteenth century. Though both of them chronicled the extensive social changes that were being wrought upon nineteenth-century life; though both of them demonstrated in their writings that the origins of modern social estrangement lay in Romanticism; and though both of them depicted the disjuncture between ideals and actuality that subsequently was to become an element in the modern world view; they returned inevitably to pre-Romantic values and schemes for assessing human conduct. Surely their critiques of contemporary literary foibles are as devastatingly shrewd and as engagingly conceived as any from the early part of the century. By temperament, both men stood outside the bourgeois culture of their time. Their strength as comic writers lay in their reductiveness. But Peacock and Thackeray ultimately circumscribed the range of their comedy and reduced the generative potentiality of their art by returning to cultural positions that lacked contemporary vitality. As alternatives to what they so shrewdly observed to be narrow and disintegrative in early nineteenth-century England, they retreated to what were essentially aristocratic concepts—to the values of the "classics" and to the idea of the gentleman. To a certain extent, this can be accounted for by the inclinations that we can detect throughout the loftier reaches of British letters at the time; to a certain extent, also, their positions are products of their personal natures—of the reticence and conservatism that was so much a part of Peacock's behavior and of the ambivalence that was so characteristic of Thackeray.

Douglas Jerrold, one of the founders of *Punch*, does not share this predisposition to anachronistic cultural position. Having apprenticed himself over many lean years writing farces under contract to theatre managers, and having developed an abiding sense of the social injustices inflicted upon the lower classes, he is very much a creature of his time. Although apparently a clever and genial companion, he bore the reputation for most of his life of being an embittered man—a reputation encouraged perhaps by the toll that rheumatism took on him physically, for at age fifty-two he was described as prematurely aged, harsh in visage, and with a back bent "almost to deformity." His writing was guided by an intense and rather simple moralism; there were none of the slack accommodations that we find at times in Thackeray nor the patrician withdrawal of Peacock. Jerrold's first writings in *Punch* seem to give the lie to the proposition that English comedy of the nineteenth century was never severely critical of English social assumptions. He is unsparing in his assault on the received ideas and sanctified institutions of the Victorian Establishment. "Inquire of many an Alderman what is Life. He will tell you that it is a fine, dignified, full-bellied, purple-faced creature, in a furred and violet-coloured gown," sneers Jerrold.[28] His target here is a particularly vulnerable one, for he addresses the occasion of Alderman Peter Laurie's infamous prohibition against suicide in which he warned that he would "look very narrowly" on poor persons who wantonly took their own lives. All sorts of callousness provoked Jerrold's bile, however, especially the sort of brutality that some of his countrymen seemed to take for granted, such as public hangings so that the fates of the condemned could be "morally instructive":

> If we might suggest an enlargement of Newgate hospitalities, we would propose that all ladies admitted to the condemned sermon should be invited to behold the galvanic battery applied to the corpse of the murderer as early as possible after execution. Certain we are that the exhibition would be equally interesting, equally pleasurable to the nervous system. . . . And more, what a wholesome, moral fillip it would give them, if, at midnight, they were to attend the burial of the assassin, and, to show their horror of his deeds, were to cast within his unblest, unsanctified grave, a handful or so of lime. . . . They would—bless their delicacy!—scatter their lime, as the *Queen* in *Hamlet* scatters the flowers upon *Ophelia's* tomb,—with the same tenderness, the same pathos![29]

Such writing, in its relentlessness, conveys the impression that *nothing* in words and images can quite reach the insensitivity of such a public.

Jerrold's manner was to carry the outrage to its furthest gradation in the hope that it would at last penetrate thick hides and thick skulls. In the sketch "The President and the Negro," he screws tight the ironies of a report that President Tyler was saved from injury when his runaway carriage was arrested in flight by a Negro:

> We know not whether, according to American notions, we can courteously congratulate the President on his escape,—seeing that it makes him a debtor for his life to a black—a mere human chattel—a thing of sale and barter. . . . Thus considered, it would have been a sublime spectacle to behold President Tyler prepared for death, and loudly forbidding the approach of the negro, as a creature with whom he had nothing in common . . .

whose compassionate help brought odium on the assisted. Thus dying, the President would have asserted a great principle.[30]

At times, this method got Jerrold into irksome complications. When he seized upon the *Morning Post*'s use of the term "gentleman Jews" to complain sarcastically that in the past few decades Jews have risen "from 'accursed dogs,' . . . to 'individuals of the Jewish persuasion,' 'persons of the Hebrew faith,' and so on" to "gentleman Jews," and to ask, "What . . . are we to expect when we find all our pet prejudices taken from us? The truth is, we then cease to be a people worth saving,"[31] Jerrold then had to cope with complaints to the *Times* and the *Morning Chronicle* about his alleged anti-Semitism. It took another article to set this absurdity aright. Thackeray would never have lost his readers to quite that extent; he would have invited complicity at every step.

But Thackeray never laid about him like Jerrold does. The birth of the Prince of Wales, in Jerrold's hands, is just an occasion for heavy drinking and for gorging oneself with food. Thackeray would not have touched such a sanctified occasion. Nor would he have ridiculed the bishops of England by suggesting that if more were appointed, there would be "such a superfluity of goodness" that England could export it. Indeed, Thackeray quarreled with Jerrold for attacks of that kind on the clergy; he found them rather excessive.

Yet for all that, we cannot deny that Thackeray's is the richer writing; it is more inventive in imagery and in comic exaggeration; it is verbally more stimulating; it is more supple and poised. Although Jerrold can execute a deft attack on occasion, he buries it in convolutions of heavy-going prose. In the essay on the virtue of English bishops, Jerrold is able to dispatch the national hero, the Duke of Wellington, and the prominent Whig statesman Lord Henry Brougham, whom he considered one of Wellington's most egregious toadies, in an aside: "Did [the Bishops] not one and all [proclaim the horrors of war] with such fearful eloquence, that even 'the iron Duke' wept drops of burning metal (which Lord Brougham in his admiration of the warrior has since had mounted for shirt-studs)?" But this is the only adroit line in a set of paragraphs containing sentences like the following: "Is there one Bishop of the whole Bench, who is not a very Nathan pleading with resistless speech for the one 'ewe lamb' of the English pauper, outraged and despoiled by the tyranny of wealth?"[32] Jerrold leans on his readers in these writings, thrusting home his issues, while Thackeray convivially engages us in worldly insinuation, mingling the glee of verbal invention with attack.

The contrast between the sketches of Thackeray and Jerrold suggests that as comic writing on social issues becomes more direct and demands a more committed response from its readers, it is inclined to be less artful and to contain less of the virtuosity and play that we normally associate with comedy. Similarly, as we sense greater psychological involvement by the author in his cause, we must be less easygoing in our attitude toward it. Thackeray's manner allows the reader to be safely cynical and to repair to the enjoyment of the comic production itself. Jerrold's manner forces the confrontation that is normally (by my earlier definition) the indication that the work is to be considered "serious" and not "comic." Indeed, Jerrold complained that his fellow humorists were often out of perspective: "After all, life has something serious in it. It cannot all be a comic history of humanity. Some men would, I believe, write the Comic Sermon on the Mount. Think of a comic History of England; the drollery of Alfred; the fun of Sir Thomas More in the Tower; the farce of his daughter begging his dear head. . . ."[33] As such a statement (and many others) indicates, Jerrold is a moralist—and one who has come by his morality through an independent struggle with the causes of evil in his time.

He relies on none of the received pieties and sanctities that comfort readers of Thackeray; indeed, Jerrold rebukes them. Thackeray, in any event, was really more often a moralizer than a moralist.

Most comic theories work on the assumption that the more oblique the social attack and the more adroitly it is insinuated, the more influential it will be, for readers pull away from confrontation. Such theories—and Freud's, Bergson's, and Meredith's are among them—put a premium upon the artistic expression of comic attack. Certainly, it can be argued that sophisticated readers, who are likely to be those in position to work greatest change in attitude and institutions, prefer sophisticated comedy. We can also contend that oblique presentation of injustice, say, through the inventions of comic allusion and suggestion does not mean that the writer is any less angry nor any less determined that his writing shall have social effect. As a writer identifies his target audience with greater sureness, he adapts his writing to reach them. Thackeray apparently gauged his audience correctly from the outset and took the method he felt most congenial to it. But changes in Jerrold's writing indicate that he developed his sense of the "ideal reader" slowly. As he did so, his writing became noticeably less strained and blunt, noticeably more artful. We can argue that it became more indulgent, too, for his greatest success, "Mrs. Caudle's Curtain Lectures," is a prime example of domestic comedy.

Jerrold's situation is an interesting one, for it can be read as an instance of the ineluctable forces of accommodation that push even the most vitriolic of social critics away from radicalism. His career is not like Pierce Egan's, for instance, for Egan was never a searching social critic; and it is not like Thackeray's, for Thackeray appears to have been yearning for a personal concept, such as the one of the "gentleman," that could synthesize what he knew of the world and what he held as an ideal of human behavior. Jerrold is the best example we have of a man whose social criticism changed in accordance with the changing social position of the Victorian middle class.

Whatever adjustments Jerrold made to his reading public, however, he made without compromise. Though he evolved from a writer taking angry potshots at the great to one who sympathetically satirized the everyday concerns of the lower middle class, and though this would seem to be an accommodation to the bourgeois banality and materialism that turned Victorian England into a cultural desert, according to later comic critics, Jerrold did not accept the comforting myths that floated through the period and he never constructed the dubious syntheses about human nature that Thackeray did. The series of "Punch's Letters to His Son" serves, in fact, as a bracing tonic to Thackeray's attempt to resuscitate eighteenth-century morality. Jerrold's series spoofs the Earl of Chesterfield's letters to his son written in the early and mid-eighteenth century, which were classic statements of the code of the gentleman. But where Chesterfield bids his son to be true to his best nature, Jerrold's Mr. Punch urges his boy to go along with the affectations of modern life. "By these means, although you are most efficiently assisting in the hypocrisy of life, you will be deemed a sociable, a most goodnatured fellow. Be stone-blind, and you will be benevolent; be deaf, and you will be all heart. . . . No: though you meet with men scruffed with moral leprosy, see not the scales, but cry out lustily, 'What perfect gentlemen!' "[34] What Thackeray observed of the opportunistic insincerity of modern life and could not abide, Jerrold unearths in great detail and, though disliking it, lays it down as the truth of human behavior in the modern urban world.

Play the Thackerayan gentleman, by all means, Jerrold says slyly, for it is the key to idleness. Punch chides the young man who refused at school to copy the sentence, "Command you may your mind from play" and based his refusal on the argument that it would be insincere and stifling to write a dictum in which one does not believe. Feign

seriousness, says Punch; humbug is the key to success. "It
will, I hope, impress upon your mind the necessity of taking certain sentences current in the world for precisely
what they are worth, without hallooing and calling a crowd
about you to show their cracked and counterfeit condition."[35] Mastering a little aristocratic brutality would also
help, so the lad is encouraged to smash bird's nests, hunt
down hares, shoot the cornered stag, and otherwise engage
in "manly sports." And above all, remember that to be a
gentleman is to acquire no substantive qualities:

> Again, then, I say it, my son, be Nothing! Look at the
> flourishing examples of Nothing about you! Consider
> the men in this vast metropolis whose faces shine with
> the very marrow of the land, and all for doing and being
> Nothing! Then, what ease—what unconcern—what per-
> fect dignity in the profession! Why, dull-brained, horn-
> handed labour, sweats and grows thin, and dies worn
> out, whilst Nothing gets a redder tinge upon its cheek, a
> thicker wattle to its chin, and a larger compass of abdo-
> men.[36]

Jerrold sees through that favorite recourse of men like
Bulwer, Peacock, and Thackeray—the withdrawal to medi-
tative philosophy. Punch becomes a hermit (not entirely in
the interests of philosophy, however; as it happens there is
also a warrant out for his arrest on the charge of his forg-
ing his Aunt Abishag's name to a check). This enables him
to reach the noble self that the vicissitudes of life had compelled him to subdue. "I have learned another trick in this
solitude. I have learned to separate the twin natures with
which, it is my belief, every man is born, and to sit in
judgement upon the vices, the follies, the high feelings,
and grovelling appetites, that make up the double *me*."[37]
He derives mock comfort from the notion that the self he
has constructed for the outer world is no reflection upon
the benevolent person within. Jerrold's series of letters

strips naked the deceit of the old theories of human nature.

"Punch's Letters to His Son," and the companion series of "Punch's Letter Writer," develop a quality in Jerrold that was lacking in his earlier occasional pieces of social satire—a more accessible, relaxed human voice. Such a direction is predictable in comic writers of this period, for it enables them to assume a more personal relationship with the reader in place of the detached coldness of the nonindividualized observer. Those personae who emerge, however, are riddled with the inconsistencies, blindnesses, and foibles of ordinary men. Jerrold is creating, in a limited way, *characters*. They are more ambivalent by the very fact that they are more human. Hence the hard, remorseless wrath of the impersonal satiric voice disappears; a softer, more complicated observer-narrator replaces it.

The change of tone that we find in Jerrold roughly parallels a shift in his area of interest to the established and largely suburban middle class that was attaining greater numbers and cultural dominance in the mid-Victorian years. The relative affluence and general social calm of the 1850s allowed people to turn their attention away from larger political issues to more immediate ones of ordinary life. The sense of instability that governed the 1820s and 1830s was on the wane; Victorian solidity became the image of the times. *Punch* reflected that change by tempering its satire and by concentrating less of its energy on major public figures and more on the nature of life in the ranges of the middle class. The evolution was gradual because *Punch*'s chief writers during the 1840s were people like Jerrold and Mark Lemon who had an eye for the prominent target and an abiding sense of social injustice. Jerrold's series of sketches called "Mrs. Caudle's Curtain Lectures," purporting to be the bedtime harangues by a frustrated wife of her lower middle-class husband, had a strong influence on the change in the locus of *Punch*'s humor. They are of a piece with his earlier unsparing realism but they introduce a whole new strain of English comedy. We will put off an analysis of the "Curtain Lectures" until chapter five, when their cultural position may be clearer. It is time now to turn to the greatest of the critics of English society, Charles Dickens.

3

Early Dickens: Metamorphosis, Psychic Disorientation, and the Small Fry

"Here's a Jolly Life! Catch hold."
—*The Artful Dodger*

I

*C*harles Dickens is the great comic writer of the middle class. "All the resources of the bourgeois epic were in his grasp,"[1] as his friend George Henry Lewes observed. In this one writer we see how comedy is turned from social schematization to the expression of an evolving personal experience and how subtly it serves to convey the ambiguity of one man's relationship to the middle class of which he was a part. Dickens' career bridged the euphoric social expansiveness of the 1830s and the mid-Victorian internal disillusionment of the 1860s. His early *Sketches by Boz* creates the freewheeling impression of the quasi-comic cultural expression that we examined in chapter one; and his late work betrays the sense of paradox and extreme alienation that we find in Oscar Wilde. For all of Dickens' remarkable ability to impose his own vision of his world, he is the first writer we observe whose comedy adequately reveals the anguish and perplexity of being caught *within* bourgeois assumptions. And in Dickens we can perceive the manifold workings of the comic process itself—the self-parody and reduction of comic material, the elaboration of it, the variation and incremental repetition.

In this chapter, we encounter a Dickens—the early

Dickens—who, if anything, vaunts the middle-class myths:
his character Pickwick stands as the ultimate expression of
one such myth; and his early sketches, and to a certain extent his early novels, put the whole unnerving upheaval of
social change in comforting, controlled perspective. But we
encounter almost at the same time a Dickens who revels in
the play of the chancy city, who discovers the powers of the
comic to invent fictions and celebrate the world of contingency. His great villains, like Quilp of *The Old Curiosity
Shop*, lead grotesquely vital and charmed lives in the most
horrendous chaos. Yet there is a nightmare in the city,
too—a nightmare of disequilibrium, of psychic and social
instability, of phenomenal overflow—and it invariably
catches up with even the wiliest of those villains. It also sur-
rounds and threatens the little people of the city, for whom
Dickens created a comedy of compassion, and it is they who
must build personality constructs, or elaborated fictions, in
order to survive. All through this chapter, we deal with the
Dickens whose eye is on his middle-class audience, but by
chapter's end, we perceive him beginning to harden
against that same public, especially as he chafes under the
comic formulas that he has exploited so well. In chapter
four, we will consider the direction that his writing took
beyond this critical turning point.

His early writing—the *Sketches*—is surprising considering
what we know of Dickens' searing childhood experiences,
his rugged initiation as a reporter, and his own lifelong
vulnerability. As introductions to the sordid realities of the
city, the *Sketches* have remarkably little bite and almost
never carry home any accusative thrust. Boz is "Your Town
Correspondent," a bluff, congenial man with a shrewd eye
for the grotesquely telling gesture and the comic-pathetic
pretension. He is inclined to be ironic and expansive by
turns, to be easily "unmanned," but equally ready to seek
out any incident that is curious, entertaining, and bracing
to the healthy sentiments. His venture into "a filthy and
miserable . . . part of London [that] can hardly be imagined

by those (and there are many such) who have not witnessed it" is memorable not so much for the barefoot girls playing in the swills of gutter refuse but for the tableau of a brace of young dandies giving the girls the eye, and the fast talk at a gin-shop counter. Though the sketch ends with a solemn warning of the havoc of the bottle, what actually sticks in the mind are the names on those gin casks—The Out and Out, The No Mistake, The Celebrated Butter Gin, The Real Knock-me-down.[2] The *Sketches* are city color for the home edition and were praised not for exposing the underside of London, but for their "discovery of 'everyday life' in neglected but immediately recognized pockets of urban and suburban society."[3]

The *Sketches* are fanciful introductions to the strange urban scene, as Pierce Egan's Tom and Jerry episodes were. They tend, as does other literature of the 1820s and 1830s, to fulfill middle-class expectations and to be schematic in their moral observations. In the sketch "The Prisoner's Van," for instance, Boz describes two girls in handcuffs: one is sixteen and already hardened to her sins, jeering back defiantly at the crowd; the other, her younger sister, is being brought in for her first offense and hangs back in humiliation. "What the younger girl was then, the elder had been once," Boz comments, "and what the elder then was, the younger must soon become. A melancholy prospect, but how surely to be realised; a tragic drama, but how often acted!"[4] So familiar is this parable—another Hogarthian Progress of the kind that Boz's illustrator, George Cruikshank, rendered so often—that almost any reader could have constructed the appropriate moral scenario. We cannot but reflect that if every instance of human degradation has so sure a source and so inevitable a progress, if it has so obviously a "story," then it is not, as Boz darkly warns, a proof of a spreading "pestilence" of urban social decay. Rather, it is another instance of failure by the poor to interpret and respond to their situation in the light of the proper morality.

Similarly, the mishaps of the lower middle-class clerks and grocers are attributable to their hapless attempts to arrogate themselves into a higher social station without having any sense of the values and outlook of the middle class. "The wish of persons in the humbler classes of life to ape the manners and customs of those whom fortune has placed above them, is often the subject of remark."[5] Consider the delightfully instructive case of the Tuggses, a grocer's family, who inherit some money and try to effect a mercurial rise from the petite to the haute bourgeoisie. It proves to be one thing for the younger Tuggses to change the spellings of their names—from Simon to the more elegant Cymon and from Charlotte to the exquisitely Europeanized Charlotta—thereby magically assuming the hauteur that surely befits a superior social station. And it is equally within the realm of possibility (indeed, of absolute necessity) to bully Father and Mother into some manners so that they will not wolf down their shrimps in public, heads, tails, and all. But it is quite another thing to be able to see through the pretenses of the swindlers that lay about for such vulnerable prey. Comic humiliation can only await the Tuggses' ill-conceived sally into more elevated spheres; Cymon carelessly and tragically falls in love with a con man's accomplice, is discovered "compromised" behind the curtains of her room; and only 1500 pounds in blackmail can get him out of the scrape. The moral is that there are some matters of substance and sound judgment that cannot be affected. A similar fate awaits poor Horatio Sparkins, who plays a headier game as the romantic, "metaphysical" wooer of Theresa Malderton, daughter of the Malderton of Lloyd's, the Exchange, and the Bank.[6] Sparkins gets as far as he does in this venture only because the Maldertons themselves have ascended too precipitously, have "affected fashion, taste and many other fooleries in imitation of their betters." Sparkins is ultimately found out to be nothing grander than a clerk in a "cheap shop," however, and it is probably just as well. Dickens is telling his readers that the whole City can be analyzed in terms of middle-class criteria; everyone falls into some construct, whether a pathetic one of moral decline or a comic one of social pretension.

In addition, Dickens shows the ability, even as a young man, to transmit the sense of openness and change that is so appropriate to this heady time of unlimited social horizons. Like Thackeray, he induces the reader to indulge in imaginative speculation, to seize the typical situation and "fill it in" with variation and story. In Dickens, however, this creates a unique sense of metamorphosis. Thus, in his earliest sketches, we see his mind wandering beyond the described scene or event to the possibilities for change. The very faculty of imagination that can conjure up ·a scapegrace's Progress from the contemplation of discarded boys' clothes hanging in a shop on Monmouth Street—the inevitable downward slide that begins with the young pup's neglect of his doting mother, carries him through hours spent in the taproom, to abuse of his wife and children, into a career of crime, and finally to the gallows—can turn in an instant, "by way of restoring the naturally cheerful tone of our thoughts," to a fantasy of clothes coming alive in an antic dance to the tune of a street organ.[7] And even when one cannot resist the hard truth about the unhappy lot of London's most heart-wringing creatures, the chimney sweeps, the truth comes only reluctantly. Boz muses first on the quaint old beliefs that the sweeps were the lost children of wealthy gentlemen, put on a "probationary term" from which they would be released after years of sorrow and suffering and restored to "their ranks and titles."[8] Who then can look upon those sweeps again without recalling the legends or taking a measure of solace for one's own feelings in those possibilities of romantic transformation? Social metamorphosis is in the air and it gives one a feeling for the dynamics of multifarious change, even when the movement is one of disintegration. Boz watches a street address decline through stages: it is first a linen draper's shop, then given over to a bonnet-maker, after that to a tobacconist, a hairdresser, and finally to a shabby ladies' school, when he says, "we thought . . . that the house had reached its lowest pitch of degradation. We were wrong. When we last passed it, a 'dairy' was established in the area, and a party of melancholy-looking fowls were amusing themselves by running in at the front door, and out at the back door."[9]

We get this impression of dynamism despite the sterility that characterizes so many individual lives in the *Sketches*. Dickens accomplishes this paradox again in *Martin Chuzzlewit*, where a world of individuals encased in tight personality constructs seems to be delightfully freewheeling. The effect is more explainable in *Chuzzlewit*, where the Pecksniffs, Tiggses, and Mrs. Gamps are richly imagined and given amplitude in their roles; it is more problematical in the *Sketches*, where the characters are caught in narrower stereotypes. But as E. H. Gombrich observes in his study of the processes of art: within certain circumstances, the most stereotyped schemata may induce such recognition that we have the impression of vitality.[10] The varying of literary forms in the *Sketches* (Dickens alternated scenes, character sketches, and stories), the stress upon social transformation and metamorphosis, and Boz's wide ranging imagination and hearty manner, all contribute toward the sense of vitality. It may be literally true, as Chesterton says, that "all that *moving* machinery exists only to display entirely *static* character," but the illusion of movement is there.[11]

There is another element of Dickens' early imagination that prefigures the characteristic quality of the great comic vision to invent and exploit its own self-parodic tensions. Dickens is entranced with the mimicking, expanding powers of art. Thus, when Boz wanders through the Vauxhall gardens in the uncomplimentary daylight, his initial response is one of disillusionment with what *really* lies behind the romance of the gaudy night: "*That* the Moorish tower—that wooden shed with a door in the centre, and daubs of crimson and yellow all round, like a gigantic watch-case! *That* the place where night after night we beheld the undaunted Mr. Blackmore make his terrific ascent, surrounded by flames of fire, and peals of artillery. . . ."[12] Yet the essay concludes with a glorious balloon ascension from the fireworks ground as if restoring the spectacle that Boz had set out to demystify.

J. Hillis Miller has noted an oscillation back and forth between figurative and literal interpretations of experience in many of the *Sketches* and in Cruikshank's illustrations of them. Within individual Cruikshank drawings, he remarks, there are disconcerting "works of art," busts, and wall portraits that mock the depiction of "reality" in the drawings.[13] Similarly, Dickens alludes to our formulaic literary expectations of situations and the recurring tendency of art and life to transpose each other. He betrays none of the uneasiness toward this that Bulwer does, however; the hearty comic tone rarely slips. Instead, he creates a subtle internal tension as if to compel the reader to be creatively receptive to the interchange of illusion and reality, to the way in which fictitious assumptions necessarily penetrate our conceptions of actuality. This tension is felt through all of Dickens' writing; we become sensitive to the interplay of several visions in Dickens—the romantic, the disillusioned, the sentimental, and the skeptical.

Even in *Pickwick Papers*, we can perceive the sources of such tension. Pickwick is the great culminating work of the English humor tradition of the eighteenth and early nineteenth centuries. This tradition celebrates the individual and encourages appreciation and affection for the unique oddities and eccentricities that characterize human nature—especially English human nature. Its tone is gentle and tolerant, in contrast to the reductiveness of wit. And it is comfortably bourgeois, accommodating eccentricity so long as the behavior is socially harmless. Parson Adams of Fielding's *Joseph Andrews* and Uncle Toby of Sterne's *Tristram Shandy* are the great paradigms of the tradition; and no more harmless, indeed sentimental, "originals" could be found.

As we observed earlier, Pickwick epitomizes a fond literary myth of the middle class as it enters the less robust and more confining circumstances of Victorianism and modern urban/suburban existence. Pickwick packs his bourgeois habits and predilections—his propriety, his sensibility, his love of the creature comforts—in his portmanteau and sets out on the open road. As Chesterton says, he is "the type of this true and neglected thing, the romance of the middle classes."[14] There is nothing sterile or confining about being stoutly middle-class in *this* novel's world; each morning that Pickwick bounds out of bed, another adventure waits for him—a hunting party, a fancy dress ball, a ride pell-mell through the countryside, a convivial round of drinking and eating to excess at yet another cozy inn. Unlike his successor Jorrocks, Pickwick is no crude upstart trampling down hedges; he is the eccentric uncle whom we are fond of; he is, indeed, the childlike, respectably antisocial impulse in all of us. The creation of such a character advances Dickens beyond the *Sketches* where this kind of movement and openness had to be conveyed by the very incompleteness of the sketches and the shifting of forms. In keeping with his greater literary powers, Dickens here embodies the motifs in a single character. *Pickwick Papers* is a grand assertion of expansiveness, riding over discordant social facts like a runaway coach.

Yet even in *Pickwick*, the discordant social facts still exist; and they rise up from time to time. Pickwick himself is buffered from raw actuality by Sam Weller, his man from the respectable lower classes. Sam wonders at times whether Pickwick is "half-baptized," so naive is he; most of the time it is Sam who must traffic with the real world. Significantly, then, when Pickwick determines to have real contact with degradation and despair, when he faces up to the conditions of life in the Fleet Prison, he dismisses Sam. So radical a departure is this prison experience from the others, that

Dickens entitles the chapter in which Pickwick is committed, "Scene in the Great Drama of Life" (chap. XLII). Everywhere else in the novel, the harsher dimensions of human existence are insulated from the realm of Pickwickian action. Only in the encapsulated tales are we introduced to the horror of insanity, for instance, and even then, we take it as a bedtime thriller; Pickwick reads "A Madman's Manuscript" when he cannot sleep. And only in tales like "The Queer Client" (chap. XXI) do we encounter human evil that goes beyond the kind of quixotic, casual rascality of Jingle or Dodson and Fogg to the deadlier, more trying level of action on which men deal with each other ruthlessly, in unrelenting earnest.

These brief exposures of another scale of human behavior may betray some impatience in Dickens with the middle-class myth he is propagating. We wonder whether he senses that this great child-man, Pickwick, induces a kind of sentimental fading away to the retreat shown in later versions of the green world and to its ultimate puerility in the late century. Certainly we observe in the young novelist a struggle toward a synthesis of the middle-class urge to sentimentalize (and thus to stabilize and freeze) with his own abiding appreciation of the exciting if harrowing energy of the city. Dickens' fascination with the wild side of life is so strong that *Oliver Twist*, which follows *Pickwick*, begins as a tale of the Pickwickian lad Oliver meeting fate with the pluck and bedrock goodness of the wellborn child but the narrative is later overwhelmed by the vitality of the inhabitants of the London underworld, Fagin, Sikes, and the Artful Dodger. Dickens' real interests lie in the fortunes of the streets. He can temporarily reconcile his divided loyalties by ensuring that the point of view remains middle class. *Oliver Twist* is a little boy's nightmare of being kidnapped and held prisoner—literally cast as an infantile fantasy when in one incident Oliver wakes, supposedly safe in the Maylie cottage, to see Monks and Fagin lurking at his bedroom windows. Similarly, *The Old Curios-*

ity Shop is a little girl's specter of gross male sexuality: "such a fresh, blooming, modest little bud," gloats the hunchbacked Quilp to Nell's Grandfather Trent, "such a chubby, rosy, cosy little Nell."

Dickens' delight, though, springs from his characterizations of those who thrive in the phenomenal world, those who enact the comic vision, rolling with the contingencies of life, hoisting elaborate, bizarre fictions against the flux. They are the creatures of Dickens' own metamorphosing imagination. "Here's a Jolly Life! Catch hold," says the Artful Dodger to Oliver. The Dodger is the waif become con man, the lost soul who has found himself in his wits. What better expression of the resilience of the human condition? He and Charley Bates have their own kind of perambulating Club and their own pint-sized versions of evenings of conviviality, lounging in Fagin's den—that parody of snugness—and discoursing in a mellow mood over pipe and beer about retiring on one's property and doing "the genteel" (chap. xviii). Pickwick could not be keener on his Englishman's "priwileges," nor could Sam Weller be more cocksure in court, than is the Artful Dodger during this exchange:

> "We'll see wot the Secretary of State for the Home Affairs has got to say to the beaks. . . . Now then! Wot is this here business? I shall thank the madg'strates to dispose of this here little affair, and not to keep me while they read the paper, for I've got an appointment with a genelman in the City, and as I'm a man of my word, and wery punctual in business matters, he'll go away if I ain't there to my time, and then perhaps there won't be an action for damage against them as kep me away. Oh no, certainly not!"
>
> "Has the boy ever been here before?"
>
> "He ought to have been, a many times," replied the jailer. "He has been pretty well everywhere else. *I* know him well, your worship."

"Oh! you know me, do you?" cried the Artful, making a note of the statement. "Wery good. That's a case of de-formation of character, any way" (chap. XLIII).

A splendid case of deformation of character. No matter that the Artful Dodger is dragged out of the book by the ear; no matter that he'll not make the Newgate Calendar of infamous scoundrels. He enacts the comic vision. He lives his own elaborations.

The circumstances against which these powers of self-creation must be exerted are formidable. There is, first of all, the mob. In the last chapters of *Oliver Twist*, Bill Sikes throttles himself in trying to escape the vengeance of the London mob that climbs up every water spout and crevice in the wall, clambers to every house-top, engulfs every bridge, and batters down the door to get at him. Fagin con-fronts an immobile but no less horrible gallery of unsympa-thetic, curious eyes out of which he tries, in desperation, to select a single token of humanity. The particular Victorian nightmare that was most acutely experienced by a middle class unsure of its foundations, the specter of social anar-chy welling up from the depths of the city poor—the legacy of worry from the French Revolution, the Gordon riots, the Peterloo Massacre, and the unsettling awareness that there was another "nation" seething down there—is trans-posed in *Oliver* into one of the most primitive of horrors, that of being overwhelmed by the nonhuman.

The last days of Sikes and Fagin are exercises in melo-drama, of course; they are intensifications of latent threats for the psychological effect. But nobody does this as well as Dickens because nobody is as close to believing in it as he. Long before the anarchy of the crowd scenes at the end of the novel were written, and probably long before they were conceived, the London of Dickens begins to gather and press in upon the imagination. His City is crazy with cramped houses, pinched store fronts, and narrow little al-leys, with great beams out in the street propping up build-

ings that totter and creak and groan, and with scuttling
rats, cringing dogs, bawling children, surly whores, fish-
wives, cabmen, hawkers, and pickpockets. *Oliver Twist* gives
clear indication, for the first time, that Dickens finds aspects of the City uncanny and has simply got to cope with
them. Sketches like that of the Seven Dials—of a neighborhood in which "streets and courts dart in all directions"
and a kind of perpetual raucousness enlivens every Irish
family—transmit something of the urban chaos. But such
details and incidents in the *Sketches* are treated as bright
fragments that revolve into a series of temporary kaleido-
scopic patterns. In *Oliver*, everything settles in, precipitates
down and collects, like soot, then becomes encrusted, angu-
lar, and then antic under the fevered spell of the imagination.

The phenomenal world exploded in Dickens' generation; the pulse of life quickened;[15] the City of London,
bursting with infusions of people from the country, broke
out in rashes of individual deformations. Just to list the
subjects of Henry Mayhew's *London Labour and the London
Poor* (1851) is to gorge and tax the imagination: Street-
sellers of Pea soup and Hot Eels, Street-sellers of Gutta-
percha Heads, Street-sellers of Fly-papers and Beetle-
wafers, "Screevers" or Writers of Begging Letters and
Petitions, The Cheap Johns, Bone-grubbers and Rag-
gatherers, The Cigar-end Finders, Her Majesty's Bug
Destroyer, The Afflicted Crossing-sweepers. Charles
Manby Smith's *Curiosities of London Life* (written in the late
1840s and early 1850s) is nearly as rich. Along with this,
manufacture, mass production, expansion of trade, and a
larger affluent market caused an inundation of goods and
items, many of them grotesque reflections of the Victorian
public's taste for the ornate.[16]

Dickens' personal experience uniquely shaped his imagination to deal with such a scene. Forster says that Dickens
recollected long into adulthood the specific details of the
neighborhood of Hungerford Stairs and the routes he took

through the City as a child. Lewes calls this power in Dickens almost hallucinatory and insists that it extended even to created images, which he imagined "not in the vague schematic way of ordinary imagination, but in the sharp definition of actual perception, all the salient details obtruding themselves on his attention."[17] Such vision is at the core of Dickens' artistic method,[18] and it is this image that he is determined to transmit out to his reading public.

Dickens' villains, however, appear to thrive in the confusion of the City. It has often been noted that the villains of the early books provide us with some of the most splendid comic moments in literature. Chesterton speaks for many of us when he says that he hates to see a Dickens villain leave; if only the scoundrel could stick his head back into the doorway "and make one more atrocious remark." We dare not so misread Dickens or his Victorian public as to suppose that Quilp and Carker are to prevail over the instruments of good in Dickens' novels. But we cannot be so false to our own reading experience as to deny the fascination and pleasure that such scoundrels bring. Quilp surely is perversity incarnate, but Dickens, sharing DeQuincey's attraction to the uncanny creative energies seemingly unleashed in the anarchy of the City, makes Quilp an ambivalently intriguing exploration of the crafty diabolism of imaginative play. Quilp spins loose from cloying, enervating sublimation and reveals to us how elemental the pleasures of the perverse can be, how close to those childhood delights—those childhood *comic* delights. Quilp is a capriccio of the childlike, antisocial, semierotic urges that fuel the elaborative impulse.

Who can resist thumbing ahead to see when the next Quilp passage occurs in *The Old Curiosity Shop*? Without him the book would have an atmosphere as stifling as that in a glass jar of crushed funeral roses. He is the Scourge of Comedy, the reductive impulse that all these parlor societies seem to need periodically. He can turn every trick; when he intrudes upon Mrs. Jiniwin, his mother-in-law,

and the neighbor ladies gabbling about how they put down
their husbands, he curdles them with kindness and politeness, suggesting that they all "stop to supper, and have a
couple of lobsters and something light and palatable."
Every attack by Mrs. Jiniwin is enveloped in his insidious
mock courtesy:

> "And [your wife] has a right to do as she likes, I hope,
> Quilp," said the old lady trembling, partly with anger
> and partly with a secret fear of her impish son-in-law.
> "Hope she has!" he replied. "Oh! Don't you know she
> has? Don't you know she has, Mrs. Jiniwin?"
> "I know she ought to have, Quilp, and would have, if
> she was to my way of thinking."
> "Why an't you of your mother's way of thinking, my
> dear?" said the dwarf, turning around and addressing
> his wife, "why don't you always imitate your mother, my
> dear? She's the ornament of her sex—your father said so
> every day of his life. I am sure he did."
> "Her father was a blessed creetur, Quilp, and worth
> twenty thousand of some people," said Mrs. Jiniwin;
> "twenty hundred million thousand."
> "I should like to have known him," remarked the
> dwarf. "I dare say he was a blessed creature then; but I'm
> sure he is now. It was a happy release. I believe he suf-
> fered a long time?" (chap. IV).

We all know how Mr. Jiniwin suffered and we can all
agree that Mrs. Jiniwin deserves to be scourged. She is
pompous and overbearing and self-righteous. But why is it
so delightful to read about Quilp's torture of his wife, who
is not overbearing, nor simpering either, but just an unobtrusive little woman trying to do her best? Quilp subjects
her, as her punishment for allowing the neighbor women
in, to a night's ordeal of sitting up with *him*—in the dark, on
a hard chair, immobile, with his cigar smoke in her face.
Yet it is genuinely funny when he remarks the next morning, "Who says man and wife are bad company? Ha ha!

The time has flown." And we are quite ready to be regaled with his ill manners at breakfast where he munches his hard eggs shell and all, gnaws his forks and spoons into odd shapes, gobbles up gigantic prawns without removing the heads and tails, wolfs down water-cress with raw tobacco, and has his tea boiling hot.

The comic pleasures of a Quilp are antisocial, for he is the bane not only of the Mrs. Jiniwins, who are preposterous frauds and cheats themselves, but of goodness wherever it shows itself. "I hate your virtuous people," says the dwarf, "ah, I hate 'em every one." Few of us would like to deny him his sport with Mrs. Nubbles, another good soul, when he indulges his "taste for doing something fantastic and monkey-like" during a coach ride back to London:

> It was some gratification to Mr. Quilp to find, as he took his place upon the roof, that Kit's mother was alone inside; from which circumstance he derived in the course of the journey much cheerfulness of spirit, inasmuch as her solitary condition enabled him to terrify her with many extraordinary annoyances; such as hanging over the side of the coach at great risk of his life, and staring in with his great goggle eyes, which seemed in hers the more horrible from his face being upside down; dodging her in this way from one window to another; getting nimbly down whenever they changed horses and thrusting his head in at the window with a dismal squint: which ingenious tortures had such an effect upon Mrs. Nubbles, that she was quite unable for the time to resist the belief that Mr. Quilp did in his own person represent and embody that Evil Power, who was so vigorously attacked at Little Bethel, and who, by reason of her backslidings in respect of Astley's and oysters, was now frolicsome and rampant (chap. XLVIII).

There is in this, of course, something of the boyish fiendishness that we left behind in our pranks of childhood. It is no surprise that the boy Tom Scott sticks so close to Quilp despite cuffings and taunts. There is good fun to be had. Who has not experienced the glee of sneaking up on someone unawares and scaring the wits out of him? And when Tom informs Quilp that his wife, mother-in-law, and the lawyer Brass think he is dead and are right this minute lugubriously savoring his demise, the two pranksters are momentarily helpless with the rich prospects: "They both stood for some seconds, grinning and gasping, and wagging their heads at each other, on either side of the post, like an unmatchable pair of Chinese idols." The tension is exquisite as we listen in, along with Quilp, to the vultures as they fill themselves with his liquor and pick over the bones of his memory:

> "With regard to the descriptive advertisement," said Sampson Brass, taking up his pen. "It is a melancholy pleasure to recall his traits. Respecting his legs now—?"
>
> "Crooked, certainly," said Mrs. Jiniwin.
>
> "Do you think they *were* crooked?" said Brass, in an insinuating tone. "I think I see them now coming up the street very wide apart, in nankeen pantaloons a little shrunk and without straps. Ah! what a vale of tears we live in. Do we say crooked?"
>
> "This is an occupation," said the lawyer, laying down his pen and emptying his glass, "which seems to bring him before my eyes like the Ghost of Hamlet's father, in the very clothes that he wore on work-a-days. His coat, his waistcoat, his shoes and stockings, his trousers, his hat, his wit and humour, his pathos and his umbrella, all come before me like visions of my youth."
>
> "His linen!" said Mr. Brass smiling fondly at the wall, "his linen which was always of a particular colour, for such was his whim and fancy—how plain I see his linen now!" (chap. XLIX).

Oh, what a rattling they are all going to get for that! It is hard to say which is most delightful, the prospect of Quilp's revenge or Brass's gleeful recollection of Quilp's dirty linen. The scene is a masterpiece of the crude pleasures of comedy elaborated to their limits. And what fun Dickens must have had writing it.

One aspect of the enjoyment of childhood play is its ostensible freedom from social restraints, even if just in fantasy. Quilp can stay up all night if he wishes, always has liberty for extended tricks and deviltry, and simply moves out on his wife in order that he might enjoy the pleasures of bachelorhood. In 1840, while *The Old Curiosity Shop* was appearing in serial, Dickens wrote Forster, "I saw the Responsibilities this morning, and burst into tears. The presence of my wife aggravates me. I loathe my parents. I detest my house."[19] The comment was written in the context of offhand joking, but Edgar Johnson thinks it has "deeper overtones."[20] At any rate, Quilp has all the license for unconventionality that anyone could wish for. *He* is not trapped in any middle-class construct of respectable behavior. His "monkey-like" habits are not altogether grotesque exaggerations; they suggest a sort of manic flexibility. He sleeps with his head hanging down from the bed like a dog or curled up on a desk like a hedgehog, so free from the average mold is he.

One cannot dance on the live wire forever, alas. The villains thrive for a while in that field of psychic disorientation and contingency, but it is a dangerous sphere. They are villains because they have nothing of principle, or even of lasting personal interest, to hold onto. Their obsession with the main chance, the headiness of their own spontaneous diabolism, has driven out almost all other human characteristics and values. And always in Dickens they prove the most vulnerable to the City's Powers of Dissolution. The demise of Carker, the witty devil of *Dombey and Son*, characterizes the fate of Dickens' villains. And symbolically, he is done in by all of the constellation of elements that make up the nightmare vision of Dickens' early novels—the breakdown of the integral personality, the overwhelming of man by the brute force of the unleashed machine energy of the

Industrial Revolution, and the literal fragmentation that is symbolized by material flux. As Carker races across France and England trying to escape his guilt in a fever of total disorientation, he is tumbled along in a stream of phenomena:

> The clatter and commotion echoed to the hurry and discordance of the fugitive's ideas. Nothing clear without, and nothing clear within. Objects flitting past, merging into one another, dimly descried, confusedly lost sight of, gone!

> Of rolling on and on, always postponing thought, and always racked with thinking; of being unable to reckon up the hours he had been on the road, or to comprehend the points of time and place in his journey. Of being parched and giddy, and half mad.

> A troubled vision, then, of bridges, quays, interminable streets; of wine-shops, water-carriers, great crowds of people, soldiers, coaches, military drums, arcades. Of the monotony of bells and wheels and horses' feet being at length lost in the universal din and uproar.

> Disordered with wine and want of rest—that want which nothing, although he was so weary, would appease—these ideas and objects assumed a diseased importance in his thoughts. When he went back to his room, which was not until near midnight, they still haunted him, and he sat listening for the coming of another [train].

Finally, weary, distracted, paranoically convinced that he is being pursued by a stranger, he staggers out onto train tracks:

> He heard a shout—another—saw the face change from its vindictive passion to a faint sickness and terror—felt

the earth tremble—knew in a moment that the rush was come—uttered a shriek—looked round—saw the red eyes, bleared and dim, in the daylight, close upon him—was beaten down, caught up, and whirled away upon a jagged mill, that spun him round and round and struck him limb from limb, and licked his stream of life up with its fiery heat, and cast his mutilated fragments in the air (chap. LV).

There is the unique Dickens nightmare. *There* is what threatens all of his alienated souls if they lose control in the overwhelming City.[21]

Still, even the Powers of Dissolution seem to regret the loss of the Dickensian villain's manic glee for life. When Quilp is finally driven down, the narrator solemnly proclaiming the close of his "malignant career," the old bluebottle nonetheless capers in the imagination. Though he has gone to his death in the Thames, the waters of the river are said to have "toyed and sported" with his body, handling it as an "ugly plaything" before tossing it ashore. And on Quilp's carcass "the hair, stirred by the damp breeze, played in a kind of mockery of death—such mockery as the dead man himself would have revelled in when alive" (chap. LXVII).

"His wit and humour, his pathos and his umbrella"—*Sampson Brass*

II

Martin Chuzzlewit is very likely Dickens' greatest expression of the comic impulse and one of his most ambitious attempts to embrace the widest possible variety of City experience. In it he tried to bring under his domination an entire social milieu and a teeming field of individual comic characters. He felt his full powers as he wrote it; no story was launched, Forster asserts, "with a stronger heart or confidence."[22] "I think Chuzzlewit in a hundred points immeasurably the best of my stories. . . . I feel my power now more than I ever did. . . . I have a greater confidence in myself than I ever had," Dickens writes.[23] Even though the statements were made partly in defiance when Dickens learned that the sales of the novel were inexplicably lower than those of previous books, they accord with all he expressed of this work that made him "laugh very much" in the writing of it.

The nature of the novel itself, with its sprawling, casual accommodation of character after character, indicates that it was a product of the elaborative impulse—and Dickens confirms it. The book was begun without a sense of "the main track of his design," according to Forster, and Dickens soon caught himself up in inventive characterization, especially of Pecksniff and Mrs. Gamp: "as to the way in which these characters have opened out," he tells Forster, "that is to me one of the most surprising processes of the mind in this sort of invention. Given what one knows, what one does not know springs up; and I am as absolutely certain of its being true, as I am of the law of gravitation."[24] But to account for *Chuzzlewit*'s other salient characteristic—its plethora of characters and incident—we must understand something more of the quality of Dickens' imagination.

Dickens' novels fall more properly into the English literary form of the anatomy than Peacock's do, primarily because Dickens was responding, as other great comic artists did, to the effusion of ideas, knowledge, and tangible goods that marked the Victorian era, by gathering them under the covers of his book and exploring the possibilities of playful experimentation with them. The encounter with a fugacious reality full of things does not necessarily produce a comic response, as we can see in the nausea of Jean-Paul Sartre's Roquentin.[25] The prevalent reaction, indeed, as

W. J. Harvey argues, is alienation. But the attempt to embrace an entire field of experience often does lead to comedy. Possibly this is because the writer perceives the humorous futility in it all; we sense such an awareness in Flaubert's *Bouvard and Pecuchet*, especially when we recall Flaubert's long-harbored disgust with the material excrescences of modern bourgeois life. In many other cases, however—in Rabelais and Dickens and Joyce—the enterprise is comic because it signifies the pleasure of temporarily dominating the outer world, of being able to engage in a sort of play with it.

Hugh Kenner calls this the Comedy of Inventory, drawing on Joyce's concept that joy rises out of the satiation of desire.[26] Kenner's study of Flaubert, Joyce, and Samuel Beckett shows how narrow the division is in modern writers between play and alienating futility. The English tradition of the literary anatomy, on the other hand, is more properly seen as a masterly exercise of domination over diverse materials. It is closer to those instincts of play which figure so fundamentally in the growth of the comic manner. The idea of the anatomy—which reached Dickens through Laurence Sterne's *Tristram Shandy* (although also through Carlyle's *Sartor Resartus*, and even through Fielding and Smollett)—had been to collect all knowledge, when that still seemed possible to do, for the purposes of demonstrating the fecundity and reach of the individual mind and accumulating a treasure trove of curiosities for the anatomist's personal amusement. The objective, in a man like Sterne, clearly seems to be play, an opportunity to exhibit one's wit and virtuosity by juggling known material through inventive analogies and clever juxtapositions. Earlier scientific knowledge was especially rich in comic possibilities, for it had a nonabstract, pithy quality about it. The old physiology, for instance, retained a pictorial specificity in its accounts of the functions of phlegm and liver and spleen.[27]

Dickens had more than a casual interest in scientific

knowledge, but he can hardly be said to stand directly in the anatomist tradition. He was not absorbed with ideas, as such. Rather, his artistic objective was to embrace the widest possible range of human *experience*—to identify each character and situation and to capture each specific detail. This was a superhuman task, however, for experience is not only multiple, it is changing. It requires constant interpretation and analysis. Hence we have some of the structural agonies of Dickens' fiction—the attempt, in novels such as *Bleak House*, *Little Dorrit*, and *Martin Chuzzlewit*, to introduce scores of characters as if just to include them all; to stretch the action through city and country, rich area and poor, England, Europe, and America; and then, especially in the later books, to compress it all into tighter and more arbitrary conceptual frameworks.

Only in this way could Dickens master the flux of the changing phenomenal world, the nightmare into which human beings with less firm self-control are plunged. Cataloguing and naming and including are not enough, however. When Fagin confronts a courtroom full of strange, impersonal souls, he illustrates Dickens' personal method of dealing with the mass:

> He looked, wistfully, into their faces, one by one, when they passed out, as though to see which way the greater number leant; but that was fruitless. . . .
>
> He looked up into the gallery again. Some of the people were eating, and some fanning themselves with handkerchiefs; for the crowded place was very hot. There was one young man sketching his face in a little note-book. He wondered whether it was like, and looked on when the artist broke his pencil-point, and made another with his knife, as any idle spectator might have done.
>
> In the same way, when he turned his eyes towards the judge, his mind began to busy itself with the fashion of his dress, and what it cost, and how he put it on (chap. LII).

The roving eye searches the mass for detail; the slightest recognizable object is seized upon and intensified to almost hallucinatory vividness; then the mind tries to probe behind and around it for human context, for a story or a situation that will differentiate it from the thousand other particles. George Santayana puts his finger on Dickens' method when he distinguishes it from that of Walt Whitman, who also attempted to subsume a large and teeming continent in a swiftly moving time by experiencing and describing everything in it. Whitman, Santayana says, had "a sort of transcendental philosophy which swallows the universe whole," gathering up everything and swirling it into a gigantic mix, a "nebula." Dickens, on the other hand, visualized his world not as a nebula, but as "a concourse of very distinct individual bodies, natural and social, each with its definite interest and story."[28]

In Dickens, human beings remain not only discrete but highly personalized. We observed the story-making tendency in the *Sketches by Boz* where the artist's imagination could not be restrained from creating a "background" of lineage, habits, and attitudes for every denizen of London. In the *Sketches*, however, the story tended to be a schema; in *Chuzzlewit*, each human being has his unique personality, even if a stylized and fantastic one. This makes Dickens predominantly a comic writer rather than a satirist. "The scene of satire," Alvin Kernan states, "is always disorderly and crowded; packed to the very point of bursting. The deformed faces of depravity, stupidity, greed, venality, ignorance and maliciousness group closely together. . . . The scene is equally choked with things: ostentatious buildings and statuary, sedan-chairs, clothes, books, food, horses, dildoes, luxurious furnishings, gin-bottles, wigs."[29] That surely resembles Dickens' underworld in many respects. The satirist, however, rarely tries to make us understand the humanity behind those deformed faces. The satiric persona, Kernan maintains, contemplates his scene with barren detachment. This Dickens could never do. He could not stare down the horror of the anarchic, degenerated City life; he could not condemn the weak; and he tended even to soften his excoriations of those whose neglect or indifference he held accountable for the human rot. Ambivalence distinguishes comedy from satire, and because, as we shall later see so vividly illustrated in Dickens, ambivalence usually characterizes the attitude of a middle-class writer toward his society, Dickens remained a writer of the comic mode.

Dickens' shading of his urban types accounts for the particular characteristics that we associate with the Dickensian comic figure. The little people of the City exhibit the same kind of elaborative imagination that the Quilps do: they construct fictions by which they operate, often with great gusto and verve; and they are as assuredly exposed to the contingencies of a chancy life as are any of the villains. They differ, these true victims of the upheaval of social transformation, from the Quilps and Carkers in not being really immoral (albeit a bit casual in their ethics) and in their use of the comic imagination for self-protection rather than for exploitation. Their appearance marks rather a bold advance in Dickens' own vision, for he now clearly perceives what urban existence has forced upon the human psyche and he is trying, through them, to enlarge the imaginative powers of the middle-class audience, which he senses is gradually shrinking away from the realities of that urban existence.

The purpose of what we saw to be Dickens' individualization of his people, his projection of a unique story and personality for each, has been to compel the middle-class reading public to reach out in sympathetic imagination toward souls who are completely alien to them. The act required is not simply one of expanded awareness; the spectator is called upon to heighten and enrich the life he either ignored or shied away from. A possible theoretical foundation for this rests in the early nineteenth-century, literary-critical position referred to as "idealism." In contrast to "realism," idealism portrayed the generalized, the universal, or the "ideal," rather than the particularized portrait of an individual. The idealist artist drew a character who may have been slightly exaggerated or abstract, but who was representative of generalities in human nature. Dickens has been called an idealist in his characterization, for despite the uniqueness of his portraits, especially of comic grotesques, they are more intensified than one is likely to encounter in actual experience. In addition, his creations are infused with his own vision. Bulwer was influential here; in an important essay, he states that the function of art is to "allure us to transport ourselves for the moment into the place of those who are passing through events which are not familiar to our actual experience." We must engage in imaginative projection: "the real truthfulness of all works of imagination . . . is so purely in the imagination, *that the artist never seeks to represent the positive truth, but the idealized image of a truth*."[30] Hence we only learn of women like Mrs. Gamp by applying our imagination to the "fetch and ghost of her," as we have seen Dickens do. We project her story, her lively case, her gestures and devices— intensified and exaggerated, *idealized* in Bulwer's sense—all to get at her spirit and essence.

The thesis of idealism, in Bulwer's and Dickens' hands, has even more interesting implications. Bulwer was one of the first of his time to attempt to elicit sympathetic comprehension of the poor, "little folk" of the City. He was also one of the first to sense the prevalence of self-fictions, which were particularly necessary for survival in an urban environment. Idealism's justification for an artistic method that emphasizes the role of imaginative projection adjusts our sight so that we can not only see vividly the characteristic quality of human beings who are alien to our immediate experience but we can also grasp the facility for self-projection that such people are required to make. The objective of it all is to broaden the reader's sympathies.

It is still more important for dramatic effect, that the *dramatis personae* should embody attributes of passion, humour, sentiment, character, with which large miscel-

laneous audiences can establish sympathy; and sympathy
can be only established by such a recognition of a something familiar to our own natures, or to our conception
of our natures, as will allure us to transport ourselves for
the moment into the place of those who are passing
through events which are not familiar to our actual
experience.[31]

Then, tellingly, Bulwer chooses Don Quixote as one of his
illustrations, a figure whom the nineteenth century considered a comic eccentric, a man cherishing his fantastic illusions and acting out a comic/pathetic role—but a man who
is all the more true to "certain qualities which are largely
diffused through human nature."

By the time of *Oliver Twist*, the locus of Dickens' comedy
was shifting to the lower classes. Dickens treats his lower-
class and lower middle-class people comically because this
is the way to engage our sympathetic imagination. In the
Preface to *Martin Chuzzlewit*, Dickens defends those very
characterizations, arguing that "What is exaggeration to
one class of minds, is plain truth to another. That which is
commonly called a longsight, perceives in a prospect
innumerable features and bearings non-existent to a
shortsighted person. I sometimes ask myself whether there
may occasionally be a difference of this kind between some
writers and some readers; whether it is *always* the writer
who colours highly, or whether it is now and then the
reader whose eye for colour is a little dull?" The great
achievement of Dickens' comic powers in *Chuzzlewit* is in
bringing out the color of the personalities of the forgotten
or neglected of the City—the night-nurses and innkeepers
and errand boys whom we would otherwise assume to be
drab and dull. By exaggeration and intensification, by
the free run of the imagination, he teaches us, as the
caricaturist does, to see things with different eyes. The ex-
istences of the lower classes in London are no longer of a
depressing, devitalized sameness, for we invest them with
antic and sometimes manic life. We see people we would

miss otherwise; we humanize them. The achievement is thus much different from what Henri Bergson's theory of comedy would imply; no matter how eccentric and compulsive the actions of these people are, Dickens has breathed more life into them, not less. Samuel Taylor Coleridge, whose critical influence on Dickens appears to have been substantial, laid to Art the very power of "humanizing nature." Coleridge's invocation of a vision that is humanly sympathetic was, as Carlyle and others could observe, in conflict with the Benthamite viewpoint that sees people functionally. Nowhere but in the culture's conception of the lower classes of the City could that conflict be more vividly observed.

Dickens' objective is to make us appreciate that much of the stunted and imitative behavior of the little people in his novels is contrived and maintained as a protection against demoralization and psychic disintegration in the hard world of the modern City. The marvelous dinner of the Small Fry in *Bleak House* is a respite, a moment of mock elegance snatched out of the abasement of their everyday lives. Three very junior clerks, Guppy, Jobling, and the younger Smallweed (who is described as a "town made article, of small stature and weazen features"), after a day of slouching on the stools at the law firm of Kenge and Carboy, repair to an ostentatious dinner, washed down with innumerable pints of half-and-half. The elegance and expansiveness of their manner is appropriately awesome:

"Will you take any other vegetables? Grass? Peas? Summer cabbage?"

"Thank you, Guppy," says Mr. Jobling. "I really don't know but what I *will* take summer cabbage."

Order given: with the sarcastic addition (from Mr. Smallweed) of "Without slugs, Polly!" And cabbage produced.

"Now, Small," says Mr. Guppy, "What would you recommend about pastry?"

"Marrow puddings," says Mr. Smallweed, instantly.

"Aye, aye!" cries Mr. Jobling, with an arch look. "You're there, are you? Thank you, Mr. Guppy, I don't know but what I *will* take a marrow pudding."

Three marrow puddings being produced, Mr. Jobling adds, in a pleasant humour, that he is coming of age fast. To these succeed, by command of Mr. Smallweed, "three Cheshires;" and to those, "three small rums" (chap. xx).

No gentleman of Lloyd's or the Exchange, no potentate, could exceed their self-satisfaction, could attain, in their Small Fry's estimation, to the liberality with which marrow pudding, rum, and cigars are ordered or to the sharp exactness with which Smallweed cautions the waitress, Polly, that slugs in the summer cabbage will not pass. For a moment, in a pocket of the City, the life of leisure and superiority can be emulated. And necessary it is, for these are the souls who are closest to that nightmare of disintegration into which Carker fell. It is Guppy and Jobling, lounging against the window sill in the apartment above Krook's shop, who first touch the "thick, yellow liquor" that is the nauseous residue of Krook's spontaneous combustion.

The celebrations and pleasures of the little people in London are staked out in the grimmest of circumstances— like the comic repasts of Pecksniff, Mrs. Gamp, and Mould's mutes in the death chambers of Anthony Chuzzlewit:

they kept quite a dainty table during this melancholy season; with sweetbreads, stewed kidneys, oysters, and other such light viands for supper every night.

Nor did Mr. Pecksniff alone indulge in the creature comforts during this sad time. Mrs. Gamp proved to be very choice in her eating, and repudiated hashed mutton with scorn. In her drinking too, she was very punctual and particular, requiring a pint of mild porter at lunch, a pint at dinner, half-a-pint as a species of stay or holdfast between dinner and tea, and a pint of the celebrated staggering ale, or Real Old Brighton Tipper, at supper; besides the bottle on the chimney-piece, and such casual invitations to refresh herself with wine as the good breeding of her employers might prompt them to offer. In like manner, Mr. Mould's men found it necessary to drown their grief, like a young kitten in the morning of its existence; for which reason they generally fuddled themselves before they began to do anything, lest it should make head and get the better of them. In short, the whole of that strange week was a round of dismal joviality and grim enjoyment; and everyone, except poor Chuffey, who came within the shadow of Anthony Chuzzlewit's grave, feasted like a Ghoul (chap. XIX).

Well they need to, for all about them is chaos: Mrs. Gamp must maintain her decorum in a room full of bandboxes where one can hardly move without barking one's shins or having the pippins of the bedposts come tumbling down to knock one dizzy. Every corner of the City is packed with objects, from Poll Sweedlepipe's warren full of bantams, ewes and hutches of rabbits, to Jonas's dirty, warehouselike offices. The neighborhood around Todgers's is a clutter of the bizarre:

> one of the first impressions wrought upon the strangers' senses was of oranges—of damaged oranges, with blue and green bruises on them, festering in boxes, or mouldering away in cellars. . . . Strange solitary pumps were found near Todgers's hiding themselves for the most part in blind alleys, and keeping company with fire-ladders. There were churches also by dozens, with many a ghostly little churchyard, all overgrown with such straggling vegetation as springs up spontaneously from damp, and graves, and rubbish (chap. IX).

These are the folk who live in the twilight region of rationality, where animism and sickening metamorphosis

take place. The physical toll is inevitable; as Mrs. Todgers
reflects, "Presiding over an establishment like this, makes
sad havoc with the features. The gravy alone is enough to
add twenty years to one's age, I do assure you."

The psychic toll would be greater if most of the individuals did not erect personality constructs to ward off the potential dissolution that such a life brings. The constructs
are, like Mrs. Gamp's half-a-pint of porter between dinner
and tea, a species of stay or holdfast. We have seen from
Dickens' analysis of his villains that it is essential that some
personality be established and rigidly adhered to if one is
to survive. The lamentable career of Augustus Moodle in
Chuzzlewit is another example; he is perpetually bursting
into tears and snuffling with despair; his final letter to
Cherry Pecksniff is all distraction, for Moodle has not
erected a Self that will resist the effects of life. Instead, he
sighs at one point, "The Elements may have me when they
please. I'm ready."

Montague Tigg and Mrs. Gamp, on the other hand, have
heroically put together self-constructs. Their personalities
are almost entirely cases of the comic elaborative power
spinning out its own web. They are classic instances of the
creation of fictions as a way of coping with the contingent
flux of actuality. Tigg, when we first encounter him, is woe-
fully down and out, cadging half-crowns in the name of his
even seedier confederate Chevy Slyme. But language and
imagination give him an almost triumphant air:

> Sir, if there is a man on earth whom a gentleman would
> feel proud and honoured to be mistaken for, that gen-
> tleman is my friend Slyme. For he is, without an ex-
> ception, the highest-minded, the most independent-
> spirited, most original, spiritual, classical, talented, the
> most thoroughly Shakespearean, if not Miltonic, and at
> the same time the most disgustingly-unappreciated dog I
> know (chap. IV).

It is Tigg who is Shakespearean here; a creature sustained
by words. All it takes to convert him into a titan of industry

as Chairman of the Anglo-Bengalee Disinterested Loan
and Life Assurance Company, is reversing his name and
acquiring a toupee, a mustache, and a red waistcoat. The
Anglo-Bengalee is a symbol of the heady power of the
imaginative construct in this unstable, money-mad world;
no substance is required, just a Turkey carpet on the floor,
an officious porter, and the effects of prosperity.

Against the "mortal wale" of her life, against the necessity of having to sit up with the dead and delirious and
spoon physic and slime draught down the throats of the
sick, against the legacy of grievous memory left by the late
Mr. Gamp, who drank the shoes right off the feet of their
little boy, Mrs. Gamp has fabricated her entire being. Her
fictions have become almost novelistic, for she has invented
another character, Mrs. Harris, who unendingly extolls her
virtues and who has passed, as far as Mrs. Gamp is concerned, from fiction to reality: there is a picture of Mrs.
Harris on the mantle and a full history behind her, complete with husband and "one sweet infant in her own family by her mother's side kep in spirits in a bottle."

This kind of objectification is quite common in one form
or another. Pecksniff often regards his created Self as if it
were another figure: the narrator catches him "warming
his hands as benevolently as if they were someone else's."
Appropriately, two of his most treasured possessions are
the portrait of himself by Spiller and the bust of himself by
Spoker. The constructs are no less real for that, however;
they accord remarkably with the Jungian concept of the
persona, which is defined as "a function-complex which
has come into existence for reasons of adaptation or necessary convenience" in coping with the outside world.[32] In
Jung, the persona is not identical with what he calls the
"individuality," the essential person. But in Dickens' characters very little exists beyond the construct, so effectively
has it taken over. Anthony Chuzzlewit remarks to
Pecksniff, "you have a way with you, as if you—he, he,
he!—as if you really believed in yourself." It would be hard
to say that Pecksniff does not actually believe in his self-

image. Dickens says that whatever the self-transformation that occurs when Montague Tigg becomes Tigg Montague, "still it was Tigg; the same Satanic, gallant, military Tigg." When, in fact, the constructs are threatened or de-molished, the psychic damage is severe. Upon being re-buffed by Mary Graham, Pecksniff "seemed to be shrunk and reduced. . . . His shoes looked too large; his sleeve looked too long; his hair looked too limp; his features looked too mean. . . . For a minute or two, in fact, he was hot, and pale, and mean, and shy and slinking, and con-sequently not at all Pecksniffian" (chap. xxx). The implica-tion of this is that the Pecksniffian construct *is* Pecksniff; take that away and there is no person at all. What a trauma it is, then, when Betsy Prig tells Mrs. Gamp that she be-lieves "ther's no sich a person" as Mrs. Harris. Mrs. Gamp is struck momentarily speechless, gasping for breath, and for days afterward she can barely sleep. "The words she spoke of Mrs. Harris, lambs could not forgive . . . nor worms forget."

To be sure, Mrs. Gamp, Montague Tigg, and Seth Pecksniff are a gamy, ragtag troupe. Their personality con-structs are jerry-built out of such material as their wit and situation provides them, seemingly unstable bulwarks against the calamity of the City. But they have, for the most part, fended off life with art and they awaken in us the inimitable pleasures of their specious beings. Garrett Stewart, in his analysis of Dickens' style and its imaginative sources, contends that such creatures symptomize a prog-ress since *Pickwick Papers* of imagination gone wrong. He cites Pecksniff in particular as a member of a "naughty company" of hypocrites and grandiloquent frauds, whose sleights of rhetoric only illustrate the insubstantiality of the individual self. He contrasts Pecksniff with Pickwick, who emerged at the end of his adventures "as a more than oratorical being, a moral agent whose essential goodness and humility waited only to be cured of too much talk. No such essence can be thought to lurk beneath the verbal surface of a Pecksniff."[33] That is exactly the case, for Pickwick is that eighteenth-century figure, the man of humor, whose eccentricity is only an aberration of integral selfhood. Pecksniff is the new dispensation of urban life—a persona, a creature obliged to fabricate a self through language and role. And I would argue that Pecksniff, Mrs. Gamp, and Tigg, though more tenuous beings, are nonetheless more poignantly heroic in this harsher nineteenth-century reality. They are, in a way, more exhilarating examples of the power of the comic imagination on the part of their creator.

They also partake of certain habits of thought, certain attitudes, that we shall come to identify as Victorian middle-class. They fashion their lives to a great extent around the appurtenances that a modern bourgeois could appreciate so well—the sumptuous repasts of Guppy, Jobling, and Smallweed, the ghoulish company at Chuzzlewit's laying out, the gathering of objects about one (even if birdcages and hand-me-downs) as a kind of signification of establishment, the affectation of piety and gravity of manner. Indeed, John Forster tells us that Pecksniff was intended to be a specimen of the middle class:

> Pecksniff was all our own. The confession is not encouraging to national pride, but this character is so far English, that though our countrymen as a rule are by no means Pecksniffs the ruling weakness is to countenance and encourage the race. When people call the character exaggerated, and protest that the lines are too broad to deceive anyone, they only refuse, naturally enough, to sanction in a book what half their lives is passed in tolerating, if not in worshipping.[34]

He says that if he had not dissuaded Dickens, the point would have been made bluntly on the title page of the novel, for Dickens originally proposed as its motto: "Your homes the scene, yourselves the actors, here!" "Something more pestiferous now was the aim of his satire," recounts

Forster, "and he had not before so decisively shown vigour, daring, or discernment of what lay within reach of his art, as in taking such a person as Pecksniff for the central figure in a tale of existing life."

As these insights suggest, Dickens appears to be generating some misgivings about the culture he is addressing just at the time when he seems most successfully to have achieved a synthesis between his delight in the vitality of lower-class life and the assumptions of his readership. At the beginning of the next chapter, we shall demonstrate how strong these misgivings were: from this point on, Dickens works in uneasy antagonism with what he defines as the English middle-class Establishment. In conjunction with this, he chafes at the formulas that he finds himself operating by, sensing that they are in essence sociopolitical. Northrop Frye identifies it as the classic "comedy of humors" pattern in *Martin Chuzzlewit* under which falsity is exposed, humbug defeated, and the prevalent social order reaffirmed.[35] *Chuzzlewit* executes that scheme faithfully, as Pecksniff, Tigg, and even Mrs. Gamp are stripped of their pretensions, and the solidly bourgeois Martin Chuzzlewit installed in their place. But we as readers regret the loss of vitality and imagination that this entails. And so, surely, must the Dickens who could not write enough of Mrs. Gamp. After such condescensions, what forgiveness? In addition, Dickens' imagination ultimately rejects schemata. He is remarkable for his impulse to undercut, reverse, even ridicule his own propensities and positions. His powers of metamorphic elaboration can scarcely be restrained; they will work upon his own attitudes as well. It is this aspect of the comic imagination, working hand in hand with his own ambivalence toward the middle class, that we will examine in the next chapter.

4

Later Dickens: Disenchantment, Transmogrification, and Ambivalence

"A case of deformation of character."
—*The Artful Dodger*

I

*T*he sea change in comedy during the early and mid-Victorian period is that from the comedy of social symbolization (ideas and concerns that represent themselves through depiction of action and as relations among broad social categories) to that expressing internalized concerns. The change was taking place in several quarters, but no more strikingly than in the art of Charles Dickens, where his comic powers shaped the change. From his disillusionment with the middle class, Dickens was obliged to begin reconceiving his comic characterization. A process of transmogrification—a reworking that took his creations toward almost grotesque formations—began to dominate his art from *Dombey and Son* on. It was quintessentially a *comic* process, emerging from the reductive and elaborative impulses, but it also accords nicely with the self-reflexiveness that appears to have been characteristic of comic writing in England from the mid-century on. As we come to diagnose the nature of Dickens' ambivalence—his deepening disenchantment with what the middle class stands for and what it has wrought, coupled with his doubts about his own responses—we see that it found its most adequate expression through the comic—through paradox, transmogrification, and involution. And in all likelihood the contours of the feelings themselves were shaped by the comic disposition of the writer.

During the several years between the completion of *Chuzzlewit* and the commencement of *Dombey* (a period in which Dickens substantially broadened his outlook traveling through Europe)[1] Dickens developed a harder view of the middle class and its condescending manner toward the City poor. The issues that arise in *Chuzzlewit*—the need for sympathetic projection into the lives of the lower classes, the dangers of hypocrisy, and the misconceptions that bourgeois readers entertain about people of the lower classes—preoccupied Dickens during the years from 1844 to 1846. He confronted them in a Christmas story called "The Chimes." Forster reports that when Dickens sat down to write the story, "he was bent, as he says, on striking a blow for the poor. They had always been his clients, they had never been forgotten in any of his books, but here nothing else was to be remembered. He had become, in short, terribly earnest in the matter. Several months before he left England I had noticed him in the habit of more gravely regarding many things before passed lightly enough."[2]

To strike that blow for the poor, Dickens attempts to shake his audience free of the stultifying opinions and stereotypes that were governing contemporary reader response to comic treatment of the lower classes.[3] The impoverished hero of "The Chimes," an aged porter named Trotty Veck, has reached the point of believing all the upper class cant about the irresponsibility and haplessness of the picturesque poor and he wonders, as a New Year comes, whether he and others like him are not "intruding" into a world in which they have no place. The middle and upper classes have foisted that impression on him with their cocksure opinions about all that is wrong with life in the lower strata. Alderman Cate says that he knows how to "deal with this sort of people" and informs Trotty's daughter and prospective son-in-law that they will have a miserable, quarrelsome married life "because I tell you so." That is, after all, the kind of prospect that *must* face those with lack of breeding; the billingsgate and broken crockery is what makes low people colorful and comical. Sir Joseph Bewley, a great man of the world, is equally knowledgeable about the weaknesses of the destitute and is consequently never surprised when they turn out bad.

Rosa Dartle's and Steerforth's discussion of the lower classes in *David Copperfield* is similarly insidious. Rosa asks, "That sort of people. Are they really animals and clods, and beings of another order? I want to know *so* much." Steerforth languidly replies that certainly "they are not to be expected to be as sensitive as we are. . . . Like their coarse rough skins, they are not easily wounded." Rosa finds this comforting: "It's such a delight to know that, when they suffer, they don't feel! Sometimes I have been quite uneasy for that sort of people; but now I shall just dismiss the idea of them altogether" (chap. xx).

What a change this is from the indulgent nurturing of bourgeois social preconceptions that governed the comedy of the *Sketches by Boz*. The old soft comedy will not do because it only encourages complacency. Indeed, "The Chimes" is not amusing in the least; it is terribly in earnest. And there appears to be another crisis in the use of comedy here. Now it is not so much a question whether comedy can impart the full seriousness of the conditions of life in the City but whether comedy can free itself of those stereotyped attitudes that had so impregnated its manner and form. The underlying implications about lack of substance in certain sorts of people; the expectations that govern the reading of works clearly identifiable as comedies— that the prevailing faults are affectation and social pretension and that a corrective will be rendered at the conclusion of the work—both make it difficult to treat social conditions, especially those of the lower classes, through comedy. The very mode seems to feed the self-satisfaction of the middle-class reader who needs instead to be shaken up. A change in the tenor of comedy is clearly needed.

Certainly we can say that the comedy in both *Dombey* and *Copperfield* has been separated from the social argument, at times almost isolated. J. Hillis Miller observes that "always in Dickens there is a conflict between the comic or pathetic moment, presented with intense immediacy, for its own sake and the organization of these moments into a whole." But he takes *Dombey* as his occasion for reflecting on the lack of integration of the comedy.[4] Kathleen Tillotson writes that the "deliberate control of comic exaggeration and inventiveness marks one of the differences between *Dombey* and its predecessors; [the comedy] is in lower relief and is subordinated to the design of the whole."[5] James C. Kincaid notes a similar division of the comic-imaginative world view from social analysis in *Copperfield*.[6] The composition of *Dombey* offers even more striking evidence: Dickens cut *comic* passages for the most part when he was forced to revise; for instance, scenes with Mrs. Chick and Major Bagstock were discarded.[7] In a letter to Forster about the plan of Dombey, he talked of the comic characters as ingredients that do not constitute "the stock of the soup."

When we say that *Dombey* and *Copperfield* are less comic than Dickens' earlier works, we are speaking of comic in the sense of humorous incidents and the elaboration of antic behavior rather than what we have defined in this book as the comic world view. The imaginative, transforming, liberating aspects of that world view are still asserted in *Dombey*, but not, as in *Chuzzlewit* and the books that preceded it, through the operations of the comic characters. What is so stunning about comic characterization in *Dombey* is that almost all the individuals are broken, stunted, discarded. They are not sources of vitality, as are Mrs. Gamp, Montague Tigg, Quilp, and Pecksniff; they are moribund, or in the throes of garish decline. Instead of engaging in the heroic self-assertions of the lower classes, they act out the grotesque contortions of the middle class.

Joe, Josh, old Joey Bagstock hobbles apoplectically about, with his lobster eyes and his purple face, gorging himself like a boa constrictor. He fancies himself, "Tough, sir, tough, and de-vilish sly!," although he has "arrived at what is called in polite literature the grand meridian of life, and [is] proceeding on his journey downhill with hardly any throat, and a very rigid pair of jaw-bones" (chap. VII). He wheezes and wrenches spasmodically through all his scenes, waggling his walking stick about until his blue veins throb; each day is a series of declining convulsions: "the major's voice, what with talking and eating and chuckling and choking, appeared to be in the box under the rumble, or in some neighboring haystack. Nor did the major improve it at the Royal Hotel, where rooms and dinner had been ordered, and where he so oppressed his organs of speech by eating and drinking, that when he retired to bed he had no voice at all, except to cough with, and could only make himself intelligible to the dark servant by gasping at him" (chap. XX). The major's sometime flame, Miss Tox, had "such a faded air that she seemed not to have been made in what linen-drapers call 'fast colours' originally, and to have, little by little, washed out." She wears old weedy flowers in her bonnets and strange grasses in her hair and converses mainly with her caged bird, "a very high-shouldered canary, stricken in years, and much rumpled, but a piercing singer."

Another of the comic delights—and they *are* funny—is Cousin Feenix, who forty years ago was a man about town, but now only retains a certain juvenility of manner. While Major Bagstock's complaint is apoplexy, and another character Mrs. Skewton's is aphasia, Cousin Feenix is troubled with ataxia, an inability to control his body movements. He is "not exactly certain when he walks across a room, of going quite straight to where he wants to go." At Dombey's wedding, he turns to the wrong page of the Church register and enrolls himself as having been born that day. His wits go astray, too, as when he tells a story at one of Dombey's dinners about a man who bought his wife, and thereupon freezes the assembled company.

The Serpent of Old Nile, Mrs. Skewton is, appropriately, the prima donna of this ravaged cast. Transported in a wheeled chaise, à la Cleopatra, from promenade to boudoir to dining room, she declines before our very eyes. Her coy mind has slipped its hold on most of the petty details of rational thought long before she makes her debut: "But seclusion and contemplation are my what's-his-name——? . . . The sword wears out its what's-its-name——?" The narrator ungallantly reveals to us that Mrs. Skewton is little more alive than her famous namesake: undressed for bed, "the hair dropped off, the arched dark eyebrows changed to scanty tufts of grey; the pale lips shrunk, the skin became cadaverous and loose; an old, worn, yellow nodding woman, with red eyes, alone remained in Cleopatra's place" (chap. xxvii). She is the most macabre target of this wicked comedy of human decadence; and it is awful the way Dickens screws the point home with his cruel fancifulness. When the maid puts Mrs. Skewton's bonnet on, the artificial roses on it are said to nod to "uncommon advantage, as the palsy trifled with them, like a breeze." "It was a tremendous sight to see this old woman in her finery leering and mincing at Death, and playing off her youthful tricks upon him as if he had been the major" (chap. xxxvii). Dickens spares us no detail of her last phases, including a breakfast exchange after her stroke: " 'Now my dearest Grangeby . . . you must positively prom,' she cut some of her words short, and cut out others altogether, 'come done very soon . . . Sterious wretch.' "

Even the "good" comic characters of *Dombey* are disabled in some way. The lower-class Toodle has kept up with the times and gotten himself a good job with the railroad, but he is named Toodle, after all, and his life style is bovine, overrun with little Toodles reproduced one after the other and all munching their bread-and-butter. Toots is mentally deficient; too much Blimber fact-feeding has sprung his wits: "Some mist there may have been, issuing from that leaden casket, his cranium, which if it could have taken shape and form would have become a genie; but it could not" (chap. XII). Captain Cuttle and Sol Gills are the amiable flotsom and jetsam left high and dry by the change in the tide of industrial life. Sol laments that "the world has gone past me"; he is only "the ghost" of his marine nicknack business. And Cuttle is one of those half-grown-up men-children that populate the Dickens world, slinking about in mortal fear of adult women and most easily at home with children and half-wits like Toots, Rob the Grinder, and the Game Chicken.

Ruin and abandonment are the governing motifs of the comic underlife in *Dombey and Son*. It is as if the new world has cut a horrible swath through the land of comedy and exuberant byplay. Just as the analogue of Boz's London was the old clothes shop where waistcoats and pantaloons seemed to break into a dance at the sound of a barrel-organ, so the symbolic store in *Dombey* is Brogley the Broker's shop:

Dozens of chairs hooked on to washing-stands, which with difficulty poised themselves on the shoulders of side-boards, which in their turn stood upon the wrong side of dining-tables, gymnastic with their legs turned upward. . . . A set of window curtains with no windows belonging to them, would be seen gracefully draping a barricade of chests of drawers, loaded with little jars from chemists' shops; while a homeless hearthrug severed from its natural companion the fireside, braved the shrewd east wind in its adversity, and trembled in melancholy accord with the shrill complainings of a cabinet piano, wasting away, a string a day, and faintly resounding to the noises of the street in its jangling and distracted brain. Of motionless clocks that never stirred a finger, and seemed as incapable of being successfully

wound up, as the pecuniary affairs of their former own-
ers, there was always great choice in Mr. Brogley's shop;
and various looking-glasses, accidently placed at compound interest of reflection and refraction, presented to
the eye an eternal perspective of bankruptcy and ruin
(chap. IX).

The comic characters of *Dombey* are strewn about in the
course of the action much like these motionless clocks and
blank looking-glasses. They resemble the enchanted souls
that we meet along the way in fairy tales—the gnarled old
hags, the stunted men, the charmed children who create
something of the wonder and strangeness of the journey.
They are curiosities of the wandering imagination and, like
creatures in fairy tales, they all seem to be under the besetting ill or the evil spell of that imaginary world. That evil
spell, of course, is the hard domination of commerce.

The "enchanted" scene correlates with Dickens' own
brief attraction to the possibilities of a green world of imagination and freedom of the kind that fairy tales seem to offer. Several critics, most notably Harry Stone, have pointed
out the fairy-tale elements that exist in Dickens' art, particularly in his middle novels.[8] It is too familiar a thesis to
repeat in detail here: Dickens, bred in fairy tales and considering his own rise to success to be like a fairy tale, works
the expectations of the formula (sometimes against itself)
in novel after novel. Always straddling the deep division in
his own nature between a desire for deathlike stasis and
idealized love, on the one hand, and his delight in the rugged, contingent, City world of strife and aggressive self-
projection, on the other, Dickens comes to identify the
sphere of wish fulfillment with certain qualities that are
being choked out of ordinary life. Young David Copperfield, when the Murdstone means of practical learning
fills him with despair, turns to comic and fairy tale
literature—to Smollett, Cervantes, and Gil Blas. "They
kept alive my fancy," he says, "and my hope of something

beyond that place and time" (chap. IV). Rather vague ideals are yoked together in the image of another plane of existence—love and beauty and sentiment and death. And comedy, interestingly enough, for it is the appeal of fairy tale green worlds that happy, joyful expression abounds there, undiluted, undiminished. Northrop Frye assigns that kind of world to one of the mythos of comedy. And the connection is not difficult to discover. Comedy takes us back to childhood play, after all. And its generation from the functions of artistic imagination suggest that only where the imagination has free play, uninhibited by exigent realities, can the comic truly thrive.

As we shall see in Lewis Carroll, however, the green world of desire or transmuted childhood freedom is rarely a convincing alternative except for those who seek in it retrogression or escape. Dickens is fundamentally a writer who believes in experience; as dramatically as he recast the actualities of his time and as compelling as his romanticism could be, he was a realist. Again and again he checks his imagination against experience. Though the green world is a happy instance of a mythos, a pregeneric structuring of existence that accords with the comic elaborative power, it is not congenial with the comic vision's celebration of contingency. The vision that engendered the Quilps, Artful Dodgers, and Pickwicks, and Sairy Gamps is what sustains Dickens.

We must refine the point a bit further. What specifically begins operating in Dickens by mid-career is the tendency of comedy to undercut every premise—its reductive spirit—and its refusal to let anything alone—its elaborative as well as its reductive spirit. The shrewd eye of the comic writer for the ridiculous and his power to turn everything upside down almost inevitably means that he will start to rework his own assumptions, sometimes in a reductive and self-parodying way. Dickens could impose a tight rein on his own elaborative impulses, and he generally did so after the chaos of *Martin Chuzzlewit*, but he could not quite refrain from turning that power in against himself. Involution is a characteristic of most great comic writers. It is as readily apparent in Laurence Sterne, James Joyce, and Vladimir Nabokov as it is in Dickens. Often it functions analytically, revealing the schemata of the artist's characteristic modes of presentation, exposing tendencies of thought and design, realizing the hidden tensions within attitude and art. Because Dickens' comedy finds its premier outlet in the drawing of characters, it is in their transmogrification in Dickens' middle and late novels that we find the most striking example of comedy's analytic/reductive impulse at work.

Mr. Micawber, a celebrated Dickensian creation, for all his bounce, is a man whose sphere for self-expression is circumscribed. Caught in the muddle of his own impecuniousness and financial irresponsibility, he fluctuates through radical shifts of mood. Unlike the earlier Dickensian comic heroes, however, he cannot brazen through his misfortunes: he lacks the cheek of the Artful Dodger or Sairy Gamp and he registers too much social pain. And though his comic exuberance gives him release, perhaps in the long run a certain measure of triumph, it is a distressfully quixotic thing. "Mr. Micawber's difficulties are almost overwhelming just at present," notes Mrs. Micawber, "and whether it is possible to bring them through I don't know." It surely does appear to be problematical much of the time; and there remains hardly a teaspoon to hock at the end of the book. Both Micawbers oscillate violently between poles of feeling. David Copperfield remarks on one occasion that Micawber seems "uncommonly convivial," indeed "I never saw anybody so thoroughly jovial as Mr. Micawber was, down to the very last moment of the evening." During that last moment, however, while departing David's apartment, Micawber handed him a letter beginning, "The die is cast—all is over. Hiding the ravages of care with a sickly mask of mirth, I have not informed you, this evening that there is no hope of remittance! . . . The result is destruc-

tion. . . . Let the wretched man who now addresses you . . .
be a beacon to you through life" (chap. xvii). And David
says that "Mrs. Micawber was quite as elastic. I have known
her to be thrown into fainting fits by the king's taxes at
three o'clock, and to eat lamb-chops breaded, and drink
warm ale (paid for with two tea-spoons that had gone to the
pawnbroker's) at four" (chap. xi).

Such resilience is often taken to be the essence of the
comic spirit. The Micawbers always snap back. They find
great solace in their own rhetoric and are inveterate believ-
ers in the possibilities of transformation, those sudden social metamorphoses that seemed to keep the early Victorian bourgeoisie in high hopes. Mrs. Micawber can discourse for hours about her husband's prospects as a corn
and coals broker, or brewer, or City banker—had he but
the means. But even here there is a crucial psychological
distinction from the earlier Dickensian comic types.
Pecksniff is, except for a few crucial moments, wholly and
almost unconsciously his persona; his supposed façade is
the man himself. For Micawber at times, however, the
mirth is only a "sickly mask"; we come to know another side
of the man that is just not always up to the role. The emotional flip-flops do bespeak great comic resourcefulness,
but in order to see them as such we seem to require a kind
of arbitrary blocking off of our essential feelings. The entire man is not seized by his antic self-image. This may constitute a more "realistic" portrayal of human behavior; certainly it denotes a more complicated sensibility and enhanced self-awareness. It implies, at the same time, that
comic constructs are less efficacious because they offer only
temporary respite from pain and anguish.

Thus, in *Copperfield*, the efficacy of comedy itself is thrust
periodically to the forefront, as if Dickens were losing faith
in its sympathetic powers. In *Hard Times*, where imagination, comedy, and sensitivity are thematically opposed to
utilitarian practicality, the comic spirit of flexibility and resourcefulness is embodied in the circus people. Their

spokesman, however, is Sleary, who comes across to us, with his lisp and his occasional peevishness, as hardly a counterpoise to the hard pounding of the Coketown world. " 'People must be amuthed, Thquire, thomehow,' continued Sleary, rendered more pursy than ever by so much talking; 'they can't alwayth be a-working, nor yet they can't be alwayth a-learning. I've got my living out of the hortheriding all my life, I know; but I conthider that I lay down the philothophy of the thubject when I thay to you, Thquire, make the betht of uth, not the wurtht!' " (chap. VII). We might ask what Dickens has in mind when he makes a man like Sleary the exponent of the comic values. Why has he given him the slightly childish aspect of "pursy" speech, deference to the "Thquire," and winsome vagueness? And what solace can we take in comedy when Sissy Jupe recounts how the others treated her father, a circus clown: "sometimes they played tricks on him; but they never knew how he felt them, and shrunk up when he was alone with me" (chap. IX)? The circus clown has his own myths, of course, one being that there is a suffering soul beneath his paint and red nose. But more and more in middle and late Dickens we encounter his critical probing of comedy as a sustaining mode of dealing with experience. The Micawbers are, after all, shipped off to Australia at book's end, as if they could not continue to exist in Victorian England; and the circus is by nature an illusion for children.

Harold Skimpole of *Bleak House*, perhaps more than any other character, purports to *live* by the comic-imaginative spirit. He asks only to be permitted to breakfast at noon on a peach, claret, and coffee, which remind him of the sun, and he seems to be saying to everyone, "forget your worldly arts and come play with me." "He is all sentiment—and susceptibility, and—and sensibility—and imagination," says Jarndyce, "and these qualities are not regulated in him somehow" (chap. XLIII). Skimpole is something of a humor character—a harmless eccentric, good-natured, sensitive, but not a man of this world—requesting that everyone "suffer him to ride his rocking-horse." Specifically, the portrait draws on the blitheness of Leigh Hunt and surely on Dickens' own father, whom Dickens affectionately enjoyed despite his incorrigible irresponsibility. On the larger scale, Skimpole, like the circus people, embodies the characteristics that Dickens presumably set up in opposition to grinding materialism; he is "free and spontaneous," has "no head for detail," refuses to be drawn into competition or struggle. He speaks, at times, for the artistic sensibility itself. In a remarkable passage, he talks about how delightful "enterprise and effort" are to him: "I lie in a shady place like this, and think of adventurous spirits going to the North Pole, or penetrating to the heart of the Torrid Zone, with admiration. I dare say theirs is an unpleasant experience on the whole; but, they people the landscape for me, they give it a poetry for me, and perhaps that is one of the pleasanter objects of their existence" (chap. XVIII).

Yet there is no doubt that Dickens condemns the man. Skimpole allows his family to wallow in poverty and debt so that he may have his music and his claret. Even Esther Summerson, whose faith in human nature borders at times upon the insipid, learns of the defective overripeness of the Skimpole sensibility. It is the *beaux-arts* effeteness, the spectatorial approach to life, and the attenuation of willpower and energy that Dickens disdains. But Skimpole is so blithe a spirit, so pure a refinement of amusement and imagination, that we have the disquieting sensation that Dickens is crushing a butterfly. There is a perverse wantonness to it.

The depiction of the Smallweeds in *Bleak House*, on the other hand, proves that Dickens is not slackening his attack on crass materialism. "In respect of ideality, reverence, wonder, and other such phrenological attributes, it is no worse off than it used to be. Everything that Mr. Smallweed's grandfather ever put away in his mind was a grub at first, and is a grub at last. In all his life he has never bred a single butterfly" (chap. XXI). The Smallweeds skulk through an even narrower course of life than the pure utilitarians: "During the whole time consumed in the slow growth of this family tree, the house of Smallweed, always early to go out and late to marry, has strengthened itself in its practical character, has discarded all amusements, discountenanced all story-books, fairy tales, fictions, and fables, and banished all levities whatsoever" (chap. XXI). At the other extreme from the elegant languor of Skimpole, they exist in their own kind of near-paralysis, as raggy dolls that have to be "poked and punched like a great bolster" and propped up in their chairs. They are the incubi and succubi of the acquisitive society, lurking like a "money-getting species of spider, who spun webs to catch unwary flies, and retired into holes until they were entrapped." Theirs is the endgame of devotion to Compound Interest, and like Hamm in the Beckett play whom they prefigure, the Smallweeds endure on and on as clothesbags of hate and resentment. Hence the values that run counter to the imagination are worse than any of its excesses.

The crucial distinction between the Smallweeds and Skimpole, we can assume, is the one made by Jarndyce; in Skimpole, the imaginative qualities "are not regulated . . . somehow." Dickens rigidly regulated his own comic exuberance, expecially after *Chuzzlewit*. "Invention, thank God, seems the easiest thing in the world," he remarked on one occasion, "and I seem to have a preposterous sense of the ridiculous . . . as to be constantly requiring to restrain myself from launching into extravagances in the height of my enjoyment." He could not shake off the Victorian distrust of pure comic expression as somehow *irresponsible*; he was part of an age that admired socially effective thought and action. Comic writers of almost every age are uneasy about the implications of comedy as a mode of behavior; the comic world is a nice place to visit, but no one can possibly live there. The emphasis, though, on Skimpole's sensibility and devotion to "pure imagination" and the attention given to the issue of the efficacy of comedy in the characterizations of Micawber, Skimpole, and Sleary suggest that Dickens was working through a problem that involved the very nature of his vision.

It doesn't require a critic to tell us that too many of Dickens' adult comic characters are childish. In *David Copperfield*, Betsey Trotwood says that Mr. Dick's father realizes that the infantile Mr. Dick is "a natural," and Peggotty bursts out to Mr. Peggotty, "you're a baby!" Other such insights into his personal concerns, however, appear at first glance to be less accessible to Dickens. For instance, a strange and sensitive psychological and sexual concern seems to be arising in *David Copperfield* as we read of Agnes's affectionate mother/daughter relationship to her father and of old Dr. Strong's blindness to the infatuation of his child-bride for Jack Malden. Although Dickens indicates that he is aware of an attraction for very young or childlike women, since those aspects of both David's mother and Dora are emphasized, we cannot be sure in *Copperfield* that he has come to terms with it. In *Bleak House*, however, the blatant uneasiness that the middle-aged Jarndyce expresses about his affection for the young Esther Summerson, and the uncomfortable manner in which he tries to deny her youth by calling her Dame Durden and Little Old Woman, betrays a devastating analytical operation in movement; the author himself distorting a convention of the previous novel as if to expose its perverse potentialities.

To cite another instance of the involution of technique as Dickens moves from book to book: it has often been noted that the comic characters in the later novels seem more grotesque, more spurious than those in the heartier literature of his youth. Never one to stint himself on cast of characters, Dickens nonetheless gives the impression of overindulging from *Bleak House* on in odd characters who do little to advance or supplement the insights of the book.

Old Turveydrop of *Bleak House*, the Model of Deportment, may be tangentially related to the motif of self-concern and personal insularity, but he is not used to good effect, as Mrs. Jellyby and Vholes are. We suspect that he is there because the odd case came to Dickens' mind of a man so tightly laced and buttoned that his eyeballs creased when he bowed. Mr. F's Aunt in *Little Dorrit* stands almost alone as a devastating portrait of irrelevance: she is a crazy old woman of unbelievable spleen who spits forth vitriolic insults at total strangers or croaks out bizarre non sequiturs: "When we lived at Henley, Barnes' gander was stole by tinkers"; "The Monument near London Bridge was put up arter the Great Fire of London; . . ." "I hate a fool!"

Similarly, though Flora Finching of *Little Dorrit* is worked from Dickens' real life encounter with the vapid middle-aged version of his childhood sweetheart Maria Beadnell, she is allowed to carry on in her witless way remorselessly. "It is perfectly clear you think so, for you take it very coolly, if I hadn't known it to be China I should have guessed myself the Polar regions, dear Mr. Clennam you are right however and I cannot blame you but as to Doyce and Clennam pap's property being about here we heard it from Pancks. . . ." She emerges as less an observation of human traits seen outside the novel than a comic-satiric invention parodying itself forever. Arthur Clennam sees her as an awful curiosity:

> She left about half of herself at eighteen years of age behind, and grafted the rest on to the relict of the late Mr. F; thus making a moral mermaid of herself, which her once boy-lover contemplated with feelings wherein his sense of the sorrowful and his sense of the comical were curiously blended. . . . With the sensation of becoming more and more light-headed every minute, Clennam saw the relict of the late Mr. F enjoying herself in the most wonderful manner, by putting herself and him in their old places, and going through all the old

performances—now, when the stage was dusty, when the scenery was faded, when the youthful actors were dead, when the orchestra was empty, when the lights were out (chap. XIII).

In *Little Dorrit*, there are numerous instances of comic characters running through their Dickensian routines in this self-sustaining way. They arise as images of themselves—Pancks appears in the number plans of the novel already transmogrified into a "steam tug"—and they become relics of themselves.

The conclusive evidence, though, that Dickens himself is well aware of the persistent fault of too many exotic Dickensian curiosities is the sly reference in *Our Mutual Friend* to a book called "Kirby's Wonderful Museum," which contains page after page of ludicrous grotesques, such as General Reid, the Walking Rushlight. Here, once again, it is the contents of a shop, however, that betray the artist's vision. The old clothes shop in *Sketches by Boz* contained the fetch and ghost of various lively souls and was ready for joyful animation; Brogley the broker's shop in *Dombey*, midpoint in Dickens' career, was aclutter with shattered mirrors that reflected bankruptcy; Venus's shop in *Our Mutual Friend* is a collection of the "human warious," specimens of deformed and strange people:

Mr. Wegg gradually acquires an imperfect notion that over against him on the chimney-piece is a Hindoo baby in a bottle, curved up with his big head tucked under him, as though he would instantly throw a summersault if the bottle were large enough.

"You're casting your eye round the shop, Mr. Wegg. Let me show you a light. My working bench. My young man's bench. A Wice. Tools, Bones, warious. Skulls, warious. Preserved Indian Baby. African ditto. Bottle preparations, warious. Everything within reach of your hand, in good preservation. The mouldy ones a-top.

What's in those hampers over them again, I don't quite remember. Say, human warious. Cats. Articulated English baby. Dogs. Ducks. Glass eyes, warious. Mummied bird. Dried cuticle, warious. Oh, dear me! That's the general panoramic view" (chap. VII).

Venus's shelves of articulated English babies and other warious comprise an analogue for what I believe is a prominent quality of Dickens' comedy in the last half of his career—the analytical reduction of his own creations. The eye that has been searching the landscape of London for interesting possibilities in characterization, now scans Dickens' own fictional pages for the crucial tendency toward the grotesque, for the telltale inclination toward perversity. This is a consequence of Dickens' corresponding inclination to be introspective and brooding.

This involution is the critical difference in the use of comedy from the pre-*Dombey* period. Then, certainly he had been willing, within the controls he exercised on himself, to engage in elaboration. He played with his imaginative creations—but not so much for the purposes of analysis and refinement of their tendencies as to see what new, richer manifestations he could conjure up. He was determined to populate a great fictional field with distinct individuals. Rarely was a characterization reworked; he simply introduced a new one. After *Dombey*, however, Dickens began to take previously used portraits and hone them, sometimes to too sharp a point. As an artist, he began to doodle, and to vary his own creations, and usually for the purpose of analysis. The analytical involution of comic art is akin to more creative, speculative elaboration, for in both there is a willful exercise of the fictive powers, and in both something new is created out of old materials, but the uses are different; involution, in Dickens at least, indicates a preoccupation with understanding what he has wrought and with defining the psychological manifestations that are taking place.

One of the most fascinating instances of Dickens' involution for the purposes of understanding the psychological implications of his own characterization occurs in his reduction of idealized child-women figures from Florence Dombey on. Although this takes us into an examination of what are not properly *comic* characterizations, it illustrates the power of transmogrification in one of its most far-reaching manifestations. Furthermore, it demonstrates the complexities of Dickens' ambivalence toward social attitudes (the topic of the second half of this chapter). Dickens is notoriously least successful with his heroines—he is too rarely able to break free of the Victorian stereotype of the Angel in the House—and this may indeed explain his use of analytical involution against the problem. In the characterization of Florence Dombey, we note scarcely any indication that Dickens perceives the inherent dullness of his idealized portrait. The only evidence of authorial impatience with Florence's childish worship and self-abasement is the abrupt decision that she must "orphan" herself and leave Dombey's house after he slaps her.

Esther Summerson, however, carries visible psychic defects that hint of some dissatisfaction lying within the idealized young woman of Victorian literature. Beset by her own unworthiness, haunted by the knowledge that she had been given up for dead, she calls herself a "tiresome little creature." In Esther, Dickens sloughs away some of the slavish, virtuous devotedness that he never questioned in Florence. The little woman as the paragon of order, the source of emotional strength, Esther is subjected to the sticky inanity of Jarndyce's nursery rhyme for her: " 'You are clever enough to be the good little woman of our lives here, my dear,' he returned, playfully; 'the little old woman of the Child's . . . Rhyme. "Little old woman, and whither so high—To sweep the cobwebs out of the sky." You will sweep them so neatly out of our sky . . .' " (chap. VII). Louisa Gradgrind in *Hard Times* is even more demoralized and scarcely able to play housekeeper or wife at all—a substantive variation from Florence because she is deprived of recourse to imagination but nonetheless an indication that Dickens has moved rather far from the old Florence Dombey kind of heroine.

Little Dorrit may seem at first glance to be a relapse, and certainly Dickens is trying to draw once again from the old emotional well, but there are some uncanny reductions of her in the novel. The most arresting is in her physical stature. For much of *Dombey and Son*, Florence is a child, but she is nonetheless growing up to be the normal young woman she becomes at book's end. Amy Dorrit, though, is "Little Dorrit," and some unnerving misadventures occur because she so resembles a child. Walking with the fully grown but intellectually stunted Maggie on the streets of London, Amy is mistaken for Maggie's daughter, a queer twist against Dickens' concept. He drives home the inversion by talking of "the little mother with her big child" and by indulging Amy's sister Fanny in a degrading series of insipid names for Amy, such as "oddity," "baby," "you Mole," "Owl," "tortoise"—it goes on remorselessly—"the best of small creatures." She gets it from all sides; Flora Finching says that "Little Dorrit" sounds like a place in the country, or a favorite pony or puppy. And can it be that Dickens intends to make us as uneasy as we are when Amy, after marriage is talked about, pleads to be allowed to stay and take care of her ungrateful, self-pitying father? At this point, the virtue of filial devotion becomes tasteless and annoying.

But Dickens knows that. In *Our Mutual Friend*, the long, dreary line of chapters with women selflessly nursing the decrepit egos of old men and men-children—Florence tending Dombey, and Esther sweeping for Jarndyce, and Amy propping up William Dorrit, and Biddy playing mother to Joe—all comes crashing down into the grotesque shambles of Jenny Wren taking care of her alcoholic father. " 'If you were treated as you ought to be,' " she tells her cowering sire, " 'you'd be fed upon the skewers of cats' meat; only the skewers, after the cats had had the meat. As it is, go to bed.' When he stumbled out of the corner to comply, he again put out both his hands, and pleaded: 'Circumstances over which no control—' 'Get along with you to bed!' cried Miss Wren, snapping him up" (chap. II, bk. II). She cuffs and abuses him as "a bad old boy! Oh-h-h you naughty wicked creature" in what the narrator calls a "dire reversal of parent and child." And in keeping with the novel's self-consciousness about the Dickensian specimens it contains, she says on one occasion that he is "a muddling and swipey old child, fit for nothing but to be preserved in the liquor that destroys him, and put in a great glass bottle as a sight for other swipey children of his own pattern" (chap. x, bk. III). Jenny Wren is herself a crippled, half-mad child-woman with beautiful long blond hair and, of course, the name of the ideal English heroine. She is of the cast from which Florence Dombey was molded, but she has come out deformed. She has the kind of imagination that could, in another person and another context, transport her out of the City to country smells and sights, but here it only enhances her poignancy; "And yet, as I sit at work, I smell miles of flowers. I smell roses till I think I see the rose leaves lying in heaps, bushels, on the floor. I smell fallen leaves till I put down my hand—so— and expect to make them rustle." She is in tune, as all the Dickensian Angel figures are, with the restful sea-borne voices of existence beyond life's concerns, but for her it is a desire engendered by her physical agonies:

"How do you feel when you are dead?" asked Fledgeby, much perplexed.

"Oh, so tranquil!" cried the little creature, smiling. "Oh, so peaceful and so thankful! And you hear the people who are alive, crying, and working, and calling to one another down in the close dark streets, and you seem to pity them so! And such a chain has fallen from you, and such a strange good sorrowful happiness comes upon you!" (chap. v, bk. II).

Thus Dickens' character concept twists around in a diminishing, tighter circle, exposing new sides of itself. In *Drood*, his last novel, Rosa Bud (condemned to that dreadful name) is physically and mentally whole once again but highly self-conscious that she is an adored doll, a "mite," compared to the emotional maturity of Helena Landless. In Rosa at least, there appears to be a new infusion from Bella Wilfer, who is also unusually self-aware for a Dickensian heroine. Edmund Wilson probably correctly identifies Ellen Ternan as the source of this new infusion, which may be the beginning of what would have been a new process of character involution. There are also possibilities that some of the later heroines are divisions of previous portraits, for by the time of *Dombey*, Dickens was experimenting with paired characters such as Edith Dombey and Alice Marwood; and it is only a slight step from that to, say, the division of the Florence/Esther figure into Louisa Gradgrind and Sissy Jupe (Louisa records something of Esther's emotional toll; Sissy keeps alive her cheerful, active aspect). There are enough intriguing interconnections through the women of all the later novels to indicate that Dickens was varying and experimenting, working insights that he had gained from previous portraits.

Such tinkering with one's own artistic product is what leads to changes in man's perception of physical reality, according to E. H. Gombrich:

> The artist's gift is of this order. He is the man who has learned to look critically, to probe his perceptions by trying alternative interpretations both in play and in earnest. . . . Similes, metaphors, the stuff of poetry no less than of myth, testify to the powers of the creative mind to create and dissolve new classifications.[9]

Dickens' advance toward what many critics believe is the greater psychological complexity of his later fiction may very well have occurred almost as much through such analysis of this own fictional creations and the attitudes they embody as from disillusioning personal experiences. The writing did come harder for him, and the Muse seemed less exuberant, but this could very well have been a consequence of taking harder looks at what he was producing.

Dickens' consciousness of schemata—in evidence as early as the *Sketches by Boz* when he was employing stereotypes, and at issue in middle-class preconceptions about lower class behavior, especially when such behavior is depicted in comic format—also contributes to the analytical process, as Gombrich suggests. Similarly, the vision that sees human personalities as self-created constructs is more likely to take the liberty of involuting those constructs, even in "realistic" fiction, because it involves a less radical departure from "reality." This will be even more the case if the writer believes that some of the constructs are imposed by people not for self-protection or self-expression, as in the case of the Small Fry in *Chuzzlewit*, but for deception and self-promotion. This may also contribute to the reductive-analytical tendency we have noted in the second half of Dickens' career. The conviction that personae are now being assumed for predatory purposes inspires Dickens to some of his most wicked satiric-comic operations. No longer is Dickens' purpose to induce sympathy with the personality constructs that little people must assume; rather it is to dissect the motives and appetites that have dictated the aggressive personae of elements of the English middle class.

Mrs. Jellyby, a pleasant enough middle-class woman, is probably in too much disarray to be called "assertive," except vicariously, through the thrust of all her missionary projects. Mrs. Pardiggle, however, has acquired a quite formidable persona. It is clear from the way she marches in and out of brickmakers' cottages with the Infant Bonds of Joy in tow that the purpose of the exterior she puts up is to browbeat everyone around her with her Muscular Christianity. This is a far cry from the antic selves assumed by the likes of Mrs. Gamp as a holdfast against psychic dissolution. Chadband turns the characterization another notch to a positively oppressive use of spurious moral authority. Dickens' analysis through characterization makes the point even clearer; Mr. Vholes, the image of respectability, with a father in the Vale of Taunton and three daughters at home, is manifestly predatory behind his mask of law and moderation and is caught looking at his client Richard Carstone like a "Vampire." He makes "hay of the grass which is flesh," as the narrator says.

The basic observation is then continued through models in the subsequent novels—the Patriarch Casby in *Little Dorrit*, who presents a cherubic presence to cover his rent gouging; Mrs. Merdle of the same book, who is known generally as The Bosom; Bounderby of *Hard Times*, who brags of his supposed past poverty; Miss Havisham of *Great Expectations*, who "creates" Estella as an instrument of revenge on the world. Jaggers and Wemmick of the last of these novels represent a variation on the idea, for their hard and cold public personalities protect their essential vulnerability. Podsnap, in *Our Mutual Friend*, finally caps the analysis so triumphantly that "podsnappery" has become a term for Victorian middle-class crassness. Immersing all his guests in the "haunch of mutton vapour-bath" of pretended largess, he bullies a Frenchman for his accent: "In England, Angleterre, England, We Aspirate the 'H,' and We say 'Horse.' Only our Lower Classes Say 'Orse! . . . Ours is a Copious Language." He puts everything behind him that is "Not English" or that might offend the ear of the Young Person in its disagreeableness. His aggressive self-construct is symbolized by the Podsnap plate:

> Everything was made to look as heavy as it could, and to take up as much room as possible. Everything said boastfully, "Here you have as much of me in my ugliness as if I were only lead; but I am so many ounces of precious metal worth so much an ounce. . . ." For silver winecoolers, each furnished with four staring heads, each head obtrusively carrying a big silver ring in each of its

ears, conveyed the sentiment up and down the table, and handed it on to the pot-bellied silver saltcellars. All the big silver spoons and forks widened the mouths of the company expressly for the purpose of thrusting the sentiment down their throats with every morsel they ate (chap. XI, bk. I).

Perhaps the solidification of podsnappery into the Podsnap plate represents a kind of objectification of the personality trait that Dickens had been developing, as Venus's shop and Jenny Wren capture the deformed essence of other involutions of characterization. But podsnappery seems to me such a triumphant imaginative expression of an idea that it illustrates that analytical involution, like every other comic operation, contains within its reductiveness a potentiality for creativeness. Out of the analytical variations has emerged a quintessence, a comic original. The immense power of the Dickensian imagination, working on its own creations, turning up the false sides of its own cherished characterizations, running through a gamut of reductive images and counter images, testing its inventions against observed reality, may very well have generated the ultimate triumph of transmogrification—a new and deadly truth.

"Something is wrong, somewhere; but what something, what may come of it, to whom, when, and from which . . . unheard of quarter . . ."—*Snagsby*

I I

Comic analytic reduction indicates that an author is turning in upon himself. His attention is focusing upon his art and upon the attitudes that it reflects. This is the case with Dickens in his later fiction, but it does not mean that he lessens his concern for the state of society. If anything, he steps up the rhetorical tempo of his attacks on identifiable evils and on bourgeois pretensions; the authorial harangue becomes more frequent in later novels. And in *Hard Times*, appropriately dedicated to a master of irate rant, Thomas Carlyle, we are hit full in the face with a continuing tirade from the narrator and subjected to stentorian speechifying from Bounderby, Gradgrind, Sissy Jupe, Sleary, a labor organizer, and Stephen Blackpool.

Yet the analytical involution of Dickens' own vision and his compulsion to return to self-examination—in *Copperfield* and *Great Expectations* and in countless incidents and characterizations embedded in the rest of the novels—display what biographical evidence reveals: Dickens was engaging in a sometimes agonizing self-scrutiny. Though few people could lash back so curtly in self-vindication as Dickens did whenever he was publicly attacked, no man can be crueler with his own soft spots than a comic artist who pokes at them and pinches them into new shapes. This is a characteristic paradox of the comic writer working from within the middle class: he is both sharply critical of that class and keenly aware of his own weaknesses. This can undoubtedly be attributed to the sense of being a turncoat, but that feeling has never appeared to inhibit the bourgeois artist from laying about him with a fury. Rather, the source lies in an ambivalent attitude toward the accomplishments of middle-class culture. Such a culture in Victorian England did, after all, produce affluence on a broader scale than ever known and a heady, satisfying sense of human progress and national power. How much, therefore, *could* the culture be faulted when the very principles that made it so obnoxious were the ones that had achieved so many generally appreciated goals? And how unequivocal could the author himself feel about his own assumptions if the relentless process of reduction and introspection revealed dissatisfaction and doubt, if it produced, as in Dickens' case, no savoring of the fruits of success, but instead, a debilitating sense of something wanting? The ambivalence that we discover in the writers of this period—in Dickens, Thackeray, Carroll, Meredith, Wilde—necessarily affected their manner of social commentary: it prompted the evasive worldliness of Thackeray, the obliqueness of Carroll, the sophisticated mask of triviality in Wilde. In Dickens, ambivalence did not weaken social critiques but led him to present his critiques in contexts that revealed searching personal material.

Dickens' social critiques go to the heart of the middle-class ethos—to the vaunted English practicality and to getting on in the world. Chancery Court in *Bleak House*, the Circumlocution Office in *Little Dorrit*, and Utilitarianism in *Hard Times* all represent the society's concern with means at the cost of ends, the short term "advancement of society" at the cost of spiritual and emotional wholeness. Certain comic characters of the middle and later novels are grotesque embodiments of the sensibility that goes along with such values.

" 'I am well aware that I am the umblest person going,' said Uriah Heep, modestly; 'let the other be where he may. My mother is likewise a very umble person. We live in a numble abode, Master Copperfield, but have much to be thankful for' " (chap. xvi). With his handshake that feels as if one had just grasped a frog, his lizardlike spasticity, his involuntary writhing and screwing up of the face, and his red, shadowless eyes, Heep embodies the self-abasement that accompanies the obsequiousness by which he wriggles up the social ladder. He talks of nothing but class, class, class: "There are people enough to tread upon me in my lowly state, without my doing outrage to their feelings by possessing learning. A person like myself had better not aspire." He is therefore, as Traddles observes, completely absorbed with means, "always creeping along the ground to some small end or other" (chap. liv).

The Victorian middle class equivocates and oscillates madly in its own instability, worrying lest it slip down, thinking of where it has come, conniving to rise higher; it is as if it were nothing in itself. The caprices of its own erratic fortune are the staple of its conversation. Bounderby keeps Mrs. Sparsit on because she is related to the Scadgerses and her late husband was a Powler; and now here she is, working as housekeeper for *him*, a purportedly self-made man of the streets. Bounderby observes with complacent graciousness one morning at breakfast:

"But it's extraordinary the difficulty I have, on scores of such subjects, in speaking to anyone on equal terms. Here, for example, I have been speaking to you this morning about tumblers. Why, what do *you* know about tumblers? At the time when, to have been a tumbler in the mud of the streets, would have been a godsend to me, a prize in the lottery to me, you were at the Italian Opera, ma'am, in white satin and jewels, a blaze of splendour, when I hadn't a penny to buy a link to light you."

"I certainly, sir," returned Mrs. Sparsit, with a dignity serenely mournful, "was familiar with the Italian Opera at a very early age."

"Egad, ma'am, so was I," said Bounderby "—with the wrong side of it. A hard bed the pavement of its arcade used to make, I assure you. People like you, ma'am, accustomed from infancy to lie on down feathers, have no idea *how* hard a paving-stone is, without trying it. No, no, it's of no use of my talking to *you* about tumblers. I should speak of foreign dancers, and the West End of London, and May Fair, and lords and ladies and honourables" (chap. vii).

Mrs. Sparsit's greatest solace (other than her aquiline nose) is her decline in gentility:

True the Powlers and the Scadgerses were accustomed to splendour, "but it is my duty to remember," Mrs. Sparsit was fond of observing with a lofty grace—particularly when any of the domestics were present—"that what I was, I am no longer. Indeed," said she, "if I could altogether cancel the remembrance that Mr. Sparsit was a Powler, or that I myself am related to the Scadgers family, or if I could even revoke the fact, and make myself a person of common descent and ordinary connections, I would gladly do so" (chap. VIII).

A great and somber pleasure, certainly, to contemplate one's rise and fall, and a rich source of satiric humor; but Dickens, always touchy about class, did not like it. It was an excuse for smugness in some cases, self-pity in others, and always a case of obsessiveness with the "small ends" of business, manners, and materialism. He could be savage: "what with having no such thing as a middle class (for though we are perpetually bragging of it as our safety, it is nothing but a poor fringe on the mantle of the upper); what with flunkyism, toadying, letting the most contemptible lords come in for all manner of places, reading the Court Circular for the New Testament, I do reluctantly believe that the English people are habitually consenting parties to the miserable imbecility into which we have fallen, *and never will help themselves out of it.*"[10]

As devastating as Dickens' attack on the middle-class mentality could be, he was aware nonetheless that the possibilities of correction were frustratingly remote. Even "source" could not be simply defined in this complex and diffused modern society. As he railed against the materialism that was the sickness of the middle class, and as he wittily epitomized it in his Heeps and Bounderbys, Dickens nonetheless acknowledged that it had become increasingly difficult to pinpoint how and why it was all so bad. For the middle-class writer—and this we shall see again and again—it was something that was *felt*; it had something to do with the quality of living. Dickens' victimized characters stand in the midst of what *Hard Times*' Stephen Blackpool calls "this muddle" and grope to find its nature. Snagsby of

Bleak House, caught up as his name suggests in a tangled skein, "cannot make out what it is that he had had to do with. Something is wrong, somewhere; but what something, what may come of it, to whom, when, and from which unthought of and unheard of quarter is the puzzle of his life" (chap. xxv). Snagsby has just been taken on a journey through Tom All Alone's, the quarter of London in which chaos, disease, and neglect reign; he is for some reason implicated in social evils that he cannot quite plumb. Mrs. Gradgrind of *Hard Times* finds herself, poor old thing, overwhelmed by the social theories and the prototechnological thinking of the Industrial culture: "Ologies of all kinds from morning to night."

Such softly addled expressions of confusion and doubt are transpositions, I submit, of the author's own growing perplexity about the nature of what was going wrong with contemporary life. While fiercely knocking about him at the travesties of the social order, Dickens scourged his own sensibility for the possible faults that might have lain there. This manner is not properly that of comedy but often of pathos or irony. The two qualities, as H. P. Sucksmith has demonstrated, always lie close together in Dickens' rhetoric; indeed, for reasons we will perhaps understand better in the next chapter, they lie close together in much of middle-class Victorian comedy. Thus, in a noncomic character such as Arthur Clennam of *Little Dorrit*, we can best trace the paradox of Dickens' own relation to the middle class that he has been excoriating. Clennam is culpable of no sins of class consciousness; indeed, though a member of the middle class, he is estranged from many of its values. Essentially orphaned from his hard "mother," an outsider in London from having spent the bulk of his life abroad, puzzled and depressed by what he witnesses as he wanders from Marshalsea prison to the cottage of the Meagleses and from the Circumlocution Office to Bleeding-Heart Yard, he expresses a strong sense of alienation from his society. We know this to be Dickens' own alienation, for

Clennam is a filtering consciousness for some of the experience of the novel and he speaks as a middle-aged man (Dickens himself is now in his late forties). Like Dickens, he believes himself to have been orphaned and robbed of part of his childhood; and again like his creator, missed opportunities, lost old loves, and a deadening lack of will crowd his mind. Further like Dickens, Clennam expresses a curious division within himself: he is estranged from what his class represents and dreads complicity in it; yet he is painfully aware of the weaknesses of his own spirit.

Clennam seeks punishment—almost wallows in it—by refusing to help himself. Behind his self-hatred is the gnawing anguish of his own impotence: "I have no will," he tells Meagles, "what is to be expected from *me* in middle life? Will, purpose, hope? All those lights were extinguished before I could sound the words" (chap. II). He attributes his weakness to being ground "in a mill I always hated"—middle-class, work-ethic Puritanism. The ambivalence of Dickens himself toward exercise of the will permeates his characterization of Clennam; it is an ambivalence that is intensified by Dickens' sense that his struggle has brought him only dubious happiness, that so many well-conceived efforts have turned to ashes.[11]

When Clennam laments that "all the lights were extinguished" long ago in his life, Meagles, the hearty, practical embodiment of the bourgeois spirit, rejoins, "Light 'em up again!" No matter how oppressive life seems to be, no matter how justifiable the grounds for depression, it is countered with that Dickensian bounce. The ambiguity in the fiction grows more perplexing. Clennam's is a long, sensitively rendered portrait of alienation and the draining of psychic energy; he is never reintegrated into his society. Yet he, too, is saved "from the whimpering weakness and cruel selfishness of holding that because such a happiness or such a virtue had not come into his little path, or worked well for him, therefore it was not in the great scheme. . . . A disappointed mind he had, but a mind too firm and healthy for such unwholesome air" (chap. XIII). Deep in the core of Dickens' disillusionment with Victorian England, and crimping all his social criticism, is the suspicion that a weakness or fault in *him* compromises his position. Something disturbs him as he responds to all the great moral and emotional crises of his life. An episode from his childhood that took place in a blacking warehouse, for instance, was suppressed until mid-adulthood, enveloped in a sense of shame. The break with his wife was confused and exacerbated by convulsive attempts to justify himself, including the placement of a self-wounding and undignified notice of justification in the press. Dickens in his last years is described by all his biographers as a relentlessly self-punishing man, driven to prove his popularity through a series of exhausting public readings. In all these actions, as in all of Arthur Clennam's, there is an ambivalence about his own motives, or behavior, that goes far to account for the complexly varied modes (and targets) of comedy in the late fiction.

The self-effacement is simply too wretched when Clennam falls in love with Pet Meagles. The passion of a middle-aged man for a young girl is resonant with all those uneasy cases of older men—father-figures and actual fathers—living off the attentions of pure young things in Dickens novels. It goes beyond poignancy here, however, with Clennam's insistence upon negating himself as a Nobody and disqualifying his affection as a nothing. The chapters of his anguish are titled "Nobody's Weakness," "Nobody's Rival," and "Nobody's State of Mind." As he takes leave of Pet in the chapter "Nobody's Disappearance," apparently his last chance for love now gone, and an older love, Flora, in ghastly resurrection before his eyes, he slowly plucks the petals from a handful of roses and drops them into the river where, pale and unreal, they float away in the moonlight: "and thus do greater things that once were in our breasts, and near our hearts, flow from us to the eternal seas" (chap. XXVIII).

Dickens' ambivalence surfaces in more savage portraits. Gone, essentially, is that lively cast of lower-class Small Fry from the early fiction; in their places now appear the petit bourgeois, those who have crossed or been dragged across the threshold of the middle class and who are torn apart by feelings that are displacements of Dickens' own. Consider his creation of the little girl Tattycoram, adopted into the household of the Meagleses of *Little Dorrit*, treated as both their child and as servant-companion to their natural daughter, Pet. The Meagleses are bourgeois to a fault. "Mrs. Meagles and myself are, you see, practical people." They are insufferably cheery and very English in their approach to the rest of the world; traveling, for instance, consists of "staring at the Nile, and the Pyramids, and the Sphinxes . . . and all the rest of it." "Tattycoram" is not the girl's real name, in fact; when she came to the Meagleses, she was named Harriet. "Now, Harriet, we changed into Hattey," Meagles recounts, "and then into Tatty, because as practical people, we thought even a playful name might be a new thing to her, and might have a softening and affectionate kind of effect." Is it a wonder, then, that when we first see Tattycoram alone she is gnashing her teeth in frustration? "But I am ill-used, I am ill-used, I am ill-used!" She has somebody's idea of a playful name (wasn't it Dickens who enjoyed inventing playful names for his children?); and she is mainly just a playmate for the spoiled Pet Meagles. She cannot even vent her anger without Meagles advising her condescendingly to "count five-and-twenty." She is treated as a little dog or pony—or a curio. The Meagleses live by a pretty little stream in a pretty suburban cottage that contains the memorabilia of their numerous tours abroad:

There were . . . bits of mummy from Egypt (and perhaps Birmingham); model gondolas from Venice; model villages from Switzerland; morsels of tesselated pavement from Herculaneum and Pompeii, like petrified minced veal; ashes out of tombs . . . rosaries blest all round by the Pope himself, and an infinite variety of lumber. There were views, like and unlike, of a multitude of places; and there was one little picture-room devoted to a few of the regular sticky old Saints, with sinews like whipcord, hair like Neptune's, wrinkles like tattooing, and such coats of varnish that every holy personage served for a fly-trap, and became what is now called in the vulgar tongue a Catch-em-alive O. Of these pictorial acquisitions Mr. Meagles spoke in the usual manner. He was no judge, he said, except of what pleased himself; he had picked them up, dirt-cheap, and people *had* considered them rather fine (chap. xvi).

And lest we suppose that Mr. Meagles finds the people around him any less picturesque, he comments of his two rosy faced, bright-eyed, parlor maids, "As I always say to Mother, why not have something pretty to look at, if you have anything at all?"

Yet Meagles is a "good" character in the novel. He is kind and generous and honest and he intends well toward Tattycoram. Dickens describes the Meagleses in a number plan to the novel as a "New sort of *practical People*"[12]—meaning that they will not be Podsnaps. In them is epitomized the problem of criticizing the middle class, for though they are obtuse to Tattycoram's need for dignity and integrity, though they cannot even register the subtleties of taste, though they enrage us with their insensitivity to the nuances of human feeling, they are loving, decent, hard-working folk—solid citizens. Tattycoram's behavior in the novel is an intensification of the ambivalence that we discover in Dickens himself. Tattycoram vacillates between unrestrained fury: "I am younger than [Pet] by two or three years, and yet it's me that looks after her, as if I was old, and it's she that's always petted and called Baby! I detest the name, I hate her!"—and self-hatred: "They are nothing but good to me. I love them dearly; no people could ever be kinder to a thankless creature than they always are to me" (chap. II). Tattycoram rebels and runs away with Miss Wade, but when Meagles asks her to come back, she literally tears at herself in vexation. Dickens presents her petulance in a very unattractive light, as a small version of the greater perversity of Miss Wade (whose story is told in a "History of a Self-Tormenter"); yet still we have all that sure and fine data on the Philistinism of the Meagleses themselves to render the issue ambiguous.

The reductive progression of ambivalence into perversity is a fine instance of Dickens' comic disposition turning over, reworking, transmogrifying the author's attitudes. It wrenches the feeling around further and further so that the last novels explore the proposition that in a world in which men are will-less like Clennam, in which the causes of one's malaise are nearly impossible to assign—in which, indeed, the nature of the malaise itself is vague—and in which individual action seems to have no effect, perverse, even self-destructive, behavior is a kind of desperate assertion that "I am alive, I am human, I am individual." Bradley Headstone in *Our Mutual Friend*, and John Jasper in *The Mystery of Edwin Drood* assert that sickly cry. We are reminded that Dostoyevsky's Underground Man, rebelling against the same bourgeois nervelessness, called his perversity a proof that "man is made in a comical way." In Baudelaire and later Wilde, the comic vein of these dark impulses is explored with relish. Perhaps we might trace the lineage of this expression back to Quilp's manic self-indulgences, but Quilp's seem to have been comic impulses of a different kind, and the objectives of the comic presentation different. The comedy of the late Dickens stems from his personal, psychological concerns rather than from a broad, categorizing vision. The forms of comic expression are those that accommodate internalized anxieties and aspirations. They are consequently more ambivalent, more convoluted in expression, more paradoxical.

This is not to suggest that Dickens' positions were some-

how only consequences of an antic imagination twisting
itself out of shape. Rather, the quality of imagination
worked hand in hand with the changes in perspective of
the author, giving him a mode of expression for what he
had come to see and feel. Presumably, the analytical and
experimental bent in Dickens' comic imagination would
induce him toward certain modes of depiction, if not also
of apprehension, of his attitudes, and of his environment;
but as we noted at the beginning of this chapter, the ques-
tioning, the weighing of doubt, the disillusionment had already begun in mid-life, at least. The reductive and
elaborative aspects of the man's vision simply shaped the
way in which these things were registered.

Consequently, we can say of Dickens' final mode of ap-
proaching his world—through paradox—that it is both a
characteristic comic expression of a highly involuted imagination at work and Dickens' assessment of what the reality
of contemporary England was. In a society where such ambiguity reigns, the only honest assessments may be those
that are fraught with paradox. Dickens' boldness of manner, uncompromising wrath, and unabashed sentimentality do not especially predilect him to paradox, but nonetheless that is the way in which he came to view Victorian
society. Paradox, as Rosalie L. Colie points out in her study
of its Renaissance manifestations, can be both a manner of
observing life by the artist and an interpretation of that
life.[13]

Little Dorrit seems to illustrate both that manner of vision
and that interpretation. Dickens seems to have had more
difficulty beginning this novel than any of the others. His
letters indicate unusual restlessness when he set about
work. Though he contended that he was customarily edgy
and impatient with himself when he started a book, at no
other time do we find such a spate of correspondence
complaining of the problem.[14] The novel itself, one of
Dickens' best constructed, is designed to highlight contra-
diction. We learn that Mrs. Clennam is more a prisoner in

her own home than William Dorrit is in the Marshalsea. Merdle, who holds the greatest power in England, unconsciously grasps his wrists as if he were a criminal, and is, in fact, intimidated by his butler. The Circumlocution Office produces more "work" than any institution in the world—15,000 letters, 24,000 minutes, and 32,571 memoranda in a year—and accomplishes the least. Tattycoram, Fanny Dorrit, and William Dorrit all resent the people who are most kind to them, and crave companions whom they secretly fear or detest. Little Dorrit physically resembles a child, but is "mother" of dozens. Arthur Clennam has committed no crime, yet carries guilt most consciously. Everyone in the novel finds himself in a paradoxical situation.

Dickens, on the one hand, satirizes the English obsession with methods and procedures through the Circumlocution Office, and on the other, glorifies the inventor Daniel Doyce, who is a man devoted to the very science and industry that has taken people's eyes off the larger ends of life. Pancks, the human steamboat, articulates the get-ahead work ethic in the crassest terms: "Keep me always at it, and I'll keep you always at it, you keep somebody else always at it. There you are with the Whole Duty of Man in a commercial country." Asked about the importance of taste, he replies, unfacetiously, "What's taste?" It is Pancks, though, who effects the release from prison of both William Dorrit and Arthur Clennam. No more Philistine a life style could be imagined than that of the Meagleses, yet there they are for us to love. Paradoxically, the very attitudes that engender narrowness and unexamined complacency in the society produce energetic goodness also.

Such a picture of mid-Victorian England seems to accord with the assessments of later cultural historians. W. L. Burn describes the "Age of Equipoise" (1852-67) in terms of paradoxes. Jerome Buckley's way of defining "Victorianism" is to list the opposing truths about the period: the Victorians were "complacent" yet torn by doubt; mate-

rialistic but idealistic; conformists and iconoclasts; sentimental yet hard-boiled. Similarly, Walter E. Houghton's
analysis of the Victorian frame of mind is a matrix of con-
trarieties.[15] Dickens' own inconsistencies of tone and opinion have been legend for nearly a century, and the bane of
his critics. Certainly many of his attitudes remain inconsistencies; they cannot be reconciled. But just as some of his
positions can be explained by his own ambivalence as a
middle-class artist and critic of society, so some of his vision
of the Victorian world can be attributed to a recognition
that it was paradoxical itself in its expression and operation.[16]

We are speaking here not of diversity or complexity, although Dickens certainly observed both of those aspects in
his time, but of paradox, in which things are inconsistent
and often the reverse of what we would assume them to be.
Hence the apparent contradictions that the fiction
describes—the sense of complicity in those least culpable of
social evils; the sources of guilt feelings in innocent acts;
the self-doubt in the most strident critics of the time; and
the unsatisfactory life of an era of unprecedented affluence. Rosalie L. Colie's conclusions about paradox suggest
that it flourishes in times, like that of mid-century England,
of "relative, or competing value systems." Paradox is called
upon, in fact, to present to a class or a group of people the
inconsistencies and the defects in their own life styles and
attitudes; it must perform the neat trick of inducing the
audience to apply some of its own standards against itself,
as Dickens, a middle-class writer, finds it necessary to do.
As a technique, it correlates rather closely with what we
have observed of the later Dickens: it is profoundly self-
critical; it is analytical; and at the same time "the paradox
does not commit itself, nor does the paradoxist . . . afford-
ing [him] the chance to postpone a philosophical or religious choice he might live to regret. Indeed, the paradoxical form denies commitment."[17] It can mask, therefore,
any elements of self-doubt.

The shift from a comedy that exposes the excesses, imitative behavior, and the pretensions of the members of a society to one that relies largely on the exploration of paradoxes indicates not only a change in the operation of comedy toward more analytic, self-conscious study of motives and forms but also a change in the way that society is understood. The shift, though not an absolute one (for comic writers rarely discard any of their techniques), is perhaps the greatest change in English comedy in the nineteenth century.

It is worth noting that the vein of comic expression in England for the remainder of the century (and long after) has essentially been established here. Although I will have occasion to discuss this in greater detail in chapter seven, I want to draw attention at this point to the shape that English comedy takes, because, in a sense, Dickens determined that shape, and he, more than any writer, had the potential to articulate another mode of expression. A comedy of open and aggressive social criticism could have come out of Dickens. Indeed, it did in many ways—in his harangues against podsnappery, Utilitarianism, and so forth. But for all Dickens' anger and disgust, he was not radical; he did not *use* comedy primarily to overturn or undermine the fundamental institutions or the basic ideology of English middle-class society. On the contrary, he used it to analyze the discrepancies in the social picture, to explore the troubling paradoxes of it, to attempt a kind of critique of it. Even more to the point, we have seen in this chapter that once having felt his alienation from the dominant culture and seen its many faults and imbalances, Dickens' primary thrust was to pursue the lines of his art, to reanalyze and repicture his own vision of it. He was as much concerned with his own proclivities, with the involutions of his own creations, with an imaginative reworking of the terms and nature of his own alienation, as with the societal structure itself. It was not a matter of temperamental accommodation to prevailing mores as it was with Thackeray or maybe even Jerrold. In Dickens' case, the direction was determined by the quality of his comic imagination and by its strong elaborative characteristic, working in conjunction with his ambivalence and his capacity to posit and perceive the fictions of survival and accommodation by those—like his Small Fry and his disoriented petit bourgeois—who were trying to find a place for themselves in a manifold yet demanding social order. In a way, a man of such complexity and fertility of mind could probably go in no other direction; satire, for instance, as practiced in eighteenth-century English social criticism required a conservative, probably aristocratic orientation and was not premised on a vision of life made up of fictions or constructs—a vision that Dickens and others saw to be truest to the way things were in post-industrial (and post-Romantic) society. We shall have more to say on that, also, in chapter seven. But now, as we turn to the next generation of writers, we shall see how the vein of comedy working from *inside* the culture develops further.

5

Hood, Gilbert, Carroll, Jerrold, and the Grossmiths: Comedy from Inside

> No gentleman alive has written so much comic
> and spitten so much blood.—*Thomas Hood*

I

*L*ight, gentle humor set the comic tone of the mid-Victorian decades, the 1850s and 1860s. The magazines that sprang into being during the period were a far cry from the sensationalist journals of the 1830s and early 1840s. The sketches of boisterous London low life and high jinks on the road that dominated previous comic literature had virtually passed away. Replacing them were vignettes of social snobbery in St. James Park and wry observations on the types one meets in railway coaches. Political commentary tended to be arch in contrast to the slapdash ridicule of an earlier day, and instead of thinly disguised satires of prominent figures, that peculiar phenomenon of Victorian literature, the nonsense verse, appeared on the scene.

The gentler tone and demure outlook of the mid-century periodicals reflected an evolution in the nineteenth-century reading public, a public grown larger and more affluent than ever, with all that that means in increased leisure time and greater enjoyment of its status. The opportunity was at hand to muse idly on the social peculiarities of the day. And the middle-class reader could sense, with some satisfaction, that there were more people like him about; his way of life had become the dominant

way of life in England. It had become established. The
tenor of the period seemed to justify this composure, for
the 1850s and 1860s were good times—of peace, prosperity, stability, assurance—what the social historian W. L.
Burn characterizes as the Age of Equipoise. "The fifties,
sixties and early seventies were said to be relatively happy
and harmonious decades," Geoffrey Best remarks in his
history of mid-Victorian Britain—an assessment that he
readily accepts.[1] "The stirring and good-humoured fifties
had . . . a grace and lightness," says G. M. Young.[2] Those
qualities can presumably be seen in the comic touch of the
public's favorite reading material.

As Best notes, the 1850s were *relatively* happy times,
because they seemed to have left behind them the social
anxieties of the preceding decades. The 1830s and 1840s
had been turbulent with economic disorientation, and the
immanence of social upheaval was to all appearances now
safely past. "There might have been bloody work" in the
1840s, recalls Burn, "a *jacquerie* in the southern counties or
in Wales; a rebellion by the political unions or the Chart-
ists; a great Irish revolt in 1848. None of these things happened, but only a very unimaginative man, in the mid-
century, could deny that some or all of them might well
have happened. The so-called complacency of the 'fifties
and 'sixties (and even in that we shall see many fissures) was
based on the fact that they had not."[3] The recollection of
potential violence avoided, contributed to the sense of ease
and relief that enveloped the 1850s.

Such a rapid change in social climate and in popular
literary tastes could not take place without catching some
sensibilities in situations in which they felt strangely out of
synch. Men of an older generation that came of age in the
1830s and 1840s, like the poet Thomas Hood, found themselves writing comic verse that was somehow serving to
mediate the disorder that characterized the beginnings of
the social revolution and the need of the new middle class

for equanimity. Required to' write in a manner that was true to the jarring discrepancies of the changing times and changing sensibilities, such writers developed a mode of verse in which discordance was the dominant character-istic—the nonsense poem. Other men whose maturation coincided with the good times, men such as W. S. Gilbert and Lewis Carroll, were simply unable to share wholeheart-edly the national euphoria. Some vague dissatisfaction stirred within them, a discontent with the prevailing life style of the period, and they sought, through the most ob-lique forms of comedy, to register these feelings. They did so, however, without breaking with the bourgeois audience of which they felt a part. Thus, the light humor of the mid-Victorian period was made to accommodate two broad purposes—that of reflecting the preoccupations of the ex-panding middle class, both before and after the Equipoise, and that of articulating the muted, deflected estrangement of individual writers within that middle class.

Thomas Hood was very clearly a figure from the pre-Victorian and early Victorian period. Writing from 1815 to 1845, he personally experienced the insecurities of the quixotic fortunes of social change in London. He was al-ways spoken of as "poor Tom Hood," and his biography is one of incessant physical pain, bad luck, and bad manage-ment. "Oh, sad, marvellous picture of courage, of honesty, of patient endurance, of duty struggling against pain!" exclaimed Thackeray of Hood. Afflicted in youth with rheumatic fever, he was a partial invalid all of his life and suffered from lung ailments, coughing of blood, fevers, and internal disorders. Work was a continual struggle for him yet necessary in consequence of his poverty and his frequent mishandling of financial affairs. The creditors' bills were always on the door. And on top of this, his daughter died at childbirth, and his only mainstay, his de-voted wife, was nearly taken away in a delirium. So morbid are some of his poems and so recurrent the motif of dismemberment that we are tempted to see in his writing an obsession with being rid of his pain-racked body. He said of himself late in life, "no gentleman alive has written so much comic and spitten so much blood."

Yet by nearly all accounts, Thomas Hood was not a morbid or self-pitying man. On the contrary, he appears to have been cheerful, funny, compassionate, and resilient. Though a living example of the old saw that the great men of humor led lives of melancholia and tragedy (see Samuel Johnson and Charles Lamb), it is only in his poetry that we find evidence of the intensity of anguish that Hood must have felt. The poems of his last years are somber, impassioned pleas against the injustice of the hard lot of common folk, "The Song of a Shirt" being perhaps the most famous of these. Prior to these last poems, Hood kept himself alive, and acquired a certain amount of fame, writing comic verse. In 1829 he published the first of his *Comic Annuals*, collections of humorous verse and prose that were issued around Christmas time. By 1844 he was editing and writing his own humorous magazine, *Hood's Monthly Magazine and Comic Miscellany*. Many of his comic poems carried direct social messages—a series of Odes assailing the earliest expressions of Victorian cant, self-aggrandizement, and narrow social or religious prescription; and a long poem, "Miss Kilmansegg and Her Precious Leg," a singeing treatment of the crass nouveau riche. But the distinguishing feature of the Miscellanies was Hood's mastery of the poem that strung together puns upon human atrocities. This kind of poem, a prototype for the later nonsense verse of Carroll, Gilbert, Edward Lear, and C. S. Calverly, displays one of the most curious conflicts of tone and content in English literature. The example that is often anthologized is "Faithless Nelly Gray: A Pathetic Ballad," the lament of one Ben Battle, a "soldier bold," whose old sweetheart, Nelly Gray, proves unfaithful to him after he has had both his legs shot off by a cannon ball:

"O, Nelly Gray! O, Nelly Gray!
    Is this your love so warm?
The love that loves a scarlet coat,
    Should be more uniform!"

Said she, "I loved a soldier once,
    For he was blythe and brave;
But I will never have a man
    With both legs in the grave!

Before you had those timber toes,
    Your love I did allow,
But then, you know, you stand upon
    Another footing now!"
                        . . .
"Why then," said she, "you've lost the feet
    Of legs in war's alarms,
And now you cannot wear your shoes
    Upon your feats of arms!"

"O, false and fickle Nelly Gray!
    I know why you refuse:—
Though I've no feet—some other man
    Is standing in my shoes!

I wish I ne'er had seen your face;
    But now a long farewell!
For you will be my death:—alas!
    You will not be my *Nell*!"[4]

The dynamics of such comedy are worth investigating. I suspect most of us are rather taken aback, even embarrassed, that Hood should joke and we should laugh at such things. For all its singsong lightheartedness, it is a rather brutal kind of humor, not likely to refine the tastes. Indeed, the involuntary pleasure that we get from wordplay of such a sanguine sort reminds us of the bloody little verses we repeated in childhood. We go directly back to the antisocial impulses lying within comedy, the Quilpian sardonic sport with forbidden fascinations. The imp of the perverse, which we seem to see lurking behind so much of the comic response to the social upheavals of Hood's generation, leaps uncannily to the forefront in Hood's verse. Poems of this sort only imperfectly fulfill Hood's presumed aim of thrusting the brutalizing facts of life and quirks of fortune directly before us; a more pronounced effect is their uneasy reflection upon the reader himself. They stir within us a consciousness of our own ambivalent response toward the grotesque in human life.

Hood is chiefly remembered as a humorist, one of the notable figures in the humor tradition—its archetypal compassionate man whose comedy masks his inner sadness. His verse attempts to accommodate the vicissitudes of human misfortune to the generally benevolent and playful manner of humor. Ambitiously, he seeks to incorporate the disquiet, even the random horrors, of the unstable urban experience of the 1830s and early 1840s, with its troubled psychological awareness, into the light comic form of another era with a different governing sense of human nature. The product is slightly savage nonsense verse that awakens the uncanny as it demolishes all seriousness in absurdity. The striking feature of Hood's characteristic comic poetry is our apprehension of the erratic perverse courses that his imagination, and our laughter, will take. The humor cannot quite contain its psychological charge.

Robert Bernard Martin, in his study of Victorian comic theory, notes the gradual critical turn away from the humor tradition toward a sharper, wittier comic theory.[5] In Hood's verse we perceive something of humor's anachronism. Yet the anomaly of this is the fact that the spirit of humor dominated popular comic expression during the 1850s and 1860s as it may never have before; and the popularity of Hood's work was partly responsible. The comic mode that Hood exploited, with puns scattering out

like grapeshot, induced the reader to accept the disconcerting attitudes and subject matter in the verse as something
antic, as wordplay with the grotesque.

The literary critic William Empson argues that Hood's
comic method is unlikely, by its nature, to produce any
other kind of effect upon its reader. Hood's poetry, he says,
places the wordplay at the "focus of consciousness . . . as a
showpiece to which poetry and relevance must be sacrificed." Our interest is always directed to the virtuosity.
Hood "uses puns to back away from the echoes and implications of words, to distract your attention by insisting on
his ingenuity so that you can escape from sinking into the
meaning."[6] And it does prove true that we find ourselves
single-mindedly tracking down puns in Hood's comic
verse. My own favorite, "Sally Simpkin's Lament; or John
Jones' Kit-Cat-Astrophe," presents us with the plight of a
young man, Jones, who has been bitten in two by a shark. A
pretty awful thought at base but not, apparently, the occasion to move us emotionally. Says Jones:

> "Oh! Sally, sharks do things by halves,
>   Yet most completely do!
> A bite in one place seems enough,
>   But I've been bit in two.
>
> "You know I once was all your own
>   But now a shark must share!
> But let that pass—for now, to you
>   I'm neither here nor there.
> "Alas! death has a strange divorce
>   Effected in the sea,
> It has divided me from you,
>   And even me from me!

And finally, the last of the ten verses, a coup de grâce:

> "But now, adieu—a long adieu!
>   I've solved death's awful riddle,

And would say more, but I am doomed
To break off in the middle!"[7]

If Empson is correct, the drawing of our attention to the mechanics of the pun has the effect of neutralizing the human experience that is described in the poem or that may lie behind it. Undoubtedly, Hood felt intensely about human pain and social injustice, and certainly much of his manner of presentation can be attributed to his quirky, irrepressible bent of mind, but the very success of such poetry may come from its capacity to pass off lightly the horrors of violence and unstable existence. The psychic charges of his puns seem to travel rapidly through the reader, firing off into release before they can be absorbed in the consciousness, before they can be *experienced* in any way. The poems are in a sense extended figures of an uneasy mind, seeking to contain its equability while taking cognizance of what worries it and what lies outside of it. Indeed, though the Victorian audience is reminded, as it reads Hood's Comic Annuals beside a yuletide hearth, that other people have senselessly visited upon them a sordid, grotesque fate, that world is nonetheless *outside*. Hood's poetry speaks not so much of real people as of caricatures well suited to punning witticism. The reality that the poems represent has been denatured. Though war was an actuality to Hood's generation and revolutionary violence a constant threat in the Europe of the 1840s, the casualties of war are already being made remote from ordinary English experience. The experience recedes into something that takes place in the Crimea, or Anglo-Egyptian Sudan, or China. It is mock ballad material now, with all the impersonality and class implications that such a form carries. Hood may play upon his English audience's ambiguous feelings toward suffering but he rarely attempts, in his comic verse, to persevere on to the broader ethical and social context that would enable the comedy to have more than a temporarily unsettling effect. And in this he clearly must suit the taste of his audience, which is as yet—in the 1830s and 1840s—too uneasy to deal with pain and instability except by treating it as grotesquerie.

To move from Hood's comedy, which keeps its sources of disquiet outside, in broadly cast, half-manic sociological vignettes, to Gilbert's comedy of the anguish of living *within* the constraints of the middle class, is to parallel, in a rather specialized mode, the development toward internalized uses of comedy that we observed in Dickens. W. S. Gilbert's "Bab Ballads" began appearing in various journals in the 1860s, after Victorian complacency had well established itself. The "ballads" are short comic poems that retained a popularity almost independent of Gilbert's collaboration with Arthur Sullivan. They are Gilbert's first sustained comic works and represented for him a phase preceding his more "significant" dramatic comedy. Gilbert is of a different generation than Hood; he came of age in the 1850s, the era of bourgeois stability, the apogee of what we tend to think of as Victorianism. Consequently, Gilbert was a man bound by the anxieties and predilections of the affluent middle-class social world, and his comedy more directly articulates the tensions within its mores.

The social historians who write of the "high Victorian" decades of the 1850s and 1860s remark on the perceptible slackening off of intensity that characterized the establishment of order and good times. "We miss the precise objectives, the concentrated purpose of the earlier time," writes G. M. Young.[8] "And not enough notice is taken as a rule of the essential simplicity of the age," says W. L. Burn. "To itself it appeared highly complex and so in a sense it was; but rather through its fecundity and diversity than through anything particularly complicated or subtle in its thinking."[9] The patterns of life, as befits a period in which social stability was becoming the rule, were more settled. And for those men who were inclined toward mediocrity, the lack of intensity and conflict permitted them to indulge the weakness.

For Gilbert, such a still atmosphere, growing heavy with smugness, was oppressive. The "Bab Ballads" register a pervasive discontent. We see it in the successful sugar broker of Gilbert's best known ballad, who had "a trusty wife and true,/And very cosy quarters,/A manager, a boy or two,/Six clerks, and seven porters./A broker must be doing well/(As any lunatic can tell)/Who can employ/An active boy,/Six clerks, and seven porters." Despite such an enviable station, the broker, who is a portly man, is overcome by a gnawing self-consciousness that takes the form of a compulsion to lose weight. He responds by dancing all the way from Brompton to the City every day, incurring the wonder and then the ridicule of everyone who sees him, including "the loud uneducated chaff/Of clerks on omnibuses." And as Gilbert notes, "Against all minor things that rack/A nicely balanced mind, I'll back/The noisy chaff/And ill-bred laugh/Of clerks on omnibuses."

> His friends, who heard his money chink,
>   And saw the house he rented,
> And knew his wife, could never think
>   What made him discontented.
>   It never struck their simple minds
>   That fads are of eccentric kinds,
>   Nor would they own
>   That fat alone
>   Could make one discontented.

And so, swept up in the blind logic of his own disquiet, the sugar broker dances and dances, his bulk and rotundity increasing with every caper, until his legs quite disappear and he becomes a round ball, unable to rise but still twitching away. The moral of the tale is this:

> I hate to preach—I hate to prate—
>   I'm no fanatic croaker,
> But learn contentment from the fate
>   Of this West India broker.

He'd everything a man of taste
Could ever want, except a waist:
    And discontent
    His size anent,
And bootless perseverance blind,
Completely wrecked the peace of mind
    Of this West India broker.[10]

The moral of almost every "Bab Ballad" is that "fads are of eccentric kinds" that invariably invite ostracism and ruin when carried to their ultimate limits. Gilbert loves to cut down to common sense the postures of love, heroism, and charismatic self-assertion. When a doting wife apostrophizes her "absent husband," she launches into that particular kind of poetical nonsense that fond nostalgia inspires:

Tell me, Edward, doest remember
    How at breakfast often we,
Put our bacon in the tea-pot
    While we took and fried our tea?

How we went to evening parties
    On gigantic brewer's drays?
How you wore your coats as trousers,
    In those happy, happy days?[11]

Another of the couple's gay, impulsive habits, alas, was to "quite forget" to pay for articles they bought. The last verse recounts how their lark gave way to harsh reality when a shopkeeper sued the couple and hauled them into Old Bailey. In the early Gilbert poem "Tempora Mutantur," economic actualities have a similarly sobering consequence. A young blade recalls how he once eagerly anticipated the billets-doux of his lovely Alice. Now, however:

Bills for carriages and horses,
    Bills for wine and light cigar,
Matters that concern the Forces—

> News that may affect the Forces—
> News affecting my resources,
>   Much more interesting are![12]

Gilbert's poetry, though making clear that vivid individual expression is bootless against the mundane realities of these material times, does not actually urge us to "learn contentment from the fate" of men like the discontented sugar broker. The "Bab Ballads" are muted outcries against something lost; they are brief, bittersweet celebrations of the extravagant, joyful sensibilities that are stifled by propriety and by the smothering dictates of conformity. What better symbol of the grey moderation of Victorian respectability could there be than "The Reverend Rawston Wright," who parts his hair down the middle, does his linen up with care, and is praised by congregation and bishop alike for his moderation, seriousness, and stern demeanor. Yet every once in a while, at night, he strikes a gigantic gong, tears his hair, leaps furiously about, and then sings this strange refrain:

> "Oh, fan an aesthetical flame,
>   And sing to the moon so bright,
> For piggy-wigs worry and maim,
> And my highly respected name
>   Is the REVEREND RAWSTON WRIGHT."[13]

It is the "aesthetical flame," the urge to go berserk, to dance and yell, perhaps even to maim as the piggy-wigs do, that is locked into the tightly constrained personalities of the respectable mid-Victorian citizen. It is these desires and impulses that we feel struggling against the confines of common sense in Gilbert's verse. In a civilization so dominated by the superego as Victorian middle-class England, its discontents follow strangely Freudian paths. In one Gilbertian ballad, "The Story of Gentle Archibald," the repressed desires take ghoulish turns in the manifest dream content of an average little boy. Archibald had always wanted to be a clown, but his papa disapproved, intending his son for the Church instead. So Archibald dreams that his wish comes true and lets out his *real* feelings:

> The change had really turned his brain;
> He boiled his little sister JANE;
> He painted blue his aged mother;
> Sat down upon his little brother;
>
> Spread devastation round,—and, ah,
> He red-hot-pokered his papa![14]

The erratic flights of looniness and violence that possess the secret lives of Gilbert's little people are symbolic of dimensions of individual freedom and self-expression that are being denied. They are oblique but unmistakable protests against the consequences of saneness and sameness. Yet the manner of their presentation, with the bursts of fancy so battened down in tight little poems in which the tone is one of quizzical disapproval, reemphasizes the oppressive restrictiveness on such expressions. There is no full release in Gilbert's poems; we are always called back to the mundane norms. The expressions of hidden desires that do emerge are made to seem excessively bizarre. They follow chaotic, manic paths with a sort of horrible inner logic. We get the impression that eccentricity, that cherished English outlet so often celebrated in light humor of this kind, has become distorted: it manifests itself no longer in the harmless, sentimental oddities of Pickwick and Uncle Toby but in self-destructive, fitful behavior. The "Bab Ballads" suggest that the molds of patterned life style in mid-Victorian England have become so tight that any unshaped human material extrudes itself in grotesque variations. In Gilbert's brief tales, we see that the impulses for expression are humane; they are desires for free movement, for doing what comes naturally, for "aesthetical" flights of fancy. But they are not expressed in recognizably humane terms; the weight of the social order has compelled these individualistic rebellions against sterility to divert themselves into perverse channels.

When Gilbert hints of the debilitating effects of public opinion and anxious conformity, he chokes off any tendency toward compassion for its victims by turning the struggle for self-expression into a parable of what grotesque departures would occur if everyone carried their frustrations to their logical extremes. "A. and B., or, The Sensation Twins," for instance, tells of twin brothers, A. and B., who grew in absurdly opposite directions:

> A. had a pair of monstrous eyes,
>   B.'s eyes were awful small;
> B.'s nose attained a fearful size.
>   A. had no nose at all.
>
> B. had a thin and taper waist,
>   A. had no waist at all;
> A. was too short for proper taste,
>   B. just as much too tall.

Tormented by social disapproval—"They meekly bore their painful lots/Men shunned them as a cuss"—they take up the fancy that if people would just add them both together and divide the sum by two, they would produce two normal people. Unfortunately, the twins take on so about that idea that it becomes a mania, their sole topic of conversation, until a Turk by the name of Ben Ouseff, finding their joke "getting stale and trite," fulfills their wish and cuts each of the twins in half. Says the dying A.:

> "This is a quibble, sir, and what
>   Sharp practice people call—"
> "It's what you asked for!" "No, it's not—
>   By no means—not at all!"[15]

Hardly a moral of being contented with yourself as you are but, on the other hand, a curiously waspish kind of treatment of the issue.

Gilbert's ballads, like the little people they describe, give the impression of a certain kind of inner contortedness. The tension of warring values creates the torque of a comedy that peels open the sublimation of the prevailing culture and yet compresses the spirit of individuality into grotesquely unviable forms of expression. Gilbert's comedy is essentially the first of the muted attacks on the terms of mid-Victorian sublimation that developed as writers of the period became aware how stifling were the morals of the bourgeoisie and how banal the life style they dictated. In comparison with Hood's only erratically effective discharges, Gilbert's nonsense poems draw bead directly upon the more "refined" social anxieties of the time—the pressures of conformity and respectability, the burdens of adult responsibilities, the vague causes of dissatisfaction. The Biedermeier inclinations of English light humor— toward quietism, reverence for the small scale (earlier critics had talked about humor as producing a sort of "inverse sublimity; exalting, as it were, into our affections what is below us"), and complacency—expose themselves in Gilbert's verse. Gilbert's comic poems are curiously self-critical, for they portray anticonventional impulses as bizarre, inhumane, manic. The narrative voice sometimes worries its subject and sometimes clips it off. This is nothing like the 1820s Bulwerian oscillation between comic outlet on the one extreme and moral reaffirmation and adjustment on the other; Gilbert is worming into the process of sublimation itself. The convolutions of the Freudian comic operation—the often grotesquely antisocial impulses being assaulted by the social and moral inhibitions of the culture (and of the author) and, the unnaturalness and deadening inertia of those inhibitions being delineated and communicated at the same time—characterize the best of Gilbert's light verse.

Yet ultimately that is all we have—the dexterous workings, the curious little vignettes, the uneasy poise between repression and rebellion. Gilbert did not extend himself in this treacherously revealing and difficult-to-balance field of comic exploration. He was, in fact, a carefully guarded man. His own attitudes, full of paradoxes, are nicely summed up by James Ellis, a recent editor of the "Bab Ballads":

> "He made his reputation from comic verse and his fortune from comic opera, yet thought of himself primarily as a serious writer. He who contrived some of the most whimsical lords of misrule in all literature lived scrupulously by the rule himself and demanded that others do so, too. He who placed so many insubstantial fairy realms upon the stage lived himself in a world of strict business and high finance in which he amassed a fortune and prided himself upon his houses, his yachts, his art collection, his telephones, and his automobiles."[16]

Gilbert does not readily fit the pattern of the sentimental and anguished comic writer toughening himself through wit. Although acutely sensitive to the thwarted aspirations of the little fellow in the bourgeois world of conventions, Gilbert cultivated an aloofness of manner that served his own interests rather well. G. K. Chesterton, writing about the Savoy operas, says that behind Gilbert's satire there is "no particular positive philosophy," that there was in the man "a relative lack of moral conviction."[17] As Chesterton observes, Gilbert's direction was toward aesthetic detachment, a direction taken rather frequently by comic writers, such as Meredith and Wilde, in the last decades of the century. Emotional disengagement does appear to have been Gilbert's means of handling the tensions within his own relationship to mid-Victorian complacency. It was not a retreat or an evasion, for the "Bab Ballads" and the later opera librettos recurringly touch sensitive nerves within all that ample, well-toned flesh of middle-class equanimity; it was a kind of accommodation, a withdrawal to another stance.

We witness a steady progression as we move from

Thomas Hood's verse through Gilbert's "Bab Ballads" and now to Lewis Carroll's Alice books—a progression in the degree of self-revelation allowed by each author and in the degree of social amplification that characterizes each man's comedy. The fabric of attitudes and concerns has become so complex in the mid-Victorian period that any attempt by a writer to come to terms with his own share of them requires that they be explored in a context that accounts for that complexity. Carroll's estrangement, at least during the 1860s, from his culture's imperatives was surely of a different nature from Hood's, whose life straddled two rather contradictory epochs. Carroll's necessarily required a more thorough sounding of the tempo of his own times. And he was obliged to find a literary form that would be able to provide an amplified imaginative context and still permit him to register his own disquiet—hence, the Alice books.

"I seem to see some meaning in
them after all."—*The King of Hearts*

II

Alice in Wonderland and *Through the Looking-Glass* present explorations of the cultural anxieties that concentrate within the mid-century sensibility. They have traditionally, of course, invited multiple interpretations—as retreats into childhood, as mythic excursions into the unconscious, as thinly disguised expressions of black humor, and as paradigms of games and sport. The coy intellectuality of Carroll's inversions of sophisticated ideas has prompted critics to consider the Alice books as paradigmatic works of self-contained logic (or illogic) that bear no resemblance to the outer social world. Such interpretations, though valid with respect to one dimension of Carroll's writing, cannot account for the remarkable impact that the Alice books have had upon adult readers for over a hundred years. They are explorations of an adult life that ventures as far as Carroll could risk going toward freedom from the duties, responsibilities, and arid self-limitations of modern society.

What a pleasant change the caucus-race would be from the competition of most "games" and adult occupations: "they began running when they liked and left off when they liked," and at the end of the race "*everybody* has won and *all* must have prizes." How nice it would be to sit, as the Mock Turtle does, on a shingle by the sea and sentimentally ruminate on one's experiences, to surrender to all the self-indulgence that seems too rarely possible in modern life. It is always teatime for the Mad Hatter, the March Hare, and the Dormouse, and people they don't like just aren't invited; "No room! No room!.," says the Hare. And when Humpty Dumpty uses a word it means what *he* chooses it to mean, neither more nor less.

We cannot say exactly what was included in the original, oral version of *Wonderland* that Carroll spun for the Liddell sisters while boating on the Thames, but we do know that many of the additions that he made to the tale when writing it out for publication were those episodes of comic indulgence, such as the Mad Tea Party and the reminiscences of the Mock Turtle.[18] Common to these additions is the sense of a poignant need to retreat to personal patterns of play and whim, as if to escape from the narrowing pressures of a life in society. In the years just before *Wonderland* was published, Carroll himself chafed and despaired under what seemed to him the onerous burdens and anxieties of adult life. At the end of each year, he sadly assessed himself and recorded in his diaries his failures to live up to his responsibilities as a scholar, teacher, and man of religion. "Great mercies, great failings," he wrote at year's end in 1855, "time lost, talents misapplied—such has been the past year."[19] In 1863 he made this self-appraisal:

Dec. 31 (Th). Here, at the close of another year, how much of neglect, carelessness, and sin have I to remember! I had hoped, during the year, to have made a beginning in parochial work, to have thrown off habits of evil, to have advanced in my work at Christ Church. How little, next to nothing, has been done of all this! Now I have a fresh year before me; once more let me set myself to do something worthy of life 'before I go hence, and be no more seen.'[20]

He pleaded with God, "make me hereafter such a worker! But, alas, what are the means?"[21] Characteristically, in February 1863, he bemoaned, "This year has given no promise as yet of being better than its predecessors: my habits of life need much amendment"; he then listed four ways (including "denying myself indulgence of sleep in the evening") by which they could be improved.[22] Distracted by his amusements, unambitious, eyed suspiciously by the parents of his little girls, and nagged by a sense of failure for forsaking a religious vocation, Carroll looked for life possibilities in which these concerns and burdens did not exist. In his own life, he found respite in his many hobbies and avocations; he was an inveterate riddler, game-maker, rhymester. But in the Alice books, he could render through imagination the fragments, at least, of a desired life style, a life style that had the freedoms and satisfactions of adult play.

It was through play, in fact, that Carroll developed the talents for which he is most remembered. He began writing nonsense as a boy for his own amusement and that of his brothers and sisters. As he acquired a special, self-conscious skill at it, his play developed into an art—but an art that retained its child's play quality. Nonsense, to be successful, must keep that precarious balance between childlike whimsy and the capriccio of a trained artist showing off his skills. Like caricature, it is apparently casually rendered; but it is often swept up in the exuberance of comic creation, the writer improvising and piling on richer and wilder creations and scenes for his own delight in them (like Dickens indulging himself in more and more of Mrs. Gamp).

The exuberance of play, however, is often deliberately restrained by an arbitrary order of rules invented by the player, and this was especially important to Carroll. In this quality of personally devised order—the brief moments in the Alice books of creatures rehearsing their individual delights—one captures the pleasure of personal control of one's life, and perhaps achieves the stasis that so many Victorians sought in a rapidly changing world.

Even more important is the relief that play brings from the officious moralizing of other people. The "moral" of *Wonderland* is drawn by the Duchess (although she doesn't practice it): "If everybody minded their own business, the world would go round a deal faster than it does." Victorian comic writers from Thackeray to Butler tried to fend off the ponderous forces that were bent on dictating ethical, social, and even psychological conformity. In moments of play, at least, one can operate, as Johan Huizinga has noted, "outside the antithesis of wisdom and folly . . . of good and evil."[23] In later years, Carroll could rhapsodize about his dream Alice because she was living in the happy hours "when Sin and Sorrow are but names—empty words signifying nothing!"[24] The homiletic hymns and rhymes that Alice tries to recall in *Wonderland* but cannot—"The Old Man's Comforts," "Against Idleness and Mischief," "The Sluggard," and "Speak Gently"—all share three elements—an injunction to be industrious and responsible, the reminder that we shall all grow old, and an invocation of our religious duties. Significantly, these banished thoughts are those we try to forget in play.

Carroll could not forget them for long, however. Wonderland's imaginative projection as a possible variant life style was at the same time an opportunity to register and somehow work out the very anxieties that gave rise to the search for a new life style. In dreams we are often able to do all these things, and *Wonderland* is such a dream.

True to the realm of dreams, most things in Wonderland do not happen in a logical and chronological manner. There is no "plot" to the book; instead, dream thoughts pull seemingly disorganized elements together. Almost immediately the anxieties Carroll recorded so often in his diaries come to the surface in the behavior of the White Rabbit, who's late, who's lost his glove, who'll lose his head if he doesn't get to the Duchess's house on time.[25] The Rabbit will later act for the Crown in the surrealistic trial of the knave at the book's end, thereby explicitly linking such social anxieties with the arbitrary punishment and the dread of fury that persistently flash along hidden circuits of Wonderland's dreaming brain and periodically seize Alice and the creatures. At the end of the innocuous caucus-race, the Mouse tells Alice his "tale"; it is about Fury and it prefigures the terrifying dissolution of the Wonderland dream itself. According to the tale, personified Fury, who this morning has "nothing to do," imperiously decides he'll prosecute the Mouse: " 'I'll be judge, I'll be jury,' said cunning old Fury; 'I'll try the whole cause and condemn you to death.' "[26]

Time and again the delights of play are cut off suddenly by such arbitrary violence, for we perceive that play by its nature cannot last. No wonder the Mad Hatter curtly changes the subject when Alice reminds him that he will soon run out of places at the tea table. Too soon he is dragged into Court by the Queen to be badgered and intimidated, despite his pathetic protest, "I hadn't quite finished my tea when I was sent for." Play can only temporarily remove us from outside reality, as Carroll himself repeatedly discovered, because authority (characterized in those adult women—Queens and Duchesses) will interfere and impose its angry will. This is why I believe it is inaccurate to assert, as Hugh Kenner and Elizabeth Sewell have, that Carroll's books are "closed" works of art, literary game structures that are deliberately isolated and fundamentally unrelated to the Victorian social world outside them.[27] On the contrary, they show Carroll's reluctant conclusion that totally independent life patterns were impossible and even dangerous; they are Carroll's paradigms of the way social power was achieved and how it operated in Victorian England.

Inherent in the very freedom of play is its weakness. Functioning by personal whim, it is potentially anarchic and thus vulnerable to the strongest, most brutal will. Halfway through the book, Alice unaccountably must enter Wonderland a second time and she finds its tenor radically different. Instead of the pleasantly free caucus-race, she plays in a croquet game where "the players all played at once, quarrelling all the while." All order has collapsed; hedgehog balls scuttle through the grass, bodiless cats grin in the dusk. And the domineering Queen of Hearts imposes her angry will more and more as she exploits the anarchy of the hapless world of play.

The antics that the Mad Tea Party group, the Caterpillar, and the other free souls had been indulging in were, in a word, nonsense. Just as nonsense writing is a form of play activity, play itself—at least as Carroll conceived it—is nonsensical in the context of the "real world"; it has been deliberately deprived of meaning, of any overt social and moral significance. Alice noted at the tea party that "the Hatter's remark seemed to her to have no sort of meaning in it, and yet it was certainly English." At the trial of the knave, however, suddenly there *is* meaning that the autocratic Queen wants attached to the words so that they can be made to serve her lust for persecution. The most damning piece of evidence, according to the Crown, is a nonsensical letter purportedly written by the defendant. Alice argues, "*I* don't believe there's an atom of meaning in it," but the King of Hearts insists, "I seem to see some meaning in [the words] after all." The individuals who assert power in society, Carroll is suggesting, decide what things shall mean. *Their* whims, prompted and carried out by an irrational fury against people who would be free, dictate our responsibilities, our duties, our guilts, our sins, our punishment.

Here, the adult victim's view nicely corresponds to the child's view of grown-up authority. If a child is called to task, told to remember some rule or duty he has forgotten about or never fully realized he was responsible for, he feels like the Mad Hatter, who is told, "Don't be nervous, or I'll have you executed on the spot." Justice from a child's perspective often does seem to function like the Queen's—verdict first, guilt later.

This vision is surely familiar to post-Kafka readers and may be one of the reasons why *Wonderland* has such contemporary appeal. If there is a difference between Carroll's rendition of social power and the view of present writers, it probably lies in Carroll's attribution of the evils of that power to the ambitions of specific unscrupulous individuals. Social authority is frequently depicted in contemporary literature as a vague but pervasive *impersonal* force—monolithic, self-sustaining, its motives obscure, its constituents unidentified. Although *Looking-Glass* implies a social order close to this, *Wonderland* delineates—as much mid-Victorian literature does—an Establishment that is made up of greedy, insensitive individuals fulfilling selfish urges for power and disguising it with moral cant. This view reflects the rise to power in nineteenth-century England of the entrepreneurs, the exploiters, and the social climbers who are so vividly depicted in Dickens and Trollope. It also reflects the abundance and variety of self-appointed moral arbiters of the time—the Churchmen, earnest reformers, and busy, bustling middle-class matrons. As W. L. Burn puts it, "One of the cardinal differences between the mid-Victorians and ourselves lies not in their optimism and our pessimism but in the much greater faith they had in the power of the human will."[28] Yet in the final analysis, Carroll's particular depiction of the way society worked stemmed largely from his own psychological makeup, the unique mix in him of fear of anarchy, self-doubt, and of sad realism about the way things were.

In the second of the Alice books, *Through the Looking-Glass*, published in 1871, six years after *Wonderland*, we can detect a significant sombering of outlook. There is a remarkable difference in the mood and strategy of the two books. In *Looking-Glass*, Carroll sees the prospects for free activity in society much more pessimistically. We discover immediately that *Looking-Glass* is worked out as a chess game, in which Alice is propelled along toward a visible goal; she is no longer exploring on her own. A deterministic impulse underlies the Looking-Glass dream; indeed, it ends with the suggestion that we are all part of the dream of a godlike Red King whose own unconscious wishes predetermine our lives.

Alice's entry to Wonderland had been balked by problems of identity; she had to shed some false notions relating to size, rote-knowledge, and rules of behavior before she could participate in the dream world. On entering the looking-glass, she is confronted with difficulties in moving "forward," as if her need now is to move out, away from home and childhood and into the adult world of roles and responsibility.

While *Wonderland* is set in a spring afternoon, *Looking-Glass* takes place in mid-winter; the first book's golden aura now seems only the yellowing of age. Alice is rudely told by the flowers that she is beginning to fade. Humpty Dumpty dwells on her age and the possibility of death, and in parting, as he offers her his finger to shake, he says that he very much doubts if he'd know her if they *did* meet again: "you're so exactly like other people." How chilling it is, Carroll seems to be saying, to contemplate a dry, unsatisfying maturity like that of the Queens in *Looking-Glass*, whom Carroll later described this way:

The Red Queen I pictured as a Fury, but of another type from the Queen of Hearts in Wonderland; *her* passion must be cold and calm; she must be formal and strict, yet not unkindly; pedantic to the tenth degree; the concentrated essence of all governesses! Lastly, the White Queen seemed, to my dreaming fancy, gentle, stupid, fat and pale; . . . just *suggesting* imbecility, but never quite passing into it.[29]

The poems that frame *Looking-Glass* echo the plaint and seem to be spooned up from Carroll's deepest, stickiest treacle well:

> Come, harken then, ere voice of dread
> With bitter tidings laden,
> Shall summon to unwelcome bed
> A melancholy maiden!
> We are but older children, dear,
> Who fret to find our bedtime near.
>
> Long has paled that sunny sky:
> Echoes fade and memories die:
> Autumn frosts have slain July.[30]

Toward the end of *Looking-Glass*, the White Knight—whose resemblance to Carroll himself has often been noted—invents for Alice a nonsense verse that is a Looking-Glass distortion of *Wonderland*. This one, too, is set in a summer, now "long ago," not about a child, however, but about a pathetically aged man "who seemed distracted with his woe." Growing old, we recall, was banished from *Wonderland*; it was in the poems that Alice "forgot." In *Looking-Glass*, it is omnipresent.

Adult play, which was so vividly real early in *Wonderland*, is not seriously offered again. Humpty Dumpty, the Lion and the Unicorn, and the Tweedles carry on a bit, but their careers are predetermined by the nursery rhymes about them. By wishing for the crow of the Tweedle rhyme to come, Alice makes it come; and we uneasily suspect that if she willed it, Alice could make Humpty Dumpty fall off the wall immediately. If the Cheshire Cat of *Wonderland* is the comic spirit of play, able to go where he wishes, do as he wishes, and remain—sometimes literally—detached, the gnat that Alice meets in *Looking-Glass* is the comic spirit of that book: he can barely be heard, his humor is forced and restricted in range, and he himself is miserable.

The mood in *Looking-Glass* is close to that of the humor tradition in English letters that we have traced earlier. Although the tones of adult play and eccentricity admittedly shade into each other, it is apparent from the manner and structure of *Looking-Glass* that Carroll felt he could not go back again to an exploration of the possibilities of a free life style. As he grew older, he settled for a conventional, if less joyful, accommodation to the societal patterns of his time. The White Knight, for example, has all the characteristics of the humor tradition's amiable eccentric: he is melancholy, lovable, laughable, and very obviously modeled after Don Quixote, who, to early nineteenth-century readers, seemed a perfect specimen of the amiable humorist.[31] And he is very much part of the chessboard social pattern. Contrast the White Knight to the waspish Hare and Hatter who have no part in any larger social order. The creatures in *Looking-Glass* spend much of their time perched on walls or upside down in ditches idly contemplating—like Parson Adams or Sterne's Walter Shandy. At one point in *Looking-Glass* when Alice bursts into tears because it is so very *lonely* there, the White Queen tries to comfort her by telling her to "consider what a great girl you are. Consider what a long way you've come today." "Can *you* keep from crying by considering things?" Alice asks. "That's the way it's done," the Queen says.

Consider what a long way you've come: *Looking-Glass*, unlike *Wonderland*, has the speeded up tempo and brassy talk of the acquisitive, industrial society. Alice is flung onto a rushing train and asked where her ticket is. "Don't keep him waiting, child," a chorus of voices demands, "his time is worth a thousand pounds a minute." The land is worth a thousand pounds an inch, the smoke from the engine a thousand pounds a puff. Alice is haplessly driven on toward womanhood as an underlying anxiety constricts the dream's action tighter and tighter toward the breaking point, until at last life becomes unbearable and rapacious.

The last moments in the Looking-Glass, with the banquet guests wallowing in the gravy, are a hideous analogue of the life of an indulgent society. Just as the characters are less joyful and independent than those of Wonderland, so the society here is faster, harder, more manipulative. The Darwinian motif of survival of the fittest and of cannibalism that had shot randomly through Alice's first dream have now become almost the governing principle in a world where people are figuratively "consuming" others.

The half a dozen years between the two books had resigned Lewis Carroll to an even more muted expression of rebellion. They were years in which Victorian England grew more affluent, more wasteful, perhaps a bit more frenetic. And Carroll's own life, as the diary entries from 1866 to 1870 reflect, was more demanding, and his interests had turned more to politics and affairs of the world. Ever sensitive to changes in the quality of life, Carroll may have sensed the disillusionment that was to beset the late Victorians when the promise of a more satisfying life through progress proved empty. For all the vigor of the 1860s, "doubts and fears there were," says G. M. Young. "The roaring slapdash prosperity of a decade had worked itself out to its appointed end: overtrading, speculation, fraud and collapse."[32] Already feeling like a man hopelessly out of tune with his time, Carroll, in his oblique and highly personal way, registered these nuances of change in English culture and, sadly, in his own prospects for happiness and freedom.

Lewis Carroll has been posthumously psychoanalyzed more than any other English writer, save maybe Swift. The smug callousness with which his possible repressions and perversions have been delineated constrains one from any more inquiry into the man. Yet, the ambivalence of positions and tones in the Alice books—the odd mixture of self-pity and insouciant gaiety, of coy spoofing and mordant commentary on human foibles—does inevitably draw us to inquire into the complex of attitudes that dictated the comic expression that Carroll chose.

The madness in the Alice books is often no more than the looniness of children's literature or harmless addle-patedness, which Alice usually absorbs with considerable aplomb. But there is a more worrisome dimension to the motif. The hallucinatory qualities of the books, the sudden metamorphoses, the wayward thoughts of cannibalism and dismemberment, the hot flashes of fury—all remind us that in dreams, especially, our minds seem to wander dangerously close to insanity. Throughout his life, Carroll displayed a fascination with mental derangement. His long poem "The Hunting of the Snark," subtitled "An Agony in Eight Fits," takes us imaginatively to the borderline of dissolution: a Baker goes out like a candle at the sight of a boojum snark. An insomniac, Carroll worked off and on at a small book of mathematical "pillow problems" to take the mind, he said, off the "undesired thoughts" that fly into the head in those late-night hours before sleep. And Carroll recorded in his diary the confusion between dream and wakefulness—an observation that makes us question our very sanity:

> Query: when we are dreaming and, as often happens, have a dim consciousness of the fact and try to wake, do we not say and do things which in waking life would be insane? May we not then sometimes define insanity as an inability to distinguish which is the waking and which the sleeping life?[33]

All this is not to show that Carroll feared he would go mad, but that he was acutely conscious of the distortions of the human mind. He was preoccupied enough with the train of his own uncanny thoughts to have strong doubts about those potentially anarchic individual life styles that he concocted. He was evidently uneasy about deviation from societal norms. For this reason, Alice herself acts in *Wonderland* and *Looking-Glass* as a check on the possibly manic behavior of even the "free" adult creatures like the Hatter and the Hare. She retains throughout a nice balance of self-control and imagination, qualities of pre-adolescence which may be, in part, what made little girls so attractive to Carroll. Even at her most disoriented, Alice can declare firmly, "I'm I." Though Carroll gently spoofs Alice's literal-minded common sense, she serves to remind us that no matter how appealing some of the creatures' life styles are, any sensible child her age must see it all as silly behavior by grown-ups. When the chaos and foolishness in Wonderland get out of hand at the end of the book, it is Alice who becomes the adult by growing in size and authority; the imaginary creatures appear to be only errant children. Built into the work—a work which vividly and alluringly explores the free behavior patterns to which Carroll was attracted—is a perspective that makes it all seem puerile and pathetic. It is as if Carroll had doubts in his own mind about the sense (as well as the social wisdom) of that life style.

Carroll's ambivalence is even more in evidence when he treats religious issues. The Alice books can be easily read as subtle critiques of Calvinist tenets. *Looking-Glass*'s dreaming king seems to parody predestination, as does its policy of punishment first, guilt later. The knave's trial draws on the idea that there is something that one is guilty of but cannot remember—which may, in fact, be a primordial sin lying deep in one's unconscious. (Carroll, writing later in life of his religious beliefs, explicitly rejected the notion of punishment for original sin.)[34] And there are numerous al-

lusions in the Alice books to the burdens and anxieties that
religion places upon us through its hymns and stultifying
moral parables. Yet there is nothing we can characterize as
overt or conclusive condemnation of religious belief in
either of the books. Issues like original sin and Darwinian
survival of the fittest cut so many different ways in *Wonderland* that it appears that Carroll is expressing only something of the confusion in his own mind. The British historian G. Kitson Clark suggests that this is symptomatic of intellectuals in the 1860s, who shared "a general uneasy feeling that Christianity had been disproved by someone,
which combined with the increase in the number of secular
interests and amusements to cause a retreat from the old
habits and certainties."[35]

Carroll himself had undergone a crisis of confidence in
his ability to defend his religious beliefs in 1857, which
figured in his decision that he had no vocation for the
ministry.[36] Presumably doubt, directed perhaps as intensely against himself as against religious doctrines,
lingered during the period of the writing of the two Alice
books, even though Carroll responded then and throughout his life to any license in literary portrayal of religion
with exaggerated sensitivity. Evelyn Waugh, a religious
man who himself dealt in the comic mode with the problems of sincerity of belief in *The Ordeal of Gilbert Pinfold*,
says of Carroll:

> It seems likely to me that Dodgson was tortured by reli-
> gious skepticism; his abnormal tenderness of conscience
> with regard to blasphemy is explicable if we think of him
> as treasuring a religious faith so fragile that a child's
> prattle endangered it. He believed that the only way he
> could protect his faith was by escaping . . . from contem-
> porary life—in his scholarship into remote and fanciful
> abstractions, in literature into nonsense.[37]

Hence we have the conflicting impulses that underlie the
Alice books—a fervent desire to set up a completely free,

amoral life style of adult play, and an equally intense dread of the anarchy that would ensue; a need to assert Carroll's own, very individual way of recreating contemporary adult life, and a distrust close to fear of the mad tracks of his own fantasies; an antagonism to the life- and freedom-denying tenets of religion, and despair at the slippage of his own faith. Added to this is the ambivalence that we observed in the writings of Dickens' later years toward the society of his day (which may indeed be an ambivalence shared by many twentieth-century British and American comic writers). Though *Looking-Glass* registers, as we have noted, a decline in the quality of individual life and sharp criticism of the frenzy and the rush of industrial England, nonetheless the 1850s and 1860s were, objectively speaking, a progressive, relatively comfortable time. In an era of such excitement, hope, and affluence, how legitimately can society be faulted in what one feels is not quite right about one's own life— especially when one is as acutely aware as Carroll was of one's own shortcomings and anxieties?

Ambivalence and indirect attack, *Angst* and muted self-assertion are beautifully accommodated in nonsense. The virtue of nonsense is its obliqueness; it is ideally suited to criticism from the "inside" of a class or society by one too racked by self-doubt to engage in open assault. In nonsense, one does not have to be precise about one's target or the manifold causes of grievance. George Orwell, drawing on an observation of Aldous Huxley's, notes that nonsense poetry usually does not specifically identify the people or institutions in society that are accused of denying men their pleasure and freedom. He uses an Edward Lear nonsense limerick as an example:

> There was an old man of Whitehaven
> Who danced a quadrille with a raven;
> But they said, "It's absurd
> To encourage this bird!"
> So they smashed that old man of Whitehaven.

"To smash somebody just for dancing a quadrille with a raven is exactly the kind of thing that 'They' would do," Orwell observes.[38] We know very well who "they" are—the Establishment, the self-appointed moral arbiters of society. And what are they smashing? Harmless adult play, whimsy, dancing. Lear's verse is slight, hardly serious, yet its underlying resentment is perfectly communicated.

A further virtue of nonsense is that the author is never made vulnerable himself. The author cannot be counterattacked or criticized. Carroll can allude to his misgivings about such sensitive matters as religious beliefs, morality, and social responsibility without exposing himself to challenges to his own orthodoxy or propriety. Indeed, in Carroll's case, his contemporaries found no social criticism in the Alice books at all. His books and nonsense poems fit comfortably into the mid-nineteenth-century light comedy tradition that Donald J. Gray has analyzed in his essay "The Uses of Victorian Laughter."[39] In the vaguely liberal bourgeois magazines like *Punch* that flourished during the period, important topics were treated so gently, Gray contends, that humor did as much to confirm as to challenge prevailing social and political opinion. The newly established Victorian middle class was as uneasy about the lengths to which its comedy should go as it was about its sexual mores.

Thus, although Carroll's Alice books give us a strong sense of the anguish of the man locked up inside middle-class society, twisting in confusion and despair yet unwilling to burst out, they slid relatively easily into the light popular canon of that same middle class. Carroll's critique of his time is if anything further reaching and more intellectually penetrating than Gilbert's "Bab Ballads" or perhaps anything that Gilbert ever wrote. Gilbert, as we have noted, shrank back from the kind of extensive elaboration of his anxieties and desires that Carroll engaged in. Gilbert essentially detached himself. Carroll immersed himself progressively deeper in the popular culture's mores, almost suggesting that the further one goes in amplifying and exploring one's ambivalent personal relationship to a culture, in the context of that culture, the more resigned one becomes. Certainly the course that Carroll took involved an attempt to accommodate his personal feelings to the climate of the times in a way that Gilbert would not venture to do.

In any event, Carroll's second pair of "children's books," *Sylvie and Bruno* (1889) and *Sylvie and Bruno Concluded* (1893) comprise awkward and tonally inconsistent fusions of his older manner of whimsy and his new determination to speak seriously, of his older fascinations with erratic behavior and his new insistence on illustrating the benefits of good actions. In the preface to *Sylvie and Bruno*, he promises to show how one can combine a few hours of thoughtless merriment with some reflections on the "graver cadences of life." He descants gratuitously on the mortality of man and makes a specious case for Bowdlerization, leading at last to an argument that is little short of amazing. Positing the case of a theatrical play or other comic amusement that may be "a little too 'risky,' the dialogue a little too strong, the 'business' a little too suggestive," but that one is tempted to attend nonetheless because one has heard that it is frightfully clever, Carroll asks: how can we steel our consciences and weight the factors correctly? The best possible test, he says, is to inquire of oneself whether it is the kind of thing that one would like to make his last mortal act; "the safest rule is that we should not dare to *live* in any scene in which we dare not *die*."[40] In other words, the test for any comic bit of theatre is whether we would literally like to be caught dead there. A long, strenuous, twisted course from the playful, imaginative, mordant sensibility that was so attractive in *Alice in Wonderland*.

This development correlates nonetheless with the changes in the content, and to a certain extent the manner, of light comedy during the years 1850-1880. At the beginning of this period, we are likely to find that popular light humor deals with only the most trivial kinds of entertainments; its function is solely to amuse. More serious issues were treated in writing that had a more serious tone. Gradually, however, this division breaks down, and we find writers of humor involving themselves to a greater extent with everyday middle-class behavior patterns and social situations. We noted something of this progression in the comedy of Hood, Gilbert, and Carroll; the comedy gradually becomes more referential and begins to accommodate a broader social context. Inevitably, as a form of comic writing changes its nature to that degree, it begins to absorb more of the ambiguities of its culture. As it provides extended treatment of the mores and attitudes of its time, it runs a greater risk of becoming a means of expression of those mores and attitudes. In the case of the light humor of Victorian England, it grew more bourgeois. By the 1880s, it was heavily charged with middle-class positions; it was no longer light entertainment but the characteristic mode in which the mass of its readers found their attitudes reflected.

For all of that though, Lewis Carroll's humorous writing remained in the peculiar tradition of Victorian nonsense verse. All three of the writers we have just examined—Hood, Gilbert, and Carroll—began with grievances that were probably social in origin but immediately cast them into forms that seem to be intensely personal in expression. They launched directly into artistic caprice, into plays on words, curious fantasies, exotic variations. There is something rather elemental about the art of these three that accounts for its expression as adult play, as dream, as remote fantasy, as pure concoction. Similarly, there is something elemental about their feelings that explains the penchant for incidents of brutality, perversity, madness, and pure anguish. Such literature is ultimately an individual outcry, so intense an expression of personal estrangement from the diffusive social modes of the time as to require the self-strangulation of the odd individual forms and the antic mask of their jollity. Thus, although Carroll's social context is broader than Hood's, and his anxieties more deflected, he does not, finally, give us a projection or examination of human problems in their ordinary social matrices. His, too, is the song of the man slightly out of tune.

"I have often seen reminiscences of people I have never heard of."—*Charles Pooter*

III

Hood, Carroll, and Gilbert are, broadly speaking, Romantics. Societal problems take an intensely personal form; their art is devoted essentially to expression of the tensions within the artist himself. Douglas Jerrold, whose series in *Punch*, "Mrs. Caudle's Curtain Lectures," created the model for the mid-century comedy of ordinary living experiences, is a Victorian. He is interested in the nature of social relationships and he is a moralist. His subjects are the pressures of class and position and the tensions experienced by the ordinary man in establishing a life style.

Jerrold's sympathy for the problems of the lower middle class was unusually strong, even in a generation that included Dickens and Charles Kingsley. His approach to these problems was influenced by the literary company he kept as a founder of *Punch*. *Punch* set the tone for popular magazine and media comedy in England for the last half of the nineteenth century (and much of the twentieth century). It was the most innovative and successful journal of wit and humor of the time; all others were but imitators or detractors. Remarkable in this is the fact that English comedy was thus influenced by what were fortuitous circumstances attending *Punch*'s establishment. One of the factors setting *Punch*'s tone was the personality of its staff and, particularly, the influence of its reigning literary lion, Thackeray. Thackeray brought to comic journalism of the time those Fieldingesque qualities that so well suited his eighteenth-century tastes—a grand cultural perspective, an expansiveness, a sometimes mordant wit, and an abiding fascination with social pretension in its myriad forms. His delight in cataloguing humbug and affectation and in diagnosing the outward symptoms of social ills formed the nexus between the comedy of the Regency period, when Thackeray first turned his hand to journalism, and that of the Victorian period. If Martin Turnell's observation that British humor directs its wit only toward outward affectations is to hold true, it is probably due to the influence at this stage of Thackeray and the men of a similar sensibility who founded the comic literary journals.

Jerrold did not always hit it off with Thackeray. Jerrold was the greater radical (Thackeray found much of his vitriol excessive) and he was, as we have seen, no advocate of the code of the gentleman. But the descriptions that we have of the founding of *Punch* show that the atmosphere was one of haute bourgeois gentility. It was a clubby group, assembling for their famous editorial dinners, bandying witty remarks, whipping up amateur theatricals, getting on in an elegant way. Shirley Brooks, one of the long-term mainstays, liked to be known primarily as a man about town. And even those who, like the illustrator John Leech, began as critics of the conditions that led to the slums, moved speedily on to the gentility of country sporting scenes. An initial radicalism in *Punch* soon succumbed to a rather waspish and then a bemused tolerance, and the contributors who succeeded the founding journalists were often men like John Tenniel, who had no compelling political positions at all.[41] Jerrold himself, as we noted earlier, began to soften his lines as he developed a greater ability to sketch out social scenes. The rasping, almost tongue-tied prose of his earlier angry pieces was supplanted with a smoother, subtler (and inevitably less biting) manner as he became more novelistic. The movement within the journal during those years was away from reformist criticism toward social observation, from sarcasm toward spoofing wit.

The nature of *Punch* was also determined by the conditions of its time. The audience that it angled after was a reading public made up, as Richard C. Altick tells us, of people whose inclinations could hardly be predicted—clerks, small shopkeepers, the nouveau riche. They were men and women newly established, unsure of their politics and social judgments, rather cautious, materialistic by necessity, unlikely to throw over all they had just acquired for some disruptive political activity. The growth of the magazine audience occurred at the same time as the creation of palpable, satisfying prosperity. The political climate reflected their moderation: Palmerston and Gladstone dominated the scene, and the two major parties moved closer to the center, making any general magazine's political position a rather arbitrary thing indeed. The social historians who look at the mid-century remark on the difficulty of finding clear philosophical positions. Laissez faire and "getting on" were the rallying concepts of the day. Having just completed one of the greatest changes in economic order in man's history, the English were in no mood for additional disruptions.

Indeed, what were really absorbing most people's attention were not grand political and social issues, but immediate domestic concerns. We have ample evidence of Victorian domesticity and the refuge of the home. It is here that the efforts for self-definition were taking place. Economic change brought on a new range of adjustments; affluence necessitated new life styles, and none of the problems had been sufficiently articulated in ways that made them understandable. From our twentieth-century perspective we can recognize the causes of dissatisfaction in unexciting lives—the alienation from real power and influence, the boredom, the atrophy of intense passions. But for the Victorian lower middle-class householder, these were all puzzling and vague sensations, diffuse and highly personal. There is a kind of embarrassed comicality in the half-understood plights of obscure people who are experiencing unreasonable disquiet in what seem to them to be perfectly ordinary circumstances. The light comic vignettes of the popular magazines, through what we now call "situation comedies," drew off some of this vaporous self-confusion and distilled it into a familiar, palatable potion.

Jerrold's "Mrs. Caudle's Curtain Lectures" are the harangues of a lower middle-class housewife, Mrs. Caudle, delivered to her hapless spouse at bedtime each night. Her primary worldly grievance when we first encounter her is Caudle's determination to have a pint each evening at the neighborhood pub with a few of the boys. "It's enough for a wife to sit like Cinderella by the ashes," complains Mrs. Caudle, "whilst her husband can go drinking and singing at a tavern."[44] Caudle, as we can imagine, is harmless enough—pathetically limited, really, in ways of expressing his manly urges for adventure and freedom. Indeed, one of the couple's more ludicrous flaps occurs when Caudle joins the Masonic Order. Mrs. Caudle writhes in anguished speculations of what must go on in "secret" meetings. There could hardly be a more socially conservative way to take one's "mysteries" than in lodge meetings, but Jerrold's "Curtain Lectures" series reflects just that—the settling in to diminished possibilities for individual expression that is characteristic of what we call the petit bourgeois way of life and the strains of such adjustment. The Caudles must express themselves through the fabric of the new post-industrial life—no manic outbursts or "aesthetical" gyrations for them.

Were we to try to define what we mean by the term "bourgeois," we would probably point to something of this nature—a kind of experience that is primarily safe and that poses a minimal threat to personal stability and to social equilibrium; a kind of experience that displays a contraction of imaginative breadth (visible to us in the transition from Pickwickism to Jorrock's jaunts to Caudle's night out with the Masons); and a kind of experience that can be accommodated within the dominant mores of the society. Mrs. Caudle's besetting worry is that timeworn one of propriety, and it is this that she drums into her husband until there is no doubt that it rings in his ears each time he takes a drink and each time he slinks home from the pub. "No: nor I won't have discredit brought upon the house by sending for soda-water early, for all the neighbourhood to see, 'Caudle was drunk last night.' No: I've some regard for the dear children, if you haven't" (205). We know enough of Victorian life to understand that the notorious prudery and love of the home of the lower middle-class people, especially, were necessary indicia of their elevation about the lower classes and of their qualifications to remain there. In a time when the rise in station takes place in a single generation, as it does with the Caudles, the anxiousness over it is quite justifiable.

The Caudles, who steadily ascend during the course of the series from lower middle class to a more solidly comfortable station, experience the advent of our modern economy of mass production and mass consumption. The very magazines in which comedy like Jerrold's appears are beginning to be filled up with advertisements for personal goods. We are familiar enough with the syndrome of stepping-up that this induces, and the Caudles, especially Mrs. Caudle, avidly use it as an outlet for their rather banal fancies. She waxes almost poetic as she contemplates with envy the new livery that Chalkpit, the milkman, has acquired: "He used to drive a green cart; and now he's got a closed yellow carriage, with two large tortoise-shell cats, with their whiskers as if dipt in cream, standing on their hind legs upon each door, with a heap of Latin underneath. You may buy the carriage, if you please, Mr. Caudle; but unless your arms are there, you won't get me to enter it" (279).

From our twentieth-century perspectives, such insights into the bourgeois mentality do not appear particularly perceptive, even if Jerrold was one of the first to turn them into comic material. What is remarkable, though, is Jerrold's ability to penetrate to the affecting pathos of the situation—to catch for a moment, before such domestic comedy sunk into the comforts of its own conventions and unexamined complacency, the psychic desperation of people being irrevocably committed to the social order that Gilbert and Carroll were at least able to fend off through their playful oddities of expression. Jerrold perceives that all the accoutrements and routines of the bourgeois life style that so preoccupy Mrs. Caudle are being rummaged through by her every night as a means of constructing new contexts for a self-expression that she dimly senses is gradually escaping her. Indeed, Mrs. Caudle's nocturnal diatribes serve a purpose beyond keeping her husband in line; they give her the chance to *talk* her way into an understanding of who she is and what she feels. The confusing welter of prejudices and fears, of slanderous opinions and timorous conventionalities, the preoccupation with banal routines of housekeeping—all these constitute a matrix of judgments and interests that form the fabric of her very existence:

> "You hate cold mutton. The more shame for you, Mr. Caudle. I'm sure you've got the stomach of a lord, you have. No, sir; I didn't choose to hash the mutton. It's very easy for you to say hash it; but *I* know what a joint loses in hashing: it's a day's dinner the less, if it's a bit. Yes, I dare say; other people may have puddings with cold mutton. No doubt of it; and other people become bankrupts" (215).

What a marvelous texture there is to Mrs. Caudle's speech. What a readiness to come up with the practical detail, to rally and rout anyone else's position when it comes to domestic matters. But talking down life is not always enough; some things may slip away. The poignant side of Mrs. Caudle's great career of vivid harangues is the haunting sensation that she may be losing touch with what is more important about human life. We are almost surprised when she tells Caudle, "Sometimes at the seaside— especially when the tide's down—I feel so happy: quite as if I could cry" (260). The comment reveals depths of Mrs. Caudle that we didn't think were there. But on reflection, we realize that her nightly berating of Caudle is in part a desperate attempt to establish contact with him. She can only corner him when he is in bed. Caudle has dimensions to his life that his wife cannot share, whether it be business in the city or evenings at the tavern. And Mrs. Caudle senses that her limited existence is relegating her to a position of irrelevance. Her besetting concerns about the house and family and the budget and the neighbors have put things out of proportion. Hers is not the alienation of the "refined" sensibility of a man like Carroll who feels out of step with the march of his time; hers is the terrible isolation of the circumscribed experience and dulled relationships that characterizes small, ordinary lives.

As the "Curtain Lectures" progress, we develop compassion for this shrewish, materialistic woman. Her need to break through to her husband's consciousness grows more acute. She talks about dying before him. Already she imagines Caudle's temptations to remarry, possibly to that scheming neighborhood flirt, Miss Prettyman, and she fears that she will be lost from his memory. In her last lectures, as she suffers from a cold acquired (naturally) from sitting up late in a draught worrying about Caudle, she relentlessly seeks to make a lasting claim upon his memory. The means that she has would seem haplessly inappropriate. She bullies and cajoles, she sinks into self-pity and rises into accusation, all the time trying to build the basis for a lasting attachment out of sentimentality, loyalty, guilt, habit, and, if necessary, out of Caudle's love for domestic order, her pickles, her all-sorts, her well-done mutton-chops—anything. The means for creating an emotional reality from such conventions and such materiality is difficult, but she is a master of strategic use of her resources. And Caudle, after her death, gives not the slightest thought to any Miss Prettyman; "he never ceased to speak of the late partner of his bed but as either 'his sainted creature,' or 'that angel now in heaven' " (296).

The last days of the comic Mrs. Caudle are pathos, of course. Jerrold's "Curtain Lectures" move inexorably, and remarkably swiftly, from social critique into affectionate tolerance and emotional identification. The descent into pathos necessarily accelerates the progression; hence comedy of this sort cannot ultimately maintain its critical edge. Indeed, the English humor tradition, so fond of the pathetic interlude, had been effecting a rather substantial change in the relationship between the reader and the comic subject for almost a century. Traditionally, comedy had been aggressive in manner, a means of upsetting the overbearing and the pretentious and ridiculing aberrant behavior. Its targets had been authoritarian figures holding moral and social power, "blocking characters" in Northrop Frye's formulation. And often their comic characteristics had assumed unreal proportions. Thus, whatever might be a failing common to all men took on grotesque dimensions in these comic targets. We all may share some of the meanness and weakness of a Tartuffe or an Alceste, but nowhere near so completely or so intensely. Their vices and foibles became abstractions. Though there might have been a secret kind of identification with the comic figures' excesses (I suspect there always is) the figures were objectified and removed from us in a way that made them distinctly other people. Whatever one might share of their weaknesses, it was hardly likely that such comic representation ever effectively functioned to relieve or purge its audience of any anxieties about their own behavior. The English humor tradition, however, began gradually to narrow the distance between the reader and the comic targets and their activities. Beginning with Sterne's Walter Shandy, the comic figure tended to be a person whose behavior was more like that of the average man. His excesses were no longer so aberrant, and he himself became less of an abstraction. As one would expect, the tone of such comedy was modulated from ridicule and satiric observation to indulgent humor. By the middle of the nineteenth century, the favorite comic subject was a person much like us, doing the foolish or funny things that any of us might do, and the prevalent tone was soft and benevolent. When such subjects are at stake, the attending emotions are likely to be a certain amount of embarrassment and also a certain amount of sentimentalization— these, after all, are the sorts of things *we* would do. Consequently, the literary effects that are in keeping with such emotional investments are humor and pathos.

The classic nineteenth-century comedy of the ordinary man's ordinary experiences began appearing in serial in *Punch* in the May 26, 1888 issue. The series was later published as a book and has remained in publication to the present day. It is called *The Diary of a Nobody*,[43] written by the brothers George and Weedon Grossmith, and it is their only claim to literary fame (although George Grossmith was a celebrity of his time as the lead in the first productions of several Gilbert and Sullivan operas). *The Diary* is the recollection of events—"adventures" would be too strong a word—in the daily life of a small-time suburban clerk named Charles Pooter. Pooter asks, by way of beginning, "Why should I not publish my diary? I have often seen reminiscences of people I have never even heard of, and I fail to see—because I do not happen to be a 'Somebody'—why my diary should not be interesting." Bolstered by that marvelous ingenuousness, Pooter illustrates that even the most mundane of affairs can offer tonic delights. A typical entry opens on a controversy with the butcher, recounts a debate over the shade of chocolate brown needed to touch up the stairs, and closes with: "planted some mustard-and-cress and radishes, and went to bed at nine." Pooter likes to spend his time around the house, fixing up this and that, maybe trying out Pinkford's new red enamel that is said to work "wonders": it does so nicely on the flower pots that Pooter goes on to paint everything in the maid's room red, then the coal scuttle, the backs of his Shakespeare set, and then—why not?—the inside of the bathtub. Even vacations are spent in the same resort year after year, with old friends like Gowing and the Cummingses near at hand.

Our own pleasures in reading such a book are those of amused self-recognition:

> *April 6.* Eggs for breakfast simply shocking; sent them back to Borset [the butterman] with my compliments, and he needn't call any more for orders. In the evening, hearing someone talking in a loud voice to the servant in the downstairs hall, I went out to see who it was and was surprised to find it was Borset . . . who was both drunk and offensive. Borset, on seeing me, said he would be hanged it he would ever serve City clerks any more—the game wasn't worth the candle. I restrained my feelings, and quietly remarked that I thought it was *possible* for a City clerk to be a *gentleman*. He replied he was very glad to hear it, and wanted to know whether I had ever come across one, for he hadn't. He left the house, slamming the door after him which nearly broke the fanlight; and I heard him fall over the scraper, which made me feel glad I hadn't removed it. When he had gone, I thought of a splendid answer I ought to have given him. However, I will keep it for another occasion (31).

How familiar those little battles are to us; the upshot of a clash with a tradesman can make or break the mood of our entire day. And how galling it is that we, like Pooter, too often come up with that coolly scorching rejoinder only after the moment has passed.

The comedy in *The Diary* verges closely upon our own social apprehensions. In one incident, it is Pooter's friends who lead him, as so often happens, into a humiliating predicament. Pooter, for some reason he cannot quite account for, obligates himself to buy a dozen bottles of wine that he does not want from his old friend Gowing's smooth-talking associate Merton, who claims to be able to get things considerably off price. The only saver in the deal is that Merton assures Pooter that any time he needs theatre passes, he can supply them since his name stands "good for any theatre in London." What better opportunity for Pooter to impress his wife Carrie's friends from the country, the Jameses, than to take them to a play on Merton's passes. Suavely ushering his company into the theatre, Pooter is told by a very rude ticket-taker that not only are Merton's passes utterly worthless but that no one there ever heard of the man. Then, to Pooter's dismay, while he is still exchanging heated words with the management, James goes to the box office and *buys* tickets for the four of them.

> This was humiliating enough, and I could scarcely follow the play, but I was doomed to still further humiliation. I was leaning out of the box, when my tie—a little black bow which fastened on to the stud by means of a new patent—fell into the pit below. A clumsy man not noticing it, had his foot on it for ever so long before he discovered it. He then picked it up and eventually flung it under the next seat in disgust. What with the box incident and the tie, I felt quite miserable. Mr. James, of Sutton, was very good. He said: "Don't worry—no one will notice it with your beard. That is the only advantage of growing one that I can see." There was no occasion for that remark, for Carrie is very proud of my beard.
>
> To hide the absence of the tie I had to keep my chin down the rest of the evening, which caused a pain at the back of my neck (51).

How close to our own most uncomfortable memories. And who has not experienced the anguish of Pooter and Carrie when on another occasion they are invited to the mayor's ball and find that they don't know a soul there—except their local ironmonger to whom they had never before deigned to speak? Or the horrible few moments when Pooter, a guest at the home of an old school friend, observes judiciously of a large picture done in crayons that there is "something about the expression of the face that [is] not quite pleasing. It looks pinched," and the host sorrowfully replies, "Yes, the face was done after death—my wife's sister." And who has not had a dream like Pooter's on the night that he is having his employer, Mr. Perkupp, over to dinner for the first time: that all kinds of low people come to the party without invitation and start throwing things at Mr. Perkupp until Pooter is obliged to hide him in the boxroom with a bath towel over his head?

These times of agony over social gaffes, lapses of taste, and unforeseen humiliations, reveal how closely comedy works with the anxieties that the audience must surely share. The very fact that we laugh sometimes without quite knowing why—almost unexpectedly—suggests that the comic incident may have brought sudden recognition and relief of an anxiety of which we were scarcely conscious. Certainly we are laughing *at* Pooter, whose ineptitude transcends whatever ours might have been, but we are also registering our sense that he is playing out the very social traumas that most of us endure. The kind of comedy in *The Diary of a Nobody*, which treads such familiar home ground, and in which we feel an affectionate identification with the comic characters, is brought into the area of our own emotional experience. Its virtue, its great appeal, is its ability, through obliquity and a light touch, to insinuate us into that inner awareness and release into laughter.

The drift into a comedy of self-recognition is a prominent characteristic of nineteenth-century English literature. It marks the great dividing of the ways of comedy during the last three decades of the century. The division occurs as almost an emotional versus intellectual opposition and it has, as we shall examine in the next chapter, significant *class* connotations. We can see certain inchoate indications of the warring tendencies in Gilbert's nonsense verse, where low-key petit bourgeois sentiments are confounded by an acerbic disengagement. Significantly, Gilbert himself walks away from such problematic verse to his more witty, detached comic opera. Even Jerrold retains a certain amount of detachment, although the encroaching pathos of the Caudles surely charts the evolution toward comedy of involvement and recognition. The Grossmiths, though, write from well within an established comic manner: the foibles of the ordinary little fellow and of the everyday domestic ambiance are well on their way to the favored position in popular culture that domestic comedy and its more sophisticated variants of comedy of the victim or nonhero will occupy for the next century.

When we compare Pooter's world with that of the Caudles thirty years earlier, we can detect some notable changes in emphasis. Pooter devotes a substantially greater portion of his attention to products like Pickford's new red enamel and to the vagaries of fashion. A nation of consumers has become trend conscious and it is preoccupied with the transitory things of modern life.

> The first arrival was Gowing, who, with his usual taste, greeted me with: 'Hullo, Pooter, why your trousers are too short!'
>
> I simply said: 'Very likely, and you will find my temper "*short*" also.'
>
> He said: 'That won't make your trousers longer, Juggins. You should get your missus to put a flounce on them.'
>
> I wonder I waste my time entering his insulting observations in my diary (118).

The 1880s and 1890s were years when style—in dress, behavior, and literature—seemed particularly unstable. Max Beerbohm, in a *Yellow Book* essay on the 1880s, caricatured it as a period of almost manic floridity. Mr. Punch, especially, filled his columns with derisive gibes at fashions. One historian of *Punch* has noted that class consciousness seemed particularly acute then.[44] And alas, it was true that a man or woman betrayed his or her social station in manners and dress. Comedy, at least, could palliate the haunting doubts about the cut of one's clothes and enable one to laugh off the perplexities and disruptions of shifting and often ephemeral social values.

In Pooter's generation, one's eye is no longer on the insecurities of social class. With the economic situation relatively stable, one runs less danger of falling in station. Pooter does not give way, as Mrs. Caudle does, to disquieting thoughts of alienation, of the possible irrelevance of his daily obsessions, and of the diminishment of human communication that seems to be part of a materialistic life. On the contrary, Pooter represents the suburban consciousness, which almost revels in its isolation from the City and from the frenzied great issues of the day. A significant new quality of life is emerging with the unprecedented rate of growth of suburbia. As H. J. Dyos points out in his book *Victorian Suburb*, "the outer ring of suburbs of Greater London grew by about 50 per cent. in each of the three intercensal periods between 1861 and 1891 and by 45 per cent. in the decade 1891-1901." Life in suburbs, as in the Grossmith's rendition of the suburb of Holloway, created an attitude toward one's position in life that is much different from that of the Caudles. The suburb, Dyos suggests:

> is the product of a whole social and economic process set in motion by a curious blend of romantic idealism and hard-headed realism. It was romanticism which created in suburbia the apotheosis of the Englishman's castle. . . . To most middle-class Victorians, and to a rapidly growing proportion of the working classes, the suburb had a meaning which was little less than idyllic. It was not only the seat of respectability but . . . a world of fantasy in which dreams of self-importance and fulfilment could become tangible in the management of some doll's house estate and in the occupation of a unique social niche.[45]

We have also been told, by more than one commentator, that the vitiation of traditional morality began to accelerate significantly during the last two decades of the century. Charles Pooter, however, is debilitated by no such doubts; he never stops to question. He bristles at any discourtesy to Carrie, fumes at his son Lupin's refusal to go to church and his la-de-da attitude toward serious employment, and ruffles with his own sense of dignity through the shambles of pratfalls, slights, put-downs, and gaffes. Pooter's structure of traditional personal values is another larger context against which any instability on the day-to-day level stands in shallow relief. In this respect, *The Diary*'s brand of humor is a far cry from that irreverent older comedy of social attack and change; it is complacent with and protective of middle-class values and strongly conservative.

Shadows nonetheless touch even these rooms of sunlight and glowing hearth. There are moments in *The Diary* when Pooter's complacency can be strained in the debacle of events and the insecurity that is the source of the humor can dizzy him briefly. Son Lupin, who appears to be already anticipating some of the Edwardian insouciance, leads an unsparing assault upon the old way of life; *his* style is casual personal attachments, easy irreverence, fast slangy talk, mod clothes, and heady speculation in shady stocks "simply as a matter of biz—good old biz." So home one night he trots his new friend Burwin-Fosselton, who does imitations of the famous actor Irving. Burwin-Fosselton does his imitations relentlessly, in fact—all evening and all the next evening. And as if it weren't bad enough to have an extended run of Irving imitations in his front parlor, Pooter is suddenly plagued by the most aggravating friend of Gowing's, "a fat and I think, very vulgar-looking man named Padge." Padge comes in, plumps himself down in the best chair in the house, lights up an unusually foul-smelling pipe, and says nothing more, even when addressed, than "That's right." Pooter and Carrie are near despair when, on the third evening:

Of course, Burwin-Fosselton came, but Lupin never turned up, and imagine my utter disgust when that man Padge actually came again, and not even accompanied by Gowing. I was exasperated, and said: "Mr. Padge, this is a *surprise*." Dear Carrie, fearing unpleasantness, said: "Oh! I suppose Mr. Padge has only come to see the other Irving make-up." Mr. Padge said: "That's right," and took the best chair again, from which he never moved the whole evening (134-35).

This is, obviously, the material from which Harold Pinter and others make such ominous comedy: domineering boors and strange, uncommunicative Padges invade one's home, stay forever, monopolize one's time. At these moments, the apprehensions about preserving one's cherished equilibrium can venture close to the surface. Odd things suddenly begin to happen to Pooter: he discovers that someone has been ripping pages out of his diary; Carrie invites her garish friend Mrs. James to give séances in the drawing room; Pooter receives a distinctly insulting Christmas card in the mail. The perspective that is so essential to the comfort of domestic humor—knowing where you are, what values count, what things are important—is lost for a minute. Even games seem to get out of hand: at dinner one night, Lupin and his current fiancée Daisy Mutlar begin throwing rolled-up bread balls at each other, someone pinches out the gas, and Pooter receives a sharp crack on the head. Pooter, suddenly paranoid, suspects a plot to humiliate him: "The person who sent me that insulting postcard at Christmas was here tonight," he tells Carrie ominously. It is alarming how quickly this most devotedly petit bourgeois atmosphere can give way to instants of the grotesque. It seems to suggest a certain uneasiness and catches us all the more off guard because of the psychological commitment we have been induced to make by the easy, gentle manner in which such self-doubts have been treated. Our involvement in domestic humor is not at all like that with mystery stories and ghost stories, which are also often set in the most comfortable and established of circumstances, for in the latter, we deliberately seek the temporary sensations of terror and insecurity; here, we cannot quite adjust to the swift change in feeling. In *The Diary of a Nobody*, this is quickly smoothed over—things never get out of hand; the contexts, values, and motives are still what we understood them to be.

Such contexts and values are essential to the comic effect of works like *The Diary*, for without them the relatively inconsequential anxieties that trigger laughter can get out of hand. Without our sense that Pooter does, for all his occasional obtuseness, keep his domestic problems in perspective, the daily preoccupations and small fears would proliferate and go to seed. Unless the dimensions of his activities are understood against the backdrop of larger social, ethical, and political concerns, they assume uncanny prominence. Pooter's travails would become nightmarish if we believed that the surrounding world of the Grossmiths' book were so different from ours that a sense of proportion was not possible. The insecurities and doubts of Pooter are too much our own; the comic subject matter has been brought dangerously close to home. Happily, though, Charles Pooter has sense enough to style himself a "Nobody" and retains, after all is suffered and done, a good idea of what counts most in life.

The comedy of domestic trials and tribulations is, in fact, comforting. We watch ourselves in a slightly distorted glass, the quaint specimens of the bourgeois world. The saga of a Charles Pooter proves that eccentricity and quirky individualism lives, but within a sphere that is essentially conforming and familiar. Those brief rebellions and occasional losses of dignity are all the more endearing because we share the impulses behind them. A literature of harmless human mediocrity builds up as a kind of analogue to the presumed diminishment in scale of most human lives. From all evidence, the possibilities for enriching self-

expression were no more restricted for most people in the
1880s than they had ever been. We can argue, in fact, that
such possibilities were greater. But rarely before had a culture been able to make limitation and even failure so attractive. As Hugh Duncan notes, the versatility of modern
popular art lies in its ability to accommodate the public
mind to human restrictions that the nature of the social
structure compels.[46]

The middle-class point of view is somewhat more complex than that, however, for accommodation and identification is probably never quite complete. Even as the late
nineteenth-century middle-class reader may laugh from
the pleasures of recognition of Pooter's characteristic foibles, he withholds a certain measure of psychological par-
ticipation in the experience. We have noted, of course, that
Pooter is more obtuse and less self-aware than we suppose
ourselves to be, whatever he may signify about our lives.
But beyond that, Pooter, as do many of the more famous
victimized little people and nonheroes of modern comedy,
demonstrates an impotency in dealing with his circumstances that I suspect a few bourgeois readers of the late
nineteenth century would acknowledge as their own. We
can surmise, in fact, that in responding to all such literature—H. G. Wells' *History of Mr. Polly*, Evelyn Waugh's *Decline and Fall* or *Vile Bodies*, and perhaps Samuel Beckett's
novels and plays—a middle-class reader half-consciously
retains a secret conviction that *he* would not be so impotent
and ineffectual, so lost and buffeted about. And the reader
may nonetheless consciously accept the premise that the
author's account is philosophically true and an essentially
accurate picture of the way life actually is. In other words,
the reader may be so temperamentally skeptical of art that
he can accept its premises while at the same time retaining
a refusal to concede its relevance to *him* individually. Comedy accommodates this ambiguity—provoking laughter of
recognition, inducing acceptance, yet still allowing preservation of one's other visions of self.

The Grossmiths' book furnishes an apt case in point, for it was addressing a middle-class audience that continued to believe that it could make things happen. The middle-class attitude was by its very nature one of self-confidence in the ability of the individual to control his destiny and attain essentially what he aspired to. The agony that Carroll registered in the Alice books is attributed precisely to the assumption that he could and should dominate his situation and to his sense of shame for not being able to do so. Weakness, insufficiency, and failure were inimical to the class self-concept, even as the culture recorded and accommodated people to mere mediocrity. It was one of the most difficult issues that faced the end of the Victorian period. Fatalism and a sense of futility were considered lower-class characteristics. Interestingly, there was a marked increase in literature by and about the lower classes at the end of the century. Much of such literature chronicled the incapacity of the individual to control the course of his welfare. The picture of individual life in the lower-class novel was drawn up into the middle-class comedy of the little man, producing humor of a significantly different ontological viewpoint from *The Diary of a Nobody*. For us to pursue the development of this comedy in the twentieth century and its implications about reader attitudes is obviously beyond the scope of this book. We shall, however, be able to explore other aesthetic responses to the larger issue of faltering middle-class self-image in the works of Samuel Butler and Max Beerbohm in the next two chapters.

6

Meredith and Butler: Comedy as Lyric, High Culture, and the Bourgeois Trap

[He] read deeply in her eyes. He found the man he
sought there, [and] squeezed him passionately.
—*George Meredith*

I

*I*t is inevitable that an exotic type from a
Peacockian dinner party should turn up and say
unnerving things in George Meredith's first major
novel, *The Ordeal of Richard Feverel* (1859). Meredith was
Peacock's son-in-law for a time, and they apparently spent
many a difficult moment with each other. But the two had
genuine literary affinities. Meredith, like Peacock, was the
literary skeptic who always stood outside the dominant cultural tradition. He was, like Peacock, a player with ideas
and a mordant connoisseur of social foibles and Romantic
posturing. They differed in one crucial way, however:
while Peacock's comedy never touched him personally,
Meredith's comedy seems always to have been bound up in
his personal tensions.

The Peacockian figure in *Feverel* is a prematurely cynical
young man named Adrian Harley, "a fat Wise Youth, di-
gesting well: charming after dinner, with men or with
women: soft, dimpled, succulent-looking as a sucking pig:
delightfully sarcastic: perhaps a little too unscrupulous in
his moral tone."[1] He is a figure, in other words, who could

have just adjourned from a dinner at Peacock's Crotchet
Castle, well fed with his own aphorisms and Horatian observations, which are almost never quite comprehensible
but always apropos. Casually, in the mellow effulgence of a
select *digestif*, Adrian makes observations that penetrate the
confusion of the novel's world in a haunting way; and it is
he who proposes what will prove to be the surest insight
into the nature of Meredith's comic impulse: "You shall
find great poets, rare philosophers, night after night on the
broad grin before a row of yellow lights and mouthing
masks [at the comic theatre]. Why? Because all's dark at
home."

The Meredith who is successor to Peacock's manner and
literary position is the first Meredith we see. His fiction, like
Peacock's, is the work of the study. His novels are elaborately wrought, baroque designs of reality that parody and
confound the mainstream English novel's means of presenting life: *Feverel* is a *Bildungsroman* manqué; *The Egoist*, a
stylized social comedy; and *One of Our Conquerors*, an extravagance of psychological drama. The vital action in
these works remains frustratingly outside our grasp, the
motives somehow not correlated with all the dazzling narrative analysis and byplay. We are never quite grounded in
any social actuality. People are posturing; people are haplessly acting out obsessions; people are being obliterated in
the frenetic interaction of ideas and concepts. Over a long
writing career of some sixteen novels and romances,
Meredith never left off being experimental. His works always seemed to be testing something, be it an idea, a new
departure in form, or an obscure psychological state.

And Meredith, the person, emerges, despite his literary
prominence (at the end of the nineteenth century, he was
thought to be the greatest novelist of his generation), as a
latter-day embodiment of the Thomas Love Peacock who
was remote and unreachable during the last decades of his
life. Meredith associated at one time or another with many
of the eminent writers and critics of his day—the Rossettis,

Hardy, John Morley—yet none of them leaves us reminiscences or vignettes that really bring him to life. We are amazed to learn that he once shared lodgings in London with Swinburne. The man of many apparently intimate friendships comes down to us as a strangely guarded, inaccessible figure. A photograph of him in old age captures the enigma of the man: it is the profile of a face that suggests an almost delicate sensitivity—frozen into hauteur. Virginia Woolf, whose father Leslie Stephen was one of Meredith's close friends, recalls Meredith at that time, in his cottage Box Hill:

> Visitors who went down to Box Hill reported that they were thrilled as they walked up the drive of the little suburban house by the sound of a voice booming and reverberating within. The novelist, seated among the usual knick-knacks of the drawing-room, was like the bust of Euripides to look at. Age had worn and sharpened the fine features, but the nose was still acute, the blue eyes still keen and ironical. Though he had sunk immobile into an arm-chair, his aspect was still vigorous and alert. It was true that he was almost stone-deaf, but this was the least of afflictions to one who was scarcely able to keep pace with the rapidity of his own ideas. Since he could not hear what was said to him, he could give himself whole-heartedly to the delights of soliloquy. It did not much matter, perhaps, whether his audience was cultivated or simple. Compliments that would have flattered a duchess were presented with equal ceremony to a child. To neither could he speak the simple language of daily life. But all the time this highly wrought, artificial conversation, with its crystallised phrases and its high-piled metaphors, moved and tossed on a current of laughter. His laugh curled round his sentences as if he himself enjoyed their humorous exaggeration. The master of language was splashing and diving in his element of words.[2]

This is the image of Meredith that we keep—stone-deaf, totally isolated from his puzzled audience, and forever talking. He was the Peacockian dinner guest—preoccupied with his own ideas and speaking wittily to no communicative purpose.

Yet the difference between Meredith and Peacock comes out at once in *The Ordeal of Richard Feverel*. Meredith's comic writings are about feelings and concerns that he has deeply absorbed into his own experience. In fact, Meredith is highly critical of the kind of disengagement that characterizes Peacock. He dismisses it as Epicureanism. Adrian Harley, the transplanted Peacockian figure, functions as a critique of the old man: "The wise youth, then, had the world with him, but no friend. Adrian was an epicurean; one whom Epicurus would have scourged out of his garden, certainly; an epicurean of our modern notions. To satisfy his appetite without rashly staking his character was the wise youth's problem for life. He was a disposer of men: he was polished, luxurious, and happy—at their cost."[3] There is a complex irony in this, as we shall see, for Meredith eventually proposes a theory of comedy that has more than its share of detachment and Epicureanism. But the vital element, the governing drive, of Meredith's comic expression is the personal element—the darkness in the spirit's home.

Feverel and *The Egoist*, Meredith's major comic novels, share the same curious quality: they are explorations of the most devastating experience of Meredith's life, the break-up of his marraige to Mary Ellen Peacock. The precise circumstances of the estrangement are not clear, and the fault difficult to assign. Mary Ellen was widowed before she married Meredith and was six and a half years his senior. She was by all accounts an accomplished, beautiful, sophisticated woman, emancipated by her admiring father from the Victorian woman's submissiveness and introduced through him into literary circles. Meredith was struggling as a poet and then a novelist during their marriage; he had been essentially an orphaned child, raised in Germany, and was presumably solitary and intense even then. Mary Ellen was too frequently pregnant and the one child that survived was a burden because they were poor; she was apparently suffering from what later proved to be a fatal kidney disorder; Meredith demanded to be left alone to write; and old Peacock was no help—the chronicle has its inexorable implications. Mary Ellen fell in love with a family friend, the genteel minor artist Henry Wallis, had Wallis's child, and the two went to Capri. Meredith's response was to seek to "annihilate" her. He refused to allow their son to visit her and never acknowledged her when she came back to England, miserable and sick. The public mask settled on and he never spoke of his emotions during the long years of their breaking up. But for the next twenty years, he continued to search through his feelings, his pain and humiliation, and his motives for the part he played. The sonnet sequence "Modern Love" records the process of marital love turning into resentment; the imagery is of anguish like gaping snakes, of wounded pride lying still like a small frozen bird, and of the terrible, ludicrous posturing of people who cannot communicate.

The Ordeal of Richard Feverel was composed during the years of the marriage's rupture; and there, to our surprise, in the second chapter of the novel, is a recreation of the author's own experience. We are introduced to Sir Austin Feverel, a wealthy baronet who is a thorough, out-and-out misogynist. He is a rather preposterous man who lives by aphorisms that he has gathered into a little book called The Pilgrim's Scrip. And yet, we discover that his experience is Meredith's: for he too had a young wife whose emotional needs he could not adequately respond to; and she too ran off with another man, the poet Diaper Sandoe, leaving Sir Austin with the care of their son. And he too sheathed his pain and humiliation in a hard show of will: he was "a stern cold man, it was said: touched in his Pride—nowhere but there." The novel is a refraction of Meredith's personal experiences in other ways as well. Sir Austin has difficulties raising his son Richard, much as Meredith was said to have had with his boy. Yet Richard is also a reflection of Meredith in some respects, for we know that Richard's resentment of his elders is like Meredith's toward his own parents. And Richard reenacts the drama of male selfishness and irresolution. He treats his young wife abominably and dallies with an older woman—a woman like Mary Ellen, perhaps?—who is worldly and cruel and who betrays his emotions. As if he were pushing shafts deep into the sources of his own nature, Meredith strikes various faces of it; yet, ultimately, we are never quite sure that the dimensions of the subterranean mass are fully gauged. The insights into personal experience do not cohere. They do not adequately chart the deep-lying psychic pattern, nor on the surface is there satisfactory dramatization of the tensions. As V. S. Pritchett remarks, "the weakness of intensely personal novels is that they do not wholly transfigure the personal experience. . . . As shadows, his wife and her lover appear in the novel; so that we are blatantly invited to see that under the comedy there is an unresolved torture and that real life is grimacing unassimilated."[4]

The Ordeal of Richard Feverel thus presents a Krisian venture into the very depths of Meredith's most disturbing, unresolved concerns and a confusing integration of it into literary expression. The problem is attributable in part to the curious interplay that Meredith is trying to achieve in his novel. Not only is he seeking to dramatize, in some partial and perhaps self-protective way, his own emotional conflicts, but he is trying to join together two apparently inconsistent impulses—those of comedy and those of lyricism—in the hope of ultimately finding an adequate expression for those inchoate emotional conflicts.

Feveral is a bewildering virtuoso piece of involution. *The Pilgrim's Scrip*, for instance, houses all the notions about women, ethics, and education that lead to disaster in the novel. Sir Austin's principal failure as a father is set forth immediately: "Sin is an alien element in our blood. . . . To treat Youth as naturally sinful is, therefore, false and bad." Consequently, Sir Austin spoils Richard and leaves him vulnerable to the treachery of experience. Yet if we recall the many accounts of miserable Victorian childhoods that the old Puritan notion of a child's innate predilection for sinfulness produced, we are inclined to think Sir Austin's dogma a refreshing departure. We encounter this sort of paradox repeatedly: ideas that are fundamentally progressive and unconventional engender ludicrous or catastrophic effects. Sir Austin's fondness of theory makes him into a hapless figure of fun, yet the theories are often so close to what we know Meredith himself believed that we are presented with the discomforting spectacle of a man making fun of himself. When we discover, as Gillian Beer has in her research on Meredith, that he in fact kept his own notebook containing many of the same observations that appear in *The Pilgrim's Scrip*—some of them even attributed to "Sir A. Fev."—and did so for several years after the completion of *Feveral*, we are further teased along.[5] What are we to make of the knowledge that many of the positions taken in the *Scrip* are ones Meredith held with apparent conviction much of his life? Sir Austin's entry, rhapsodizing "the ultimate victory of good within us, without which nature has neither music or meaning," accords perfectly with Meredith's meliorism and his sense of the inspiriting powers of nature, visible in much of his poetry. Similarly, the vision by Sir Austin of an Intellectual Aristocracy does not too greatly misrepresent Meredith's thinking, as we shall see in the next section of this chapter. Even the ridiculous poetry of the Wallis figure, Diaper Sandoe, contains some of Meredith's own youthful lines.

This is involution with a vengeance, involution not born, though, as Dickens' is, of the analytical disposition to rework one's artistic motifs. Rather, it is play with literary invention and thought, producing a state of continual imbalance, teaching us to distrust formulations of morality and philosophy and even language itself. It is akin to the laugh that Virginia Woolf describes, curling around Meredith's own expression.

This involution introduces a nervous quality into *Feverel*. Consequently, when moments of intense lyricism arise—and they frequently do—they are often in an intolerable tension with the undercutting comedy. *Feverel* has passages that are utter debacles of ironic counterpoint in romantic expression. Take, for example, the description of Richard musing on the way his first young love, Lucy, looks when she half-closes her eyes:

> Know you those wand-like touches of I know not what, before which our grosser being melts, and we, much as we hope to be in the Awaking, stand etherealized, trembling with new Joy? They come but rarely; rarely even in love, when we fondly think them revelations. Mere sensations they are, doubtless: and we rank for them no higher in the spiritual scale than so many translucent glorious polypi that quiver on the shores, the hues of heaven running through them. Yet in the harvest of our days it is something for the animal to have had such mere fleshly polypian experiences to look back upon, and they give him an horizon—pale seas of luring splendour (177).

Forgiving for a moment the characteristic Meredithian extravagances—the shimmering polypi—we must remark that the passage quivers in its own excesses of sensibility: apparently Meredith does want to evoke something of the epiphanal quality of first love's sensations, but he unrelentingly tears at it with sarcasm and common sense.

It would be easy for us to dismiss this as the ineptitude of an overambitious beginning novelist. Yet I am convinced that something more complicated and sophisticated is going on here. As I said earlier, Meredith wants to find an expression that can be both lyrical and comic. Lyricism is a vital mode of expression for a man who would use literature as a refinement of his own experience. It is a mode that conveys an individual state of feeling or of mind. And it does so in a way that incorporates fluidity, process, attunement with the flow of feeling or intuition. Meredith began his literary career as a poet; and in his poetry and almost all of his fiction, we can observe the effort to capture the nearly epiphanal moments of union with the flux of nature, of transcendence beyond persona and society and present time. If one is to reach beyond pride and self-pity and social inhibition, if one is to break free of the rigid husks of self, only lyricism will suffice.

Lyricism is not a socially referential expression. Nothing annoyed Meredith more than a feeling that was dictated by social concerns, that found outlet only in those charades of behavior that we call social intercourse. Socially referential expression produced sentimentalism and middle-class banality. Lyricism is pure. And this is where it joins functions with comedy. The comic, especially the shrewdly parodic and involuted comedy of a man alert to his own foibles and predilections, is also a purifying agent, reaming out the smug, the sentimental, and the romanticized. In the Prelude to *The Egoist*, Meredith asserts of comedy that "she is the ultimate civilizer, the polisher, a sweet cook. If . . . she watches over sentimentalism with a birchrod, she is not opposed to romance. You may love, and warmly love, as long as you are honest. Do not offend reason."[6] If, unfortunately, comedy and lyricism do not work together in *Feverel*, but rather work at cross-purposes, the novel nonetheless breaks new ground. Meredith will not go along the road that Dickens briefly explored, and that Carroll and others seemed to travel, toward a romanticized green world where comedy often seemed to become puerile and escapist. Instead, he attempts to achieve a mode of self-expression that is self-critical while it is expansive, and that can be a means of refining the uniquely individual complex of emotions, anxieties, and yearnings that energizes his art.

With his other major comic novel, *The Egoist* (1879), he comes closer to realizing his objectives.

The Egoist is a drama of the struggle between Clara Middleton, a young woman who has fallen into a loveless engagement, and her fiancé, the egoist, Sir Willoughby Patterne, a young aristocrat. In the course of the novel, Clara discovers that she does not love Sir Willoughby; indeed, she comes to loathe him for his distasteful possessiveness. The dynamic of the story is the internal struggle of Clara to discover the strength and integrity within herself to break from her fiancé's clutches, a bold move for any young woman of the Victorian era, for it risks scandal. As Clara wrenches herself free, Sir Willoughby holds on more desperately, not wanting to face the hidden horror of a devastating wound to his exceedingly tender pride. Meredith reenacts again in his fiction the traumas of his own past, delving once more into the psychology of estrangement, humiliation, and self-pity.

In *The Egoist*, however, Meredith's control of his techniques and his perception of the human situation is surer than it was in *Feverel*. The elements of the comic vision emerge with a purity and force that is rare in nineteenth-century literature. Clara's struggle is clearly one toward freedom, openness to life's flow, liberation from the restricting conventions of her society. The rhythm of the novel accords with the primary rhythm of comedy—the breaking down of fictions that have become ossified and rigid, the acceptance of life's contingency and the invocation at novel's end of a pattern of existence that allows for individual constructs that are truly fictions, temporary, clear-sighted, dissoluble. And now Meredith's concept of lyricism accords with his comic vision, for Clara's near-epiphanal moments of lyric experience and transcendence awaken her to the need to be liberated, to be at one with nature's flow. On one occasion, Clara, still confused and distraught, observes the young man Vernon Whitford, one of the few relatively free spirits in the novel, sleeping under a cherry tree in blossom. The lyricism of Clara's perception of what Vernon stands for can now be expressed in a prose that is free from nervous self-consciousness:

> She turned her face to where the load of virginal blossom, whiter than summer-cloud on the sky, showered and drooped and clustered so thick as to claim colour and seem, like higher Alpine snows in noon-sunlight, a flush of white. From deep to deeper heavens of white, her eyes perched and scanned. Wonder lived in her. Happiness in the beauty of the tree pressed to supplant it, and was more mortal and narrower. Reflection came, contracting her vision and weighing her to earth. Her reflection was: "He must be good who loves to lie and sleep beneath the branches of this tree!" (94).

Again, when Clara is near defeat, ready to succumb to society's pressure to conform, she looks upon the dawn and takes new heart from her lyrical communion with nature:

> The lovely morning breathed of sweet earth into her open window and made it painful, in the dense twitter, chirp, cheep, and song of the air to resist the innocent intoxication. O to love! (96).

Such lyrical impulses move through a novelistic setting that is curiously structured. *The Egoist* adheres to the unities of the old drama: it is confined to one setting for the most part, Patterne Hall and its grounds, to a limited time period, to a tightly drawn cast of characters, and to a single human issue. The movement of people in the novel is mannered, and the narrator frequently calls attention to the minuetlike meeting and withdrawal of partners, the sweeping of Clara from hand to hand, the divisions of the company into balanced groups. We come upon Sir Willoughby on the veranda of Patterne Hall, "tripping, dancing, exactly balancing himself, head to right, head to left, addressing his idolaters in phrases of perfect choice." He is "rich, handsome, courteous, generous, lord of the Hall, the feast and the dance." His role resembles that of an elegantly plumed figure in a highly civilized, but also icily rigidified, mating dance: "to play incessantly on the first reclaiming chord which led our ancestral satyr to the measures of the dance, the threading of the maze, and the setting conformably to his partner before it was accorded to him to spin her with both hands." The novel, though set in contemporary England, endeavors to reproduce the quality of another age, one that is baroque, formal, ostensibly more elegant. We are explicitly recalled to the French-influenced Restoration court of Charles II, to that brief efflorescence of wickedly sophisticated comedy that defied the English Puritan bent. The narrator, expanding on a casual remark that Sir Willoughby is a man with a "fine leg," half-seriously muses of the time, "through mournful veneration of the Martyr Charles, a coy attachment to the Court of his Merrie Son, where the leg was ribanded with love-knots and reigned. Oh! it was a naughty Court. Yet we have dreamed of it as the period when an English cavalier was grace incarnate" (13). Sir Willoughby, astride his horse Black Norman, reminds one of a figure of "the old French court. . . . He did not wish the period revived, but reserved it as a garden to stray into when he was in the mood for displaying elegance and brightness" (112). Thus, half-teasingly through such allusions, and more concretely through the manner of Patterne society, the novel acquires a highly stylized fabric. The sphere in which the comic impulse toward flux and openness must operate is one of ceremony and a special kind of social expression.

Meredith's objective is not to recreate a latter-day Restoration Comedy. Indeed, he criticized that period of English drama for its licentiousness and lack of feeling in "An Essay on Comedy," delivered shortly before the publication of *The Egoist*. But Meredith defined comedy in the first

line of the novel's Prelude as "a game played to throw reflections upon social life, . . . it deals with human nature in
the drawing-room of civilized men and women." *The Egoist*
intends to demonstrate the classic dynamics of comedy—
freedom versus containment, and openness versus form.
Meredith's significant departure from other writers of the
Victorian period is marked by his realization that the highest satisfactions for a civilized audience come when the
comic impulses work within a contained pattern of artistic
and social form. Meredith revives the pleasures of comic
celebration, pleasures so little in evidence in English
humor's individualistic, erratic solo song or in the irreverent slashings of satire. Comedy, with its origins in rites of
spring, with its long tradition of formal expression in
drama from Aristophanes through Molière, carries added
power and added human satisfaction when its impetus for
the anarchic and freewheeling can find scope within a contained aesthetic mode. Then the full release of comedy's
dissolving force can be implied, but can be balanced by the
gratifications of control. The spring winds tighter in the
watchcases of artistic discipline.

Finally, the setting and manner of the novel also carry
implications about cultural position. Sir Willoughby's
milieu is that of aristocracy in effete decline; Clara's temperament is that of the middle class who would shape their
own way. Molière's comedy can attribute part of its greatness, Meredith asserts in the "Essay," to a similar social
conflict.

[Louis XIV] was a boon to the comic poet. He had that
lively quicksilver world of the animalcule passions, the
huge pretensions, the placid absurdities. . . . A simply
bourgeois circle will not furnish it, for the middle class
must have the brilliant, flippant, independent upper for
a spur and a pattern; otherwise it is as likely to be in-
wardly dull as well as outwardly correct. Yet . . . it is not
to the French Court that we are indebted for [Molière's]

unrivaled studies of mankind in society. . . . In all countries the middle class represents the public which, fighting the world, and with a good footing in the fight, knows the world best.[7]

It is vital, if we are to understand *The Egoist* and Meredith's writings on comedy, that we appreciate his setting for the novel. The mannered movement and baroque quality of the book are not further instances of Meredithian excess; they are integral elements of the comic operation.

Thematically, of course, Sir Willoughby's "courtly" world does not carry such rich connotations. It is the society of complacent self-absorption, the petrification of social fictions into snobbery, vanity, boorishness. Sir Willoughby represents a mentality that is the deadliest of the English. He thrives on British adulation of rank and privilege and converts the national pride in self-sufficiency and independence into the vice of insularity. It is a case of a fiction hardening into a self-serving myth, and Meredith makes clear how much of this rests on haute bourgeois fondness for moribund ways of life. Willoughby sets himself up as a prince in the old patrician manner and corrupts the long outdated virtues of the English gentry. He wants to absorb Clara into a marriage that will be entirely isolated from life's give and take. Hypocritically pretending to dislike public weddings, he reveals his fundamental rigidity: "If we might say the words and pass from sight! There is a way of cutting off the world." Clara, on the other hand, praises the living world, "I am sure it is our duty to love it" (52). The narrator reveals Sir Willoughby's genuine hostility toward experience:

> This was the ground of his hatred of the world: it was an appalling fear on behalf of his naked eidolon, the tender infant Self swaddled in his name before the world, for which he felt as the most highly civilized of men alone can feel, and which it was impossible for him to stretch out hands to protect (233).

Remembering for a moment that this is very likely some-thing of his own past egoism and protectiveness that Meredith is describing, we can discern how tightly the comic operation is bound up with the process of personal insight. Society may be the arena in which comedy per-forms, and celebration may be an aspect of its effect, but comedy's workings here are psychological in a way that could not have been true of Molière. Almost everything that transpires in *The Egoist* is linked to an emotional and mental process. Clara's struggle against the rigid social order and her movement toward the flux of the "real world" is representative of the comic vision in its broader aspects, certainly; but characteristic of Meredith as an artist is the concentrated psychological dramatization of it. He came to comedy as a way of discovering his own motives and feelings; he employed comedy in his novels as a proc-ess of self-discovery.

The subtlety of Clara's drama, therefore, derives from our realization that this is not simply a story of will toward freedom in the face of social tyranny, nor a story of the natural versus the artificial, but the charting of Clara's state of mind as she discovers her own desires and powers. Clara has "fallen into" betrothal at the beginning of the book without recollecting exactly how or why—"in a dream somehow." She soon becomes aware of the vaporousness in Sir Willoughby's manner, but for some time we observe her "vainly sounding for the source and drift" of what she senses. When Willoughby whispers "come," an inexplicable "lightning terror" shoots through her. Clara cannot under-stand why she all of a sudden develops an irresistible urge to yawn, to drift off in aimless thought when her fiancé talks with her: "She compressed her lips. The yawn would come" (83). And the "glorious" infinity of love that Wil-loughby describes for the two of them raises in her the per-verse image of "a narrow dwelling where a voice droned and ceased not" (39). Such queer tricks of her mind are signals from her unconscious that her marriage to Willoughby would be unending sleep, a death in life. Yet at the same time, she is inclined just to give in to him. Meredith's imagery grows more explicit; on two occasions Clara feels a chill "as if someone were walking over my grave." And ironically, it is Willoughby who haplessly makes the connection for her. "Most marriages ought to be celebrated with the funeral knell," he says, to her amazement. On another occasion, he presses her to pledge that she will be faithful to him should he die before her and inadvertently alludes to the practice of Suttee in which the widow throws herself on her husband's funeral pyre. Then, what had seemed previously to be lover's talk about the two of them becoming one is understood in its true light. Sir Willoughby is gripped in a clear Freudian narcissistic condition; his "sexual overestimation" of Clara is simply a means of reflecting back his love of himself. Clara had sensed this relatively early in their relationship:

> She would not burn the world for him; she would not, though a purer poetry is little imaginable, reduce herself to ashes, or incense, or essence, in honour of him, and so, by love's transmutation, literally be the man she was to marry (40).

But she is slower in perceiving that there is within her an equally strong and deadly pull to acquiesce. She is gripped with what she calls, "a sense of shame at my natural weakness" (131). Through her lack of nerve, she evades what her inner impulses have been telling her. "The false course she had taken through sophistical cowardice appalled the girl; she was lost" (163).

The comic vision, which opens up our capacity for seeing life as contingent and enables us to establish those personal fictions that give us freedom rather than bondage, is in Meredith's novel a vision that develops only with the understanding of our own psychic dispositions toward death in life, toward stasis. Clara Middleton's drama illustrates the importance of that insight, especially in women, who are, in Meredith's opinion, particularly predisposed by their culture and position to cowardice and sentimentality. This accounts for the stress that Meredith places in his "Essay" on the necessity for an audience of cultivated women to receive comedy. The workings of comic analysis are tough and intellectual; comedy teaches women to see in ways that are not falsely emotional: "the heroines of comedy are like women of the world, not necessarily heartless from being clear-sighted; they seem so to the sentimentally reared, only for the reason that they use their wits, and are not wandering vessels crying for a captain or a pilot" (15).

The other side of the comic vision in *The Egoist* is more difficult to explain. That is the portrayal of Sir Willoughby, the symbol of rigidity and the old dead ways. He is more than just a symbol; he is a characterization of remarkable intensity. He has a grotesque force, prancing through the story like some hallucinating specter of maleness. Characters—and readers—confess to being "baffled, from not knowing the heart in the centre of him." He is, and is treated as, a specimen. The light on him is harsh and penetrating; the faults of the man, faults presumably that Meredith found once in himself, are writ uncommonly large, in bold caricaturing strokes. For many a reader, the absorption of Sir Willoughby in his self-pity, in his protectiveness, and in his gargoyle of a manner has seemed to be obsessive.

The characterization of Sir Willoughby can best be explained by the poetic disposition of his creator. It is a disposition that compels Meredith to intensify his creations into essences of the nature they embody. (Meredith spoke admiringly in his "Essay" of Shakespeare's "poetically comic" characters like Jacques, Falstaff, and Benedick, who have what he called more "blood life" than ordinary figures of literature.) As we have noted, *The Egoist*, and specifically the portrait of Sir Willoughby, display the achievement that Meredith fell confusingly short of in *The Ordeal of*

Richard Feverel—the joining of the comic and of the lyric. Meredith seeks to bring certain of his comic creations to the kind of agonizing and exhilarating self-expression that lyrical poetry reaches. He strives to depict the quintessential state of mind and feeling. In the "Essay," Meredith praises a comic work because in it "we feel the power of the poet's creation; and, in the sharp light of that sudden turn, the humanity is livelier than any realistic work can make it" (29). He cites Menander and Molière as "comic poets of the feelings and the idea. In each of them there is a conception of the comic that refines even to pain. . . . These two poets idealized upon life; the foundation of their types is real and in the quick." The Prelude to *The Egoist* further defines the objective of comedy: comedy "condenses whole sections of the Book [of Life] in a sentence, volumes in a character" (6); comedy is "the inward mirror, the embracing and condensing spirit . . . required to give us those interminable mile-post piles of matter . . . in essense, in chosen samples" (5). The characterization of Sir Willoughby constitutes the distilled essence of the state of mind that was Meredith's own in his months of trauma, doubt, and egoism; he is the comic rendition of that state, heightened to lyric intensity.

Meredith brings the powers of comedy into such intimate expression because comedy promotes intellectual detachment; it is the mode for dispassionate treatment of volatile material. Beyond that, the comic bent is to exaggerate, to heighten the actuality, and to pare away the ambiguousness of circumstance in order that we may get the subject in its sharpest, most ridiculous outlines. Comedy, for Meredith, lent itself to the conceptual. But further, comedy was the means that he and many others before him used to explore the uncanny, forbidden areas of the human psyche. It enabled him to divulge the quirky, almost manic impulses that nineteenth-century psychology had no terminology or framework for. Therein lies one of the great objectives of Meredith's art—to prompt his audience to new valuations of human behavior by showing them the unique transmutations of the individual mind.

Robert Langbaum's description of the "poetry of experience" as exemplified by Meredith's contemporaries Robert Browning and Alfred Lord Tennyson provides a useful insight into Meredith's objectives in works like *The Egoist*. Langbaum suggests that the objective of such poetry, which often takes the form of the dramatic monologue, is to "awaken fresh responses that exceed formulation." Such a poem communicates not a general truth but a particular experience. It is the modern disposition, Langbaum argues, to believe less in accepted moral and emotional truths and more in the notion that there are only perspectives toward truth. We come to expressions like that of *The Egoist* with the assumption that human situations are problematical and will remain so, but with the determination to learn "the perceptive or genetic process, to learn the psychology and situation in which ideas are perceived or generated." Hence the expression may be highly subjective in its presentation, as Meredith's is of the process of his own traumatic response, but nonetheless objective in its rendition of the nature and form of a problematical situation. Intriguingly, the characteristic subject matter of the poetry of experience of Browning and Tennyson, of their dramatic monologues, is comprised of extraordinary moral positions and extraordinary emotions. Langbaum notes, "Most successful dramatic monologues deal with speakers who are in some way reprehensible . . . characters who have taken up their extraordinary positions through an act of will."[8]

The direction taken by Meredith toward the presentation of intensely dramatized and psychologically oriented individual experiences as a perspective on the truths of the human situation diverges significantly from the pattern of nineteenth-century comic literature that we noted in the 1830s and 1840s. Meredith's comedy can scarcely be called sociological in the sense that such earlier comedy had been, because it attempted to delineate the broader outlines of social classes and groups and it served the need of the middle class for sustaining myths. We have already observed the more subjective inclinations of comedy in late Dickens and in Carroll and Gilbert. Much of their expression was ambivalent, however, in the face of the dominant social order and the success of English middle-class culture. Meredith's is not. Meredith is critical of that culture and he is generally uninhibited by considerations of it. As we shall examine in the next section of this chapter, Meredith is one of the principal figures in a generation of literary men who sought to establish a cultural outlook that was not determined by the materialistic conventions of the bourgeois majority.

The Egoist does not succeed, finally, in establishing the detached perspective on problematical reality because of the very intensity of Meredith's treatment of such personally charged experience. Meredith once said that "to know oneself is more a matter of will than insight," and we sense that Sir Willoughby is too much a creation of will. Meredith's understanding of his own faults in his relationship with Mary Ellen never seems to have simply come forth in quiet moments of reflection or honesty or regret; the subject always seems to have been an obsession. Apparently it brought him no rest until he could *drive* the motives and weaknesses out into the open with the lashes of comic wit. Consequently, we witness, with a certain horror as civilized readers, the excoriation of the old Meredithian husk Sir Willoughby Patterne. In the final chapters of the novel, Sir Willoughby is a galvanic puppet trying to jerk the strings of his own predicament. He is likened to an insect or spider; his arm contracts sharply, the muscles of his mouth pull back "sourly" showing his underteeth; he has stretching fits that terminate in violent shakes of the body and limbs; and at one point he involuntarily flaps his arms "resembling for the moment those birds of enormous body

which attempt a rise upon their wings and achieve a hop"
(399). There are grinning imps of ridicule, Meredith tells
us in the Prelude to the book, that surround the wounded
game of the exposed egoist and jeer at him. The imps are
projections of the paranoia of the jilted lover, the voices
outside that Sir Willoughby fears above all things.

Where, we might ask, is the spirit of disengaged comic
analysis that Meredith describes in the "Essay?" The late
nineteenth-century literary figure William Ernest Henley
said it well: "Meredith writes with the pen of a great artist
in one hand and the razor of a spiritual suicide in the
other." The portrait of Sir Willoughby exceeds its presumed objective as a presentation of the quintessence of
male human nature in a certain stressful position. It relentlessly extends the dimensions of a human nightmare.
Various explanations come to mind for such a thoroughgoing denunciation of what must once have been, in some
form, the author's own thoughts and feelings. Perhaps by
cutting up his effigy so, Meredith assumes he can achieve
absolution. Perhaps this is another of that coldly contained
man's protective diversions. Perhaps he is giving in to the
temptations he described in a letter to his good friend William Maxse: "Much of my strength lies in painting morbid
emotion and exceptional positions; but my conscience will
not let me so waste my time. My love is . . . not for cobwebs
in a putrid corner; though I know the fascination of un-
ravelling them."[9] None of these explanations quite satisfies
us. The crucial connections between the author's state of
mind and the literary product are absent.

Similarly, we must admit that in spite of the brilliance
and boldness of the novel's conception, the crucial connection between the novel's operations and its stated objective
of prompting refined, perceptive self-analysis in a cultivated reading audience is probably not made. *The Egoist*
was for its time, and for all of us since, a difficult book. The
critic Dorothy Van Ghent complained in a famous essay
that the transference of the meaning we perceive in the

novel to ordinary experience is nearly impossible.[1] She, however, was asking of *The Egoist* that it present an integrated *social* picture, and we know that such was not Meredith's intention. Rather, it is a way of looking at oneself and one's experience, a way of thinking, a skeptical but open disposition, a unique *cultural* quality that Meredith sought to instill in his audience. It is questionable whether this quality can be inculcated in the reader by a novel so intense in its dissections and abstract in its setting and methods. We need, however, to explore the cultural outlook that Meredith had come to share in the 1870s before we can fully understand the nature of the difficulties we have with his comic masterpiece.

"You mean, then . . . that a man of the highest culture is a sort of emotional *bon vivant?*"
—*Miss Merton*

I I

In 1877, two years before the first publication of *The Egoist*, George Meredith read a paper on "The Idea of Comedy and the Uses of the Comic Spirit" to the London Institution. It has been subsequently published as "An Essay on Comedy," and read and widely quoted to the confusion of thousands of people who find it incomprehensible. In this essay, we have the most extended statement of comic theory in the nineteenth century—by a major comic artist—and at times, it appears to be chiefly a long expostulation, a chance for Meredith to indulge in his love of high flown rhetoric. His principal point is clear enough: the English are overdue for dispassionate, cultivated comedy. The message of the "Essay" is the same as that of the Prelude to *The Egoist* in which he talks of the comic as the "ultimate civilizer." "The comic is a different spirit" from

English humor and satire: "the laughter of comedy is impersonal and of unrivaled politeness, nearer a smile—often no more than a smile. It laughs through the mind, for the mind directs it; and it might be called the humor of the mind" (47).

But how are we to reconcile this concept of a generous, capacious, primarily intellectual comedy with the relentless dissection of Sir Willoughby, or with our observation that so much of Meredith's comedy comes from the probing of his own sensibility's darker realms? Indeed, one discovers in the "Essay" itself glimpses of the more malignant animus in Meredith. The Comic Spirit "has the sage's brows, and the sunny malice of a faun lurks at the corners of the half-closed lips drawn in an idle wariness of half-tension." "The slim feasting smile" of the Spirit is called "humanely malign." And when we are told, "you will, in fact, be standing in the peculiar oblique beam of light, yourself illuminated to the general eye as the very object of chase and doomed quarry of the thing obscure to you" (47-48), we recognize the compulsion to self-dissect that makes Meredith's own comic explorations so punishing. Yet there is a strangely complex consistency here. Meredith is saying that only the acutely self-aware can be "civilized." The comic operation requires a special quickening of sensibility, acquired by the reaming of one's own emotions and beliefs by sharp comic tools, before it can attain to the civilizing enlightenment that the culture so desperately needs. Comedy's objectivity proceeds from the sensitizing of the self.

Still, we wonder how one can accommodate these strains—on the one hand, a comic operation that is basically self-analytical, a lyricizing of what are often uniquely composed, sometimes aberrant, individual expressions; and on the other hand, a critical theory that calls for dispassionateness and cultural perspective. We wonder, given the broadly uplifting meliorist tone of Meredith's "Essay," whether it is not indeed largely rhetorical. Ultimately, the cultural context must account for this piece of comic theory. It is a classic instance of the point I made in this book's Introduction: comic expressions can only be understood fully in their literary and social contexts. "An Essay on Comedy" is as much an essay on culture as on comedy. It is a document of the "high culture" movement of the 1870s and 1880s, a concerted attempt to define "culture" as a set of ideals of judgment, taste, and action that surmount the crass, materialistic, mundane processes of ordinary life, as a means of introducing into English life the perspective afforded by the best that has been thought and done in human history. Matthew Arnold's *Culture and Anarchy*, which appeared in 1869, is the most famous statement of the position. And Walter Pater, whose influence peaked in the 1870s and 1880s, was vitally instrumental in attracting a significant group of intellectuals and artists toward high culture. Meredith's "Essay" acquires coherence and cultural relevance when we examine it in terms of Arnold's and Pater's thought. And, paradoxically, the easiest way to understand the "Essay" seems to be through the harshest and most pertinacious criticisms that were made of the high culture movement.

Three sorts of accusations have been levied against Arnold's and Pater's position, and the first points directly to Meredith's emphasis upon the quickening of individual sensibilities as the way to refined comedy. The favorite ground for dismissing high culture was that it was an idealization of the sensuality and aestheticism that Arnold and particularly Pater loved so well. All that lofty discourse was about refinement, all right, but the refinement of the two men's sensuous experience, merely an elevation into dogma of a hedonistic taste for the "aesthetic moment." Although such hostile characterizations are unfair, it is in part true, as Raymond Williams notes, that culture in Arnold's and Pater's hands referred "back to an area of personal and apparently private experience."[11] The crucial point, though, is that both men, like Meredith, were trying to achieve a synthesis of intensified subjectivity with a more altruistic ideal. David J. DeLaura, in his studies of Arnold and Pater in *Hebrew and Hellene*, defines Pater's struggle as one to reconcile the dialectic of the "Apollonian vs. Dionysian, one tending toward realization of an inward, intellectual idea, more sensuous, the other for order, sanity, proportion."[12] Pater could not ask himself or his followers to forsake the awakening, the keening of individual natures that was essential to full awareness, yet he was plainly troubled by the widespread contention that this led only to a personal philosophy of sensualism and absorption with one's own feelings and moods.

The burden of attaining such a synthesis seemed greater because Pater was conscious of the charges that had been made about Arnold's cultural writings being simply elevated justifications for "hedonism, aestheticism, uselessness, and self-centredness." And Pater could never quite shake off the popular indictments against him—Pater, the Oxford don, poisoning the springs of young minds with his potions of distilled sensuality. The most celebrated caricature of Pater appeared in a Peacockian novel, *The New Republic* (1877), by William H. Mallock (himself an intriguing casualty of the high culture movement of the period). In a series of extended debates by thinly-disguised caricatures of the "great thinkers" of the time on such topics as the "Aim of Life" and the "ideal New Republic," Mallock's stand-in for Matthew Arnold stentoriously pronounces that "culture is the union of two things—fastidious taste and liberal sympathy." The character representing Pater flutters precariously on the edge of the discussion, a hummingbird of sensuality: "I would compare the man of culture to an Aeolian harp," he says at one point, "which the winds at will play through—a beautiful face, a rainbow, a ruined temple, a death-bed, or a line of poetry, wandering in like a breath of air amongst the chords of his soul, touching note after note into soft music, and at last gently dying away into silence."[13]

Raymond Williams points out that it is inevitable that any

cultural position should also be entwined with an artistic position. "Aesthetic and social judgments are closely inter-related," in English thought in the nineteenth century—in Ruskin's writings and in Pugin's architectural theory, to cite two examples.[14] The merger generally took the form of arguments for the need to introduce moral considerations of the society into its art. But Pater and Arnold—and to a certain extent, Meredith—were reversing that proposition. They proposed that the society should inform its culture through its aesthetics. As DeLaura establishes in his book, an evolution took place by which the "conservative humanism" of Cardinal Newman was converted into the "fluid, relativistic, and 'aesthetic' humanism of Pater."[15] The shift of direction (for it is that, rather than a mere shift of emphasis) is a highly important one; it not only worked to liberate art from Victorian moralism but it took into account the new perception of human experience that we observed in Meredith's comic writings—the perception of it as fluid and relativistic. Meredith's interest in the problematical quality of human nature accords with Pater's invocations to become highly responsive and treat experience as an end in itself. Both men began with a highly sensitized aesthetic in the belief that only in this way can one's mind and feelings register fleeting and metamorphosing experience. Hence, both the highly self-conscious (sometimes even morbid) sensitivity to the moment and the posture of openness and receptivity that is the cultural ideal can be reconciled. In a world of flux, the latter can only proceed from the former.

The second general criticism made of the high culture movement of the 1870s and 1880s followed from the very emphasis that Pater, Arnold, and others put upon savoring experience and upon breadth of vision. The art historian Arnold Hauser, charting the social history of Impressionism during the later decades of the nineteenth century in Europe, observes that any aesthetic position that places stress upon personal receptivity to impressions, upon the transitoriness of phenomena, and upon the truth of the moment of apprehension inspires a passive approach to life. The artist acquiesces in the role of spectator.[16] He becomes a sampler of experience, a philosopher-poet. This complaint was made of the entire generation of artists and philosophers who adhered to a position close to Pater's and Arnold's. The term "Epicurean"—a term that for many centuries had held both positive and negative connotations—surfaced with intriguing frequency during the period. We recall that the dilettantish, disengaged Adrian Harley in *The Ordeal of Richard Feverel* was characterized negatively as an Epicure. Pater quite obviously uses the term more ambivalently in *Marius the Epicurean*. "Epicurean" describes the pleasure-lover, the "emotional *bon vivant*"; but more crucially, it implies a detachment from the give-and-take of ordinary life. As we shall develop in our discussion of Samuel Butler in the next section of this chapter, a disposition toward stoicism and self-distancing was already present in many late century writers; Epicureanism gave it a certain elevated and refined twist.

The consequences that such a stance might hold for the ability of art to affect its audience is of special significance to our concerns here. First of all, it may induce in writers a social vision that is removed from the actuality of the times, that lacks concreteness. Raymond Williams attributes the difficulty that Arnold encountered in implementing his cultural doctrines to the absence of any vividly apprehensible, compelling social model. Edmund Burke had been able to draw upon an existing social order as a ground for his thinking about culture; Coleridge upon the recent image of such a society; Cardinal Newman upon his vision of divine order; but Arnold, distanced from any such society, and secular, had no such model to draw upon, and his ideas became abstractions. "Culture," as defined by Arnold, ineluctably develops into an aspect of "feeling" and "knowing" rather than an aspect of "doing."[17] Culture becomes "poise" in both senses of the word.

We notice the same lack of social concreteness, the same detachment from the normal order of experience in the concept of civilizing comedy in Meredith's "Essay." Judith Wilt, in her study *The Readable People of George Meredith*, advances a valuable argument about Meredith's literary objectives that ties in with our observations about his cultural position. She contends that a great deal of the ordinary reader's difficulty with Meredith arises from the fact that he is not directing his prose to the *ordinary* reader at all but is attempting to cultivate an audience of sophisticated, extraordinary readers. "Meredith," she says, "like many another artist, was convinced that he was at the expanding frontier of a civilization ready in the near future to fulfill itself." He addresses, therefore, a special audience that can apprehend his edited "texts" or "books" for interpreting life. His "anticipated community of homo *legens* . . . [consists] of minds in . . . a stance whose qualities are capaciousness born of distance, sympathy born of analysis, skepticism born of the experience of the malleability of reality, the story, the intuition, the Book. This is the mind that Meredith calls philosophic."[18] Wilt goes on, however, to wrestle with a criticism made by Sartre of English comic literature, that it "perpetrated the falsehood of tranquillity, absoluteness, the noncontingency of existence right at the crucial period of the forming of the bourgeoisie, and hence became its tool, promoting the editing and reading of experience rather than experiencing itself." After pointing out that it is doubtful whether any fiction can give the reader more than an interpretation or "editing" of experience, Wilt nonetheless concedes that "in fact, Meredith comes close sometimes to describing . . . the novel as an addiction to thought, promoting [thought] at the expense of [action] out of some naive faith that the simple multiplication of thoughtfulness in the world solves problems" (37,

40). Surely one cause of Meredith's difficulty in attaining a wide general readership is the disposition of his work to fulfill itself in the presentation of "its idea." We find it difficult to make the necessary connections between the portrait of an Austin Feverel or a Willoughby Patterne and ourselves; we cannot achieve the vital relationship with them as "living" beings, as we can with some other writers' characters. It is the only explanation for the curious paradox of Meredith's closing observations in the "Essay," in which, after extolling comedy's power to break through the false forms of the social order, he goes on to complain about the "directness of the study of actual life" in contemporary French comedy. The French writer, Meredith contends, "has but painted from the life; he leaves his audience to the reflections of unphilosophic minds upon life" (55-56). Comic art, in Meredith's concept, must be, above all, "philosophic."

The case of Meredith's contemporary William Mallock becomes poignantly instructive here. The humor of *The New Republic* and Mallock's later satire *The New Paul and Virginia, or Positivism on an Island* very clearly induces what Meredith calls "laughter of the mind." By his own account, Mallock modeled his works on those of Peacock, but with a significant difference. Where Peacock's motif is the inability of his thinkers and visionaries to translate their ideas into action, Mallock portrays a body of intellectuals who are not in the least concerned with the realm of action. His people are content with their ideas and sometimes with just the sounds of their ideas. If the works of Peacock and Mallock can be taken as reasonably accurate representations of English intelligentsia at different periods of the century, then a crucial estrangement from the practical sphere has taken place. Comic art itself reflects the change, for it concentrates not on the disparity between thought and action, but on isolated thought itself. Mallock seems to have been close enough to the dispositions of the figures whom he parodied to understand their substantial difference from the generation of Shelley and Coleridge; and he adjusts his comedy in a way that corresponds with that difference. And Mallock himself, with brains and wit enough to be a devastating social satirist, was dogged by the problem of "irrelevancy" all the rest of his life. His literary and philosophical output over the years became more and more tangential, absorbed in its own preoccupations, as the almost comical titles—*The Nation as a Business Firm* and the winsome *Religion as a Credible Doctrine*—suggest. When Mallock died in 1923, pensioned for many years "in consideration of his distinguished literary work and straitened circumstances," it was one of those occasions on which most observers were surprised to learn that he had still been around. The prominent critic George Saintsbury, who believed that he had encountered Mallock only once, in a club (which he said "relieves me from the risk of having felt that rather modified personal affection which I have been told he sometimes excited"), wrote in a retrospective essay that Mallock had once enjoyed a reputation of brilliance. "Yet how little came of it. He might have been accused—he actually did seem, I believe, to some—to have in him the makings of an Aristophanes or a Swift of not so much lessened degree. . . . And yet after the chiefly scandalous success of *The New Republic* he never 'came off.' Exactly what was the flaw, the rot, the 'dram of eale,' I do not know—it lay in faults of taste and temper, perhaps."[19]

There was no "fault" there, and no "rot." It was simply that Mallock would never have sought to be another Swift, goading the public's conscience with satire. He was pitching his comedy (and later his noncomic treatises) to a different level of reader and was concerned not with inspiring action or concrete change, but a certain kind of elevated *thinking*. His audience, presumably part of the Oxford-centered cultural elite from which he had come, at some point simply forsook him.

And this brings us to the final charge that was pressed against the high culture movement of the 1870s and

1880s—the accusation that it was addressing an aristocratically oriented audience. DeLaura notes in Newman, Pater, and Arnold "the emphasis all three place on an *elite* culture; that is, their shared sense of the highest organization of the human powers was 'aristocratic,' a privileged mode of perception endangered in a rapidly democratizing society."[20] Williams, too, observes that, when speaking of culture, Arnold tends to allude to a small "remnant" in each class that is not disabled by the notions and habits of the majority. And Meredith, as we noted earlier, calls for an interpenetration of an educated, sophisticated middle class and the upper class, saying that the latter would serve as a "brilliant, flippant, independent . . . spur and pattern."

The high culture movement appears to have had aristocratic inclinations because only the English upper classes were believed to have had enough independence from the dominant bourgeois moral inhibitions to indulge in the intense self-absorption essential to the refinement of one's sensibility. For most of the century, it had been a common assumption that the blooded class was so securely beyond concern over appearances that its members could indulge their tastes in literature and behavior. And certainly much of the sensational material of literature and art entered England during the mid-Victorian period only through upper-class channels; it was the aristocratic Lord Houghton and Algernon Swinburne who were reading French writers like Baudelaire and DeSade. And now, presumably, Meredith, Pater, and the other high culture proponents were advocating a kind of hedonism. All that blather about quickened senses and Hellenism was a cover for the devotion to individual gratification. (Pater's self-proclaimed disciples were, in fact, notorious for their excesses and, in the popular mind, they were doing in public what the upper classes had the decency to do behind closed mansion doors.) The high culture movement was altogether too "refined" for the ordinary man, and the books themselves were nearly inaccessible—polished intellectual exercises like *Marius the Epicurean*, stylized social comedies like *The Egoist*. And isn't this a rather characteristic English direction for avant-garde art to take? In reacting to bourgeois crassness, a middle-class British intelligentsia will simply seek an outlet for expression in another *social* milieu—that of the hedonistic aristocracy.

We would misread *The Egoist*, however, if we were to go on to make the corollary assumption that Meredith aspires to English aristocratic ways of living and perceiving things. The structural dynamics of the novel reside in the efforts by the middle-class sensibility of Clara Middleton to break through the elaborate façades of Patterne Hall aristocracy; the tension inheres in the struggle of middle-class open-ness against Sir Willoughby's upper-class sterility and self-indulgence; and the middle-class way does triumph at the book's end. Rather, what Meredith calls for is the interpen-etration of characteristically middle-class and upper-class sensibilities in his audience. He is seeking to develop, as was Arnold in *Culture and Anarchy*, a sophisticated stratum of readers who are drawn from the middle class. He seeks an audience for "true comedy." As he proclaims in the "Es-say," "a perception of the Comic Spirit gives high fellow-ship. You become a citizen of the selector world, the high-est we know of in connection with our old world, which is not supermundane. Look there for your unchallengeable upper class!" (49).

It is interesting to note that in the three most significant theoretical statements on comedy by men of the generation that came of age in the latter half of the nineteenth cen-tury—those by Meredith, Freud, and Bergson—we find the same insistence that excellent comedy can only thrive in a sophisticated culture. It is repeated again and again; sometimes in the dubious contexts of Western cultural superiority, but the conviction of it is deep and solid. Here it is useful to turn once again to Freud's theory of comic structure, for I think we can make a connection between this call for sophistication and an important shift of emphasis in the nature of comic writing toward the end of the century.

Freud, as we recall, premises his theory on the notion that pleasure can only be achieved if the social and psychological inhibitions felt about a tendentious comic attack can be sublimated by the artful presentation of the joke or comic expression. He then goes on to stress the particularly strong pleasure that comes from effective wit work, from the manner in which the anticipation of laughter and the cathexis is postponed through the art of the telling of the joke. Building upon the observation that games intensify pleasure by putting obstacles in the way of our final gratification—creating a "psychical damming up" that heightens the pleasure achieved in its final release—Freud suggests that sophisticated audiences prefer comedy that prolongs such a release through artful presentation. In fact, the emphasis shifts in certain social contexts to the "fore-pleasure" of comedy; that is, the pleasure that comes from the joke-teller's or comic writer's creation of a form that withstands critical judgment and exploits our desire to play with words and thoughts. It is the form of the joke or comic expression, then, that appeals to certain audiences—the elaboration and the success in prolonging tension through artful presentation.

When Meredith speaks of a civilized audience for his comedy, when he speaks of a selector world, when he speaks of the laughter of the mind, he too is writing from an assumption that the richest pleasure in comedy arises from our delight in its form. He is, however, going beyond that. If Freud's analysis of the nature of comedy and comedic response is valid, then it seems inevitable that under certain circumstances it is likely that the tendentious thrust of comedy will atrophy, be lost sight of, or at least become so oblique as to be inconsequential to its effect. When that happens, the source of delight will shift predominantly to comic wit work. Meredith's comic theory marks such a shift among certain writers in the last half of the nineteenth century. His call in "An Essay on Comedy" is for a comedy that is not savage, that is essentially not tendentious. His emphasis on the "idea," on dispassionateness, even his insistence that one work through one's own psychological dispositions and poetically refine them to the point at which one can treat them with artistic objectivity, all point to a comedy whose richness comes from its manner of presentation rather than its tendentious thrust. An important shift of balance occurs in Meredith's generation of comic writers that inevitably affects the nature of a large body of English nineteenth-century comedy.

Now we can see why it is useful to approach Meredith's "Essay," as we have, through a review of the charges leveled against high culture. It helps define the new emphases in comic expression. The complaint, for instance, that the cultural position was in reality an aesthetic position highlights the greater attention devoted to artistic expression in a comedy that puts primary value on its form of presentation rather than on its object of attack. The focus in such comedy is transferred to wit work and elaboration. Similarly, the charge that high culture developed into an aspect of "thinking" rather than "doing" and that its art often fixed upon the static, governing "idea" rather than upon moving its audience toward action accords with a comedy whose weight is upon its form. Indeed, if the pleasure of comic expression is heightened by the obstacles in the way of psychic release, then a highly complex and ideational comic presentation is likely to make that pleasure more exquisite, at least among certain readers. And, finally, the accusation that the high culture movement is elitist and pseudoaristocratic in its manner of expression and in its appeal no longer seems so telling. Such an audience is, after all, presumably ideal for a comedy that puts emphasis on its manner rather than upon its target of attack, or upon its sublimative operations. This is the audience that Judith Wilt suggests has been Meredith's objective all along.

A further consequence of the redirection of comic expression toward its manner, art, and ideas is the diminishment of the sublimative operations that Freud stressed so heavily. We observed that in writers like Bulwer the sublimation of moral objections was so predominant a concern that the comedy was constantly oscillating in tone; the expression was largely the sublimation itself. Only in the isolated instance of Disraeli did we find a writer free enough of the worries of the hypersensitive superego to be able to give free play to the elaborative process. In Meredith's generation, we encounter a group of artists who are breaking out of the society's ethical inhibitions. They do this by appealing to an audience that is not as dependent for its self-assessment upon morality—the aristocracy and the established upper middle class. They also try to enlarge this audience by instilling a cultural ideal that is not "Hebraistic," not grounded in primarily moral referents. And they take advantage of the changed intellectual climate of the 1870s and 1880s, the post-Darwinian atmosphere of religious skepticism and doubt, which makes it easier for a sophisticated upper class to talk and laugh about issues without nagging worries of impropriety.

As early as *Feverel*, Meredith began to make fun of the Puritan nature of contemporary society. He gingerly works himself free of moral inhibitions against comic expression, opening the "Essay" with a complaint against the "tenacity of national impressions" that has, since Restoration days, "caused the word 'theatre' . . . to prod the Puritan nervous system like a satanic instrument" (6). In *The New Republic*, Mallock is even more incisive, for he identifies the sublimative operations in comedy and facetiously laments the decline of religiosity because of the effect it will have on the nation's humor. One of his characters, a hedonistic voluptuary, bewails the passing of "Christianity, and that marvellous system of moral laws and restraints which, although accredited through imposture, elaborated by barbarism, and received by credulity, has entirely changed the whole complexion of life":

> It has cunningly associated everything with the most awful or the most glittering conceptions with which the imagination can soar or intoxicate itself—with Hell, Heaven, Judgment, and so forth. . . . The enchantment quite deludes the vulgar; it a little deludes the wise; but the wise are for ever in various ways secretly undoing the spell, and getting glimpses of things as they really are. Here lies the sense of humour—in the detection of truth through revered and reigning falsehood. . . . Christianity, with a miraculous ingenuity, has confined and cramped it into so grotesque and painful a posture, and set such vigilant guardians to keep it there, that any return to . . . natural freedom is a rapture.[21]

Moral concern had been, of course, symptomatic of English bourgeois humor in the nineteenth century. It is the source of sentimentalism, and the reason why so much humor lacks "idea." Meredith complains that the middle-class cultural denominator is "a rosy, sometimes a larmoyant, geniality, not unmanly in its verging upon tenderness, and with a singular attraction for thickheadedness." His "Essay" is significant for its direct attack upon "humor," the benevolist comic form. "If you laugh all round [your comic subject], tumble him, roll him about, deal him a smack, and drop a tear on him, own his likeness to you, and yours to your neighbor, spare him as little as you shun, pity him as much as you expose, it is a spirit of Humor that is moving you" (42). The contempt Meredith feels for such tomfoolery is barely sheathed. Robert Bernard Martin, in *The Triumph of Wit*, notes a gradual evolution among critics and intellectuals toward the position that Meredith takes openly. "Humour had nearly total sway in the nineteenth century until the late 1860s," Martin says. "Wit and intellectual comedy had been universally agreed upon as arrogant, cold, and unpoetic, but when they had almost disappeared in practice, the suspicion grew that they might be a cool refreshment from the sticky and unrelieved sentimentality of what had been passing as comedy."[22]

We sense, though, that it was more than just the tone of humor that Meredith objected to: it was the entire galaxy of beliefs and attitudes that characterized English middle-class humorous expression. Meredith repeatedly went beyond criticism of tone to criticism of attitude and orientation. According to him, the fault of humor lay in its tolerance of qualities of "dullness," in the "malady of sameness, our modern malady." All that Meredith argued for—an intellectual comedy, a nonsentimental comedy, a comedy that penetrates and demolishes the indulgences of the self, a comedy that emphasizes its art, a comedy that speaks to a cultivated audience—indicates that it was the petit bourgeois disposition of English humor that he disliked. His determination to yoke his comedy to a high cultural standard strongly suggests that his purpose was to disentangle English comic expression from bourgeois concerns and attitudes. Meredith's comic ideal was intended to bring his audience to a different way of thinking. One must shake loose of the middle-class values of moralism, sentimentality, obsession with material concerns, and narrow pragmatism to a new mode of responding and living, to an elevated "culture." Raymond Williams has remarked that the definition of culture emerging in this period incorporated not only "a state or habit of mind, or a body of intellectual activities; it means now, also, a whole way of life."[23] We shall have occasion to emphasize this point in the next chapter. It is crucial to note here, however, that Meredith's call for a civilized comedy in a civilized cultural environment signifies more than a change in comic manner: it was an attempt to articulate a different approach to life, a different orientation, a different life style.

At this point in the century, English comedy divides radically. One branch continues along the line of the humor tradition and constitutes much of the popular comedy. We have traced that line in chapter five, noting the tendency of such humor to become indulgent of bourgeois tastes and values. The other branch, beginning essentially with Meredith, takes a high culture line, becoming more sophisticated, aesthetically oriented, amoral, witty—premised upon a style of life that is "refined" and antimaterialistic. The division reflects the estrangement of a group of comic artists from the prevailing middle-class social order. Such an alienation has been noted in various contexts before, but not in terms of comic expression. Indeed, it seems as if the concerns of comedy accelerate the division. We have witnessed how difficult it was for Carroll to continue his original comic vein in the humor tradition, how much he was forced to hedge and sentimentalize. Meredith very clearly could not have used comedy as he wanted had he been required to work within the value system and social orientation of bourgeois humor. The necessity for such a radical conceptual dislocation is no more vividly illustrated than in the work of Samuel Butler who tried to rebel against bourgeois values from *within* the bourgeois cultural and conceptual framework.

Its notion of Heaven is hardly higher than a
transformation scene at Drury Lane.
—*Samuel Butler*

III

With the appearance of Samuel Butler, oblique attack and cultural displacement in nineteenth-century comedy seems to come to an end. Butler's posthumously published novel *The Way of All Flesh* has been described as a time bomb, set in the last decades of Victorianism, ticking away in Butler's aggrieved mind through the 1870s, 1880s, and 1890s. Meredith's identification of Puritanism as the archenemy of comedy and wit has to be inferred to a certain extent; it is there, but it really has not been spelled out except in his remarks about its consequences for comic theatre. Not so with Butler: in *The Way of All Flesh*, the Puritan model of serious self-examination and spiritual conversion is blown inside out. The novel describes a spiritual struggle and a conversion experience, all right, but it is a struggle against religion and its supports and a conversion to self-regarding pleasure. The protagonist, Ernest Pontifex, wades through a slough of temptations just as did Christian in John Bunyan's paradigmatic work of the Puritan ethos *Pilgrim's Progress* (in fact, we are told by Butler's companion and biographer Henry Festing Jones that Ernest was originally to be named "Christian"), but they are the temptations of the hypocritical religiosity of his parents and his society. He must be tested against his weak-willed inclinations to become an Evangelical reformer and a God-fearing, home-worshipping prig. He must constantly guard himself against the lures of earnestness and avoid backsliding into solemnity.

"*Pilgrim's Progress* consists mainly of a series of infamous libels upon life and things," Butler wrote in his notebook; "it is a blasphemy against certain fundamental ideas of right and wrong which our consciences most instinctively approve; its notion of Heaven is hardly higher than a transformation scene at Drury Lane."[24] The only way to dispel the baleful effects of Puritanism is through comedy. Reduce it to an idle farce, suggests Edward Overton, the narrator of *The Way of All Flesh* and the author's frequent spokesman:

> I had also dramatised Pilgrim's Progress for a Christmas Pantomime, and made an important scene of Vanity Fair, with Mr. Greatheart, Apollyon, Christiana, Mercy and Hopeful as the principal characters. . . . Hopeful was

up to as much mischief as I could give him; he wore the costume of a young swell of the period, and had a cigar in his mouth. . . . Christiana did not wear much of anything; indeed it was said that the dress which the stage manager had originally proposed for her had been considered inadequate even by the Lord Chamberlain.[25]

Butler's point of view seems to bring together the various motifs of the English comic disposition that we have traced through the century. He speaks of life as if Fortune, comedy's sometime presiding spirit, were the only operative force. Luck has more to do with an individual's situation than anything else; in his dystopian satire of contemporary society, *Erewhon*, Butler makes unluckiness a crime, because that is what it amounts to in real life. And in *The Way of All Flesh*, he relentlessly exposes the ossified beliefs, the sterile life patterns, the deadening conformity of respectable existence. The novel reaches back three generations to show how social myths set in on an English family and how self-fictions petrify in the name of consistency and social status. Ernest's characteristically Victorian parents, Christina and Theobald, become such dead vessels of old self-concepts, so dully lacking in vitality, that when death overtakes them, it is barely noticeable. Christina's passing is likened to "the blending of sea and sky in mid-ocean upon a soft hazy day when none can say where the earth ends and the heavens begin" (335). And of Theobald the narrator remarks that he only presented the phenomena of death: "This is not more than half-dying, but then neither was his life more than a half-living. He presented so many of the phenomena of living that I suppose on the whole it would be less trouble to think of him as having been alive than as never having been born at all" (350).

While comically disposed writers earlier in the century were uneasy about the implications of human nature as a series of self-constructs, Butler accepted it as psychological actuality. Ernest Pontifex's adult personality takes shape through the adoption and discarding of what the narrator calls his "selves," various personae that represent not only stages in his development but also aspects of his "nature." Ernest's nature is an amalgam of inherited characteristics (it is for this reason that Butler takes us three generations back to show their source) and adaptations to his Victorian social environment. Butler's expression of the workings of heredity and culture takes an unusually radical form. Overton toys with the analogy that "there is no life save as a succession of deaths" (26), and Ernest reflects that "sensible people get the greater part of their own dying done during their own lifetime" (91). The story of Ernest's development is one of the trying on of numerous personae. He assumes the role of St. Paul, prompted by the Simeonite religious fanatic Gideon Hawke and by the stirrings within his own blood of his mother's fondness for dramatic martyrdom. When that persona collapses in ridicule, he assumes the nature of his ancestor John Pontifex and becomes, briefly and disastrously, a man of simple, workingman's tastes. Butler's own sense that he has been different men at different times—his abiding wonder that the self-assured man of independent, iconoclastic mind that he has become as an adult, could once have been the weak-willed, deluded youth and young man that he was—informs the entire story of Ernest. Overton, the novel's narrator, is an "idealized" depiction of what Butler feels he has become as an adult; Ernest represents what he had been and has at least partially overcome in his own character. The novel, attempting to bridge the author's two "selves," is as autobiographical a piece of fiction as we have seen. Overton partly confesses this: "Every man's work whether it be literature, or music, or pictures . . . is always a portrait of himself, and the more he tries to conceal himself the more clearly will his character appear in spite of him. I may very likely be condemning myself all the time that I am writing this book, for I know that whether I like it or no I am portraying myself more surely than I am portraying any of the

characters whom I set before the reader" (55-56). Festing
Jones confirms this: "Both Ernest Pontifex and Edward
Overton are portraits of Butler, the narrator being Butler
as a man of sixty-five, and the hero being also Butler as a
child, a boy, a youth, and a man."[26] And the conviction that
human nature is a process of adoption and rejection of
personae is also Butler's conviction: it governs every effort
he made to strip great men of their façades and to expose
all dominant individual characteristics as poses.

The language and associated imagery used by Butler is
telling. By describing the change of self-constructs as a "dying off" of old selves—he even speaks in his letters of such
changes being "pro tanto deaths"[27]—he invests the process
with implications of pain and loss. The toll on Ernest Pontifex, like the toll on his creator, has been immense. The
molting process, the shedding of the skins of old sensibilities and dashed aspirations, finally debilitates Ernest.
At the end of the novel, he emerges as a diminished person, content with the sedate pleasures of bachelorhood, a
sufficient income, and an indifferent reputation. Butler's
point is clear: "they" will get you in the end—your parents,
the Church, the moral arbiters, the middle-class social establishment. They will abase you, stifle your imagination,
break your spirit, devalue your objectives. And just as
surely as Butler's novel had seemed to contain all the elements of the nineteenth-century comic vision—with its
emphasis on fictions, on change, on the resistance to Puritan moral censorship—it concludes in a portrait of defeat,
or of victory that is Pyrrhic to say the least. The comic response to Victorianism that is most iconoclastic proves to
have been costly to Ernest, and therefore presumably to
Butler himself. It is comedy turned ironic, comedy turned
essentially aggrieved; it is a picture of the comic "hero" as
victim. It is as if we had a source here for all the novels of
the little man by H. G. Wells, Evelyn Waugh, and Kingsley
Amis.

Butler's novel demonstrates the complexities of trying to

work free of the dominant middle-class social and ideological framework when one cannot be the high-culture intellectual that Meredith and Arnold are. Ernest Pontifex has not only had to revise his expectations in the face of his experience but he has, almost unintentionally, been obliged to revise his essential values. He has adjusted his lens in such a way that losses appear to be gains and diminished possibilities appear to be victories of sorts. Overton and Ernest thus make a positive virtue out of the destruction of normal human relationships. Ernest farms off his children; he alienates himself from his family; he "cuts" all his old friends.

> At first it had been very painful to him to meet any of his old friends, as he sometimes accidentally did, but this soon passed; either they cut him, or he cut them; it was not nice being cut for the first time or two, but after that it became rather pleasant than not. . . . The ordeal is a painful one, but if a man's moral and intellectual constitution is naturally sound, there is nothing which will give him so much strength of character as having been well cut (284).

> For society indeed of all sorts—except of course that of a few intimate friends—he had an unconquerable aversion. "I always did hate those people," he said, "and they always have hated and always will hate me. I am an Ishmael by instinct as much as by accident of circumstances, but if I keep out of society I shall be less vulnerable than Ishmaels generally are. The moment a man goes into society, he becomes vulnerable all round" (336).

That is the idea—to keep from being vulnerable. Butler lived the idea himself; ensconced in cranky semireclusiveness, he admitted only Festing Jones to his intimacy because, Butler wrote, "I found he did not sit upon me, nor bully me." Having been thwarted for so long in such perverse ways by his own parents, the demands of emotional expression were simply too agonizing for him. A moving case in point is his relationship with Eliza May Savage, a woman who seemed to inspire Butler to his finest moments of self-expression in the composition of *The Way of All Flesh*, who was a fond and spirited sometime confidante, who probably loved Butler—and to whom he could not respond. "She rarely left my rooms," he wrote, "without my neck swelling and my head for a time being all wrong from the effort it cost me to conceal the fact that she had been too much for me."[28] He closed off their relationship, too, but brooded in later years about his inability to cope with his feelings toward her. Regrets of this kind do surface now and then, but fleetingly. In *The Way of All Flesh*, Butler has taken his public position on the issue of personal attachment: it is a puerile, sentimental sort of yearning and an invitation to be hurt.

Public positions on such matters are important because Butler seems to be convinced that qualities of life are largely a matter of assuming positions about them. It is probably the infirmity of a lifelong iconoclast to believe that everything that had been set up as desirable was done so by manipulating its appearances. P. N. Furbank notes that in all Butler's writings, even the most private ones, "it is the desire to appear happy, rather than the attainment of happiness, of which we are most conscious."[29] Yet never do we intimate that Butler is covering up, that he secretly yearns or suffers and is putting on a brave front. Rather, the man holds to the importance of assumed positions as a rationally derived, emotionally confirmed truth, whatever those positions may lack in joyousness and vitality.

The Way of All Flesh, and the life of Samuel Butler behind it, make nice dramatizations of Freud's concept of the evolution of the "pleasure principle." Freud says that at first the human ego seeks pure pleasure in order to satisfy the urges of the libido, but that eventually the harsh experiences of reality force the ego to make adjustments in its goals. Avoiding pain becomes as important as seeking pleasure, and as a way of accommodation, the ego settles for a delayed and diminished pleasure.[30] As Overton puts it in *The Way of All Flesh*, "the utmost that can be said is that we are fairly happy so long as we are not distinctly aware of being miserable" (171). Indeed, in a little-known essay on "Humour," Freud links our appreciation of comedy to the process of accommodation made in the pleasure principle. Comedy preserves us from psychologically taxing feelings aroused by contact with reality, in particular feelings of anger or despair. "The ego refuses to be distressed by the provocations of reality—It signifies not only the triumph of the ego, but also of the pleasure principle."[31] Freud also stresses that human activity "is attended by pleasure in proportion as . . . it approximates to complete stability, and is attended by unpleasure in proportion as, beyond a certain limit, it deviates from complete stability."[32]

Accordingly, we discover in Butler not only the attempt to acquire stability by evading upsetting human exchanges but also a remarkably strong emphasis on the stability that presumably inheres in certain material surroundings. "I will live as I like living, not as other people would like me to live; . . . I can afford the luxury of a quiet unobtrusive life of self-indulgence, . . . and I mean to have it," announces Ernest toward the end of the novel. His digs—his room and furniture—acquire a curious stress in the book, as if we were to understand something of unusual significance from the comfort that Ernest derives from "the fireplace with a fire in it, the easy chairs, the Times, my cat, the red geraniums in my window" (266). One reading to give this, I suppose, is that having been hurt so badly, Ernest gathers strength from the simplest elements of life. Another implication is that an existence revolving around material, self-indulgent concerns has attained a necessary importance to men with Ernest's experience.

In this respect, *The Way of All Flesh* registers one sense of things in the 1880s. G. M. Young observes in the last quarter of the nineteenth century "a greater care for the amenities of life, natural and domestic; and, behind this, a far more critical attitude towards the structure of society."[33] Lewis and Maude record the same phenomenon: "rising standards of consumption and comfort became very marked in the last years of the century."[34] The reasons were diverse; most immediately, in the 1870s and 1880s there had been economic reverses that, as the historian R.C.K. Ensor notes, destroyed the economic complacency of Victorianism and drove more people toward tending their own gardens.[35] Beyond that was a general disquiet over the apparent failures of the Victorian liberal experiment, which had now run a long course but had not produced what men like Butler might have looked for—a greater richness to life, the uplift of dramatic challenge, a true "culture" as it was now coming to be defined. More difficult to account for, but equally prevalent, was an atmosphere of stoical withdrawal among certain members of the intelligentsia (most notably Hardy, but also Kipling, Henley, and Butler). In consequence, as David Daiches argues in his study of *Some Late Victorian Attitudes*, many a writer eschewed any direct engagement with the issues of his time and took refuge in various outlets of personal conservatism, ranging from Kipling's jingoistic celebration of strenuous effort to Wilde's flamboyant amorality.[36]

As Daiches observes, some of Butler's pronouncements could have stood as well for Wilde: "sensible people will get through life by rule of thumb as they may interpret it most conveniently without asking too many questions for conscience sake" (265); "no man's opinions can be worth holding unless he knows how to deny them easily and gracefully upon occasion" (356); "the one serious conviction that a man should have is that nothing is to be taken too seriously." But as Daiches also points out, Butler differed from Wilde in being "incorrigibly middle class."[37]

This is the factor that begins to link up all the elements of Butler's position that we have seen so far and that eventually sets the tone of an attitude toward life that appears superficially to share our comic vision. Butler's outlook is conditioned by the middle-class set of values that he spent so much of his life opposing. His orientation is bourgeois in such a deep-seated way that not only does it determine what he must fight against but it also shapes the nature of his "triumph" over it. The terms by which his life is defined are middle-class, or are the products of a deadly struggle against the middle class. The observation that much of Ernest's vaunted independence seems to be grounded in material welfare—in comfy digs and a settled income—is easy enough to make. But other dimensions furnish more crucial indicators of the way in which middle-class orientation affects Butler's self-definition, and, ultimately, his comic art.

Daiches describes Butler's ethos as "a mocking version of Benthamism." That is, it carries to absurd extremes the Benthamite emphasis on laissez faire and on judging actions in terms of an economic "pleasure principle"—that which provides the greatest balance of pleasure over pain for the most people. As is often the case with Butler, however, it is a mockery that has difficulty freeing itself from the contours and the logic of its target. Benthamism's influence on the Victorians had been to shift the stress, in judging political and social acts at least, from the intention of the act and the ethical ideals of it to its effects. The gauge of correct action was not its inherent philosophical significance, but its demonstrable practical consequences. If it produced sufficient socially definable "pleasure" to a sufficient number of people and was in accord with the realities of the situation, it met the basic test. We cannot really judge the extent to which such thinking influenced the literature of the Victorian period. Surely the Victorian novel's emphasis on society and its interest (in Trollope and George Eliot and many others) in situations and effects, owes something to the Benthamite orientation in the social and political areas of the culture. On the other hand, the literary mind would seem to be naturally inimical to that orientation, for writers are generally inclined to pursue the complexities of intuition, psychology, emotion, and of nonobjectifiable values that prompt human expression and behavior. We can sense this struggle between the intuitive and the "Benthamite" in writers like Dickens who stress qualities of inner nature yet show how much of a man's makeup is his social role. Butler, in any event, comes at the end of a culture in which Benthamism played an integral part and is, moreover, not a man of a literary bent of mind. His frame of reference is a logical, fairly pragmatic one; as a novelist he is a social critic. In consequence, there is ingrained in him a disposition to interpret matters in the Benthamite way, to look upon man as a socially conditioned animal, to lay heavy emphasis upon outward behavior. He puts less weight on intuitive factors in an individual's makeup and more on the adjustments a man makes to social pressures. Accordingly, he is inclined to describe human nature in terms of the assumption of social roles.

I have argued earlier that during the century, the changing view of human nature (in which an individual "personality" is redefined as a series of constructs or personae) was a product of observation of man in an urban milieu rather than a product of Benthamism or any other single, identifiable philosophy. This is certainly the case, although we can see now that a variety of factors could have been contributing to each other in this regard. Butler's position relies more than most on Benthamism because he tends to equate those personae with recognizable social roles, and even at times with occupations, rather than defining them in terms of personal constructs, some of them reactions against social roles, as did Dickens. Butler draws all his values and definitions out of people's life styles. Ernest Pontifex, for instance, has defined himself almost entirely in terms of the *way* he will live. And every supposedly inherent quality, every value, is ultimately tested in terms of

its sufficiency to that way: "For most men, and most circumstance, pleasure—tangible material prosperity in this
world—is the safest test of virtue" (76). Behind the shock
value of this and numerous other similar statements in *The
Way of All Flesh* and in Butler's other writings stands a firm
operating principle, the essence of the "ad hoc" philosophy. This, I suggest, is Benthamite; and this, in nineteenth-century England, at least, is at the heart of the
bourgeois orientation.

In all the important ways, Samuel Butler defined the
human situation in terms that his fellow writers and social
critics characterized as bourgeois. While Arnold and others
urged an escape from the enthrallment of materialism,
Butler made statements of this sort through his alter ego,
Overton: "Granted, then, that the three most serious losses
which a man can suffer are those affecting money, health,
and reputation, loss of money is far the worst; . . . a man
may grow a new reputation as easily as a lobster grows a
new claw, or if he have health and money may thrive in
great peace of mind without any reputation at all" (251-
52). While such a remark may simply seem to turn the
middle-class preoccupation with money upon its head,
anyone who looks very long at Butler will have a firm conviction that he means what he says. Like Ernest Pontifex,
Butler felt himself to be constrained in vital ways by money
problems—so much so that it became difficult to think
about self-expression in any other terms.

The Way of All Flesh is a semiautobiographical depiction
of the subtle ways in which the bourgeois scheme of values
works in a man. There are parallels to Ernest's struggle for
financial independence in Butler's own youth: there is a
long-rankling instance when Butler believed that his own
father had taken unfair advantage of him by persuading
him to dispose of a remainder interest in family property;
and there is, in letters to Butler from his father, the same
niggling manner that he so expertly parodies in *The Way of
All Flesh*.[38] Theobald's letter to Ernest concerning the pos-

sible deductions he may be obliged to make from Ernest's legacy from his grandfather is a tour de force:

> "From the legacy, however, large deductions must be made. There will be legacy duty, and I do not know whether I am not entitled to deduct the expences of your education and maintenance from birth to your coming of age; I shall not in all likelihood insist on this right to the full, if you conduct yourself properly, but a considerable sum should certainly be deducted; there will therefore remain very little—say £1000 or £2000 at the outside, as what will be actually yours—but the strictest account shall be rendered you in due time" (148).

This passage masterfully captures all the browbeater's insidious implications: Theobald is generally aggrieved; deductions from the legacy for Ernest's education from birth will depend on the boy's good conduct; in any event there will be precious little left at the end; and he anticipates the unjust and cruel charge that he misappropriated his son's funds and will, therefore, protect himself by "the strictest account." Butler's novel renders, as few others have been able, the real narrowness of mind that an existence predicated on material concerns creates. He can show how such dealing debases the father as well as the son, how pettiness and meanness soak into the very fabric of daily existence and turn it such ugly colors.

"Moral force is like physical force," Overton remarks at one point, but *The Way of All Flesh* illustrates how much more difficult it is to throw off. Moral force applied by Theobald and Christina, and their infinite accomplices in English society, on their young son is like the administration of a slow poison. Relentlessly they impress upon Ernest his weakness; he is an ungrateful wretch who will not return to his parents the love and respect he owes them. "It is an unnatural thing for a boy not to be fond of his own father" (108), Christina chides Ernest, and since he cannot find that fondness within him, he shrinks into self-doubt.

"Papa does not feel," she continued, "that you love him with that fulness and unreserve which would prompt you to have no concealment from him, and to tell him everything freely and fearlessly as your most loving earthly friend next only to your Heavenly Father. Perfect love, as we know, casteth out fear: your father loves you perfectly, my darling, but he does not feel as though you love him perfectly in return. If you fear him it is because you do not love him as he deserves, and I know it sometimes cuts him to the very heart to think that he has earned from you a deeper and more willing sympathy than you display towards him" (152).

No wonder the boy asks himself in despair, "when should he learn to love his papa and mamma as [other boys] loved theirs" (110). No wonder the grown man so doubts his capacity for love that he insures himself against the embarrassment by cutting all his friends and denying normal human relations. And no wonder also that he becomes an iconoclast of religion when he perceives how subtly the notion of sin has been woven into all those family bullyings. The religious cant—"perfect love," "next only to your Heavenly Father"—reinforces Ernest's sense of guilt. Indeed, Ernest found all those dull Sundays, vacuous sermons droning on while the yellow sun played upon the brown walls, equally meaningless. Butler knew how the Victorians used their false piety and burdensome morality to crush the vitality out of life.

When Ernest grows up and achieves some perspective on the situation, he discovers that all those factors have constituted a *way of life*. As such, it carries its own scheme of values and its own orientation. Arnold and others complained not so much of the necessary preoccupation with material concerns that every person's daily existence required of him but of the frame of mind that it established. The categories of thought—money, parental duty, conventional morality, creature comforts, and, finally, one's occupation and social position—became categories of value; this is what he and others meant when they used "bourgeois" pejoratively.

The tragedy of this orientation can be seen in Ernest's story and in Butler's own case, for it inevitably reduces the scope of the individual personality. The self-doubts lead to retreat and usually to mediocrity; the intensity of material concerns, hedged in by quasi-religious cant, produces narrowness of spirit. The anguish of *The Way of All Flesh* derives, as P. N. Furbank says, from "recognizing that the forces that have brought the victim to this point are too strong to lose their hold merely by being recognized for what they are. The pain is not merely in the contrast between [this and a richer way of life], but in the sensation of the impossibility by now of any complete conversion from the one to the other."[39] Such was Samuel Butler's anguish, for his acute self-consciousness never engendered real self-awareness. His hatred of his bourgeois upbringing and surroundings could never be converted into the spaciousness of mind and spirit that would truly have been a liberation and fulfillment. He acknowledged this when he claimed, later on, "the main desire of my life was to conceal how severely I had been wounded, and to get beyond the reach of those arrows that from time to time still reach me." "I HAVE HAD TO STEAL MY OWN BIRTHRIGHT. I stole it and was bitterly punished. But I saved my soul alive."[40] Perhaps. But all things intellectual and spiritual were turned into Philistinisms in the process. He never laid to rest the petty hatreds; instead, he grew to be something of a brilliant crank.

Furbank shrewdly perceives that even thought itself acquired the aspect of a material possession for Butler. His unconventional opinions about art and other things were adopted because they could be his alone, like a suit of clothes or a particular plot of land. For example, "he understands and enjoys a good deal of Beethoven, but not all Beethoven. Beethoven, therefore, has to be given up. What is not Butler's own Beethoven is somebody else's, and the 'somebody else' is bound to be an enemy. Butler cannot share his property in Beethoven with another"[41]—consequently, the fanatic espousal of Handel as the greatest composer of all time. Samuel Butler thus becomes one of the century's most poignant instances of the difficulties faced by the comic spirit in breaking out of the bourgeois enthrallment. Every recourse that he chooses seems to have its inescapably bourgeois form and manner. The independent way of life is bachelor apartments and a concern with one's own comfort. Radical thought is the appropriation of a set of opinions that one can call one's unique property.

Similarly, Butler's grand concept of human behavior is simply another social role, and an enviously distorted aristocratic one at that. Wandering through *The Way of All Flesh* is the ill-defined figure of Towneley, an insouciant, hedonistic young man of good breeding who appears to represent all that Ernest aspires to. "Towneley . . . is not only a good fellow, but he is without exception the very best man I ever saw in my life. . . . Towneley is my notion of everything which I should most like to be." Towneley is *cultured*; he is self-confident; he has aplomb; he has style. Towneley has no besetting grievances and presumably no limiting doubts of taste.

Ernest "cuts" Towneley along with all the rest of his acquaintances because he knows that he will never *be* a Towneley and he is afraid of losing the man's good opinion of him. A complex attachment of Butler's lies behind Towneley's portrait, but it is of no great matter; the crucial point is that this ideal of Ernest's and of Butler's is simply a shadowy social role. One is finally condemned by one's bourgeois orientation to aspire after social behavior, after a life style. The complicated and fervently advocated notion of "unconscious memory"—which was Butler's theory that certain acquired traits of one's social life were genetically passed on to future generations—amounts, it seems at times, to little more than an imaginative way to escape from the limitations of one's orientation. Ernest will never really be able to think and feel and behave as anything but a half-transformed bourgeois, but maybe his children will. Subliminally, Butler transmits how limited his sense of his spirit is by proposing that only in new lives will things be different. Unintentionally, he casts that "new self" in the most patently bourgeois terms—a classier social position.

The range of Butler's comedy is inevitably determined by the same factors. Butler excells in mimicry of the bourgeois voice. Theobald speaking solemnly on dispositions of legacies, Christina on revering thy father as one would thy God—these are authentic voices of respectable middle-class hypocrisy. Butler can render the cant of religiously phrased solipsism with the sureness of one who finds it ringing forever in his ears. For him, the task has been to squirm free through those narrow channels of thought, and it has required that he feel out for himself the contours of the thinking that restricted him. Butler's method in his comedies, satires, and philosophical treatises is to work from inside, to follow the logic, to scout out the implications, to develop the analogy of the social or philosophical positions that he is overthrowing. His favorite rhetorical device is the *reductio ad absurdum*, and he proved so successful at it that one of his antireligious pieces, *The Fair Haven*, passed for some time (to Butler's immense glee) as a defense of religion.

Such a procedure invites special dangers, of course. It is a primarily reductive mode that may never disengage itself from the object of its attention, may never rise to creative, elaborative heights of its own unique expression. It may also breed a profound disenchantment with expression. Butler's great discovery was that people were frauds and that they used language and position to promulgate their fraudulence. Ernest Pontifex is taken, for instance, to meet the esteemed schoolmaster, Dr. Skinner, whose whole being rests upon falsity: Dr. Skinner's "moral character—a point on which so many geniuses were weak—was absolutely irreproachable; foremost of all, however, among his many great qualities, and perhaps more remarkable even than his genius, was what biographers have called the simpleminded and childlike earnestness of his character—an earnestness which might be perceived by the solemnity with which he spoke even about trifles" (98). That is the trick, you see, to inflate yourself. The middle class is sustained by aggrandizing its banal, petty business. Ordinary language thus becomes radically denatured. Dr. Skinner, for example, announces "in a tone of almost superhuman solemnity," that he will take nothing for dinner. "By and by, however, I had a sense come over me as though I were nearer the consummation of all things than I had ever yet been. The room seemed to grow dark as an expression came over Dr. Skinner's face which showed he was about to speak. . . . 'Stay—I may presently take a glass of cold water—and a small piece of bread and butter.' " The cold water turns out to be a strong potion of hot gin, and the bread and butter, a sumptuous repast of oysters, potatoes, a scallop shell of minced veal nicely browned, some apple tart, and a hunk of bread and cheese. "Nor should his words be taken without searching for what he used to call a 'deeper and more hidden meaning.' Those who searched for this even in his lightest utterances would not be without their reward. They would find that bread and butter was Skinnerese for oyster patties and apple tart, and 'gin hot' the true translation of water" (99-101).

Butler perceives, as Lewis Carroll did, that the oppressive figures in English society have the power to invest insignificant things with "meaning." His response to this is to smash down anything that the culture has inflated. He goes out of his way to debunk every so-called "important" idea and to flout every great reputation. Iconoclasm takes on aspects of personal rigor: "this obsession," David Daiches contends, "led him to attack father-figures wherever they appeared—not only parents and schoolmasters, but even the great masters in art, music, and literature. Italian Renaissance painters, Shakespeare, Milton, Beethoven—any figure esteemed by the Establishment had to be sneered at or at least depreciated in some way."[42] Greatness is just another humbug:

> What, then, it may be asked is the good of being great? The answer is that you may understand greatness better in others whether alive or dead, and choose better company from these, and enjoy and understand that company better when you have chosen it. . . . This, one would think, was substantial gain enough for greatness without its wanting to ride roughshod over us (84).

"Who but a prig would set himself high aims or make high resolves at all?" (311). Consigned to fight the false English establishment on its own terms, even through mimicry of its language and ways of thinking, and sensing deep down that they had made him small and peevish like they were, Butler seems to have had no recourse but such denial.

Flaubert had recognized sometime before that bourgeois cultures pose ironic challenges to the modern artist. If one is to work with the materials of such a culture, if one is to retain some degree of mimetic representation of the life around one, then one must cope in some way with the conservatism of that life style and the treachery of its self-serving language. Flaubert resents the banality and cheapness of bourgeois values and manners as intensely as Butler does. His response, however, is to seek a dispassionate prose style that will not be cankered with his own distaste and grievance. He takes great pains to appear, at least, to negate himself, lest the tone of recrimination creep in. In letters to Louise Colet during the composition of *Madame Bovary*, Flaubert speaks of trying to be "impeccable"; "No lyricism, no comments, the author's personality absent." "Nowhere in my book must the author express his emotions or his opinions." "I refuse to consider Art as a drainpipe for passion, a kind of chamberpot."[43] Though irony often devastates its subject in *Madame Bovary*, the novel seems to be less dominated by the bourgeois disposition for reproach than Butler's *The Way of All Flesh*. Butler himself was conscious of his inability to disengage himself from the old ways of thinking and responding, for he observed:

> If in my books, from *Erewhon* to *Luck or Cunning?* there is a something behind the written words which the reader can feel but not grasp—and I fancy that this must be so—it is due, I believe, to the sense of wrong which was omnipresent with me, not only in regard to Pauli, the Darwins, and my father, but also in regard to my ever-present anxiety about money.[44]

Flaubert's response to bourgeois culture differs significantly from Butler's in another respect. The greatest challenge confronting a novelist of the modern middle class is to find adequate means of articulation in the debased language of the time for the grander expressions of the human spirit. How can one speak in language so crude and hypocritical of the thoughts that elevate the human condition? How can one find images in the mundane existence of the ordinary petit bourgeois—in his clumsy furniture, his collection of dull material objects, his meals of soup and ale—for rich aesthetic expression? When Emma Bovary's crass lover Rudolphe must mouth the words of love, they seem to lay "bare the eternal monotony of passion." He struggles vainly to divest a debased language of its hollowness, to summon up an expression that is not simply an inventory of "empty metaphors": "The human tongue is like a cracked cauldron on which we beat out tunes to set a bear dancing when we would make the stars weep with our melodies." The sum of Emma's very life constitutes poignantly little when the bailiffs arrive to sieze her goods: "the plates, the saucepans, the chairs, the candlesticks, and in the bedroom all the nick-nacks on the wall-shelf. They examined her dresses, the linen, the dressing-room; and her whole existence, to its most intimate details, was stretched out like a cadaver in an autopsy."[45] How can the artist of the everyday life make gold of such dross?

Flaubert, as Hugh Kenner has observed, led the realistic novelist into an apparent cul-de-sac in which art somehow had to deal with material that was banal, debased, enervating.[46] The essential problem is as old as art itself—the need to express the ethereal through the mundane, the intangibles of feeling and spirit through the gross physical matter with which any artist must work. It seems it would have been more difficult to a writer of Flaubert's time, but Flaubert was still a firm enough believer in the power of art to transmute its materials, that he had to attempt the process. The greater disparity between art's objectives and its bourgeois subject matter simply means that for Flaubert—and, as we shall see, for Wilde—the enterprise had to be undertaken with the spirit of irony or comedy.

For Butler there was no such opening of the cul-de-sac. Butler did not essentially believe in the capacity of art to transform its materials and thus he could not transcend their limitations. Like Ernest Pontifex at the end of *The Way of All Flesh*, he denies the reality of all the grander and more spacious qualities of the human soul and along with it denies art. "I do not know or greatly care whether they are good or not," says Ernest of his books, skulking off to his reclusive life of self-confessed mediocrity and cursing the "literary swells." In rejecting the way of art, Butler condemned himself to the way of all flesh. He was caught up, in the end, in the *reductio ad absurdum* of the materialistic, bourgeois culture he had spent himself opposing.

7

Wilde and Beerbohm: The Wit of the Avant-Garde, The Charm of Failure

Only the great masters of style ever succeed in
being obscure.—*Oscar Wilde*

I

*I*n this chapter, we shall look principally at what is known as *fin-de-siècle* literature and at two writers in particular, Oscar Wilde and Max Beerbohm, whose faith in the powers of elaboration exceed any we have seen in later Victorian artists. This move toward elaboration appears to be a logical one; we noted that Meredith's manner of involuting his own positions differed from Dickens' in that it was more reflexive; Meredith's was a comedy that worked off itself with less attention to social implications. Presumably, as appreciation for the transformative capacities of art grows and the artist begins to sense (and even flaunt) his separation from the bourgeoisie, there will be a movement toward the detached, involuted comedy of the twentieth century.

The formative factor in English comedy has been the perception by the writer of his relationship to his social situation. Feeling out of tune in various ways, yet highly self-critical, the figures we have studied developed a comic mode that accommodated their doubt, hesitancy, alienation, disquiet. The comic mode has often deflected the immediate opposition of individual and society. This too would presume a trend toward more distanced comic expression. The trend has indeed been set and it is furthered by Wilde and Beerbohm, yet the most striking thing we shall observe about these two writers is their continuance of social formulations. Even as they flourish their artistic elaborations, they display a high degree of social consciousness. They speak in terms of alternative life styles, of art's influence on *life*, of the play of human social behavior.

Oscar Wilde was the great dandy of the *fin-de-siècle*—the master of wit and epigram, thriving in scandal, ever ready to live by the slogan, "Épater le bourgeois." The image of Wilde that we retain is the one from the Max Beerbohm caricatures—the grand, lascivious, hulking figure in morning coat and pumps, the gaily festooned balloon of a man, displaying touches of mauve and "decadent" yellow, riding above the common swell, blithely throwing overboard the ballast of conventions. And yet, as splendid a picture as he seems to have been of the free spirit, of the soaring outrageousness that is so bracing after decades of Victorian pedestrianism, we have devoted the last eighty years to pulling him down again to mundane reality. "Wilde was a conventional man," sniffed George Bernard Shaw in a sententious piece he did for Frank Harris in Harris's characteristically pugnacious and mendacious biography of Wilde. Wilde's "unconventionality was the very pedantry of convention; never was there a man less an outlaw than he," asserts Shaw.[1] Biography after biography reconstructs the "unrecorded life," the "demon universe," the haunted man of guilt, itching for punishment, and masking himself as the irreverent boulevardier. Even so presumably sympathetic a critic as Richard Ellmann passes through Wilde's ideas to a slightly morbid fascination with Wilde's life, remarking that the man intended to be a scapegoat but succeeded only in being a scapegrace. We seem to like that idea: that Wilde's anticonventionalism was only a gesture, his dandyism only a mask. Like Algernon in "The Importance of Being Earnest," Wilde was simply "Bunburying" as a flippant scoundrel when in his heart of hearts he wanted to be Earnest.

Criminals who want to be caught out, as Wilde allegedly

did, invariably leave clues. Wilde's writings are tantalizingly strewn with instances of exposed masquerades, of moral resolutions, of Christ figures. But Wilde was also a great mocker, a master of the forms, a parodist who knew intimately the conventions he would overturn. The clues are sometimes too obvious, as we shall see when we examine the moral decline of the protagonist in Wilde's novel *The Picture of Dorian Gray*. Perhaps they were not meant to point to the life of the artist after all or perhaps they were meant to point to the paradox of reality's relationship with art, to a more abstract principle than the author's secret consciousness of guilt for his covert homosexuality and his flagrant amorality. "We live in an age when men treat art as if it were meant to be a form of autobiography," Wilde writes, shortly before becoming the most notorious instance of that predilection. It is time we take Wilde's art on its own terms; it is time we take his art, not seriously, for that is not its tenor, but comically as it is meant to be taken.

Wilde's notorious belles-lettristic manner did not come to him immediately. In his first fictional works, the volumes of fairy tales published under the titles of *The Happy Prince* (1888) and *A House of Pomegranates* (1891), the interrelationship between art and reality is problematical and the tone often dispirited and sentimental. Their recurring theme suggests an equivocation about the powers of the imagination that gives way at times to simple despondency. In "The Happy Prince," a swallow on its way south for the winter is detained by the pleas of a statue of the Happy Prince. The statue convinces the bird to pluck out the statue's jeweled eyes and his gold leaf and give them to the many families of the poor. Each day that the swallow lingers to perform his tasks, he increases the risk of perishing in the northern cold. Finally the bird chills and dies. When an art professor notices that the statue is "no longer beautiful" and therefore "no longer useful," it is melted down as scrap. In the epilogue to the tale, God welcomes into heaven the swallow's soul and the statue's heart, which somehow did not melt, but spirit and art have clearly been sacrificed to the material world. Another tale, "The Nightingale and the Rose," expresses the same theme: a nightingale, a symbol of Romantic joy, learns that a poor student seeks a red rose to give to the girl he loves. Falsely assuming that a human heart could harbor true love, the nightingale pierces its own breast on the thorn of a rose bush so that its heart's blood can pour into the plant's fibers and stain a white rose red. The student is elated to find a red rose and, brushing aside the body of the dead bird, he takes it to his girl. She rejects it, and the dejected student callously tosses the rose into the gutter, concluding that love is "quite impractical and in this age to be practical is everything." It is a pity, he notes, that art does not really *mean* anything.

Wilde's animus against a diseased world that wants only practical things dominates the fairy tales and burdens them with poignant futility. While Samuel Butler's defeat by society followed from his inability to conceive of the transformative powers of art, Wilde understands the powers but seems to be unable to exercise them. Metamorphosis occurs again and again in the fairy tales, as if a driven magician were frantically turning his tricks, but invariably we are left with the dispirited impression that the ills and evils of the world prevail. In a story in the second volume, a beautiful boy, a "star-child," undergoes disfigurement and abuse in order to learn that beauty is in the soul. Through a series of sacrifices, he becomes a good man, his beauty is restored, and he goes on to rule the kingdom. But the strain had been telling: "so great had been his suffering, and so bitter the fire of his testing, [that] after the space of three years he died. And he who came after him ruled evilly."[2]

The very images of beauty in the tales are ambivalent. The art is lapidary: Wilde's imagined heaven is cast as a city of gold; paradise on earth is envisioned as an Egypt in which the eyes of lions are like green beryls; and the star-child's own unearthly beauty is described as a whiteness like sawn ivory, his eyes like violets. The concreteness of the images binds them to the material world; they are inlaid in diadems of descriptive prose, rarely able to suggest the transcendent, fluid nature of the beauty they symbolize. We know that Wilde's artistic aspirations leaned toward those of the symbolist poets of France, whom he studied and whose theory of imagination he expresses in his essay "The Critic as Artist."[3] Like the symbolists, he is engaged in an attempt to spiritualize literature, to evade the old bondage of rhetoric, the old bondage of exteriority. He is in revolt against an English literary tradition that simply rearranges and reinterprets material things in accordance with mundane values. Symbolist art takes, as must all art, the concrete and existent as its symbols but conceives of them as representations of a higher order of transcendent meaning, as elements in an organic and truly imaginative expression. The images in Wilde's fairy tales, however, do not seem to radiate with the spirit of that higher order. They remain grounded in a sensibility that only futilely struggles to transmute and transcend.

The curiously strong Christ motif in the fairy tales further confirms this limitedness, for Wilde's Christ is the human sufferer, the victim. In a later essay, "The Soul of Man Under Socialism" (1891), Wilde uses Christ as a representative of individualism and of the nature that will not fit into the hard-paced, acquisitive society. Christ simply stands for the idea of rejecting private property. And even in the fairy tales, Christ figures, such as the little boy in "The Selfish Giant" who has "the prints of two nails" on the palms of his hands and on his feet or the Young King who forsakes wealth and pomp for a crown of thorns, are for the most part examples of the importance of selfless compassion in the real world and poignant reminders that relief from pain will only come after death. This obviously furnishes rich material for the clue-hunting "autobiographical" critic, but not instances of religiously oriented symbolism.

The crux of the matter is that Wilde is neither a symbolist nor a religious mystic. There is scant evidence of his belief in the transcendent, nor does spirituality inform his art. He is, as he must have recognized in writing the fairy tales, grounded in the oppressive material world. Imagination must work for him in another way—to change and confound the nature of the mundane. It transmutes, but in an agonistic way, turning objects and attitudes about and elaborating them. Wilde's writing illustrates what may be the particular nature of the comic impulse—the tendency to rework the existent rather than to enfigure the transcendent. Certainly, for him at least, the only means of liberating himself from the poignancy of the human condition is to use art agonistically. Play is the thing he does so incomparably well. And once he discovers the wonders of the comic—as he does in the short story "Lord Arthur Savile's Crime" (1887)—he is winging on his way.

In comedy, one can kill middle-class seriousness and get away with it. Lord Arthur Savile's crime is a representative crime. Lord Arthur, a slim, elegant young man of breeding, on the verge of marriage to the exquisite Sybil Merton, learns a terrible secret when his palm is read at one of Lady Windermere's soirées: he is destined to commit murder. Thrown into a bourgeois funk by this prediction, he starts to think as the bourgeois do and fancies that he is "fated," a victim of circumstances. The world, which had previously been a refined aristocratic one, now appears to be grotesque in its want of meaning, full of the incoherence that dominates the middle-class sense of actuality. He begins to reason like a shopkeeper and conceives it his "duty" to commit his destined murder *before* marrying Sybil lest he bring a stain upon her reputation. It is no wonder that he thinks in this way, for the awful prediction was made by a character called Podgers. And as if a name like "Podgers" weren't enough to typify him as middle-class, we are told that "he is a little, stout man with a funny, bald head, and great gold-rimmed spectacles; something between a family doctor and a country attorney."[4] He has a coarse, fat face that perspires all the time, a business card, regular office hours for palmistry from ten to four, and he offers discounts for families. His soul is pure bourgeois; when Lord Arthur offers 100 pounds for the prediction, Podgers haggles it up to guineas.

Lord Arthur sets about his crime, nonetheless. He first attempts to poison his Aunt Clementina with a bonbon of aconitine disguised as a homeopathic for heartburn. Vexed when Aunt Clementina dies of natural causes, he next resolves to blow up his uncle, the dean of Chichester. Through the offices of a Russian friend who is a nihilist, he contacts one Herr Winckelkopf, who lives in a French laundry and produces bombs on order. Winckelkopf provides the device—a round cake of dynamite placed in a "pretty little French clock, surmounted by an ormolu figure of Liberty trampling on the hydra of Despotism"— and it is sent to the dean, timed to go off during his regular lunch hour. The dean is pleased, thinking it a gift from a anonymous admirer of his remarkable sermon "Is License Liberty?" But alas, on the fatal hour, the clock makes a whirring noise, a puff of smoke blows out of the pedestal and the goddess of Liberty falls off and breaks her nose on the fireplace fender. Disdaining Herr Winckelkopf's substitute offer of an even more devilish invention just arrived from Geneva, an explosive umbrella that goes off as soon as it is opened, Lord Arthur is plunged into despair. Sulkily walking a bridge over the Thames one night, he encounters Podgers: "no one could mistake the fat, flabby face, the gold-rimmed spectacles, the sickly feeble smile, the sensual mouth."

> Lord Arthur stopped. A brilliant idea flashed across him, and he stole softly up behind. In a moment he had seized Mr. Podgers by the legs, and flung him into the Thames. There was a coarse oath, a heavy splash, and all was still.[5]

The crime is never discovered, Lord Arthur marries Sybil, and the two live happily ever after in grace and style.

The criminal who slays the bourgeoisie must do it in a manner that dispels all suspicion, of course. Even so violent a move as overturning the Podgerses of the world must not be noticed for what it is. Comedy is naturally the disguise. We have seen many instances of the uses of comedy to dissemble when antisocial acts are being perpetrated. Oscar Wilde is the archcriminal of the nineteenth century, and from "Lord Arthur Savile's Crime" on, he performs his most deadly deeds under the cloak of the comic.

Consequently, the truly revolutionary document of comedy during the century has passed with relatively little critical notice. The document is Wilde's essay "The Decay of Lying," published first in 1889 and reissued in 1891 in revised form in his collection called *Intentions*. It seems to be a trivial enough piece, a mock dialogue between two precious aesthetes, Cyril and Vivian, who break up their conversation to descant on the artificialities of Nature and smoke slim imported cigarettes. Vivian belongs to a club called "The Tired Hedonists":

> *Vivian*. We are supposed to wear faded roses in our button-holes when we meet, and to have a sort of cult for Domitian. I am afraid you are not eligible. You are too fond of simple pleasures.
>
> *Cyril*. I should be black-balled on the ground of animal spirits, I suppose?
>
> *Vivian*. Probably. Besides, you are a little too old. We don't admit anybody who is of the usual age.
>
> *Cyril*. Well, I should fancy you are all a good deal bored with each other.
>
> *Vivian*. We are. That is one of the objects of the club.[6]

Quite. Yet "The Decay of Lying" is the century's manifesto of the liberation of comedy from the inhibitions of English Puritanism. As we have noted, for over a hundred years, comedy had operated evasively under the censure that it was the quickest way for a man to lose sight of the ways to salvation. Comedy was the mode of the self-

deceiver, the builder of fictions, the fabricator. It was accused of working hand in hand with the illusions of art to
construct a false and relativistic reality; indeed, the Puritan
critical mentality had long perceived the nexus between the
fabricating elaborative aspects of the comic and the operations of art. Carlyle, we recall, condemned the novel as a
form of lying for this very reason; Trollope expressed his
fear of art's licentious powers of invention when he ex-
coriated Disraeli; Thackeray assumed it when he articulated his distrust of the comic-fictive impulse; Dickens
struggled with it as he fitfully curtailed and then unleashed
his comic imagination; Carroll fretted over it in his brief
and disturbing dream fantasies. Only Wilde was bold
enough to confront the issue openly. He strode directly
into the face of the Puritan fire; he asserted the cause of art
in the very terms by which Puritanism had so long dismissed it:

> Lying and poetry are arts—arts, as Plato saw, not uncon-
> nected with each other. . . . Many a young man starts in
> life with a natural gift for exaggeration which, if nur-
> tured in congenial and sympathetic surroundings, or by
> the imitation of the best models, might grow into some-
> thing really great and wonderful. He either falls into
> careless habits of accuracy . . . or takes to frequenting the
> society of the aged and well-informed (294).

"The Decay of Lying" is not the first or the only
nineteenth-century defense of art but it is the first to confront at the same time the prejudices against art with those
against comedy. And by doing so, Wilde makes clear the
connection we have noted between the comic impulse and
the elaborative qualities of artistic experimentation. Indeed, the terms in which Wilde speaks of art indicate that
he has in mind its comic expressions: "Art itself is really a
form of exaggeration; and selection, which is the very spirit
of art, is nothing more than an intensified mode of over-
emphasis" (302); "The aim of the liar is simply to charm, to

delight, to give pleasure" (305). In a slightly later essay, "The Critic as Artist" (1889, 1890), Wilde does speak in a symbolist vein of a broader power of art to transmute its materials and create a higher apprehension. But "The Decay of Lying" is essentially a defense of what we have identified as the elaborative impulse—it is the manifesto of the comic creator.

It is also Wilde's attempt to educate the English reader and critic to appreciate artistic creation and improvisation for its own sake. The national tendency to find or to insert social meaning into every human expression is ridiculed by Vivian and Cyril. The bourgeois inclination toward mimetic portrayal creates, they say, a literature absorbed with the doings and properties of people "who would pass unnoticed in a third class railway carriage." British expression is hopelessly realistic; even Robert Louis Stevenson's arabesque, "Dr. Jekyll and Mr. Hyde," reads dangerously like an experiment out of the medical journal *Lancet*. Consequently, the reading public does not understand that "art finds her own perfection within, and not outside of, herself. She is not to be judged by any external standard of resemblance" (306). Only when the critical climate changes so that mimetic standards are not applied to every piece of art, and only when people stop trying to find social, ethical, or autobiographical meaning in every creative expression, will elaborative art be appreciated.

The irony of this, of course, is that Wilde himself has subsequently been plagued by a critical reception that claims to read sermons and conventional social comment into his purest comic caprices. "The Importance of Being Earnest," for example, is as transparently agonistic as any work in English literature. Can we possibly translate into a commentary on English society a drawing-room comedy in which one of the principal characters was discovered in a handbag in the cloakroom at Victoria Station and is therefore denied marriage to the woman he loves because, as her mother puts it, one could hardly imagine a girl brought up with the utmost care forming "an alliance with a parcel?" Is there resounding psychological truth in the traumas of two young men whose response to crisis is to wolf down muffins and tea cakes? Can anyone seriously invest ethical content into the romance of young Miss Cecily Cardew whose life has been entirely composed of sensational entries in her diary? Does the fact that both Algernon Moncrieff and John Worthing desire to change their first names to Ernest in order to marry two flighty young women who have a fancy for that name prove that Oscar Wilde is subtly denying his own dandyism and poignantly communicating his wish to be an earnest, respectable bourgeois? Yet George Bernard Shaw rants that "The Importance of Being Earnest" was a "heartless play," "essentially hateful" toward women, a sign of "real degeneracy."[7] Eric Bentley scours it for meaning: it is "almost a satire . . . forever on the point of breaking into bitter criticism."[8] And Mary McCarthy, in a strangely boorish review of what must have been a bad production of "The Importance of Being Earnest," alleges that "Depravity is the hero and the only character, the people on the stage embodying various shades of it."[9] Never have so many teeth been found in a butterfly.

Wilde faced this anomaly all his life, and it is for this reason primarily that his definition of art is a definition of the elaborative operations of the comic. There may be certain truth in the contention that all his comic works were directed to the contemporary culture, but not in the literally satiric and morally charged way that his critics allege. Wilde's objective was transvaluation. When a culture has so soberly elaborated coarse materiality and mirthless Grundyism into its primary values, it must be instructed in the art of transposing all values.

The great moments in Wilde's comedies occur when people talk about "important" things in a heedlessly inappropriate way. When Lord Arthur Savile approaches Herr

Winckelkopf in search of an explosive clock, Winckelkopf naturally assumes that Lord Arthur is bent on revenge against the police, and protests:

> "I am afraid I cannot do anything for you. The English detectives are really our best friends, and I have always found that by relying on their stupidity, we can do exactly what we like. I could not spare one of them."
>
> "I assure you," said Lord Arthur, "that it has nothing to do with the police at all. In fact, the clock is intended for the Dean of Chichester."
>
> "Dear me! I had no idea that you felt so strongly about religion, Lord Arthur. Few young men do nowadays."
>
> "I am afraid you overrate me, Herr Winckelkopf," said Lord Arthur, blushing. "The fact is, I really know nothing about theology."[10]

The motif of "The Importance of Being Earnest" is much the same. Everything that the society puts forward as its sanctities is treated with delightful casualness. Only trifles seem to matter. Algernon, accounting for his habit of Bunburying—escaping from responsibilities—says, "Well, one must be serious about something, if one wants to have any amusement in life. [You, Jack, are serious] about everything, I should fancy. You have such an absolutely trivial nature."[11] "Serious" and "trivial" lose their customary meanings in the Wildean world. "Important" matters, from murder to religion to love to politics, are divested of their significance, and we seem to find that amusing—liberating, in fact. Wilde described "The Importance of Being Earnest" as "a trivial comedy about serious people"; (his critics, of course, persist in trying to make it a serious comedy about trivial people). The title gives away the issue: it takes up "importance" and "earnestness" in the most flippant manner possible. What more apt comic tack to take when dealing with a society that does, as we have seen with the Caudles and the Pooters, attribute significance and value to the wrong things? Deprive a utilitarian nation of its cherished valuations and you have knocked it off balance.

Wilde's method for this is paradox, for paradox is the essence of transvaluation. In Wilde's most successful paradoxical epigrams—"Ambition is the last refuge of the failure"; "Wickedness is a myth invented by good people to account for the curious attractiveness of others"; "It is only the superficial qualities that last"—the statements have a ring of truth to them and yet are not quite true. We can never fully accept Wilde's outrageous remarks but we retain a sneaking suspicion that they are more honest to life than we care to allow. When he says, that "in all unimportant matters, style, not sincerity, is the essential," and "in all important matters, style, not sincerity, is the essential," we recognize that although such nonsense contradicts our normal assumptions, it awakens disquieting thoughts. We are thrust into a mode of thinking that is disturbingly unstable, into the uneasy poise of a proposition that is neither true nor false. When such paradox treats of value as in the remark, "ambition is the last refuge of the failure," then Wilde has succeeded in starting up the habit of mind that doubts itself and begins to transfer value back and forth. Erskine, a dinner-table wit in Wilde's novel *The Picture of Dorian Gray*, says that "the way of paradoxes is the way of truth. To test Reality we must see it on the tightrope. When the Verities become acrobats we can judge them."[12] Social and emotional "truths" in such shifting balance reveal their essential relativity, and the human mind is released from the tendency to reify that is the source of prejudice, insensitivity, and sentimentality.

With characteristic brazenness, Wilde puts his method to the test in the most stereotypically formulaic of genres, the novel of moral decline. *The Picture of Dorian Gray* (1890) is ostensibly the tale of an indulgent young man, Dorian Gray, who devotes himself to greater and greater excesses of hedonism. His essential spiritual depravity is reflected in

a portrait that was painted of him in the flower of his spot-
less youth, for the portrait corrupts and deliquesces with
his every perverse act while he himself retains his un-
blemished beauty. *Dorian Gray* contains all the elements of
the sensational account of a lost soul—indulgence of the
murkiest desires, trafficking with tempters, a desperate
need for moral reform discovered too late. But it is the
moral novel manqué, for it is ultimately a parodic treatment of the quintessentially bourgeois fantasy fiction and is
built on a series of paradoxes that open up our conceptions
about the interrelationship of art and reality and about the
nature of personality.

"The Decay of Lying" explicates *The Picture of Dorian
Gray*, establishing the initial concept that governs the novel:
"Paradox though it may seem—and paradoxes are always
dangerous things—it is none the less true that Life imitates
Art far more than Art imitates Life" (307). "Life holds the
mirror up to Art, and either reproduces some strange type
imagined by painter or sculptor, or realizes in fact what has
been dreamed in fiction" (311). Wilde's concept is not as
paradoxical now as it seemed then, for we have come to acknowledge the power of art to shape our visions of reality.
But it was a stunning and frankly outrageous pronounce-
ment for a nineteenth-century English critical figure—
revolutionary in the way it predicted the conclusions of
E. H. Gombrich and other twentieth-century aestheti-
cians—radical because of its typically Wildean bravura:

Things are because we see them, and what we see, and
how we see it, depends on the Arts that have influenced
us. To look at a thing is very different from seeing a
thing. . . . There may have been fogs for centuries in
London. I dare say there were. But no one saw them,
and so we do not know anything about them. They did
not exist until Art had invented them. Now, it must be
admitted, fogs are carried to excess. They have become
the mere mannerism of a clique, and the exaggerated

realism of their method gives dull people bronchitis. Where the cultured catch an effect, the uncultured catch cold (312).

Wilde goes on to suggest that art not only shapes our seeing, but shapes our being. How surely the ironies of Joseph Conrad's *Under Western Eyes*, or Wilde's own mock novel of crime and punishment *The Picture of Dorian Gray*, fall into place when Vivian, in "The Decay of Lying," says that "The Nihilist, that strange martyr who has no faith, who goes to the stake without enthusiasm, and dies for what he does not believe in, is a purely literary product. He was invented by Tourgénieff, and completed by Dostoieffski. Robespierre came out of the pages of Rousseau as surely as the People's Palace rose out of the *débris* of a novel. Literature always anticipates life" (308). Indeed, the germ of *Dorian Gray*'s subtle paradoxes lies in an account by Vivian of a young woman of "curious exotic beauty" whom he had once known. "What interested most in her," he says, "was not her beauty, but her character, her entire vagueness of character. She seemed to have no personality at all, but simply the possibility of many types" (310). By chance the woman read a melodramatic story in which the heroine resembled her perfectly and, yielding to an "absolutely irresistible impulse," she began to imitate the fictional life in all its "strange and fatal progress." She became her fictional model; her own life attained, with tragic consequences, to the pattern of a work of bad art.

And so it is with Dorian Gray. When we initially learn about Dorian, Basil Hallward, the distinguished portraitist, speaks of his "fascinating personality." Yet we soon discover that Dorian is an unformed being—young, beautiful, and impressionable. In the first of the complex series of paradoxes about the role of art in shaping the human personality, Basil acknowledges to his friend Lord Henry Wotton, "you might see nothing [in Dorian]. I see everything in him. He is never more present in my work than when no image of him is there. He is a suggestion, as I have said, of a new manner" (10). Lord Henry's curiosity is piqued and he lingers on until Dorian comes to sit for his portrait. Lord Henry, the epitome of the cynical, amoral disposition, then mesmerizes Dorian with his bon mots, his cutting wit, his elaborations upon sensuality. He is the Oscar Wilde of the legendary poses and the studied but fascinating grace. Gradually, he acquires a dominating influence over the young man and begins to invest him with a sensibility that is clearly Lord Henry's own. "To influence a person is to give him one's own soul," he observes; "He becomes an echo of someone else's music, an actor of a part that has not been written for him" (17). Ironically, Dorian believes that it is his own true nature that is responding to Lord Henry's suggestions: "He was dimly conscious that entirely fresh influences were at work within him. Yet they seemed to him to have come really from himself. The few words that Basil's friend had said to him—words spoken by chance, no doubt, and with willful paradox in them—had touched some secret chord that had never been touched before" (18). "Seemed" is the crucial word here, for so insidious has been Lord Henry's seductive power upon the youthful Dorian that Dorian has literally convinced himself that he *is* the person that Lord Henry has artfully created him to be.

Lord Henry amazes even himself. As his influence on Dorian grows, he exhilarates in it:

Talking to [Dorian] was like playing upon an exquisite violin. He answered to every touch and thrill of the bow. There was something terribly enthralling in the exercise of influence. No other activity was like it. To project one's own soul into some gracious form, and let it tarry there for a moment; to hear one's own intellectual views echoed back to one with all the added music of passion and youth; to convey one's temperament into another as though it were a subtle fluid or a strange perfume; there was a real joy in that (35).

Lord Henry has achieved, so he believes, a rare creation—
a living work of art. "Now and then a complex personality
. . . assumed the office of art; was indeed, in its way, a real
work of art, Life having its elaborate masterpieces, just as
poetry has, or sculpture, or painting" (57).

But nothing in Wilde's paradoxical world is as simple as
that. Dorian can only exist as an unaging, undeteriorating
work of human beauty because Basil Hallward has painted
a portrait of him in his instant of most glorious youth that
absorbs all the effects that the living person would normally
suffer. As Dorian stuns the social world of England with his
personal glory, the portrait sits in a locked room of Dorian's attic, gathering cynical lines about its mouth, tinting
itself florid with sensuality, twisting its features horribly as
the jowls sag, the lips grow tight, the eyes glaze in voluptu-
ousness. Basil Hallward had adored Dorian before Lord
Henry lured him away, and there is a suggestion that all
the intensity and beauty that Basil had put in the portrait is
now being drawn out of it by the living subject. Dorian is
therefore Basil's creation also, for it was "as if he had recognized himself for the first time" (24) when he saw Basil's
portrait of him. And Lord Henry, for all his pride of authorship, acknowledges at times that the real-life Dorian is
the realization of Basil's artistic vision of him. Basil, however, is a bourgeois moralist. He is only slightly amused at
Lord Henry's cynicism and often appalled at what his witty
friend says. A kind of good-natured Podgers with talent,
Basil frumps through the novel in overcoats and galoshes,
a sincerely moral man. Thus it is that the portrait pays the
penalty for all of Dorian's evil and debauch; for it is the re-
pository of Basil's influence for good in Dorian. It is his
Puritan conscience, and as Dorian sinks deeper and deeper
into crime, the portrait in the attic haunts him as an
emblem of the sin and guilt for which he rarely physically
suffers.

And thus, in what passes with most readers for a fancifully melodramatic exercise in the old Puritan staple of crime and punishment, sensationalized with a bit of Jekyll and Hyde and some heavy doses of Huysman and the French "Art for Art's Sake" literature, Wilde has set into play his radical ideas about the influence of art on life. We can now see how far the development of the slowly evolving concept of human nature as a form of willful projection has come. In the seventy or so years from the Silver Fork novel's tentative explorations of the idea, Wilde can now propose it as one of his paradoxical truths. If it is masked, as ever, in comedy and artifice, it is not done so out of timorousness, but now out of slyness. And it is an *assertion* of the elaborative phase of the comic in English nineteenth-century literature. Not only is Lord Henry the embodiment of that spirit—"he played with the idea, and grew willful; tossed it into the air and transformed it; let it escape and recaptured it; made it iridescent with fancy, and winged it with paradox. The praise of folly, as he went on, soared into a Philosophy. . . . It was an extraordinary improvisation. He was brilliant, fantastic, irresponsbile"— but it has come alive as a central truth of human nature. We *are* improvisations—our own and those of others who influence us. We are creatures of art.

The elaborative qualities of *The Picture of Dorian Gray* do not end here, for the entire novel is a parodic arabesque upon the bête noire of the comic spirit—the Puritan notion of moral consequence. Like his contemporary Butler, Wilde is seeking to dispose of the paradigm by mockingly reconstructing it, and then throwing it by its own weight. *Dorian Gray* is, I am convinced, the melodramatic tale of a soul's progress manqué. But I acknowledge that most readers may find my theory difficult to accept. Perhaps the novel *begins* playfully, they will admit, for the opening scenes are Wilde at his casual best—flippant, excessive, paradoxical—but, they argue, the manner of the novel surely changes as we follow Dorian's gradual decline.

When Dorian becomes a fallen soul, he grows melodramatic in his posturing. And worse, the prose itself in the last half of the novel becomes overwrought, as if Wilde had changed his mind and were now trying to be serious. Passages like the following abound:

> He knew what was waiting for him there; saw it, indeed, and shuddering, crushed with dank hands his burning lids as though he would have robbed the very brain of sight, and driven the eyeballs back into their cave. It was useless. The brain had its own food on which it battened, and the imagination, made grotesque by terror, twisted and distorted as a living thing by pain, danced like some foul puppet on a stand, and grinned through moving masks (167).

Bad writing, certainly. Enough, indeed, to drive the eyeballs back into their cave. Bad art. Once again, though, "The Decay of Lying" supplies the key to Wilde's method. Vivian says:

> "Art begins with abstract decoration, with purely imaginative and pleasureable work dealing with what is real and non-existent. This is the first stage. Then Life becomes fascinated with this new wonder, and asks to be admitted into the charmed circle. Art takes life as part of her rough material, recreates it, and refashions it in fresh forms, is absolutely indifferent to fact, invents, imagines, dreams, and keeps between herself and reality the impenetrable barrier of beautiful style, of decorative or ideal treatment. The third stage is when Life gets the upper hand, and drives Art out into the wilderness. This is the true decadence, and it is from this that we are now suffering" (301).

A work of art, whether it be a novel or a human being's manner of existence, ceases to be good art when it proposes to model itself after life. "And as for Life, she is the solvent that breaks up Art, the enemy that lays waste her house" (300). "All bad art comes from returning to Life and Nature, and elevating them into ideals" (319).

The thesis is depicted within *Dorian Gray* in the story of the young actress Sybil Vane, whom Dorian worships when she plays Shakespeare's great heroines. Dorian communicates his adoration to Sybil, and at once she, now in love and now playing her own real-life drama, becomes a wretched actress. So long as she could model herself after the great art of Shakespeare, she was herself a vessel of fine art. But once she turns to life and nature, her personality dissolves into bad art. Her last days, which culminate in her suicide when she learns that Dorian will have no more to do with her, are, in fact, melodrama, for that is the kind of second-rate art that life produces (69-72).

Lord Henry Wotton is therefore, surprisingly, the real villain of the piece. For he, we learn, is an observer of life. This flaw in his artistic sensibility passes almost unnoticed in the early stage of the novel, even when he breaks off his enchantment of Dorian saying, "All I want now is to look at life" (43). It inches into our awareness, though, for we find him musing more and more on the experience around him. "Human life—that appeared to him the one thing worth investigating. Compared to it there was nothing else of any value" (56). He is fatally inclined toward the mimetic, and consequently his artistic masterpiece—the creation of the living art work, Dorian—will inevitably disintegrate into bad art. Fascinating, charming, witty, Lord Henry defines himself when he remarks that "the only artists I have ever known, who are personally delightful, are bad artists. Good artists exist simply in what they make, and consequently are perfectly uninteresting in what they are. A great poet, a really great poet, is the most unpoetical of creatures. But inferior poets are absolutely fascinating" (239).

The taint emerges in Lord Henry's creation, Dorian, for with his love of Sybil Vane, he becomes a devotee of life: "And, certainly, for him Life itself was the first, the greatest, of the arts" (289). Dorian immerses himself in real experience, indulging in long debauches in the under-world of London, and as he does so, the pattern of his existence falls more and more into that of the melodrama. Correspondingly, as the model of bad art shapes the final course of Dorian's career, the prose of Wilde's novel becomes increasingly melodramatic, the plot more formulaic, the imaginative play less vital, and the events vulgar and dispiriting. Dorian corrupts half the youth of London, arranges the murder of Basil Hallward, writhes in his sleep with nightmares of guilt, is stalked by the revenge-bound brother of Sybil Vane, and meets, finally, a ghastly end by his own hand. Next week, "East Lynne."

My point, of course, is that *The Picture of Dorian Gray* evolves—intentionally—into bad art. Wilde created an elaborate parody of the conventional tale of moral decline, much as Vladimir Nabokov fifty years later rendered up pseudo-Dostoyevsky in the last phases of the plot of *Lolita*. The problem, of course, is that Wilde forsook the controlled mockery, the elegance and *jeu d'esprit* in the last third of the book that had been the hallmark of the comedy in the earlier chapters. Nabokov, on the other hand, sustained his manner throughout. Consequently, we cannot be fully convinced that Wilde knew what he was doing; and the essential elements that would confirm the author's comic intention are missing. Nor do Wilde's post-mortems in response to critics help us, for he cautioned the hostile editor of the *St. James Gazette* that "there is a terrible moral in *Dorian Gray*" and at the same time regretted that the editor had gotten Puritanism and "art matters" all confused.[13] The tendentiousness plus some of the old emotionality of the Wilde of the fairy tales probably reasserted itself in *Dorian Gray*'s last half, when the comic elaboration could not be sustained. The paradox of the man and his art reemerges.

> "There is a nobility in fearless truthfulness, is there not? and about the magic of his personality he could never be induced to tell a lie."—
> *Narrator*, The Green Carnation

I I

William Butler Yeats said of Wilde that he was "essentially a man of action, that he was a writer by perversity and accident, and would have been more important as soldier or politician." Wilde, however, never took the slightest interest in politics. He was indolent to a fault. And when disaster overtook him in the series of trials that led to his imprisonment, he proved to be constitutionally unable to act to his own benefit and curiously naive. When Wilde learned of Yeats' assessment of him, he observed laconically, "It is always interesting to hear Yeats' opinion about one."

Yet is it true that Wilde is almost more important as a literary figure than as an artist. He is remembered in English letters for the spectacle of his life, which persistently threatened to overwhelm his creative and critical work. His was a flamboyant presence. André Gide recalls hearing of him at Mallarmé's house: "Wilde had at the time what Thackeray calls 'the chief gift of great men': success. His gesture, his look triumphed. He was portrayed as a brilliant talker, and I wished to know him, though I had no hope of managing to do so."[14] Yeats recollects that "my first meeting with Oscar Wilde was an astonishment. I never before heard a man talking with perfect sentences, as if he had written them all overnight with labour and yet all spontaneous."[15] The studied artificiality of Wilde's manner enhanced the impression he made and contributed to the notion that the art work Wilde was making of his life was as compelling as anything he wrote. He himself quipped, "I have put all my genius into my life; I have only put my talent into my works."

Such an emphasis on style of life seems to be there in Wilde's aesthetic. Even as he makes a case in "The Decay of Lying" for a pure art, unsullied by nature's lack of form, we sense that it is all intended in the end to lead to a way of living. As the social and moral inhibitions of the bourgeois Puritan ethos are cleared away from art, a new stylish life, modeled after the best art, can emerge. The decision to present his ideas on art through the conversations of dandies and to dramatize his paradoxes in works like *Dorian Gray* and "The Importance of Being Earnest" indicates that the Wilde's real fascination lies in the ways art is reflected in and influences individual behavior. How rarely are we invited to examine art objects rather than people; how much more fascinating is Dorian Gray the character than his portrait, or is Lord Henry's social "art" than Basil Hallward's painting; how often is the controversy couched as one of individual style in antagonistic tension with the dominant culture rather than creative elaboration following its own intrinsic courses. This is not the same as saying that Wilde's works are autobiographical confession pieces —for that simply travesties their parodic and comedic intentions. It is to say, rather, that a mode of living and a pure aesthetic are concatenated in Wilde; they are yoked together in a vital alliance for freedom and style.

Wilde's aesthetic thus seems to be a very *English*, very Victorian formulation. The translation of art into social activity epitomizes the nineteenth-century English critical sensibility. What was the high art Epicureanism if not the search for a culture that was also a cultivated life style? Is not Pater's invocation at the close of *The Renaissance*— which Wilde called his "golden book"—to burn in life with

a hard gemlike flame? We distinguish Meredith's artistic
elaborations from those of the late Dickens by noting that
Meredith worked toward the opening up of new life styles
while Dickens experimented with the creation of new possibilities for artistic invention and permutation. Wilde's
affinities—his comedic heritage, if you will—are with
Meredith and the high culture movement; this presumably
is what Yeats had in mind when he called Wilde "essentially
a man of action."

Still, there is a crucial difference between Wilde and
Meredith. Although both are seeking a purity of individual
expression, a quintessence of self, in their comic studies,
Meredith was also searching out the social and psychological causes of his being. His intensified dramatizations are
wrapped up in issues of social behavior: Why does the male
ego react with such coldness and anguish to social humiliation? What are the sources of that tension? *The Ordeal of
Richard Feverel* and *The Egoist* explore psychic stress
through its *social* manifestations. Meredith was also interested in social consequences, and *The Egoist* in particular
was written with an eye for its social and psychological impact on its readers. Wilde, in his notorious life style and in
his art, seeks, like Meredith, to define and elaborate on the
inexplicable, the random courses of the self, but with none
of Meredith's intensity. The tension between the comic
manner (which normally reduces or deflects psychic immediacy) and its underlying content that we find in many
comic works of self-exploration is rarely felt in Wilde. And
just as the psychic force is obscured or omitted from
Wilde's expression, so also are the social factors and the social consequences diminished and even trivialized. Personality is at play in Wilde. It is expressed for its own sake and
its own fascinations. Instead of dredging up the sources of
his behavior in the darkly complex struggles of personal
emotion and inhibition, and instead of projecting those issues into a dramatic social context, Wilde gives his personality a kind of free run. Self-presentation is undertaken not

for analysis, but for display. The object of the art, and the artificial behavior, of Oscar Wilde is a demonstration of the caprices, the vagaries, the encounters, the perverse and the pleasureful courses of the self. "Throughout the whole of his life," explains Holbrook Jackson in his vivid chronicle of the 1890s, Wilde "tried to live up . . . to an idea of personality; and the whole of his philosophy is an attempt to prove that personality, even though it destroy itself, should be the final work of art."[16] Consequently, the presentation of the Wildean self carries with it none of the preoccupation with social effects that we see in Meredith. Whatever social implications there are remain casual and incidental, for the interest is in the self-expression, in the often uncanny and always entrancing performance of the elaborately indulged personality. Wilde does not write, nor did he behave, for maximum social impact in the sense of seeking to move the audience. There is a kind of ideal comic disposition in him. No wonder he was so stunned when his performance *did* have its awesome social and psychological impact.

Wilde is the first writer we have looked at who has the *avant-garde* sensibility. Renato Poggioli propounds what he calls a theory of the avant-garde in Western culture and argues that it is a phenomenon that appears first in its true form in the last quarter of the nineteenth century.[17] Poggioli contends that one of its essential qualities, a celebration of artistic experimentation and elaboration for its own sake, is not characteristic of earlier "Bohemian" or "Dandy" movements. We can surely see from our own study of the 1820s and 1830s in England, when exotic self-display and licentious behavior seem to have flourished briefly, that a genuine commitment to artistic experimentation could scarcely be said to exist in a body of expression that was as anxiety-ridden about conventional morality as was the Silver Fork literature. The interplay of art and life, also, was handled differently by, say, Bulwer than by Wilde. For Bulwer it was a disconcerting interaction of spheres, a troubling indication that values were in flux and that attitudes were being distorted by the instability of fashions. Fictions were slipping into realities almost against one's wishes. Wilde, on the other hand, cultivates the interaction. Looking across the channel to the avant-garde movements in late nineteenth-century France, Wilde can see that he is in line with witty, humoristic experiments by Alfred Jarry and others to break down the rigid frames between the art work and life.[18] Comic artificiality in life style is accompanied by the playful introduction of incongruous bits of "real life" into art works—mock commentaries written into paintings, newspaper clippings assembled in collages, snippets of advertisements and public speeches interspersed in poems. The arbitrary boundaries between art and life are broken down in both directions in order to achieve ultimate liberation from all conventions.

Style is a trait of the avant-garde mentality. It counters middle-class cultural eclecticism with a mystique of purity; it surmounts the discursive and empirical qualities of "ordinary" art by essentializing form, manner, and aesthetic position. Almost invariably, as Poggioli suggests, it evolves into an *ultra* attitude, for it is agonistic—both antagonistic and playful—and therefore by its very nature need not be bound in its expression.[19] Hence, though it is often grounded in intellectually estimable ideas, it appears to be a posture; and, indeed, in part it is. Arthur Symons, as good a critic as the English *fin-de-siècle* produced, thus saw in Wilde a set of attitudes rather than aesthetic or social positions. Symons recognized that Wilde was interested in the display of personality—"he made of himself many souls, souls of intricate pattern and elaborate colour;" he was a "showman of souls"—but he could discover no real intellectual or aesthetic concept behind it. "His intellect was dramatic, and the whole man was not so much a personality as an attitude. Without being a sage, he maintained the attitude of a sage; without being a poet, he maintained the attitude of a poet."[20] When a man replaces belief with an attitude, he is treating ideas as one would fashions. Symons was perplexed by that lack of commitments; it seemed to him almost as if Wilde regarded aesthetic positions as something to dress up in for evenings in advanced intellectual or artistic circles.

To the observers of his time, and particularly to the ordinary middle-class man and woman, Wilde thus seemed to be intellectually as well as morally irresponsible. They were provoked by his apparent ability to carry his beliefs loosely. There was never anything insidious about Wilde—a better hearted man could scarcely be found—and that seemed to be why he troubled the English so. The humorism, the apparent lack of commitment, the readiness to treat even art as if it were the latest modish vogue, seemed to gall people more than if he had been a ferocious incendiary. Perhaps they sensed that Wilde was a strange new product of the intensified media orientation and fashion consciousness that characterized the last two decades of the nineteenth century.

Wilde's generation operated in a cultural situation that none before them can have faced. The expanded reach of newspapers and magazines—especially into strata of the middle and even lower classes that had not generally been caught up before in the interests of news, social gossip, and fashion—and the relatively established quality of the Victorian social order, which allowed its citizens to seek stimuli in popular culture, contributed to a high degree of cultural receptivity. By the 1880s, the English were absorbing and reprocessing ideas, events, and modes of behavior with a rapidity that could not have been possible even twenty years earlier. Wilde and a few others, particularly Max Beerbohm—reflected in essays such as "A Defence of Cosmetics" (1894) and "1880" (1895)—were aware of the way media was sensitizing the general public. Wilde, especially, knew how to exploit their receptivity to any sort of stimuli, to anything "new" (that adjective particularly came into force during the *fin-de-siècle*), for he had not only the detachment and aplomb to sacrifice some of the content to style but he also had the wit to keep his positions ajuggle in perpetual light-handed play.

The curious question is why the English reacted so violently to their entertaining artist-critic, while the French endured many more instances of this from their avant-garde *provocateurs*, who were exploiting the faddism of the popular culture in the same witty manner. Even the immediate answer, Wilde's sodomy conviction, does not really explain English sensitivity. Most Frenchmen were just as stolidly bourgeois in their attitudes as most of the English seem to have been. Roger Shattuck, in *The Banquet Years*, his study of aspects of the later nineteenth century avant-garde, offers the suggestion that it is the monolithic conservatism of the French, oddly enough, which accounts for their longtime tolerance of a series of antibourgeois movements.

> The premise of all extreme protest and censure in France seems to be not change but permanence: nothing will change irretrievably or change faster. . . . France tolerates extremes of heterodoxy and outrageous behavior because it knows that ultimately no one will be harmed: the life of the nation will scarcely be touched. The avant-garde formed first in France because there was an artistic tradition of defiance, and it has lasted longest there because the country as a whole has only reluctantly taken to heart the lessons of its own most venturesome talents. France is inoculated against itself.[21]

England, on the other hand, because its social structure had been in such flux through most of the nineteenth century, proved more volatile. An edginess remained in the English consciousness, an edginess provoked not so long before by Dickens' attacks on middle-class smugness. And as we have seen in the domestic comedy of the Grossmiths, a substantial portion of the middle class had just settled into their new station when they were almost immediately

beset by the instability of tastes and the excitable fashions
of a media-responsive culture. Our survey of English comedy preceding and during the Victorian age shows, in fact,
that it was the middle class more than any isolated group of
artistic rebels that was wrestling with the problems of
change and value while still attempting to achieve
equipoise. The bulk of the English nation could not "inocu-
late" itself against these fevers; it was the carrier of the disease.

Wilde, then, was touching an acutely sensitive area. The
body politic, which handled socialism and various minor
challenges to it with relative equanimity, roused itself to
squash Wilde and what he seemed to represent. The Government felt constrained to prosecute him to the hilt and
followed up an initial mistrial with another, better directed
action. The downfall of Wilde effectively destroyed the
Bohemian avant-garde in England almost in a matter of
months. *The Yellow Book*, which had come to symbolize the
"yellow nineties," faded away in 1897, two years after
Wilde's conviction, despite its genuinely innocuous propriety and its publisher's assiduous attempts to divorce himself from any association with Wilde. The entire vivid little
movement, of Aubrey Beardsley and Ernest Dowson and
Lionel Johnson, vanished overnight. By the end of the
decade, there was almost no trace of the phenomenon that
had been the scandal and rage of London in 1894. When
Wilde was released from Reading Gaol, he found nothing
but cold rancor in his old English audience and exiled himself to France and Italy for his last few pathetic years. His
effect has been a remarkably lasting one, reaching writers
from James Joyce to William Faulkner, but there was scant
evidence in the deathly quiet of the last days of the century
that this would be the case.

Wilde's own reaction to his downfall offers intriguing
clues to what it was about Wilde's manner, about the spectacle of his performance of his personality, that so
threatened the English way of life. From the first, his

friends were struck by the seeming nonchalance with which he confronted what promised at best to be a dangerous venture. Having made the first foolish move, suing the Marquis of Queensberry for the slanderous remarks he had been making about Wilde's relationship with the Marquis' estranged son Lord Alfred Douglas, Wilde seemed to raise no energy to free himself from a degenerating situation. After the failure of the slander suits, an offended government began its moves against him. Still Wilde continued to look upon the entire thing as if it were a publicity program for his aesthetic theories. He refused all urgings that he flee to France. He allowed Douglas to involve him in ruinous courses of action. At the trials themselves, he bandied with the opposing counsel about art and amorality, infuriating a scandal-hungry public with his apparant disdain for English values. The good-natured indolence that characterized all his previous social behavior continued almost unabated through the anguish of his public humiliation, and his friends (a dwindling number) searched in vain for the motive of it. He was by no means a crusader for homosexual rights; in fact, he never looked upon the trials as a case for that. Certainly some of his behavior is attributable to bad judgment—he was horribly naive—and undoubtedly a great deal of it was simply a natural continuation of the postures to which he had so inured himself. Nor can we disregard the element of conscious martyrdom in his course of action: how fitting a closure that would make to a life which was a performance; it would furnish a kind of mock moral ending as in the old reformed sinner literature. Wilde rather savored the idea that his story resembled Christ's and developed that notion at greater length in prison afterward. But the more fundamental explanation is that Wilde for the most part did not appear to treat the episode as if it had significant social or psychological consequences. He acted as if it would have no impact on him other than as another stimulating encounter in the soul's search for realization. Even after completing his sentence, he entertained the idea that there would be no serious social effects from his disgrace, and that he could resume his place as presiding wit of English culture.

In my Introduction, I suggested a working definition of the comic—an expression in which the author handles the subject in ways that avoid emphasizing or intensifying its more psychically upsetting aspects or that reduce the intensity of the reader's confrontation with its social implications. And I used, as an example of a noncomic presentation, Wilde's lengthy letter written to Lord Alfred Douglas from prison, later published as *De Profundis*. Wilde wrote the letter because he had become aware of Douglas's treachery, Douglas's exploitation of him. But *De Profundis* signifies a different, deeper awakening: Wilde recoils from the sudden revelation that human life has social consequences and searing psychological impact. So blinding is the light of this revelation that *De Profundis* conveys every incident, every nuance, every feeling in a clarity that is hallucinatory: "each detail that accompanied each dreadful moment I am forced to recall: there is nothing that happened in those ill-starred years that I cannot recreate in that chamber of the brain set apart for grief and for despair: every strained note of your voice, every twitch and gesture of your nervous hands, every bitter word."[22] *De Profundis* records the awful instant of the shattering of the comic. From this document, so far on the other side from comedy, we can perceive—and probably Wilde can perceive—what the essential nature of Wilde's performance was and why it was an anathema to English middle-class culture.

At the outset, Wilde is horror-struck at Douglas's ability to manipulate him. Time and again, Wilde maintains, he tried to break from Douglas, who was a petulant lover and sycophant, and yet he could not. "I had always thought that my giving up to you in small things meant nothing: that when a great moment arrived I could assert my will-power in its natural superiority. It was not so. At the great moment my will-power completely failed me" (430). Almost as if it were unreal, he puzzles over the force of Douglas's will, the hate that impelled it, the determination it showed.

> I thought life was going to be a brilliant comedy, and that you were to be one of many graceful figures in it. I found it to be a revolting and repellant tragedy, and that the sinister occasion of the great catastrophe, sinister in its concentration of aim and intensity of narrowed will-power, was yourself, stripped of that mask of joy and pleasure by which you, no less than I, had been deceived and led astray (444).

How revelatory this passage is! "Concentration of aim and intensity of narrowed will-power"—these constitute the socially absorbed, anxious aspirations that are the driving force of the English middle class. And this is the ethos of the noncomic. The middle-class mentality and the noncomic merge in this vision. He charges Douglas with having

> brought the element of Philistinism into a life that had been a complete protest against it, and from some points of view a complete annihilation of it. The Philistine element in life is not the failure to understand Art. Charming people such as fishermen, shepherds, ploughboys, peasants and the like know nothing about Art, and are the very salt of the earth. He is the Philistine who upholds and aids the heavy, cumbrous, blind mechanical forces of Society, and who does not recognize the dynamic force when he meets it either in a man or a movement (492).

The "mechanical" quality he defined in this way: "The more mechanical people, to whom life is a shrewd speculation dependent on a careful calculation of ways and means, always know where they are going, and go there. They start with the desire of being the Parish Beadle, and, in whatever sphere they are placed, they succeed in being the

Parish Beadle and no more" (487). If this does not define
the middle-class consciousness of social class and social position, nothing does. It defines, as well, the fixation of purpose and meaning that characterizes "seriousness" in life.

These passages reveal not only the nature of the mentality that Wilde was contending with, and which he had just
come to understand in all its deadly self-determination, but
Wilde's sense of what his own vision and role had been. He
had been living and dramatizing the comic ethos: "I
thought life was going to be a brilliant comedy." Indeed, he
saw his life as "a complete protest against" Philistinism
"and from some points of view a complete annihilation of
it." Nothing quite explains Wilde's lifelong performance
and his curiously casual, detached behavior—his apparent
lack of concentrated psychological commitment, his disregard of the conventional social effects—except the admis-
sion that he was living according to the essentially comic vision. Wilde's ability to separate himself emotively from his
own performance of the self, and his unconcern about social sources and social manifestations of his desires and
whims, which differentiates him from Meredith, devolve
only from a world view that is comic.

To champion his "individualism" as Wilde does in *De
Profundis* is to suggest also that such a position is solipsistic.
Wilde's insistence that "the artistic life is simply self-
development" and his reiteration of the importance of
being "realized" are explanations of what we have already
identified in Wilde's behavior: his ultimate purpose in all
he did was to indulge and then to observe the operations of
the personality. If that *is* solipsistic, it is so in a way that
would be difficult to apprehend by normal middle-class
standards. For it is not solipsism with a readily comprehensible purpose in mind. Wilde loved his celebrity, but it almost fell upon him. He gave away his money faster than he
earned it and he did not have that goal-orientation that
normally goes along with solipsism. By his own account,
"those whose desire is self-realization never know where

they are going" (488). How incomprehensible this must be
to his fellow countrymen.

Although the force of social consequences and the anguish of psychological distress were revelations to Wilde,
the self-definition as prophet of the comic attitude was not
the product of his sudden hindsight from a cell in Reading
Gaol. As early as 1883, he had been carving out a definition
of the comic as a contrast to intensified emotions.[23] He observed to the artist Philip Houghton in 1894 that "as seriousness of manner is the disguise of the fool, folly in its exquisite modes of triviality and indifference and lack of care
is the role of the wise man."[24] On another occasion he remarked that "Art is the only serious thing in the world.
And the artist is the only person who is never serious." In
Wilde's vocabulary, "Art" and "the comic" are often
equated, for in his idiom they both represent agonistic opposition to what the middle class in England takes seriously. "The only beautiful things," Vivian observes in "The
Decay of Lying," "are the things that do not concern us. As
long as a thing is useful or necessary to us, or affects us in
any way, either for pain or for pleasure, or appeals
strongly to our sympathies, or is a vital part of the environment in which we live, it is outside the proper sphere of
art. To art's subject-matter we should be more or less indifferent" (299).

A threatened body politic seems to sense innately what is
most dangerous to it. Late Victorian England generated its
own antibodies to the fevers of the Decadence in a set of
"Young Men" who clustered around William Ernest Henley and his *National Observer* (Beerbohm called them the
"Henley regatta"), counteracting the poisons of aestheticism with doctrines of healthy celebration of nature,
and invigorating assent. One of the "Young Men," G. S.
Street, sought to isolate Wilde for witty extermination in a
parodic satire called *The Autobiography of a Boy* (1894). The
book consists of a series of episodes narrated by a hapless
young aesthete named Tubby, each one of which, Tubby

supposes, redounds to his glory, but which in truth subjects him to humiliating put-downs and exposures. The humor, of an obtuse little man unaware of his gaffes, resembles that of the Grossmiths' *Diary of a Nobody*; it is almost as if the culture were summoning up its other branch of comedy, domestic humor, to counteract Wilde. From this other vantage point, we observe again that what troubles the prevailing culture about Wilde's operation and his ideas is his alienation from the assumptions of its life style. In a typical episode, Tubby, who has spent his days frittering away his father's money, meets an old school chum who has settled down in a job, assembled a family and modest means, and become thoroughly middle-class. Tubby attempts to lord it over his old friend with talk of art, his immoral posturing, and his airy disdain, and then is squashed by the suggestion that he "do some honest work" and quit humbugging. Street's satire develops a kind of reverse spin, for it becomes offensive in its defensiveness; the relentless humiliation of Tubby's affectation indicates that what Street is trying to pass off lightly is of deadly importance to his class. It offers further proof that Wilde's comic program has struck a raw nerve.

The sensitivity is acute because England at the end of the nineteenth century can be inflamed so readily in the very areas that Wilde touches. Lewis Carroll had perceived that "meaning" was so arbitrary a creation that it could be considered little more than cant for asserting power by those best able to grasp power. A society dimly conscious of this could scarcely tolerate a mode of expression that purported to treat all activities as if they had no social significance. A society raised on the Puritan work ethic and troubled by its own attractions to leisure could scarcely be expected to respond with equanimity to a style of behavior that seemed indolent and uncommitted. A society strenuously treading against the drift in values could scarcely be expected to welcome a system of paradox and transvaluation. A society concerned that many of its citizens were losing their individual crispness, and yet dedicated to the middle-class ethos of upward mobility and aspirations toward self-improvement, could scarcely enjoy a literary expression that openly reduced psychic intensity altogether. A society charged with the excitability of changing fashions, news, and the onset of rampant consumerism could scarcely absorb the avant-garde notion that its meaning lay in its trivialities as much as in those concerns that it had marked out as important. Several years after his release from prison, having reflected on how this society had scored upon him, Wilde looked back in wonder at his comic works and his comic life style of the 1880s and said, with what was probably as close as he could ever come to a sense of awe, "It was extraordinary. . . . How I used to toy with that Tiger Life."

> Failure, if it be a plain, unvarnished, complete
> failure . . . has always a certain dignity.
> —*Max Beerbohm*

III

The last word on English nineteenth-century comedy should be pronounced by Max Beerbohm, the avatar of turn-of-the-century sophisticated humor. Beerbohm drew off the vapors of the overheated culture of the 1890s more deftly than anyone else possibly could and decanted it in cool little essays beginning with "A Defense of Cosmetics" in *The Yellow Book* in 1894 and in limpid short stories published as *Seven Men and Two Others* in 1919. A reviewer of drama for the *Saturday Review*, a friend of Beardsley, and an acquaintance of Wilde, Beerbohm is the belles-lettrist of a movement that never, perhaps, could have exceeded that form—and never could have been captured in any other.

Let us consider as our representative figure Enoch

Soames, title character of a short story in *Seven Men*. Beer-bohm recalls meeting Soames for the first time in the Cafe Royal, a "pagan" haunt of Decadents and artistic types: Soames "was a stooping, shambling person, rather tall, very pale, with longish and brownish hair. He had a thin vague beard—or rather, he had a chin on which a large number of hairs weakly curled and clustered to cover its retreat.... I was sure this man was a writer.... He wore a soft black hat of clerical kind but of Bohemian intention, and a grey waterproof cape which, perhaps because it was waterproof, failed to be romantic."[25] Beerbohm admits that he was "immensely keen" on the *mot juste* at that time, and the *mot juste* for Soames seemed to be "dim." Enoch Soames was not an arabesque upon, but an attenuation of the Wildean artist-personality. He had written two thin volumes of third- or fourth-rate poetry called *Negations* and *Fungoids*. But, alas, he had not been able to create the fiction of a personal identity for himself.

Soames casts himself in all the affectations of the unap-preciated genius: he moodily inhabits shabby cafes, drink-ing absinthe (called by him, dramatically, his "glaucous witch"); he assumes the insolence and pettishness of a great man irritated by the banality of lesser souls; he despises Shelley and can barely countenance Keats. He has im-mersed himself in Baudelaire and apparently sunk right to the bottom. Nonetheless, the capacity to establish his exist-ence eludes him ominously. Perhaps it is the waterproof cape, Beerbohm keeps thinking. No, it is something more critical. Soames exists so marginally that there is an acute possibility that he will vanish from men's minds altogether. English comedy's version of modern human nature—a col-lection of roles and multiple selves, a fabric of its own fictions—has worked itself too fine with poor Soames. There is nothing here; he is nearly his own mirage. He in-eptly begins conversations with, "You don't remember me!" Haplessly, his best opinions fall apart in their deliv-ery. And his poetry, which is quite bad, is fixated on nonexistence: *Thou art, who has not been! Thou hast not been nor art!* When the noted portrait painter Rothenstein does a pastel of Soames, Beerbohm observes, "it 'existed' so much more than he; it was bound to."

Soames harbors one last hope. Perhaps his work, neglected in his own time, will endure, and will establish his existence through reputation. At the Restaurant du Vingtième Siècle, he meets a "Mephistophelean" character who offers him a "business" proposition: he will grant Soames an afternoon at the Reading Room of the British Museum one hundred years hence (June 3, 1997) at which time he will be able to look himself up in the card catalogue to see if he has cut any figure at all with posterity. Beerbohm, who is present on the occasion, shudders with the realization that this man is the Devil himself and that he is asking Soames to barter his soul for that glimpse into the future. Beerbohm shudders even more because the Devil shows such bad taste: he twirls his waxen mustache and swings an ebony cane, overdresses in a black sheeny outfit that makes him look like a diamond merchant, and persists in employing grotesque French expressions such as "dans le highlif." Beerbohm winces when the Devil jocosely refers to Hell as "home . . . be it never so humble!"

Now for the final twist of Beerbohm's comic involution of the Decadent reliance on gesture, of the Dorian Gray variations on the theme of Faust: when Soames is transported into the next century, he discovers that the only reference to him is Beerbohm's short story "Enoch Soames"—the one we have been reading. And in the account of that story he is described as an imaginary character. Soames is furious. Returned briefly to the nineteenth century before the Devil whisks him away, he reproaches Beerbohm for having incompetently deprived him of his existence: "You aren't an artist. . . . And you're so hopelessly not an artist that, so far from being able to imagine a thing and make it seem true, you're going to make even a true thing seem as if you'd made it up. You're a miserable bungler. And it's like my luck" (31). There is no denying that Beerbohm, the character-narrator, has botched the job; he is not even sure, by story's end, that Soames has really been seized by the Devil: "After all . . . London was a very large place, and one very dim figure might easily drop out of it unobserved—now especially, in the blinding glare of the [preparations for Victoria's] Jubilee" (33). Even were Enoch Soames to pop up (as he assuredly will in the British Museum on the afternoon of June 3, 1997), his nonexistence has been prefigured for him by the comic fiction of Max Beerbohm. There is no way off the involuted moebius curve of the story, for when Soames does appear in 1997, he will have been dead a hundred years and therefore only the ghost of himself, thus *still* not proof that he ever existed. Everything Soames has done to control his fate is a mockery.

Beerbohm's Enoch Soames is thus victim not only of the modern comic mentality that tells us all life is a fiction and that personality is a radically unstable construct but also of another aspect of the modern vision—the sense that individual will cannot control events. The outlook on life that generated the comedy of Thomas Love Peacock becomes a familiar one in the comic fiction of the twentieth century, in the short stories of Beerbohm and the novels of Evelyn Waugh, and in the burgeoning tradition of the comedy of the little man, the Chaplinesque victim, the nonhero as protagonist.

The change in literary treatment of human will and its power to effect events is as elusive to trace and yet as sure and marked as a sea change. We need only recall Thackeray's London, where rapacious old scoundrels and entrepreneurs shoved and schemed for position, or Lewis Carroll's mid-Victorian England, where power that was achieved by imposition of will was the name of the game, in order to observe how significant a shift of emphasis it has been. Like any such evolution in outlook, the doubts about the efficacy of individual purposiveness and intention evolved gradually and seeped into different sectors of the culture in varying degrees. It is beyond the scope of this book to attempt to analyze such a process, but it is worth our noting some of the salient influences because the outlook constitutes one of the primary characteristics of modern comic expression. In fact, it has something to do with the popularity of comedy as a means of portraying twentieth-century life.

We can assign the cause principally to the tempo and character of modern life. With increasing frequency the writers of the mid and later Victorian period—Carroll, Jerrold, the Grossmiths, Butler—recorded the confusion and impersonality of operating in a society whose institutions had become circumlocutious, whose chains of cause and effect had become obscure, and whose purposes had become diffuse. The retreatist mentality of the 1880s originated in the subtle sense of impotence that the average man felt when the Victorian liberal experiment failed to redeem its earlier promises, and when it more specifically proved inadequate to deal with agricultural failures, the "Irish Problem," and labor unrest. The real jolt, the fiasco of the Boer War, was to await the next century, when the concepts that propped up Imperialism were to crumble. But all in all it had been the feeling of smallness in a modern industrial society that caused men to seem Pooteresque.

Another factor must surely be modern psychology. The fiction of Henry James, Meredith and others—including, in an exaggerated way, that of Oscar Wilde—attuned English readers to the perplexity of human motivation several decades before Freud's impact was absorbed. People began thinking differently about human psychology. The idea of the human thought process as a none-too-logical, flowing confluence of irrational, emotive, often unpredictable subjective elements had subtly taken hold. Two late nineteenth-century Continental philosophers, Friedrich Nietzsche and Henri Bergson, proceeded from what were essentially psychological observations to offer theories of

human will, and of causality, that very likely had a significant contributing influence on the set of mind that was
shaping turn-of-the-century comic expression.

Nietzsche's direct influence is problematical. He was too
little understood, and in some ways too alien, to be any
kind of force in what we have suggested is essentially a cultural change of attitude in England. Certainly, his call for
an intensified, vitalistic will to power stimulated George
Bernard Shaw and H. G. Wells, and both English writers
shared Nietzsche's diagnosis of the widespread modern
vitiation of will. Wells' comic novels, especially *The History of
Mr. Polly* (1910), constitute small, classic expressions of the
plight of the nonhero, the victimized, comic little man. Although Nietzsche came into England too late to touch
Wilde's generation, the minor *fin-de-siècle* figure John
Davidson was influenced by him, George Moore, as we
might expect, had picked up some of his ideas, and
Havelock Ellis published three articles of appreciation of
Nietzsche in, of all places, Beardsley's Decadent journal
The Savoy in 1896. Nietzsche's *The Will to Power*, which concerns us principally, did not appear until 1901, 1906, and
1911 (although the ideas in the book had been taking form
for many years and the published volume is largely a collo-
cation of material from earlier periods). It is not as essential to note Nietzsche's *influence* on the English, however, as
to note the striking parallels in outlook and attitude, indeed, in sensibility, between him and a man like Wilde. *The
Will to Power* furnishes us with an expression of the line of
thought that would produce a literature focusing upon
gesture as a kind of counter to general feelings of impotence.

Thomas Mann remarks on the affinities between
Nietzsche and Wilde in an essay in which he points out that
both writers oppose the prevailing moral world view with
an aesthetic one, that both appreciate the essential fictionality of human character, and that both espouse a vitalistic
assertion of self in a civilization that they find enervating.[26]

Nietzsche had long believed, as does Wilde, that human value systems are primarily self-generated and that one creates the concept of his being and inner nature as he goes along. In *The Will to Power*, Nietzsche reveals his particular fascination—nay, admiration—for the Wildean artistic type, the rare instance of going against the general submersion of man's natural will to power. Nietzsche's enthusiasm for " 'play,' the useless—as the ideal of him who is overfull of strength, as 'childlike,' "[27] arises out of the same spirit as Wilde's comic defiance of English utilitarianism does. And Nietzsche understands the late-century aesthete's psychology:

> The *modern* artist . . . is also distinguished by [his] morbidity of character. The hysteric is false—he lies from love of lying, he is admirable in every art of dissimulation—unless his morbid vanity plays a trick on him. This vanity is like a continual fever that requires narcotics and does not shrink from any self-deception, any farce, that promises momentary relief. . . . The absurd irritability of his system, which turns all experiences into crises and introduces the 'dramatic' into the smallest accidents of life, robs him of all calculability: he is no longer a person, at most a rendezvous of persons and now this one, now that one shoots forward with shameless assurance. Precisely for this reason, he is great as an actor: all these poor will-less people whom the doctors study so closely astonish one with their virtuosity in mimicry, transfiguration, assumption of almost any desired character.[28]

Nietzsche analyzes the condition of his contemporary German culture, as some English writers analyzed the English, as one dominated by "procrastinators *par excellence*, slow to adopt, reluctant to let go, and relatively enduring in the midst of this tremendous change and mixture of elements. In such circumstances, the center of gravity necessarily shifts to the mediocre."[29] It is precisely this kind of

judgment that inspired Shaw to take his thinking a step
further, as Nietzsche does in the later sections of *The Will to
Power*, toward an idealization of a vitalistic "superman."
But Nietzsche, despite his ultimate espousal of the need for
a kind of supererogation of will, understands something
that Shaw would never admit, and that brings Nietzsche,
for a moment, close to the vision of Max Beerbohm. As the
passage on the psychology of the modern artist reveals,
Nietzsche discovers the source of a modern culture's indulgence with mediocrity and failure: there is a kind of
charm and wit in it that "becomes entertaining, it seduces."
The modern artist of the Wildean type is, in a sense, the
imaginative creation of a culture that has denied the connection between individual will and social effect, a man
who gravitates between gesture and failure.

Henri Bergson's observations are nowhere near as mordant as Nietzsche's, nor as grounded in social judgments.
But Bergson also feeds into the new ways of thinking about
the nature of human personality. In *Time and Free Will*
(1889, 1910), he writes:

> Hence there are finally two different selves, one of which
> is, as it were, the external projection of the other, its spa-
> tial and, so to speak, social representation. We reach the
> former by deep introspection, which leads us to grasp
> our inner states as living things, constantly *becoming*, as
> states not amenable to measure, which permeate one
> another and of which the succession in duration has
> nothing in common with juxtapostion in homogeneous
> space. But the moments at which we thus grasp ourselves
> are rare, and that is just why we are rarely free. The
> greater part of the time we live outside ourselves, hardly
> perceiving anything of ourselves but our own ghost. . . .
> Hence our life unfolds in space rather than in time; we
> live for the external world rather than for ourselves; we
> speak rather than think; we "are acted" rather than act
> ourselves.[30]

Bergson's contentions are particularly interesting because his theory of human nature tends to retain something of the older notion of an integral, "core" being, while acknowledging that in modern behavior we seem to be largely absorbed in our social roles, our projections of "acted out" selves. Even though the notion of created selves and of fragmented personality takes on such authority in twentieth-century literature that we scarcely challenge it any more, we wonder whether individuals do, in actuality, conceive of themselves in such a way. Indeed, we wonder whether the concept of the integral self has ever vanished. The issue carries special meaning for comic expression because if the notion of a deep-seated but rarely grasped inner self is retained, then the outward manifestations of personality seem all the more artificial and "comic" in their disparities. Certainly Bergson's psychological assumptions accord in this respect with those of Freud, and as post-Freudian concepts penetrate Western thinking, slightly different complexities must govern the comic vision of human nature. Comic writers discover new disparities in the workings of the unconscious and the conscious that seem to give a richer sense of expression than that of the projected self, which, as we have seen, was to a great extent an aspect of the industrial, urban, specialized experience of the nineteenth century.

More germane to our immediate concerns, however, is the next step that Bergson takes. He talks about causality in human behavior in much the same way that Nietzsche does. In *The Will to Power*, Nietzsche had attempted to establish that our common impression that our motives or will produce the actions and effects that follow them in time is a subjective illusion. Our error lies in falsely transposing our "feeling of will, our feeling of 'freedom,' our feeling of responsibilty and our intention to perform an act, into the concept 'cause'." In actuality all we do, Nietzsche argues, is reconstruct a cause or an intention from the effect; "we invent all causes after the schema of the effect."[31] Nietzsche's premise is psychological, in the characteristic of the human mind to construct and create its actualities, and Bergson's similar conclusion about causality is derived from a similar psychology. He too argues that the sense we have of one act proceeding from another, or from a "state of intention," really comes from our thinking backward from the effect, abetted by our tendency to abstract and objectify what are in actuality indivisible, interpenetrating phases of consciousness, by our failure to take into account the fact that human consciousness is a continuous flow or duration, and by our tendency to spatialize what is really an element of time.[32] Bergson examines at great length the process of what appears to be "choice" and argues that there is no such stopping place in human thought, no point at which we might have taken one course of action rather than another. Because of the continuous flow of our consciousness, fed by unconscious influences that presumably guide our disposition toward a course of action, we are always inclined toward what we seem finally to have decided.

When Bergson's and Nietzsche's thinking eventually penetrates into Western literary thinking, it provides a rationale for an almost absurdist view of individual behavior. It furnishes a philosophical and psychological basis for a comedy of the hapless failure of one's presumed intention to connect with deed, and for a literature in which the ordinary man, unable to affect events, is portrayed as a victim of circumstances, a passive tool of Fortune. Such ideas presumably penetrate the literary imagination in a Bergsonian fashion, as unperceived influences, as material not consciously adapted, but absorbed in a kind of substrata of the mind. It is intriguing to note that these ideas are not only supportive of the vision that is emerging in some comedy at the turn of the century, and that they dovetail nicely into that vision at some presumably later stage, but that they emerge from a psychology, a perspective on society, a line of thinking that is remarkably similar to that of a number of the English comic writers of the time. In Nietzsche's case there is also an aesthetic disposition that is nicely attuned to the *fin-de-siècle* sensibility. In both men, an affinity of outlook on human behavior produces conclusions about causality and human will that are essentially the same as those emerging in comic studies. Perhaps this accounts for the fact that the tangential connections of Nietzsche with English writers were with people like Shaw and Wells and for Bergson's interest, during the period when *Time and Free Will* was being composed, with the nature of comedy.

One of the paradoxical truths of English cultural expression at the turn of the century is that innovative artists from the middle class were likely to seek support for their social visions in ideas from men like Nietzsche and from French thought—even if those ideas came secondhand and "after the social fact," as it were. Middle-class writers self-consciously looked to aesthetes and the avant-garde intelligentsia for the concepts of their vision, ignoring other graphic sources closer by. For instance, what richer illustrations of the chanciness and disorder of modern individual existence and of the apparent impotence of human will to change or effect the course of things could there be than a literature that depicts the lot of poor people in anarchic urban conditions? As it happens, such literature, which had been in a kind of abeyance since the early Victorian period, revived in the last decades of the nineteenth century. A spate of "working class" novels appeared in the 1880s and 1890s, coinciding with a further downward reach in literacy. The more powerful of these novels depict a lower-class existence, usually set in the East End of London, in which alienation, powerlessness, and contingency are not literary constructs, they are realities. Arthur Morrison's work, such as *Tales of Mean Streets* and *A Child of the Jago*, characterizes life for those on the lower social scales as bizarre but relentless chronicles of enervating mischance and random brutalizing violence. George Gissing's novels are softer, but the sense is the same. From the point of view of the man doomed to failure—caught up on a kind of perpetually descending wheel of fortune, listless, dispirited, suspicious—a world view in which the causes of things are undecipherable does not seem strange at all. Indeed, the vision that emerged in certain comic literature at the end of the century had its origins in the first striking portrayals of lower urban existence at the beginning of the Victorian period. Egan, DeQuincey, Thackeray, and Dickens introduced the middle-class reader to this lower plane of human experience with their depictions of the poor. Even Peacock's abstraction of the breakdown between intention and action must have been informed in some way by the perspective offered in what was an essentially new experience of the City. The first anxieties about an individual's power to shape his destiny in the modern world set in then.

Literature about the lower classes also had, as we have seen, a curious predilection to find its way toward comic expression. This held true into the last decades of the century. The habits of English literature are hard to break. So, even though the "lower class life" novels of the 1880s and 1890s were reaching a different kind of audience from those of the 1840s—an audience of middle-class readers who had grown up knowing well the actualities of the lower-class urban condition, an audience that included a significant number of people who had themselves just risen out of that sphere—and even though the thinking about social problems had radically changed over the forty years, the harsh pictures of Arthur Morrison were balanced by an equal number of indulgent, comic treatments of the same situations. Along with the graphically negative novels, the 1880s and 1890s produced a bevy of comic novels. A subgenre called the "Cockney School" flourished, portraying the same denizens of the East End in rollicking, cheery, amusing disarray. Whatever the inconsistencies of these warring perspectives, they supplied, presumably, the same inspiration to middle-class writers of the comedy of the victim, the little man. Indeed, we have posited this cross-fertilization, for as domestic humor moved its locus of interest down the social scale to the petite bourgeoisie, in the Grossmiths and others it undoubtedly adopted a perspective on social power that was similar to that of lower-class literature.

And yet, compelling as these influences must have been, there is scant evidence that a man like Beerbohm would have been consciously aware of any identity of vision between his sketches of failures and mediocrities and the fiction of the lower classes. Shaw presumably made the connection, and probably H. G. Wells, but even in them we have the impression that the primary considerations affecting their outlook came from the middle class fixedly regarding itself. It is the ingrained characteristic of the middle-class mentality—its own sense of purpose, its concern about the importance of things—that determined the course of its literary expression. The most self-conscious, anxiety-ridden, and self-directed of social strata, the middle class revolved to a great extent upon its own notions of its crises; it observed its own image. Beerbohm's elaborations of incompetence are thus arabesques upon the debilities of men like him, artists and small figures from the suburbs, not the children who grew up on the mean streets. As if to emphasize that, Beerbohm's favorite caprice was to portray himself as a small-bore near-mediocrity. He cultivated a reputation as a man of slight accomplishments and small pretensions. He rarely took risks or enlarged his scope, keeping instead to the belles-lettristic—caricatures, parodies, sketches, vignettes. At the outset of his career, he ostentatiously brought out a thin volume which he entitled his collected "Works." The final essay in the "Works" is an essay, "Diminuendo," that announces his retirement at the age of eighteen. When, long after he had established an estimable reputation as a deft and telling observer and was habitually referred to as "the incomparable Max," he protested to a would-be biographer, "my gifts are small. I've

used them very well and discreetly, never straining them.
. . . Note that I am *not* incomparable. Compare me." In
Seven Men and Two Others, Beerbohm is the "ninth man,"
and he casts himself as a hesitant, inept character—the
man who "bungles" Enoch Soames's last chance for existence; the literary arbiter who, confounded by Soames's
senseless poetry, confesses that "it did now occur to me:
suppose Enoch Soames was a fool! Up cropped a rival hy-
pothesis: suppose I was!" (9); the drama critic who, when
left with "Savanarola" Brown's uncompleted, ludicrously
bad play, composes a scenario for the last act that is even
worse than anything Brown did. As John Felstiner has observed,[33] there is more than just an extended involution in
Beerbohm's studied "slightness"; there is an "indirect self-
evaluation," overtones of an ambivalence over the measure
of his own literary output, his own passionate engagement.

Beerbohm is shadowing the middle-class self-image. He
works gingerly around and in back of its attitudinal disposition, its fixation on ambition, its sense of import. We can
sense his chariness of the middle class and its values even as
he deftly picks them apart. Like Oscar Wilde, Beerbohm
throws the weaknesses of the bourgeois orientation into relief by spoofing its pretensions, showing how much of what
it esteems is the winddrift of fashion, and how shaky is its
assumption that its will conquers all. In his own persona,
Beerbohm, like Wilde, enacts the antitheses of the middle-
class sense of purpose; he is the man of cautiously con-
served actions. He is dubious of everything, even himself.

Beerbohm, however, has relatively little of the reductive
instinct in him. His is the gentle art, the discreet charm of
the mock bourgeois. His instinct is to elaborate. Consequently, Beerbohm's most telling insights about his culture often come under the cover of something else. What
he has to say about middle-class willpower is presented in
ironically self-deprecating revelations of his own supposed
inconsequence. And when he talks about the real tensions
and difficulties of his time, he does so behind the diversion

of a spoof on the excesses of the literary imagination. *Seven Men* appears to be taking *fin-de-siècle* artistic expression to task for its notoriously overwrought sensationalism. Diabolism had become *de rigueur* since *Dorian Gray* and Huysman's *Des Esseintes*, although rarely with the perplexities of Enoch Soames's self-proclaimed *Catholic* diabolism, which gives even the Devil pause. Soames's fuddled attempts to cloud his soul are symptoms of the age; nothing worse could befall an artist than to have no real Meredithian dark spots, no proto-Wildean sins. The tendency of comic expression to probe the recesses of the psyche, to work along the Krisian double-edge of the uncanny and the disturbing, wanders ludicrously astray in its own occlusion in Beerbohm's imitations. Deftly he reminds us that Soames, for example, is the absurdly misguided product of earlier literary fascinations: Soames's rendezvous with the Devil occurs in a cafe "almost opposite to that house where, in the first years of the century, a little girl, and with her a boy named DeQuincey, made nightly encampment among dust and rats and old legal parchments" (18).

Nearly all of Beerbohm's characters brush up against that sometimes Dickensian specter, the uncanny. Take Hilary Maltby, for instance, who at first glimpse strikes us as the least troubled of men. Author of the phenomenally successful novel "Ariel in Mayfair," he is rivaled only by Stephen Braxton, whose "A Faun on the Cotswolds" enjoys equal celebrity. Maltby is disposed to equanimity: "dapper little Maltby—blond, bland, diminutive Maltby, with his monocle and his gardenia. . . . Maltby had a perpetual chirrup of amusing small-talk" (40). But the uncanny never lurks far away. In a sudden impulse to be the only literary lion on a weekend at the Duchess of Hertfordshire's *very* exclusive Keeb Hall, he tells the Duchess that his ostensible friend Braxton could not possibly come. The deception unhinges part of Maltby's mind, for at Keeb Hall, he fancies he sees Braxton everywhere—in the bathtub, snoring grossly in Maltby's bed. Jolted by the apparition of Braxton, he loses control of his bicycle and veers into the bike of the elderly Lady Rodfitten, scraping her up badly. But the worst, most disorienting moment occurs when Maltby is in a pew at Keeb Hall chapel. Braxton lumbers down the aisle and sits down on him.

"No, not down *on* me. Down *through* me—and around me. What befell me was not mere ghastly contact with the intangible. It was inclusion, envelopment, eclipse. What Braxton sat down on was not I, but the seat of the pew; and what he sat back against was not my face and chest, but the back of the pew. I didn't realise this at the moment. All I knew was a sudden black blotting-out of all things; an infinite and impenetrable darkness. I dimly conjectured that I was dead. What was wrong with me, in point of fact, was that my eyes, with the rest of me, were inside Braxton. You remember what a great hulking fellow Braxton was. I calculate that as we sat there my eyes were just beneath the roof of his mouth. Horrible!

I suppose I must have craned my head forward, for I had a sudden glimpse of things—a close quick downward glimpse of a pepper-and-salt waistcoat and of two great hairy hands clasped across it. Then darkness again. Either I had drawn back my head, or Braxton had thrust his forward; I don't know which. 'Are you all right?' the Duchess' voice whispered, and no doubt my face was ashen. 'Quite,' whispered my voice. But this pathetic monosyllable was the last gasp of the social instinct in me" (69-70).

On one level, Maltby's story demolishes the English literary imagination's enchantment with the imp of the perverse, its penchant for sensationalizing; on another level, however, it indirectly highlights another kind of element in the middle-class cultural situation. For Maltby's "horrible" experience at Keeb Hall reflects the paranoia of social position. His is the nightmare of taste. An ephemeral celebrity—he was never to write a best selling novel again—Maltby reflects, in a characteristically oblique Beerbohmian way, the real areas of radical insecurity in the English middle class. The people in *Seven Men* are suffering from the inability to orient the significant and insignificant.

In another story, "A. V. Laider," Beerbohm recalls an encounter with a man named A. V. Laider, who believed, as many reasonable men do, in the accuracy of palmistry. When Beerbohm first met Laider, at a nearly deserted seaside resort, Laider told him of an incident that had scarred him for life. He was on a railway carriage, reading the palms of his traveling companions, when it clearly appeared that nearly all of them would be killed within the next few minutes. No worse example could there be of the modern frustration over inability to control one's destiny; as Laider notes, "Suppose in fact, that we *haven't* any free will whatsoever . . . that the Power that fashioned us . . . [had capriciously decided to] jot down in cipher on our hands just what was in store for us?" (104). And then, as Laider tells it, the train wreck occurred and all those whose palm had predicted it perished. But, at Beerbohm's second meeting with Laider some months afterward, Laider denies the truth of his story and passes it off by saying that sometimes when he is recuperating from an illness he makes up things. Beerbohm, the narrator, and we, the readers, are left then with nothing but a vague disquiet. It is a disquiet that extends to the nature of palmistry, to Laider's quixotic behavior, to the curious complexity of motive itself. The story is one of Beerbohm's best because it presents us with the difficulties of getting hold of patterns in human existence, and on different levels. Why would a man gratuitously make up such a story for a stranger? What does the story itself suggest about the nature of human existence? Why does Beerbohm invite us to dismiss the entire thing as a trifling incident? And why cannot we always dismiss such things?

Beerbohm's humor registers a kind of truth about psychic patterns that is different from the "truth" in the flamboyantly sensationalizing comic writers that he ostensibly spoofs. A man who achieved his first fame with an essay on "cosmetics," Beerbohm is a product of the media-conscious, faddish, volatile cultural scene at the end of the Victorian period. A canny observer of topical delusions, of vogues and sensations, and of the the foibles that ensue upon them, he is aware of the curious potency of suggestion. A sly critic of the middle-class tendency to invest things with importance in a capricious and arbitrary manner, he is aware of the elusive displacement this has effected for the culture. Freud has made us conscious of the fact that individual repressions and anxieties do not often come out in dark, clear lines; they manifest themselves in little things—in oddities, minor obsessions, slips, habits, social tics, and so forth. The comedy writer's roving eye and his appetite for the phenomenal, the odd, and the incongruous enable him to pick up these random, abortive "signals" of the culture. Such is the case with Beerbohm, for his contribution to our understanding of the comic in middle-class culture lies primarily in his capacity of fine attunement to the oblique and deflected ways in which the tensions and disorientations of the middle class are now obliged to express themselves. And he shows us a further insight: when repressions and concerns must achieve their outlet through eccentric, and apparently trifling, crises of taste and personal style, or through incidental little manic preoccupations (see W. S. Gilbert's "Bab Ballads"), then we cannot keep them in a proper orientation. We are put in the distressing situation of not being able to gauge how real, how essential, how vital these concerns might be. Like the tale of A. V. Laider's tale, it is difficult to know how to "read" them.

If we were to think back to Samuel Butler again for a moment, we would see that to a large extent it was this sort of problem that plagued Butler. His involvement in his own grievance was so intense, his anger and pain so immediate, that he found it nearly impossible to attain the perspective that would allow him to see that it was aspects of the quality of the bourgeois life style that bothered him. Although Ernest Pontifex found oblique outlets for his tensions in his crankiness and in his love of cozy digs, Butler himself does not seem to have been aware of the necessity to diagnose and comprehend those outlets. Although acutely sensitized to the insidious convolutions of language and attitude in the bourgeois ethos, Butler does not appear to have been separately conscious of the manner in which they shaped his and other actualities. As we have suggested, only the imaginative powers of elaboration can give the writer that kind of poise.

Butler's problem guides us in reaching some conclusions about the nature of British comedy in the nineteenth century. The tenor and imaginative dimensions of the comic expression have been determined by the relationship of the writer to the characteristics of the culture; and those characteristics have been largely defined by him in terms of middle-class goals and values. We have posited other directions or emphases that comedy could have pursued—toward satire or more sweeping condemnation of English ideology and institutions; or toward a more purely ceremonial expression, either that which we find in aristocratic cultures, where form and style prevail over personal and social elements, or that which has a ritualistic function and carries a significance beyond the immediate context. The mainstream of comic writing could have been more escapist than it was, more romantic and less socially referential. Instead, English comedy has developed from the engagement of the writer with his social position. It has, we have noted, become more introspective as the Victorian period has worn on. The sociological formulas so necessary at the start of the Industrial Revolution are supplanted with a comedy that reflects the ambivalence of the individual. The shape of the comic expression has been determined by the writer's preoccupation with his stance toward the social situation, or what he has perceived as "middle classness." It revolves around the issues of life fictions that are adjusted to or alternative to the dominant modes of behavior and response; it explores the nature of the individual's disquiet with his own ambivalence; it is a critique of self and society.

All of this seems inevitable given the complexity of modern, relatively open, mobile societies, given the late nineteenth-century interest in individual psychology, and given post-Romantic relativism. But it could not have happened with quite the same thoroughness it did were there not, at base, a strong identification of the English writer with the ideology of the class he seems so disenchanted with. It is fashionable now to see all the evils of the middle class—I find myself sometimes talking about it in this book in a rather disdainful manner—but it has been, for all that, a supple and often surprisingly humane culture. It retains, within its self-satisfaction, the capacity to laugh at itself, which has produced the remarkably vital comedy of domestic humor that gains strength, rather than weakens the further you go into the twentieth century. And what may be its determining characteristic—its confidence in the capacity of the individual to shape his own destiny— assures that most of its writers will try to work within it. Furthermore, English culture's ingrained assumption that it can tolerate and accommodate all manner of eccentricity, make room for all individualism, undoubtedly induces its writers toward less radical expression.

Thus, English comedy in the nineteenth century has tended to be reflective as well as reflexive. Undoubtedly, the sociological bent of the pre-Victorian and early Victorian literature of social change had a great deal to do with comedy's subsequent emphasis on social issues, even as that comedy became more involuted. Yet surely it is the writer's fascination with the characteristics of the middle class that has been determinative. We have observed the greater social amplification as we move from Hood through Carroll, a tacit concession to the society's greater complexity. Indeed, as the social order, its values, and individual human motivation appear to have become more problematical, they have proved a richer field for comedy's play with disparities, paradoxes, convolutions. And, perhaps as a natural correlative of the comedy of the insider speaking about his own quirks, desires, and discomforts, the distance between the audience and the subject matter of comedy has been narrowed. As the comic target shifts from an objectified grotesque, or an authority figure, to the hapless ordinary man, the identification with the middle class increases.

Even among those most detached from the middle class, the concern has been social, to a great extent. Meredith's call for sophistication in comedy stems from the sense of responsibility he and others feel for the state of the culture. Again and again the formulation takes on social dimensions. The model for the high culture's comedy is found in the upper class. The alternative for Wilde is a *life* of comic freedom; his stated objective is something called "realization," which sounds in context as much a means of social expression as of artistic. Wilde, and perhaps Beerbohm in his cameos of analysis, seek realization through experimental adaption of various forms, usually forms of behavior. It is no wonder that in *Ulysses* Joyce suggests that the soul achieves entelechy, an actualizing of its potential, by apprehending other forms, particularly the forms of other people's thinking and living.

The intimate social involvement shares responsibility as well for the other distinguishing characteristic of nineteenth-century English comedy: its reflexiveness. We have seen that the only way out of bourgeois values is to transpose them. Irreverent comic writers discover for us the insidious ways in which dominant elements in a society invest certain principles or modes of behavior with meaning. To work free of this, one must work it over; and an agonistic, transvaluing, involuted comedy serves best. Disraeli and Bulwer illustrate the perils of slipping in and out of fiction and actuality without artistic control. I think that we might argue, in fact, that the heavy reliance on social formulas in the early and pre-Victorian period made writers more aware of the possibilities for comic play: Dickens and Thackeray set to writing, after all, by parodying and transmogrifying the formulas.

Finally, I think we have achieved clearer insights into the ways in which the nature of comedy itself—its vision, its dynamics, and its use of characteristic techniques—has contributed to the mode of expression that predominates in nineteenth-century English literature. The dynamics have been particularly important, for it is the push toward elaboration, the continuing interplay between the reductive and the metamorphic, that impels the expression toward reflexiveness, toward art, into new variations. The dynamics may incline writers in sophisticated societies away from the tendentious toward greater stress on "wit work" for its own sake. Similarly the techniques of the comic writer—transmogrification, parody, paradoxical statement, and so forth—contribute almost as much to obliqueness of social critique as does the writer's ambivalence. As I have contended (now for the last time), the two factors—modal characteristics and cultural context—cannot be divorced.

Notes

NOTES TO INTRODUCTION

1. L. C. Knights, "Notes on Comedy," *The Importance of Scrutiny*, ed. Eric Bentley (New York: New York University Press, 1964), p. 229.

2. Martin Turnell, *The Novel in France* (London: H. Hamilton, 1950).

3. See Raymond Giraud, *The Unheroic Hero in the Novels of Stendhal, Balzac, and Flaubert* (New Brunswick, N.J.: Rutgers University Press, 1957); and Cesar Graña, *Bohemian vs. Bourgeois* (New York: Basic Books, 1964).

4. G. Kitson Clark, *The Making of Victorian England* (New York: Atheneum, 1967), pp. 132, 119.

5. The social theorist Cesar Graña thinks that the only basis for distinguishing the middle from lower classes that would possibly accord with what both sociologists and literary men have propounded is the difference between attitudes toward immediate pleasure. Lower classes typically engage in "short-run hedonism," while the middle classes are characteristically people who defer gratification, postponing or denying themselves pleasure in order to accumulate economic resources or ensure subsequent social advance. *Fact and Symbol: Essays in the Sociology of Art and Literature* (New York: Oxford University Press, 1971), p. 66. However debatable this philosophical generalization may seem to be in the light of a century's conspicuous consumption by British and American middle classes, the preoccupation with stability and with "respectability" has surely become one of the traits we associate with the middle class. Raymond Williams's definition of the middle class in his *Culture and Society: 1780-1950* (1958; reprint ed., New York: Harper & Row, 1966), p. 326, contributes to the same sort of picture. He proposes a differentiation between middle and lower classes on the basis of the more individualistic orientation of the former. The middle-class man looked upon society with a great sense of opportunity for self-fulfillment. The laissez faire of Victorian liberalism had created for him a field of personal possibilities. But this, too, threw the individual back on his own responsibility. It was the atmosphere that produced *Angst*—all matter of concern about one's situation and ambitions—which in turn led to ambivalence and mordant introspection. Agonizing over one's prospects, over one's rise and fall, and over one's acquisitions did indeed appear to govern middle-class literary expression.

6. Graña, in *Fact and Symbol*, p. 66, sums up the dispute in this way:

The normal ways of sociology require that statements about the "values" of a culture should rest on whatever one can find out about behavior and belief among *a number of people* which, with one or another justification, might be regarded as representative. Some sociologists of culture, however, embracing what is in fact a traditionally romantic view of the relationship between social life and aesthetic expression, fall to writing as though the work of artists, the work, that is, of a minority of the uncommon, should be taken as the final testimony of a culture's true character, or as the act or gesture *defining* the quality of the social period.

Thus, the approaches range from that of Karl Mannheim, who insists that we can only determine social attitudes by exhaustively defining social substructures—in occupations, classes, neighborhoods—and then examining the nature of the aspirations within these substructures and seeing how they are modified (*Essays on the Sociology of Culture* [London: Routledge & Kegan Paul, 1956], pp. 10, 114) to Robert Nisbet, who contends that the visions and insights of artists have strikingly corresponded with and prefigured the major observations and premises of sociologists about the nature of modern social and individual life (*Sociology as an Art Form* [New York: Oxford University Press, 1976]).

7. Oscar Wilde to Lord Alfred Douglas, January-March 1897, *The Letters of Oscar Wilde*, ed. Rupert Hart-Davis (London: Rupert Hart-Davis, 1962), p. 437.

8. Frank Kermode, *The Sense of an Ending: Studies in the Theory of Fiction* (London: Oxford University Press, 1966).

9. Susanne Langer, *Feeling and Form: A Theory of Art* (New York: Charles Scribner's Sons, 1953), p. 331.

10. George Santayana, "Carnival," *Soliloquies in England and Later Soliloquies* (New York: Charles Scribner's Sons, 1922), pp. 141-142.

11. Northrop Frye, *Anatomy of Criticism* (Princeton: Princeton University Press, 1957).

12. George Meredith, "An Essay on Comedy," in *Comedy*, ed. Wylie Sypher (Garden City, N.Y.: Doubleday & Co., 1956), p. 48.

13. Alvin Kernan, *The Cankered Muse: Satire of the English Renaissance* (New Haven: Yale University Press, 1959).

14. Ernst Kris, *Psychoanalytic Explorations in Art* (1952; reprint ed., New York: Schocken Books, 1965), p. 185.

15. Arthur Koestler, *The Act of Creation* (New York: Macmillan Co., 1964).

16. Quoted in John Forster, *The Life of Charles Dickens*, ed. J.W.T. Ley (New York: Doubleday, Doran, 1928), p. 721.

NOTES TO CHAPTER ONE

1. Benjamin Disraeli, *The Young Duke* (1831; reprint ed., London: Peter Davis, 1926), pp. 16-17.

2. Edward Lytton Bulwer (later known as Bulwer-Lytton), *Pelham, or the Adventures of a Gentleman* (London: George Routledge & Sons, 1840), p. 8. Page citations hereafter in text.

3. Robert Plumer Ward, *Tremaine, or the Man of Refinement* (London: Henry Colburn, 1825), I, vi, xii.

4. Mrs. Catherine Gore, *Cecil: or, The Adventures of a Coxcomb*, 2d ed. (London: Richard Bentley, 1841), I, xi. Page citations hereafter in text.

5. Vineta Colby points this out in *Yesterday's Woman: Domestic Realism in the English Novel* (Princeton: Princeton University Press, 1974).

6. Thomas Carlyle, "The Dandiacal Body," *Sartor Resartus* [1833], ed. Charles Frederick Harrold (New York: Odyssey Press, 1937), p. 273.

7. Edward Lytton Bulwer, *England and the English* (London: Richard Bentley, 1833), II, 108.

8. Maurice Quinlan, *Victorian Prelude* (New York: Columbia University Press, 1941), pp. 3, 103.

9. Charles Greville, *The Greville Memoirs, 1814-1860* [1839], ed. Lytton Strachey and Roger Fulford (London: Macmillan & Co., 1938), IV, 116.

10. Ward, *Tremaine* I, iii.

11. R. H. Horne, *A New Spirit of the Age* (New York: Harper & Brothers Publishers, 1844), pp. 140-141.

12. Bulwer, *England and the English* I, 29.

13. See Paul Fussell, *The Rhetorical World of Augustan Humanism: Ethics and Imagery from Swift to Burke* (Oxford: Oxford University Press, 1965), p. 54.

14. See Alexander Welsh, *The Hero of the Waverley Novels* (New York: Atheneum, 1968), chap. 1.

15. Edward Lytton Bulwer, *Critical and Miscellaneous Writings* (Philadelphia: Lea and Blanchard, 1841), II, 178.

16. Cesar Graña, *Bohemian vs. Bourgeois* (New York: Basic Books, 1964), pp. 151-152.

17. Edward Lytton Bulwer, *Paul Clifford* [1830], (London: George Routledge & Sons, 188-), p. 161. Page citations hereafter in text.

18. Johan Huizinga, *Homo Ludens* (Boston: Beacon Press, 1950), p. 8.

19. Ernst Kris, *Psychoanalytic Explorations in Art* (1952; reprint ed., New York: Schocken Books, 1965), pp. 211, 182.

20. Disraeli, *The Young Duke*, p. 23. Page citations hereafter in text.

21. John Holloway, *The Victorian Sage* (1953; reprint ed., New York: W. W. Norton & Co., 1965), p. 106.

22. Anthony Trollope, *An Autobiography* (1883; reprint ed., London: Oxford University Press, 1928), p. 236.

23. John Gross, *The Rise and Fall of the Man of Letters* (New York: Macmillan Co., 1969), pp. 14, 16.

24. Hugh Dalziel Duncan, *Language and Literature in Society* (Chicago: University of Chicago Press, 1953), p. 20.

25. Pierce Egan, *Life in London* (London: Sherwood, Jones & Co., 1823), p. 69, n. Page citations hereafter in text.

26. *George Orwell,* "Charles Dickens," *Dickens, Dali and Others* (New York: Reynal & Hitchcock, 1946), p. 4.

27. P. J. Keating, *The Working Classes in Victorian Fiction* (London: Routledge & Kegan Paul, 1971).

28. Robert Kellogg and Robert Scholes, *The Nature of Narrative* (London: Oxford University Press, 1966), p. 98f.

29. C. H. Rickword, "A Note on Fiction," *Forms of Modern Fiction*, ed. William Van O'Connor (Bloomington: Indiana University Press, 1964), pp. 280-291.

30. Frederick Marryat, *Snarleyyow: or, The Dog Fiend* (Philadelphia: E. L. Carey and A. Hart, 1837), I, 29.

31. Walter Allen, *The English Novel* (New York: E. P. Dutton & Co., 1954), p. 166.

32. Eric Auerbach, *Mimesis: The Representation of Reality in Western Literature*, trans. Willard Trask (1946; reprint ed., New York: Doubleday & Co., 1957), pp. 412, 452.

33. Two sections were published in *Blackwood's Magazine* (1827 and 1839), a third section in *Selections Grave and Gay from the Writings Published & Unpublished of Thomas DeQuincey* IV (1854). Jean-Jacques Mayoux's article, "DeQuincey's Humor and the Drugs," in *Veins of Humor*, ed. Harry Levin (Cambridge: Harvard University Press, 1972), pp. 109-130, is one of the few attempts to look at DeQuincey's humor, especially in "On Murder Considered as One of the Fine Arts."

34. David Masson, ed., *The Collected Writings of Thomas DeQuincey* (Edinburgh: Adam and Charles Black, 1890), XIII, 77.

35. Robert Surtees Smith, *Jorrocks' Jaunts and Jollities*, ed. Herbert Van Thal (London: Cassell & Co., 1968), p. 1. Page citations hereafter in text.

36. V. S. Pritchett, *The Living Novel and Later Appreciations* (1947; reprint ed., New York: Vintage Books, 1967), p. 89.

37. C. L. Barber, *Shakespeare's Festive Comedy* (Princeton: Princeton University Press, 1959).

38. Northrop Frye, *Anatomy of Criticism* (Princeton: Princeton University Press, 1957), p. 185.

39. William Hazlitt, "The English Comic Writers," in *Works*, ed. P. P. Howe (London: J. M. Dent & Sons, 1931), VI, 122.

40. John Wade, *History of the Middle and Working Classes*, 3rd ed. (London: Effingham Wilson, 1835), pp. 474-475.

NOTES TO CHAPTER TWO

1. Thomas Love Peacock, *Melincourt, or Sir Oran Haut-ton*, in *Works of Thomas Love Peacock*, ed. Henry Cole (London: Richard Bentley, 1875), I, 122.

2. Thomas Love Peacock, *Nightmare Abbey* (New York: Capricorn Books, 1964), p. 17. Page citations hereafter in text.

3. Peacock, *Melincourt*, in *Works* I, 301.

4. Thomas Love Peacock, *Crotchet Castle* (New York: Capricorn Books, 1964), p. 130.

5. Mario Praz, *The Hero in Eclipse* (London: Oxford University Press, 1956).

6. G. K. Chesterton, *Charles Dickens* (1906; reprint ed., New York: Schocken Books, 1965), pp. 163-164.

7. James Spedding, "Tales by the Author of Headlong Hall," *The Edinburgh Review* 68 (January 1839): 232.

8. William Makepeace Thackeray, *Catherine: A Story* (1839-1840; reprint ed., New York: Hurst & Co., n.d.), p. 431. Page citations hereafter in text.

9. E. H. Gombrich, *Art and Illusion: A Study in the Psychology of Pictorial Representation*, 2d ed. (Princeton: Princeton University Press, 1961), p. 172.

10. William Makepeace Thackeray, "George Cruikshank," *Westminster Review* 66 (June 1840): 11. See Barbara Hardy's *The Exposure of Luxury: Radical Themes in Thackeray* (Pittsburgh: University of Pittsburgh Press, 1972) for analyses of Thackeray's use of detail and construction of scene.

11. Edwin Muir, *The Structure of the Novel* (London: Humanities Press, 1928), p. 23f.

12. "The Oxford Thackeray" (London: Oxford University Press, 1908), II, 92.

13. Ibid., p. 194.

14. Ibid., IX, 297.

15. Ibid., p. 299.

16. Ibid., p. 490.

17. William Makepeace Thackeray, "Special Biographical Edition," *Works* (New York: Harper & Brothers Publishers, 1903), XII, 470.

18. Ibid., p. 477.

19. Ibid., p. 511.

20. Ibid., p. 517.

21. William Makepeace Thackeray to Robert Bell, September, 1848, *The Letters and Private Papers of William Makepeace Thackeray* (Cambridge: Harvard University Press, 1945-46), II, 423.

22. William Makepeace Thackeray, *Vanity Fair: A Novel Without a Hero* (Boston: Houghton Mifflin Co., 1963), p. 224. Page citations hereafter in text.

23. John Bunyan, *Grace Abounding to the Chief of Sinners*, ed. Roger Sharrock (Oxford: Clarendon Press, 1962), p. 3.

24. M. H. Abrams, *Natural Supernaturalism: Tradition and Revolution in Romantic Literature* (New York: W. W. Norton & Co., 1971), pp. 307-308.

25. Gordon Ray, *Thackeray: The Uses of Adversity (1811-1846)* (New York: McGraw-Hill Book Co., 1955), pp. 13-16.

26. Chauncey Wells, "Thackeray and the Victorian Compromise," *University of California Publications in English* 1 (1929): 179-199.

27. William Makepeace Thackeray, "The English Humourists of the Eighteenth Century" (New York: Hurst & Co., n.d.), p. 384. Page citations hereafter in text.

28. Douglas Jerrold, "Sir Peter Laurie on Human Life," *Punch* I, 210.

29. Douglas Jerrold, "Old Bailey Holidays," *Punch* II, 240.

30. Douglas Jerrold, "The President and the Negro," *Punch* VI, 155.

31. Douglas Jerrold, " 'Gentlemen Jews,' " *Punch* VI, 79.

32. Douglas Jerrold, "Wanted—Some Bishops!" *Punch* IV, 226.

33. Quoted in Walter Jerrold, *Douglas Jerrold, Dramatist and Wit* (London: Hodder & Stoughton, 1914), II, 445.

34. Douglas Jerrold, "Punch's Letters to His Son," "Letter XI," *The Best of Mr. Punch*, ed. Richard M. Kelly (Knoxville: University of Tennessee Press, 1970), p. 106.

35. Douglas Jerrold, "Letters," "Letter II," p. 77.

36. Douglas Jerrold, "Letters," "Letter V," p. 87.

37. Douglas Jerrold, "Letters," "Letter VIII," p. 96.

NOTES TO CHAPTER THREE

1. George Henry Lewes, "Dickens in Relation to Criticism," *Fortnightly Review* 11, n.s. (February 1872): 144.

2. Charles Dickens, "Gin-Shop," *Sketches by Boz*, in *Works* (Boston: Estes and Lauriat, 1892), XLV, 262, 265.

3. John Butt and Kathleen Tillotson, *Dickens at Work* (London: Methuen and Co., 1957), p. 37.

4. Dickens, "The Prisoner's Van," *Sketches*, in *Works* XLV, 394.

5. Dickens, "London Recreations," *Sketches*, in *Works* XLV, 130.

6. Dickens, "Horatio Sparkins," *Sketches*, in *Works* XLVI, 63-84.

7. Dickens, "Meditations in Monmouth Street," *Sketches*, in *Works* XLV, 105-114.

8. Dickens, "The First of May," *Sketches*, in *Works* XLV, 245.

9. Dickens, "Shops and Their Tenants," *Sketches*, in *Works* XLV, 90.

10. E. H. Gombrich, *Art and Illusion: A Study in the Psychology of Pictorial Representation*, 2d ed. (Princeton: Princeton University Press, 1961), p. 111.

11. G. K. Chesterton, *Charles Dickens* (1906; reprint ed., New York: Schocken Books, 1965), p. 82.

12. Dickens, "Vauxhall Gardens by Day," *Sketches*, in *Works* XLV, 182.

13. J. Hillis Miller, *"Sketches by Boz, Oliver Twist,* and Cruikschank's Illustrations," *Charles Dickens and George Cruikshank*, William Andrews Clark Memorial Library (Los Angeles: University of California, 1971), p. 32.

14. Chesterton, *Dickens*, p. 96.

15. There are numerous discussions of this phenomenon. Walter Houghton describes it as a characteristic impression of the period in his *The Victorian Frame of Mind, 1830-1870* (New Haven: Yale University Press, 1957), p. 8.

16. See, for example, Jerome Buckley, *The Victorian Temper: A Study in Literary Culture* (Cambridge: Harvard University Press, 1951), chap. 7; and Christopher Hibbert, "Dickens' London," in *Charles Dickens, 1812-1870*, ed. E.W.P. Tomlin (New York: Simon & Schuster, 1970), pp. 73-99.

17. Lewes, "Dickens," p. 146.

18. See Taylor Stoehr, *Dickens: The Dreamer's Stance* (Ithaca: Cornell University Press, 1965), p. 15f.; and W. J. Harvey, *Character and the Novel* (Ithaca: Cornell University Press, 1965), pp. 36-38.

19. Charles Dickens to John Forster, February 12, *The Letters of Charles Dickens, Works*, ed. Walter Dexter (Bloomsbury: Nonesuch Press, 1935-38), I, 247.

20. Edgar Johnson, *Charles Dickens: His Tragedy and Triumph* (Boston: Little, Brown and Co., 1952), I, 292.

21. Although Dickens' sense of the fields of force in the City is undoubtedly a complex of factors, many of them ill-defined, Fred Kaplan's analysis of the role of mesmerism goes as far as anything yet written to explain it. *Dickens and Mesmerism: The Hidden Springs of Fiction* (Princeton: Princeton University Press, 1975).

22. John Forster, *The Life of Charles Dickens*, ed. J.W.T. Ley (New York: Doubleday, Doran, 1928), I, 274.

23. Quoted in ibid., p. 289.

24. Ibid., p. 295-296.

25. See Harvey, *Character and the Novel*, p. 43.

26. Hugh Kenner, *Flaubert, Joyce and Beckett: The Stoic Comedians* (Boston: Beacon Press, 1962).

27. One of the best discussions of the delights of the anatomy can be found in D. W. Jefferson's *"Tristram Shandy* and its Tradition," in *The Pelican Guide to English Literature*, ed. Boris Ford (Baltimore: Penguin Books, 1965), IV, 333-345.

28. George Santayana, "Dickens," *The Dickens Critics*, ed. George H. Ford and Lauriat Lane, Jr. (Ithaca: Cornell University Press, 1961), p. 141.

29. Alvin Kernan, *The Cankered Muse: Satire of the English Renaissance* (New Haven: Yale University Press, 1959), pp. 7-8.

30. Edward Lytton Bulwer, "No. xxiii—On Certain Principles of Art in Works of Imagination," in the series "Caxtoniana," *Blackwood's Edinburgh Magazine* 93 (May 1863): 549.

31. Ibid., pp. 551-552.

32. Jolandi Jacobi, *The Psychology of C. G. Jung*, 6th ed. (New Haven: Yale University Press, 1962), p. 27. I am indebted to H. P. Sucksmith's book, *The Narrative Art of Charles Dickens* (Oxford: Clarendon Press, 1970), for suggesting the connection with Jung's concepts.

33. Garrett Stewart, *Dickens and the Trials of Imagination* (Cambridge: Harvard University Press, 1974).

34. Forster, *Dickens* I, 294, 296.

35. Northrop Frye, "Dickens and the Comedy of Humors," in *Experience in the Novel: Selected Papers from the English Institute*, ed. Roy Harvey Pearce (New York: Columbia University Press, 1968), pp. 49-81. Monroe Engel makes the same observation in his *The Maturity of Dickens* (Cambridge: Harvard University Press, 1959), p. 17. See also Barbara Hardy's *The Moral Art of Dickens* (London: Athlone Press, 1970), p. 104f., for an excellent analysis of the problems of *Chuzzlewit*.

NOTES TO CHAPTER FOUR

1. For evidence of the unsettled state of Dickens himself at the time of *Dombey*, his sense of the "want of something," see Edgar Johnson, *Charles Dickens: His Tragedy and Triumph* (Boston: Little, Brown and Co., 1952), II, 606, 619, 621.

2. John Forster, *The Life of Charles Dickens*, ed. J.W.T. Ley (New York: Doubleday, Doran, 1928), I, 334-335.

3. In a letter to Douglas Jerrold dated November 16, 1844, Dickens says that in "The Chimes," "I have tried to strike a blow upon that part of the brass countenance of wicked Cant, where such a compliment is sorely needed at this time." *The Letters of Charles Dickens*, in *Works*, ed. Walter Dexter (Bloomsbury: Nonesuch Press, 1935-38), I, 637. All subsequent references to this edition.

4. J. Hillis Miller, *Charles Dickens: The World of His Novels* (1958; reprint ed., Bloomington: Indiana University Press, 1973), pp. 143-144.

5. Kathleen Tillotson, *Novels of the Eighteen-Forties* (Oxford: Oxford University Press, 1956, 1961), p. 160.

6. James C. Kincaid, *Dickens and the Rhetoric of Laughter* (Oxford: Clarendon Press, 1971), chap. 7.

7. John Butt and Kathleen Tillotson, *Dickens at Work* (London: Methuen and Co., 1957), p. 97.

8. See ibid., p. 102; and Harry Stone, "The Novel as Fairy Tale: Dickens' *Dombey and Son*," *English Studies* 47 (1966): 1-27.

9. E. H. Gombrich, *Art and Illusion: A Study in the Psychology of Pictorial Representation* (Princeton: Princeton University Press, 1961), p. 313.

10. Dickens to W. C. Macready, October 4, 1855, *Letters* II, 695.

11. Dickens to Forster, April 1856, gives an assessment of his own mood at the time: "However strange it is to be never at rest, and never satisfied, and to be always laden with plot and plan and care and worry, how clear it is that it must be, and that one is driven. . . . As to repose—for some men there's no such thing in life. The foregoing has the appearance of a small sermon; but it is so often in my head in these days that it cannot help coming out. The old days—the old days! Shall I ever, I wonder, get the frame of mind back as it used to be then? Something of it perhaps—but never quite as it used to be." *Letters* II, 765.

12. P. D. Herning, "Dickens' Monthly Number-Plans for *Little Dorrit*," *Modern Philology* 64 (1966): 23.

13. Rosalie L. Colie, *Paradoxia epidemica* (Princeton: Princeton University Press, 1966), pp. 7, 72.

14. See, for example, Dickens' letters to Maria Beadnell Winter, April 3, 1855; to Leigh Hunt, May 4, 1855; to Miss Coutts, May 8, 1855; and to Wilkie Collins, May 11, 1855, in *Letters* II, 649, 658, 659, 660-661.

15. W. L. Burn, *The Age of Equipoise: A Study of the Mid-Victorian Generation* (New York: W. W. Norton & Co., 1965); James Buckley, *The Victorian Temper: A Study in Literary Culture* (Cambridge: Harvard University Press, 1951), pp. 2-3; Walter E. Houghton, *The Victorian Frame of Mind: 1830-1870* (New Haven: Yale University Press, 1957).

16. Some excellent discussions of the complexities (and ambiguities) in Dickens' social vision can be found in George Ford, *Dickens and His Readers: Aspects of Novel-Criticism Since 1836* (Princeton: Princeton University Press, 1955); and Humphry House, *The Dickens World*, 2d ed. (London: Oxford University Press, 1942).

17. Colie, *Paradoxia epidemica*, pp. 8, 10, 38.

NOTES TO CHAPTER FIVE

1. Geoffrey Best, *Mid-Victorian Britain, 1851-1875* (London: Weidenfeld & Nicholson, 1971), p. 228.

2. G. M. Young, *Victorian England: Portrait of an Age*, 2d ed. (London: Oxford University Press, 1953), p. 154.

3. W. L. Burn, *The Age of Equipoise: A Study of the Mid-Victorian Generation* (New York: W. W. Norton & Co., 1964), p. 67.

4. Thomas Hood, "Faithless Nelly Gray: A Pathetic Ballad," published around 1829 as No. 4 of *The Ballad Singer*, according to John Clubbe in his *Selected Poems of Thomas Hood* (Cambridge: Harvard University Press, 1970), pp. 81-83, 343.

5. Robert Bernard Martin, *The Triumph of Wit: A Study of Victorian Comic Theory* (Oxford: Clarendon Press, 1974).

6. William Empson, *Seven Types of Ambiguity*, 3rd ed. (New York: New Directions Publishing, 1953), pp. 103, 109.

7. Thomas Hood, "Sally Simpkin's Lament; or John Jones' Kit-Cat-Astrophe," published in the *Comic Annual* in 1834; reprinted in Clubbe, ed., *Selected Poems*, pp. 98-100, 346.

8. Young, *Victorian England*, p. 102.

9. Burn, *The Age of Equipoise*, p. 49.

10. W. S. Gilbert, "A Discontented Suger Broker," published in *Fun* (December 1867); reprinted in James Ellis, ed., *The "Bab Ballads"* (Cambridge: Harvard University Press, 1970), pp. 133-134. All subsequent references to this edition.

11. Gilbert, "To My Absent Husband" (1865), *"Bab Ballads"*, p. 65.

12. Gilbert, "Tempora Mutantur" (1865), *"Bab Ballads,"* p. 58.

13. Gilbert, "The Reverend Rawston Wright" (1866), *"Bab Ballads,"* p. 82.

14. Gilbert, "The Story of Gentle Archibald" (1866), *"Bab Ballads,"* pp. 83-85.

15. Gilbert, "A. and B., or, The Sensation Twins" (1867), *"Bab Ballads,"* pp. 124-125.

16. Ellis, "Introduction," *"Bab Ballads,"* pp. 17-18.

17. G. K. Chesterton, "Gilbert and Sullivan" (1930); reprinted in John Bush Jones, ed., *W. S. Gilbert: A Century of Scholarship and Commentary* (New York: New York University Press, 1970), pp. 202-203.

18. Some of these were, of course, probably derived from separate stories made up by Carroll for little girls. The Mad Tea Party has such a source. Carroll himself, however, acknowledged that in writing down *Wonderland*, he added "many fresh ideas." "*Alice* on the Stage," *The Russian Journal and Other Selections from the Work of Lewis Carroll*, ed. John Francis McDermott (New York: E. P. Dutton & Co., 1935), p. 191.

19. Roger Lancelyn Green, ed., *The Diaries of Lewis Carroll* (London: Cassell and Co., 1953), I, 70. Similar assessments were entered when Carroll surveyed his habits in 1856 and 1857 (*Diaries* I, 99, 114). All subsequent references to this edition.

20. Ibid., p. 208.

21. Ibid., p. 71, entry dated January 7, 1856.

22. Ibid., p. 191.

23. Johan Huizinga, *Homo Ludens: A Study of the Play-Element in Culture* (Boston: Beacon Press, 1950), p. 6.

24. Carroll, "*Alice* on the Stage," p. 192.

25. Carroll wrote on May 18, 1856: "I am getting into habits of unpunctuality, and must try to make a fresh start in activity: I record this resolution as a test for the future;" and as a proposed improvement for the new

year, he wrote, on December 31, 1857, that there must be "constant improvements of habits of activity, punctuality, etc." (Green, *Diaries* I, 85, 136).

26. Lewis Carroll, *Alice in Wonderland*, ed. Donald J. Gray (New York: W. W. Norton & Co., 1971), p. 25. The mouse's tale is a late addition to the manuscript. In the original version of his tale, the mouse emphasized the Darwinian randomness of death in the animal kingdom; a dog and cat, in search of a rat, crushed several mice who had been "warm and snug." It mentioned nothing of a trial, or Fury. The trial itself is a late addition.

27. See Hugh Kenner, *Dublin's Joyce* (Bloomington: Indiana University Press, 1956); pp. 276-300, and Elizabeth Sewell, *The Field of Nonsense* (London: Chatto & Windus, 1952), p. 144.

28. Burn, *Age of Equipoise*, p. 21.

29. Carroll, *"Alice* on the Stage," p. 193.

30. Lewis Carroll, *Through the Looking-Glass*, in *Alice in Wonderland*, ed., Gray, pp. 103, 209.

31. Stuart Tave, *The Amiable Humorist: A Study in the Comic Theory and Criticism of the 18th and Early 19th Centuries* (Chicago: University of Chicago Press, 1960), pp. 151-163.

32. Young, *Victorian England*, p. 114.

33. Green, *Diaries* I, 76, entry dated February 9, 1856.

34. Stuart Dodgson Collingwood, ed., *The Lewis Carroll Picture Book* (London: T. Fisher Unwin, 1899), pp. 345-55.

35. G. Kitson Clark, *The Making of Victorian England* (Cambridge: Harvard University Press, 1962), p. 286.

36. Green, *Diaries* I, 102, entry dated February 2, 1857.

37. Evelyn Waugh, "Carroll and Dodgson," *The Spectator* 163 (October 13, 1939): 511.

38. George Orwell, "Nonsense Poetry," *Shooting an Elephant and Other Essays* (London: Secker and Warburg, 1953), p. 182.

39. Donald J. Gray, "The Uses of Victorian Laughter," *Victorian Studies* x (December 1966): 160. Carroll was a frequent contributor to the magazines Gray describes.

40. Lewis Carroll, "Preface," *Sylvie and Bruno*, in *Works of Lewis Carroll* (London: Paul Hamlyn, 1965), p. 384.

41. For an account of this, see R.G.G. Price, *A History of Punch* (London: Collins, 1957).

42. Douglas Jerrold, "Mrs. Caudle's Curtain Lectures" (1846); reprinted in Richard M. Kelly, ed., *The Best of Mr. Punch: The Humorous Writings of Douglas Jerrold* (Knoxville: University of Tennessee Press, 1970), p. 204. Page citations hereafter in text.

43. George and Weedon Grossmith, *The Diary of a Nobody* (first published in book form in 1894; reprint ed., London: Collins, 1968). Page citations hereafter in text.

44. Price, *A History of Punch*, p. 133.

45. H. J. Dyos, *Victorian Suburb* (Leicester: University Press, 1961), pp. 10, 22-23.

46. Hugh Dalziel Duncan, *Language and Literature in Society* (Chicago: University of Chicago Press, 1953), pp. 34-38.

NOTES TO CHAPTER SIX

1. George Meredith, *The Ordeal of Richard Feverel*, ed. C. L. Cline (Boston: Houghton Mifflin Co., 1971), p. 25.

2. Virginia Woolf, *The Second Common Reader* (New York: Harcourt, Brace & World, 1932), pp. 204-205.

3. Meredith, *Feverel*, p. 24. Page citations hereafter in text.

4. V. S. Pritchett, *George Meredith and English Comedy* (New York: Random House, 1969), p. 71.

5. See Gillian Beer, *Meredith: A Change of Masks: A Study of the Novels* (London: Athlone Press, 1970).

6. George Meredith, *The Egoist. A Comedy in Narrative*, ed. Lionel Stevenson (Boston: Houghton Mifflin Co., 1958), p. 7. Page citations hereafter in text.

7. George Meredith, "An Essay on Comedy," in *Comedy*, ed. Wylie Sypher (Garden City, N.Y.: Doubleday & Co., 1956), pp. 12-13. Page citations hereafter in text.

8. Robert Langbaum, *The Poetry of Experience: The Dramatic Monologue in Modern Literary Tradition* (New York: W. W. Norton & Co., 1957), pp. 93, 85, 87.

9. George Meredith to William Maxse, December 28, 1865, *The Letters of George Meredith*, ed. C. L. Cline (Oxford: Clarendon Press, 1970), I, 322-323.

10. Dorothy Van Ghent, *The English Novel: Form and Function* [1953] (New York: Harper & Row, 1961), pp. 183-194.

11. Raymond Williams, *Culture and Society: 1780-1950* (1958; reprint ed., New York: Harper & Row, 1966), p. xvi.

12. David J. DeLaura, *Hebrew and Hellene in Victorian England: Newman, Arnold, and Pater* (Austin: University of Texas Press, 1969), p. 253.

13. William H. Mallock, *The New Republic, or Culture, Faith, and Philosophy in an English Country House* (London: Chatto & Windus, 1900), pp. 31, 193.

14. Williams, *Culture and Society*, p. 150.

15. DeLaura, *Hebrew and Hellene*, p. xi.

16. Arnold Hauser, *The Social History of Art* (New York: Random House, n.d.), IV, 181f.

17. Williams, *Culture and Society*, pp. 126-127.

18. Judith Wilt, *The Readable People of George Meredith* (Princeton:

Princeton University Press, 1975), pp. 41, 50. Page citations hereafter in text.

19. Quoted in Amy Belle Adams, *The Novels of William Hurrell Mallock*, University of Maine Studies, 2d series, no. 30 (Orono: Maine University Press, 1934), pp. 32-33.

20. DeLaura, *Hebrew and Hellene*, p. xi.

21. Mallock, *The New Republic*, pp. 242-244.

22. Robert Bernard Martin, *The Triumph of Wit: A Study of Victorian Comic Theory* (Oxford: Clarendon Press, 1974), p. 38.

23. Williams, *Culture and Society*, p. xvi.

24. Geoffrey Keynes and Brian Hill, eds., *Samuel Butler's Notebooks* (New York: E. P. Dutton & Co., 1951), p. 204.

25. Samuel Butler, *Ernest Pontifex, or The Way of All Flesh*, ed. Daniel F. Howard (Boston: Houghton Mifflin Co., 1964), p. 99. Page citations hereafter in text.

26. Henry Festing Jones, *Samuel Butler, Author of Erewhon (1835-1902): A Memoir* (London: Macmillan & Co., 1919), I, 21.

27. Ibid., p. 431, Samuel Butler to Edward James Jones, November 6, 1884.

28. Note by Butler dated March 1885 and revised November 29, 1897, in Geoffrey Keynes and Brian Hill, eds., *Letters Between Samuel Butler and Miss E.M.A. Savage, 1871-1885* (London: Jonathan Cape, 1935), p. 364.

29. P. N. Furbank, *Samuel Butler (1835-1902)* (Hamden, Conn.: Archon Books, 1971), p. 32.

30. Sigmund Freud, *A General Introduction to Psychoanalysis*, trans. Joan Riviere (1929; reprint ed., Garden City, N.Y.: Doubleday & Co., 1953), p. 365.

31. Sigmund Freud, "Humour," *The Standard Edition of the Complete Psychological Works of Sigmund Freud*, trans. James Strachey (London: Hogarth Press and the Institute of Psychoanalysis), XXI, 162-163.

32. Sigmund Freud, *Beyond the Pleasure Principle*, trans. James Strachey (1922; reprint ed., New York: Bantam Books, 1959), p. 23.

33. G. M. Young, *Victorian England: Portrait of an Age*, 2d ed. (London: Oxford University Press, 1953), p. 166.

34. Roy Lewis and Angus Maude, *The English Middle Classes* (London: Phoenix House, 1949), p. 70.

35. R.C.K. Ensor, *England 1870-1914* (Oxford: Oxford University Press, 1936), p. 160.

36. David Daiches, *Some Late Victorian Attitudes* (London: Andre Deutsch, 1969).

37. Ibid., p. 54.

38. See letters from Canon Butler to Samuel Butler dated May 9, 1859, August 22, 1861, and November 7, 1879. Arnold Silver, ed., *The Family Letters of Samuel Butler, 1841-1886* (Stanford: Stanford University Press, 1962), pp. 74-75, 101, 164.

39. Furbank, *Samuel Butler*, pp. 11-12.

40. Keynes and Hill, eds., *Samuel Butler's Notebooks*, p. 266.

41. Furbank, *Samuel Butler*, p. 25.

42. Daiches, *Some Late Victorian Attitudes*, p. 63.

43. Gustave Flaubert to Louise Colet, January 16, 1852, February 1, 1852, and April 22, 1854. *Selected Letters of Gustave Flaubert*, trans. and ed. Francis Steegmuller (New York: Farrar, Straus, and Giroux, 1953).

44. Jones, *Samuel Butler*, II, 1.

45. Gustave Flaubert, *Madame Bovary*, trans. Paul DeMan (1857; reprint ed., New York: W. W. Norton & Co., 1965), pp. 138-215.

46. Hugh Kenner, *Flaubert, Joyce and Beckett: The Stoic Comedians* (Boston: Beacon Press, 1962).

NOTES TO CHAPTER SEVEN

1. George Bernard Shaw, "My Memories of Oscar Wilde," in Frank Harris, *Oscar Wilde: His Life and Confessions* (New York: Crown Publishing Company, 1930); reprinted in Richard Ellmann, ed., *Oscar Wilde: A Collection of Critical Essays* (Englewood Cliffs, N.J.: Prentice-Hall, 1969), p. 104.

2. All the stories referred to in text appear in *Complete Works of Oscar Wilde* (London: Collins, 1948).

3. For a description of this connection, see Enid Starkie, *From Gautier to Eliot: The Influence of France on English Literature, 1851-1939* (London: Hutchinson & Co., 1960), and Frank Kermode, *Romantic Image* (London: Routledge & Kegan Paul, 1957).

4. Wilde, *Complete Works*, p. 169.

5. Ibid., p. 190.

6. Oscar Wilde, "The Decay of Lying," in Richard Ellmann, ed., *The Artist as Critic: Critical Writings of Oscar Wilde* (London: W. H. Allen, 1970), p. 293. Page citations hereafter in text.

7. Shaw, "My Memories of Oscar Wilde," pp. 95-96.

8. Eric Bentley, *"The Importance of Being Earnest,"* in *The Playwright as Thinker* (New York: Reynal & Hitchcock, 1946); reprinted in Ellmann, ed., *Oscar Wilde*, p. 114.

9. Mary McCarthy, "The Unimportance of Being Oscar," *Mary McCarthy's Theatre Chronicle* (New York: Farrar, Straus & Company, 1963); reprinted in Ellmann, ed., *Oscar Wilde*, p. 108.

10. Wilde, *Complete Works*, p. 186.

11. Ibid., p. 367.

12. Oscar Wilde, *The Picture of Dorian Gray*, ed. Isobel Murray (London: Oxford University Press, 1974), p. 39. Page citations hereafter in text.

13. Letters dated June 26, 1890 and June 27, 1890, *The Letters of Oscar Wilde*, ed. Rupert Hart-Davis (London: Rupert Hart-Davis, 1962), pp. 258-261.

14. André Gide, *Oscar Wilde*, trans. Bernard Frechtman (New York: Philosophical Library, 1949), pp. 1-2.

15. William Butler Yeats, *Autobiography* (New York: Macmillan Co., 1916), p. 79.

16. Holbrook Johnson, *The Eighteen Nineties: A Review of Art and Ideas at the Close of the Nineteenth Century* (1913; reprint ed., New York: G. P. Putnam's Sons, 1966), p. 86.

17. Renato Poggioli, *The Theory of the Avant-Garde*, trans. Gerald Fitzgerald (Cambridge: Harvard University Press, 1968), pp. 13, 132.

18. Roger Shattuck, *The Banquet Years: The Origins of the Avant-Garde in France: 1885 to World War I* (New York: Random House, 1955), pp. 329-330.

19. Poggioli, *Theory of the Avant-Garde*, p. 201.

20. Arthur Symons, *Studies in Prose and Verse* (New York: E. P. Dutton & Co., 1922), pp. 127, 125.

21. Shattuck, *Banquet Years*, p. 42.

22. Wilde to Lord Alfred Douglas, January-March 1897, *Letters*, p. 444. Page citations hereafter in text.

23. Wilde to Marie Prescott, (?) March-April 1883, *Letters*, p. 143.

24. Wilde to Philip Houghton, 1894, *Letters*, p. 353.

25. Max Beerbohm, *Seven Men and Two Others* (New York: Random House, 1959), pp. 5, 6. Page citations hereafter in text.

26. Thomas Mann, "Nietzsche's Philosophy in the Light of Recent History," *Last Essays*, trans. Richard and Clara Winston and Tania and James Stern (New York: Alfred A. Knopf, 1958).

27. Friedrich Nietzsche, *The Will to Power*, trans. Walter Kaufmann and R. J. Hollingdale (New York: Random House, 1967), p. 419.

28. Ibid., pp. 430-431.

29. Ibid., p. 461.

30. Henri Bergson, *Time and Free Will: An Essay on the Immediate Data of Consciousness*, trans. F. L. Pogson (London: George Allen & Co., 1913), p. 231.

31. Nietzsche, *The Will to Power*, p. 296.

32. Bergson, *Time and Free Will*, pp. 157, 196.

33. John Felstiner, "Max Beerbohm and the Wings of Henry James," *Kenyon Review* (1967), 449-471. For a fuller discusson of Beerbohm's art and manner, see Felstiner's *The Lies of Art: Max Beerbohm's Parody and Caricature* (New York: Alfred A. Knopf, 1972).

Index

middle class (*cont.*)
  definitions of, 6; instability of,
    26-29, 78-79, 109, 171-173, 232,
    335; myths, 51-57, 69, 79-80,
    117-120; sensibility, 39-40, 185,
    236-237, 251, 268, 273-275,
    283-295, 322-324, 329-331, 337,
    348-352
Miller, J. Hillis, 117, 148
Moore, George, 336
Morrison, Arthur, 341-342
Muir, Edwin, 76

Nabokov, Vladimir, 17, 154
Newman, John Henry Cardinal,
  263-264, 266
Nietzsche, Friedrich, 335-338

Orwell, George, 42-44, 215-216

parody, 13-14, 79-80, 286-288
Pater, Walter, 261-264, 266-268
Peacock, Thomas Love, 60-71, 83,
  101, 108, 130, 238-239; *Crotchet
  Castle*, 61, 67, 69; *Melincourt*, 61,
  63, 67; *Nightmare Abbey*, 61-64
play, 17, 35, 203-207, 210
Poggioli, Renato, 320
Praz, Mario, 68
Pritchett, V. S., 52, 243
Punch, 102-109, 219-221, 231

Quinlan, Maurice, 28

Ray, Gordon, 96, 100
Regency period, 20-38, 62
Rickword, C. H., 44
Ruskin, John, 83, 94, 263

Saintsbury, George, 267
Santayana, George, 11, 133
Sartre, Jean Paul, 10, 130, 265
satire, 14, 133
Savage, Eliza May, 281

Scholes, Robert, 43
Sewell, Elizabeth, 205
Shattuck, Roger, 323
Shaw, George Bernard, 297, 306,
  336
Shelley, Percy, 63, 70
Silver Fork novel, 20-38
Smith, Charles Manby, 122
Spedding, James, 69-70
Sterne, Laurence, 56, 99, 117, 131,
  154
Stewart, Garrett, 142-143
Stone, Harry, 152
Street, G. S., 329
Sucksmith, H. P., 174
Surtees, Robert, 40; *Jorrocks' Jaunts
  and Jollities*, 51-57
Swift, Jonathan, 98
Symons, Arthur, 321

Thackeray, William M., 44, 57, 68,
  71-101, 220-221; *Catherine*, 72;
  characterization in, 75-77,
  84-89; comic closure, 18; "The
  English Humourists of the
  Eighteenth Century," 98-100;
  parody in, 13, 79, 80-82, 92;
  sketch writing, 71-77; "The
  Snobs of England," 77-79; *Vanity
  Fair*, 77, 83-95
Tillotson, Kathleen, 87
Trollope, Anthony, 38, 44, 54, 84,
  92
Turnell, Martin, 5, 220

Vaihinger, Hans, 10
Van Ghent, Dorothy, 258-259

Wade, John, 56
Ward, Robert Plumer, 22, 25,
  27-28, 36, 81
Waugh, Evelyn, 59-61, 214, 236,
  279, 334
Wells, Chauncey, 97

Library of Congress Cataloging in Publication Data

Henkle, Roger B
  Comedy and culture.
  Includes bibliographical references and index.
    1.   English literature—19th century—History
and criticism.   2.   Comic, The.   3.   Middle classes
—England.   4.   Literature and society—England.
  I.   Title.
PR468.C65H4   827'.8'09   79-3214
ISBN 0-691-06428-8
ISBN 0-691-10090-9 pbk.